Investigating English Legal Genres in Academic and Professional Contexts

Investigating English Legal Genres in Academic and Professional Contexts

By

Girolamo Tessuto

CAMBRIDGE SCHOLARS
PUBLISHING

Investigating English Legal Genres in Academic and Professional Contexts,
by Girolamo Tessuto

This book first published 2012

Cambridge Scholars Publishing

12 Back Chapman Street, Newcastle upon Tyne, NE6 2XX, UK

British Library Cataloguing in Publication Data
A catalogue record for this book is available from the British Library

ISBN (10): 1-4438-4205-2, ISBN (13): 978-1-4438-4205-1

In the memory of my mother and father
whose faith has brought them together again
in God's presence.

TABLE OF CONTENTS

PART II: ABSTRACTING LEGAL RESEARCH

PART III: ASSESSING AND KEEPING FACE IN LEGAL RESEARCH

ACKNOWLEDGMENTS

I am indebted to my colleagues of English language studies, faculty assistants and informants for their personal help in writing this book.

First, I am grateful to Vijay Bhatia (Retired Professor - Department of English and Communication, City University of Hong Kong) and President of the Asia-Pacific LSP and Professional Communication Association, for his intellectual support and critical comments given to my chapters in this book, despite his recent health problems. I am also particularly grateful to Rita Salvi, Professor of English Linguistics (University of Rome 'La Sapienza') for the critical reading she gave to my chapters, and the invaluable conversations we had about how this book works.

Of course, I owe a debt to Stephen J. Spedding (Principal Law Faculty Language Assistant), who has devoted time and patience to proofreading and formatting material in this book. The Team at Cambridge Scholars Publishing has been excellent in their advice, assistance, and attention to detail.

Grateful acknowledgment is made to all authors and publishers of copyright material which appears in this book, and for permission to reprint material for my research purposes. Every effort has been made to trace and contact copyright holders prior to publication but this has not been possible in every case.

—The Author

ACKNOWLEDGMENTS

I am indebted to my colleagues of English language studies, faculty assistants and informants for their personal help in writing this book.

First, I am grateful to Vijay Bhatia (Retired Professor - Department of English and Communication, City University of Hong Kong) and President of the Asia-Pacific LSP and Professional Communication Association, for his intellectual support and critical comments given to my chapters in this book, despite his recent health problems. I am also particularly grateful to Rita Salvi, Professor of English Linguistics (University of Rome 'La Sapienza') for the critical reading she gave to my chapters, and the invaluable conversations we had about how this book works.

Of course, I owe a debt to Stephen J. Spedding (Principal Law Faculty Language Assistant), who has devoted time and patience to proofreading and formatting material in this book. The Team at Cambridge Scholars Publishing has been excellent in their advice, assistance, and attention to detail.

Grateful acknowledgment is made to all authors and publishers of copyright material which appears in this book, and for permission to reprint material for my research purposes. Every effort has been made to trace and contact copyright holders prior to publication but this has not been possible in every case.

—The Author

INTRODUCTION

As I introduce the subject covered in this book, which has been both a personal and intellectual enterprise, a short literature review suffices to reveal just how the law has aroused the interest of a number of linguist scholars up to the present.

A glance at legal discourse studies

Scholars have devoted time and energy to fine-grained descriptions of legal language, which conceals the diversity of legal discourse shaped across a multitude of written and oral genres. Apart from the pioneering examples of English legal language as a complex, yet still interesting historical, social and linguistic phenomenon (Mellinkoff 1963), or as a legal language 'register' (Crystal and Davy 1969), much of the linguistic work done in this area of legal discourse analysis in English has naturally centred on different aspects of legal textuality (e.g. Palmer and Pearce 1983; Danet 1984; Goodrich 1987; Kurzon 1994; Maley 1994; Trosborg 1995, Tiersma 1999), or focused on the structural and lexico-grammatical features instantiated in specific genres of legal discourse (Bhatia 1993, 1994). The list of language and discourse-based studies is by no means exhaustive and I will not burrow through the 'forest'. The list, however, shows that each of them has importance for highlighting variation in the use of English legal language and discourse manifested in different situational genres, where the intriguing interface between law and language is deeply involved.[1]

[1] However, as a result of the interest in the intersections of law and language, research into *semiotics* (e.g. Jackson 1994; van Schooten 1999) and *forensic linguistics* (e.g. McMenamin 1993; Gibbons 2003) add to the interdisciplinary field of *legal linguistics* (Mattila 2006; Salmi-Tolonen 2008), and *legal translation* (Garzone 2002, 2007; Gotti and Šarčević 2006; Šarčević 2009; Cao 2007, among others). Such interdisciplinary focus is also evident in the recently published encyclopedic work, *The Oxford Handbook of Language and Law* (Tiersma and Solan 2012), which includes past and present research into the relationship between linguistics and law through collected papers by expert linguists and lawyers. Importantly, the firm interdisciplinary commitment to semiotics and law coincides with the publication of the *International Journal for the Semiotics of*

Yet, as early as 2000s, other vibrant investigations have appeared in the linguistic research landscape, whether as individual books or edited collections. Central to these stimulating works has been the use of text, discourse and genre analytical as well as corpus linguistics tools to analyse the ways academic, professional and institutional contexts of legal discourse are accounted for by community and discipline-specific practices and procedures influenced by cultural and other features.

For a start, analytical insights into modality enacted in English legal texts are offered in the studies of Gotti (2001) and Garzone (2001), while the question of *if*-conditionals in modern English legal texts is offered in the study of Facchinetti (2001). Moreover, coinciding with his – indeed innovative - notion of *Specialized Discourse*, Gotti (2003, 2005, 2008) examines linguistically and pragmatically the distinctive properties of English legal discourse, and addresses identity issues in legal texts (Gotti 2011). Williams (2005, 2006, 2009) focuses on legal English in terms of verbal constructions and fuzziness in prescriptive texts, alongside the changes made to such texts over the years and the possible future changes to legal textuality. The author also speculates on the simplification of legal language as advocated by the guidelines of the worldwide Plain Language Movement. Taking a dynamic view of the real and ideal written discourse in academic, professional and institutional contexts, Bhatia (2004) convincingly advocates a critical approach to the study of genre (referred to as Critical Genre Analysis - CGA), a view that the author readily assumes in his subsequent works (Bhatia 2008, 2010, 2011). In the latter elaborations, the example of *colonization* of arbitration practices by litigation becomes the author's analytical focus on *interdiscursivity* and asymmetrical power relations. In the framework of genre theory, the process of colonization comes to describe the invasion of the integrity of arbitration by litigation with the resulting appropriation of generic resources. Colonization practices thus provide the source in which to appreciate the dynamism in accounting for legal discourse and its representation in genre analysis. Indeed, inquiries into arbitration discourse manifested in multilingual and multicultural contexts are still to be found in earlier edited papers (Bhatia, Candlin, Gotti 2003), and further extended in the legal discourse of today's ADR practices and procedures appearing in recently edited papers (Bhatia, Candlin, Gotti 2010; Bhatia, Candlin, Gotti 2012), where textual, discourse and ethnographic analytical data provide explanation of some of the issues that lie at the heart of

---

Law through a series of illuminating collected papers (e.g. Wagner, Werner, Cao 2007; Wagner and Broekman 2011). As again, this list is by no means exhaustive.

dispute resolution discourses across cultural and legal systems. The positive attribute of these studies adds to the quality of other edited papers (Bhatia, Garzone, Degano 2012), dealing with the multilingual arbitration award as a discursive genre. Clearly, insightful research also resonates with other edited volumes, variously dealing with specialized genres (Bhatia and Gotti 2006), legal concepts across systems and cultures (Bhatia, Candlin, Evangelisti 2008), legal discourse across languages and cultures (Gotti and Williams 2010), or legal discourse and communication behaviour which shape professional identities (Bhatia and Evangelisti 2011).

Although, as yet, such list of the studies conducted since 2000s is not exhaustive, it shows that there are important variations in the construction, interpretation and use of legal discourse manifested in the context of academic, professional or institutional activities of genre writers. In many such approaches to legal discourse, the notion of genre is one which offers a socially informed theory of legal language, and the ways rhetorical patternings of specific genres construe varying personal and institutional purposes of writers within the 'broader social context'. The list therefore provides evidence of the vitality in advancing knowledge in the field among applied linguists, whose commitment has been to respond continuously to an agenda that the law sets in an increasingly globalized world. And while discourse and other analysts have also paid attention to how the law itself and the actors within the legal system conceive of relations between discourse, power and ideology (Wagner and Cheng 2011; Bhatia, Hafner et al. 2012, among recent ones), the analyses of today's arbitration practices manifested through the diversity of legal discourses and genres are just a token example of the need to respond to such an important agenda.

Scope of this study

The centrality given to discourse and genre analytical perspectives of legal language in the review above provides the framework for this study. Prior to describing the structure of this book, I wish to define the scope of this study by providing a grounded understanding of the nature and operation of genre that creates academic and professional legal discourse in this research.

Legal genres as social phenomena

Despite the many insightful descriptions of genre grown out of genre theories over the last twenty years or so (Martin 1984, 1992, 1998; Bazerman 1988; Bhatia 1993, 2004; Eggins 1994; Orlikowski and Yates 1994; Berkenkotter and Huckin 1995; Freedman and Medway 1994; Devitt 2004; Swales 1990, 2004; Fairclough 2003, 2004; among others), different emphasis has been given to text or context and the resulting conventions in the three main traditions of genre studies (i.e. ESP, Sydney School, North American New Rhetoric). In the ESP tradition, in particular, scholars (Swales 1990, 2004; Bhatia 1993, 2004; Berkenkotter and Huckin 1995) rest on the idea that genre as a social construct not only includes form or structure, but also content, situation, context and communicative purposes, and the varying situations, contexts and purposes account for the natural evolution of the *discourse communities* in which social genres are realized. Correspondingly, genres are not static, but are dynamic instances which result from socially recognized ways of using language in perceived rhetorical contexts and actions.

With a focus on what constitutes genre in the reviewed approaches, the analysis of legal discourse that follows therefore relates to socially recognized genres as whole texts, or parts of texts, and the social motivation of genre includes the functionally-related *moves* and *steps* (Swales 1990, 2004; Bhatia 1993) or *staging* of the content (Martin 1984, 1992, 1998; Eggins 1994). In this framework, the connection between the recognized system of *move* or *staging* of content and lexico-grammatical patterning provides the criterion for identifying texts as similar or different. Consequently, the presence or absence of common communicative forms used to achieve a particular communicative purpose/goal (or set of communicative purposes/goals) is seen as central to the analysis of academic and professional genres in the context of disciplinary practices shaped by genre writers. This way then, investigating legal discourse proves an invaluable way of looking at regularities/irregularities of form, purpose and situated social action in the legal genres, whose dynamism also coincides with hybridity forms.

However, the nature and operation of legal genres can also be seen outside *move-stage* rhetorical patternings, by investigating issues of addressivity and audience in texts which establish complex, social interactions among the participants involved. Here, the (micro) analysis of legal discourse patterns proves an interesting way of looking at the interpersonal meanings expressed through a range of *criticism and praise* (Hyland 2004) and *politeness* features (Brown and Levinson 1987), or through a range of *metadiscourse* features (Hyland 2005a). These analytical approaches not only contribute to rhetorical understandings of socially recognized language use in texts, but also shed light on the preferred patterns of socially situated discourse practices in the legal genres.

Legal genres in inter/disciplinary culture-marking schemes

In addition to the ways that methodological approaches to social legal genres influence the creation of legal discourse in this study, legal genres provide the platform from which to generate new knowledge in the context of a disciplinary and interdisciplinary culture of law.

Since the late 1980s, several authors have studied the ways knowledge is created in professional academic writing across the disciplines (e.g. Bazerman 1988, 2000; Becher 1987, 1989; Myers 1992a/b; Becher and Trowler 2001; Fahnestock 2005) by focusing on community in the social construction of disciplinary knowledge. Here, disciplines emerge as scholarly communities where the body of knowledge meets various defining criteria - i.e. assumptions, concepts, epistemologies, methods, theories – which account for disciplines to be distinguished from one another. In addition to such premise of knowledge formation in the disciplines, research into disciplinary cultures on genres has laid emphasis on "discourse community's norms, epistemology, ideology, and social ontology" (Berkenkotter and Huckin 1995: 21), "representations of legitimate discourses which help to define and maintain particular epistemologies and academic boundaries" (Hyland 2004: 11), or "'professional goals and objectives', 'generic norms and conventions', and professional and organizational identity'" (Bhatia 2004: 126). The common features suggested in the latter approaches are the distinctive rhetorical practices constructed and negotiated by different disciplinary communities, where the social context of language use defines the different epistemological, ideological, ontological, conventional and organizational features that characterize different academic/professional communities and disciplines.

In this book, investigating legal discourse proves yet another invaluable way of looking at academic and professional genres as builders of knowledge within the law in the context of a disciplinary culture. Disciplinary culture is a key dimension of genre analysis here as it helps legal writers to capitalize on epistemology, ideology, and identity features that support shared knowledge practices in the genres. While culturally-situated practices reveal the different assumptions the writers make about their texts, ultimately they are crucial in securing rhetorical objectives in the genres since they channel the efforts of writers into systematic pursuit of knowledge advancement, albeit at various levels of disciplinary inquiry.

Yet, the reference to such disciplinary culture of law needs to move from a single, conventionally rigid, description of law disciplinarity to one which is descriptive of collaborative research and becomes part of a pragmatically interdisciplinary engagement. Such engagement, observed particularly in the abstract genre, is both a knowledge-making goal and research strategy, in that a set of epistemological and social forces allows the law to have some area of proximity to other disciplines. The latter, then, shade and cross into each other by constituting new, multi-modal knowledge space and writer role beyond the exclusive boundaries of law disciplinarity. Specifically, the boundary work of interdisciplinary research is one which not only provides the focus on methodological borrowing from other contributing or neighbouring disciplines and its application to law, but also the focus on researchable topics in response to the external demands of society. Thus, for instance, the interdisciplinary understanding of Criminology or Transitional justice in empirical research article abstracts requires identifying bits of knowledge and modes of thinking from relevant disciplines in order to produce a more comprehensive view of the problem.[2] While these collaborative results serve epistemic and ontological goals necessary to organise and construct information in the generic writing practices, they are also contingent upon the wider, emerging contexts of legal research, and as a consequence create a purposeful organizational unit of interdisciplinary law in specialized knowledge and domain.

Clearly, such collaborative understanding of interdisciplinarity poses problems to "the homogeneity of disciplinary groups and practices" in knowledge-generating activity (Hyland 2004: 8), or similarly to the nature of academic disciplines (Becher and Trowler 2001, among others). Despite these important theoretical premises, there is evidence that interdisciplinarity efforts are far more common in contemporary socio-

[2] In this context, the value of interdisciplinary understandings extends to what are commonly known as Law and Economics, Law and Sociology, Law and Religion, Law and Medicine, etc. No doubt, such dual approaches emphasise the various forms taken by law in a variety of social formations, and equip the analyst with the perspective that is relevant to pose questions. But where law is placed at the meeting ground with language, as I am concerned with here, the dual approach equips as yet with the perspective necessary to pose questions that are socially relevant to the fields, and provides a dialectical understanding of the complex interaction between language functions and their expressions in the social reality of law.

legal studies and legal education (Osborn 2001; Cownie 2004, among others) as well as law journal policies, and the nature of interdisciplinary law is often described as a disciplinary continuum (Harwell 2002; Coffin et al. 2003).

To the extent that interdisciplinary writers allow for their research project to conform to a collaborative rather than obsequious, fawning knowledge engagement (as a dog does by wagging its tail), they must recreate the practices, processes, and values from other disciplines, insofar as the latter are consistent and compatible with locally organized conditions and purposes of the writers' own culture framework. Culturally-driven consistency thus provides the key to institutionalizing and legitimizing interdisciplinarity beyond the disciplinarity limits of the law, and becomes the essence for an account of academic law as an evolving intellectual construct in knowledge structures and societal values.

The structure of this book

These ways of looking at the legal genres now bring me to outline the structure of this book.

Investigating English Legal Genres in Academic and Professional Contexts situates English legal language research in the linguistics (discourse and genre) analytical framework. As such, it is inspired by the recent research across the disciplines, showing that discourses and genres are different and have important implications for genre writers in their academic, professional and institutional roles. The central goal pursued in this book is to provide a corpus-based, comprehensive linguistic description and interpretation of selected English legal genres (i.e. Case Notes, Research Article Abstracts, Book Reviews), by surveying the distinctive argument, content, structure, and interactions revealed in the construction and use of the academic and professional written genres. The series of detailed analyses offered in this volume provides the platform on which the genres are examined for their features of variability or standardization created by lexico-grammatical and discursive patterns, and for other micro-function linguistic patterns which relate the genres to their interpersonal or other contexts and meanings. The findings of this 'article-styled' research are discussed in functional terms from (meta)discourse, genre and other methodological perspectives in order to understand how legal genre writers position themselves in the academic and professional community and discipline. The varied (macro/micro)representations of genre approaches taken in this book therefore seek to expand knowledge of the chosen genres that remain largely under-investigated in discourse and genre studies within and across academic disciplines.

This book comprises three Parts. Part I consists of three Chapters where the most elaborate material is researched into Case Notes produced in academic and professional contexts. As a result, these Chapters form the backbone of the volume. The reason for devoting a wider research space to Case Notes is because they are one of the most prominent legal genres and hence most used by all, academics as well as professionals, in addition to Research Articles. The elaborate treatment in the three Chapters, instead of one as in other analyses here (however important and insightful they may be), therefore demonstrates the importance of the Case Note genre.

In Part I, Chapter 1 begins by exploring how the global patterns of rhetorical features of the Case Note genre contemporaneously construe similar and different contexts, and therefore recognizable generic identities in academic and professional writing activities. Drawing upon this research into global rhetorical structure, Chapter 2 then provides a more detailed examination of the genre in academic writing contexts, by revealing how the various rhetorical sections are constructed and used together with features of content and structure. Chapter 3 moves away from descriptions of generic content and structure to address the interpersonal dimension of academic discourse constructed in the distinguishable *Discussion* section of the Case Note through the metadiscourse typology. This Chapter therefore looks at the ways the social context of language use articulates and constructs interactions between writer and reader.

Part II provides a different avenue of generic analysis by surveying the 'abstracting' strategies in Research Article Abstracts. Chapter 4 thus examines the discursive (move-based) and lexico-grammatical patterning revealed in abstracts, and highlights the relevant features of generic variation in academic writing contexts.

Part III closes the research in this volume by focusing on the Book Review academic genre in Chapter 5. Here, I explore evaluative language as an important rhetorical site which helps legal writers organize legal discourse for the academy and express their values and those of the widest community readership. Evaluative language is investigated in combination with politeness strategies, which expand on the ideational perception of academic qualities and values in the evaluative genre by addressing positive and negative 'face' in socially and pragmatically-based conventions.

This research, conducted on context-specific corpora, is meant to be descriptive rather than prescriptive in character. Attention to details of the descriptive analyses is meant to represent the selected genres more precisely in an attempt to demonstrate how the genres create legal discourse in published legal scholarship. This book seeks to show analytical insights in systematic and clear language, and can be of interest to native and non-native readers, whether involved in English applied linguistic research or disciplinary writing instruction at both undergraduate and postgraduate levels. Any imprecision or omission in this book are mine.

PART I:

DIGGING THE GROUND OF CASE NOTES

CHAPTER ONE

CASE NOTES: ACCOUNTING FOR ONE GENRE OR ANOTHER

This book starts off with the 'expert'-authored Case Note of the legal academy and profession, one which is the most perceptible to my eye as an analyst of the genre in the law discipline. My principal concern here is with the discursive conventions and practices that construct and display the social roles of writers in this legal genre. Grounded in the Western writing culture and law tradition[1], 'expert' case notes published in English language law journals are important on two main accounts: firstly, they provide a valuable source for the widest readership to share information about decided cases in the Common Law and other territorial jurisdictions; secondly, their varying rhetorical organization becomes an interesting tool for my role as a genre analyst. As a result of the varying rhetorical activities, case notes reflect the imperatives for writing in the discursive order of this genre, as derived from the demands of disciplinary practices outside the 'mature' student body. Yet, unlike Research Article Abstracts and Book Reviews examined later in this book, the genre of the legal case note has remained at a standstill in the academic and professional research landscape for some years.

In this Chapter, I therefore examine the rhetorical and linguistic strategies employed in case notes to determine how writers situate themselves in the law disciplinary community by achieving institutional purposes. I should first acquaint the reader with the theoretical context of this analysis and indicate the empirical material and research method, before I undertake the analysis and discussion of findings and draw some preliminary conclusions.

---

[1] In the Italian law tradition, for instance, expert-written case notes are best known as *note a sentenza*.

Theoretical background

Case notes in academic and professional genre-based research

Since the 1980s theoretical insights have been provided into a variety of written academic and professional legal genres associated with receptive and productive conditions of use. The earlier works by Bhatia (1983, legislation; 1993, legal genres), Kurzon (1985, briefs), Tiersma (1986, contracts), Howe (1990, legal problem questions), Iedema (1993, case briefs/case notes), Beasley (1994, legal problem questions), Bowles (1995, newspaper law reports), Trosborg (1995/1997, contracts), Tiersma (1999/2010, legal language and technologies of communication), Feak et al. (2000, law review notes), and Salvi (2002, legal language in case notes) add to other insightful and stimulating works. In such works, the focus has been on extending previous knowledge of specific written legal genres, such as legal problem question writing (Bruce 2002, Jensen 2002, Tessuto 2011a), newspaper law reports (Badger 2003), legal essay writing (Tessuto 2011b), or otherwise extending research to other new genres such as the barrister's opinion (Tessuto 2006; Hafner 2008, 2010), or the arbitral award in national and international contexts of legal procedures (Tessuto 2008a, Tessuto 2012; Hafner 2011; Bhatia, Garzone, Degano 2012).[2]

To the best of my knowledge, the genre of the legal case note/brief has only been part of the academic research landscape formed by the three isolated but helpful works of Iedema (1993), Feak et al. (2000) and Salvi (2002), and no other linguistics research output leading to new knowledge in the field has increased since. In order to make a passing reference to this research in the disciplinary genre I am concerned with here, the focus in Iedema's (1993) analysis has been on the identification of the generic structure and conventions (moves) of legal case studies, by comparing the instructions received from the course tutor and two student case notes. In Feak et al.'s (2000) analysis, by contrast, the focus has been on the introductory sections of published student-written legal research papers

[2] Interestingly, however, the dynamism of today's professional practices outside the law discipline shows that the term case note is also used in the health care discourse study of Sarangi and Brookes-Howell (2006) to refer to "a documentation of the contractual relationship between the patient and the practitioners" (2006: 199). This reference therefore allows for the naming and function of the genre to become an essential part of interdisciplinarity approaches to the discourse procedures.

which the authors label as law review Notes, in line with the terminology used in the field (2000: 197-199). The results of their study bear similarities to, and differences from, the Introductions found in the research article genre, as described in Swales (1990). In Salvi's (2002) analysis, the focus has been on the intertextual dimension of legal English teaching, where a recorded instance of case note is used by the author in her intertextual approach to English legal language.

Outside genre-based research studies, however, the practical profile of case notes is currently gained from university websites which provide online guidelines for students to write effective, clear and professional law case notes as part of an academic assessment item and skills learning. In this context, the American *Casenote Legal Briefs* publication series by AspenLaw Studydesk, for instance, provides students with practical guidelines for briefing assigned cases. It does so by showing the basic facts and decisions from the text of the actual opinions handed down by the courts in a variety of law areas. In addition, there are legal writing textbooks (e.g. Volokh 2010; Fajans and Falk 2011) which help native law students to either master the writing of notes as part of their UK, US or other curriculum, or to participate in the 'write-on competitions' in US law schools, with the ultimate purpose of gaining membership on a (US) law review publication. Law students can thus confidently turn to such textbooks for reliable information regarding the techniques for success in the 'write-on' competition, and therefore write a winning submission paper.

The value of legal writing materials, covering case notes and other types of legal genres, has not escaped the attention of applied discourse and genre analysts, integrating different research epistemologies and methodologies in the analysis of academic and professional legal discourse (Candlin et al. 2002a), or developing resources for legal writing (Candlin et al. 2002b). In their invaluable review of the textbooks used in EALP teaching, Candlin et al. (2002b) discuss the *systems of legal genres*, and convincingly argue for the usefulness of legal writing textbooks which analyze the purpose, structure and content of this important genre. The authors (Candlin et al. 2002b: 304-305) refer to this genre as a *case brief* rather than *case note*, as used in British legal terminology.

In an attempt to expand knowledge of this manifestly neglected genre in academic and professional legal discourse research, I shall focus on the 'expert'-authored case notes and examine how the (move) rhetorical and linguistic strategies are used to frame the writers' membership to the law discourse community which pursue particular goals or purposes. In an attempt to reveal how the patterns of rhetorical features in the genre construe the relevant communicative contexts, I will therefore look at the discoursal and generic-level patterns of variability/standardization in the socially-situated writing of the genre.

Data and Method

The Corpus

For the current study, a synchronic corpus of 70 electronically retrieved case notes (CNs) shown in Table 1 were randomly selected in a set of samples from four British Online Journals published in the 2009-2011 issues: *The Modern Law Review* (MLR), *Ecclesiastical Law Journal* (ELJ), *Netherlands International Law Review* (NILR), and *European Constitutional Law Review* (ECLR). A list of case note titles and journal source is provided in Appendixes. Table 1 also shows that not many CNs were included in ECLR in a given year of publication, and the result was that a lower than 20 (but still sufficiently valuable set of) samples was decided for collection in ECLR.

Journal	2009	2010	2011	TOTAL
The Modern Law Review Blackwell Wiley Online	4	7	9	20
Ecclesiastical Law Journal Cambridge Journals Online	5	7	8	20
Netherlands International Law Review Cambridge Journals Online	8	9	3	20
European Constitutional Law Review Cambridge Journals Online	-	7	3	10
TOTAL	17	30	23	70

Table 1. Number and publication year of case notes collected from each Journal and total number of case notes.

The method for corpus selection reflects the principles of reputation and accessibility of the journals (Nwogu 1997) committed to publishing legal scholarship in a range of law topics, and interactively proliferating e-knowledge resources for a variety of international focused readers. In the case of ELJ, for instance, we read about the journal scope, which is to focus on "all aspects of ecclesiastical law. Particular emphasis is given to the regulation of the Church of England and worldwide Anglican Communion, but the range of coverage includes comparative studies of the laws of other faiths and of the interface between law and religion in a global perspective" (ELJ – Home page). Here, interdisciplinarity aspects of the law discipline come to the fore with the coverage of the case notes in this journal including the interface between Law and Religion in a national and global perspective.

Allied with the range of coverage included in the topics, corpus journals featured the same academic genres as used in other on-line disciplinary journals – namely, Editorials, Research Articles, Book Reviews and Review Articles. In addition, there were sections devoted to other variously labelled genres – namely, Parliamentary Reports, Conference Reports, Legislation, Comments, and Case Notes. In terms of naming, different nomenclatures were sometimes used for Case Notes in the corpus journals. Unlike ELJ and ECLR adopting the consistent label of Case Note in both the Table of Contents and cover page of the published texts, MLR variously used the labels of Cases or Case Notes, while NILR went some way beyond such labels by adopting the name Hague Case Law – Latest Developments.[3]

Case notes were thus chosen for collection from both academic and professional strands of the law. In the academic strand of the writing source, case notes published in MLR were written by authors who were English native speakers affiliated to UK-based law institutions in junior and senior academic positions, while those published in ECLR were written by non-native speakers affiliated to European (non-English-speaking) law institutions also in junior and senior academic positions. In the professional strand of the writing source, case notes published in ELJ were written by English native professional authors and appeared under editorship, while those published in NILR made their appearance only

[3] As a personal aside, however, a glance at the UK Supreme Court blog (http://ukscblog.com/) shows that not only are different nomenclatures used for Case Notes, labelled therefore as Case Comments, but also that networked technologies are highly valued in the law of practice since Case Comments there are automatically linked with the Supreme Court blog entries. Such 'legal blog posts' (used for News Articles and Case Previews as well) not only provide direct access to the content of Case Comments written by law practitioners (usually barristers), but also receive comments on those topics that most attract the interest of other legal practitioners or scholars. To the extent that such 'legal blog posts' provide readers with access to the content of the Case Comment without the investment of time in surfing through traditional law e-journals, the networked technology is therefore a clear example of the speedup in the amount of informal, live/on-line communication among community readers and a clear opportunity for the writers to bypass publication in such e-journals. Legal blogs form the subject of a separate investigation by this author.

under non-native professional editorship, outside author's name. In all these instances, the criteria of 'nativeness' and 'non-nativeness' as well as affiliations were established by the authors' details appearing at the beginning or end of the case notes, and confirmed by email personal communications with the journal boards. Clearly, as is customary of any journal practice, both native and non-native submissions underwent editing, as further confirmed by such e-mail communications. It becomes clear that, as a result of the academic/professional writing source in the native/non-native divide, the sources of evidence in the current corpus provide an understanding of representative texts as 'national' case notes situated in the UK context of law (ELJ, MLR), and 'European' case notes situated in the international context of law (NILR, ECLR).

Based on these criteria and requirements for corpus selection, different quantitative data were obtained in each set of CNs in the journals using the software WordSmith 5.0, as reported in Table 2. The data source for this study was a 188,216 word corpus of published CNs, excluding titles, footnotes and bibliography, where applicable.

	TOTAL	ELJ	ECLR	NILR	MLR
Tokens	188,216	5,870	58,243	4,776	119,327
Types	9,871	1,403	4,862	1,036	7,673
Type/Token ratio (TTR)	5.37	24.32	8.57	22.63	6.57
Standardised TTR	37.31	39.82	36.38	35.95	37.70
Mean word length (in characters)	4.97	5.00	5.03	5.18	4.93
Sentences	4,919	213	1,596	170	2,940
Mean (in words)	37.38	27.08	35.53	26.94	39.74

Table 2. Different quantitative data in each set of the case notes and totals as retrieved from Scott WordSmith Tool 5.0.

Footnotes were absent in two journals (ELJ, NILR), but were used extensively in the other pair of journals (MLR, ECLR).

Methodology

The analysis reported in this study offers explanatory linguistic descriptions of the writers' communicative practices investigated along macro and micro-level analytical lines.

In keeping to the relevance of genre theory for macro-level descriptions, I sought to determine the organizational macro-structure realized in journal case notes in order to provide an understanding of their rhetorical similarities and differences. For this, I looked at the case note genre in the analytical perspectives of *typified rhetorical action* resulting from *recurrent social situations* (Miller 1984; Bazerman 1994), *regularities of staged, goal-oriented social processes* known as *schematic structure* or *generic structure* (Martin 1984, 1992, 1998; Eggins 1994), or as *consistency of communicative purposes* (Swales 1990; Bhatia 1993), the latter description however incorporating the systemic notion of genre as a *schematic* or *generic structure*.[4] While the most important feature of these approaches is the emphasis on conventions, reliance on genre theories meant other theoretical perspectives which involve the dynamic rhetorical patterning of the genre "that can be manipulated according to conditions of use" (Berkenkotter and Huckin 1995: 6), or similarly involve the notions of *flexibility and innovation* of genre (Bhatia 1997a). Where flexibility and innovation are the main issues in genre theory, the result is that they "create a tension between generic integrity, on the one hand, and the possibility of appropriation of generic resources to create new forms" (Bhatia 2004: 112), and therefore become part of a more comprehensive exploration of what Bhatia (2004) calls the *social space* of genre.

As a result of this wider (social) perspective of genre analysis, I sought to theoretically frame my study in the multidimensional three-space model for the analysis of legal discourse as genre, by integrating textual space, social space, and social professional space. This framework implied the evolutionary perspective of a *Critical Genre Analysis* (Bhatia 2004, 2008, 2010) accomplished in three stages (textualization, organization and contextualization), in Bhatia's terms. Yet, awareness of such evolutionary perspective in the social dimension of genre brought with it an appreciation of the relationships with other texts and discourses (Bakhtin 1981; Fairclough 1992; Candlin and Maley 1997; Maley 1994) in the analysis of case note writing. In this framework, the rhetorical move-structure was analyzed through a manual textual reading of corpus case notes. Rhetorical macro-structure analysis was complemented with micro-level linguistic descriptions of journal case notes in the two comparable

[4] Yet, as a result of the way the use of one genre may have or depend on the use of other interrelated genres, genre theorists have described genres as *repertoires*, *colonies*, *chains*, *sets* or *systems*, and *ecologies* (Bazerman 1994, 2004; Bhatia 2004; Devitt 1991, 2004; Fairclough 2004; Orlikowski and Yates 1994; Spinuzzi 2004).

sets, conveniently labelled as Group A and Group B. However, only a hint of the metadiscourse (Hyland 2005a) linguistic descriptions was offered in Group B, since the analysis of metadiscourse typology required a larger space in which to present the relative descriptions. Thus, the decision was made to deal with metadiscourse language separately (Chapter 3), and this choice in turn helped avoid the production of a far lengthier, over-focused Chapter here.

Results and Discussion

In this section, I present the results and hypotheses from the quantitative and qualitative analysis of the written data. First, I need to provide the situational context for my results and hypotheses by establishing the varying discourse forms and functions of case notes within their production conditions in the corpus journals.

Case notes in the comparable corpora: varying discourse forms and functions

The rhetorical variable under comparison immediately came to surface by observing how case notes 'appeared as' in the publication profile of the journals. A glance at the textual level of published case notes shows in fact that they appeared under a different guise, as measured by the minimum and maximum range of words and the resulting physical amount of page covered. Figure 1 shows variability in word range (min/max).

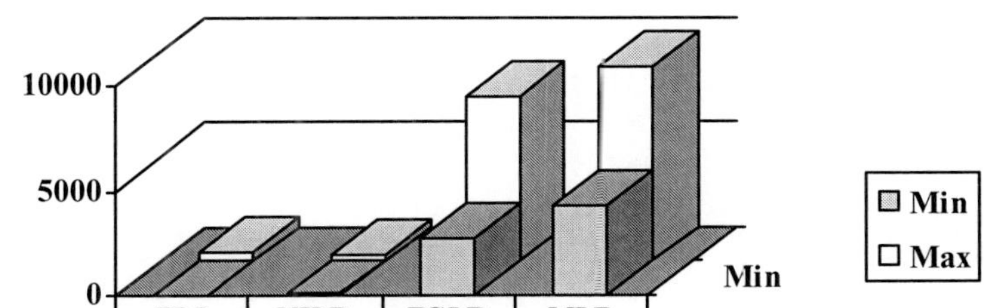

	ELJ	NILR	ECLR	MLR
Min	75	121	2766	4372
Max	511	334	7890	9260

Figure 1. Word length (min/max) of CNs across the journals.

As the reader may also infer by the total tokens in Table 2, ELJ and NILR presented the shortest case notes in the corpus. In ELJ, in fact, case note writing ranged from a minimum of 75 to a maximum of 511 words, and covered less than half of a page size, while in NILR this range went from a minimum of 121 to a maximum of 334 words, and covered half to almost two pages. In the remaining journals, however, the writing of case note progressively increased in such a range and page coverage. Thus, case notes in ECLR went from a minimum of 2,766 (six pages) to a maximum of 7,890 words (twenty-five pages), while in MLR case notes achieved a minimum of 4,372 (seven pages) to a maximum of 9,260 words (twenty-two pages).

Variability in terms of the word range and resulting content is therefore interesting to the extent that case notes under investigation reflect different forms and functions invoked by academic and professional discourse community writers. As a result of these distinguishable features in the comparable corpora, case notes were conveniently divided into:

Group A (ELJ, NILR) of professional writing activity; and
Group B (ECLR, MLR) of academic writing activity.

I shall examine each of them in turn.

Group A: generic replicability

The immediate image gained by reading the case notes in Group A (ELJ, NILR) is one of a very concise, yet comprehensive, and impartial summary of recent judgments in points of facts and law. In the case of NILR, the summary typically related to the judgments of the International Court of justice, International Criminal Tribunal for the Former Yugoslavia, International Criminal Tribunal for Rwanda, or Permanent Court of Arbitration. In the case of ELJ, the summary was typically about ecclesiastical cases determined by both secular and church courts in England.

The case round-up therefore meant that case notes built on the writer's knowledge of previous judgments by providing instant recounts of such texts through what I describe as 'generic replicability' in two closely related professional discourses. Replicability, as a process, implied that writers of case notes made use of elements from other levels of text and discourse by introducing the various notions of *dialogism* and *heteroglossia*

(Bakhtin 1981) [5] , and *intertextuality* (*manifest* and *constitutive*) and *interdiscursivity* (Fairclough 1992; Candlin and Maley 1997).[6] Viewed in these analytical frameworks, cases notes were typically expressed through explicit surface textual features (e.g. quotations through reported speech) borrowed from the previous judgments (*intertextuality*), and involved a combination of types of texts from other levels of discourse, i.e. the discourse of the parties in the case and the discourse of the judge in the current or other cases (*interdiscursivity*). By describing how previous text forms and discourse conventions conflate intertextually and interdiscursively in case notes, generic replicability was significant to highlight a feature of *interdiscursivity* (Bhatia 2004, 2008, 2010), which defines the process of "appropriating generic resources from a specific genre for the construction of another" (Bhatia 2004: 87).[7] The extent to which generic resources from

---

[5] Bakhtin's discussion of what he calls *dialogism* and *heteroglossia* is that "in this actively polyglot world, completely new relationships are established between language and its objects [...] and this is fraught with enormous consequences for all the already completed genres that had been formed during eras of closed and deaf monoglossia" (Bakhtin 1981: 12).

[6] In Fairclough's (1992) CDA framework, for instance, intertextuality is defined as "basically the property texts have of being full of snatches of other texts, which may be explicitly demarcated or merged in, and which the text may assimilate, contradict, ironically echo, and so forth" (Fairclough 1992: 84). In this framework, *manifest intertextuality* can be summarized as the employment of *content* aspects from existing texts in the creation of a new text, while *constitutive intertextuality* can be defined briefly as the use of *structural* aspects from existing texts. Using Fairclough's framework, other researchers (Candlin and Maley 1997) have carried out their studies by investigating mediation texts and accounting for the interdiscursive relations between bargaining, counselling, therapeutic, and legal genres. Here, differently related professional areas and adaptation to the requirements of diverse ideological orientations are revealed by the interdiscursivity of different social practices.

[7] Bhatia (2004) explores the phenomenon of *interdiscursivity* in business advertising, news reporting and legal texts, among others. Taking the generic variation into account, he offers a detailed account of interdiscursivity as part of the *colonization* phenomenon, which results in a *mixing* or *embedding* of genres within organizational life (2004: 87ff.). Intense colonization is accounted for by "the explosion of information technology, the use of new media and also the empowering influence of promotional activities in today's competitive world" (Bhatia 2004: 88). Indeed, *colonization* is also referred to as *commodification* (Bhatia 2004: 58, quoting Fairclough 1992: 207), as part of Fairclough's (1992, 2003, 2010) CDA approach to interdiscursivity which has important implications for social practice. According to Fairclough (1992: 200-224), interdiscursive

the judgment figured in case notes obviously depended upon the rhetorically narrowed configuration (summary format) of the case note genre, which as a consequence allowed the writers to adopt only a limited range of resources from previous judgments. Despite such limitation, replicability-as-interdiscursivity was still responsible for framing, by appropriating, the case note genre which, as will be seen, overlapped with previous and prototypical judgments in terms of structural interpretation and lexico-grammatical features, though with different social functions, as I will describe immediately below.

Group A: 'reporting' genre with intended purpose

Functional differences between the two genres (i.e. the judgment and the case note) can be seen by each type of writing existing with an intended purpose.

It is well known that the judgment serves both a *declaratory* and *justificatory* function (Maley 1994), since the judge aims to convince his/her peers of the soundness of his argument for Decision by stating the law prescriptively for the person concerned. While this communicative purpose is expressed through the different rhetorical segments (moves) in the widely configured judgment structure, the performative act of 'deciding' is also the end-result of the declaratory and justificatory function, however 'legitimate' the justification-making process may also be in nature.

By contrast, case notes built on the writer practice to present the material in a nutshell in the discursive form of 'case reports' (CRs), where recounting actions and events of previous judgments in a detached, objective tone (with no writer's intrusion) relied on reporting as a central rhetorical function of discourse. As will become increasingly clear throughout this Chapter, this function was characterized by some prototypical linguistic features, such as past tense forms used to quote earlier arguments (in summary format), and the function was sufficient to establish the specificity of case notes as the 'reporting genre', used for an overall informative purpose and overtly drawn upon within the discursive conventions and practices of the judgment genre.[8] And while the reporting

---

relations in texts reflect the "democratization", "commodification", "marketization" and "technologization" of contemporary public discourse.

[8] As an aside, similarities also exist between *case notes* here and *press releases* produced by the European Court of Judgment. Based on the essential reporting function of the genre, *press releases* provide summaries of European Court

function of case notes may be said to correspond to Bhatia's (2004) generic "value" of reporting in a variety of *reporting genres* (genre colony)[9], it comes as no surprise that the reporting activity performed in the professional case note genre also enabled the writers to act as 'reporters' of decided cases. The result here was that writing up case notes allowed the work of one person to become the conflation of the roles of 'writer' and 'reporter' in the international medium of scholarly publication.

Grounded in this specific rhetorical framework, writing the case note genre yielded sufficiently conventionalized and standardized communicative contexts, allowing for recurring rhetorical contexts through a shared set of communicative purposes achieved in the professional writing strand of the texts. Correspondingly, case notes provided the established practices of generically situated writers laying down the ways they went about achieving professional purposes in published texts.

Macro-structure

As a result of this framework, a three-move organizational structure, as proposed here, was identified of the case note genre in Group A. For the sake of clarity and comprehensiveness, this structure is outlined in Table 3, in which rhetorical moves were used by the writers to achieve their *communicative purposes* (Bhatia 1993, 2004) of Identifying the Case, Reporting Facts, and Reporting Decision, through the content criteria of move-constructing information in the social genre:

judgments by presenting issues of fact and law and the resulting decision in past tense constructions. Although *press releases* are not binding on the Court (as are indeed 'non-authoritative' Group A case notes under scrutiny), they are simply recorded communication directed at members of the news media for the purpose of announcing the court's judicial activity retrievable via the CURIA search engines. See: <http://curia.europa.eu/>

[9] Bhatia (2004: 81-84) classifies *reporting genres* as forming a colony of *news reports*, *business reports*, and *law reports*, among others.

Move	Communicative Purpose	Move-constructing information
1	Identifying the Case	Provides the name of the parties, the court or tribunal, the catchwords, and the editors' name.
2	Reporting Facts	Provides a synopsis of only the essential (material as opposed to non-material) facts of the case derived from the contentions of the parties (as in appeal), and the lower court or tribunal's decisions.
3	Reporting Decision	Provides a synopsis of the court or tribunal ruling in the case derived from the argument(s) considered by the court or tribunal in support of, or against, the principle(s) for the Decision (*ratio/rationes decidendi*), by including concurrences, dissents, primary and secondary sources of law, collateral issues or any significant observation by the court/tribunal.

Table 3. Three-move organizational structure of case notes in Group A.

Although, from other (functional) theoretical perspectives, these purposes also define the *staged* and *goal-oriented* organization of the genre (Martin 1984, 1992, 1998; Eggins 1994), the bottom-up process (as content and function categorization) was key to define the genre as:

> "a recognizable communicative event characterized by a set of communicative purpose(s) identified and mutually understood by members of the professional or academic community" (Bhatia 1993: 13).[10]

In the structural description provided in Table 3 there was little doubt that the sequential order of the rhetorical moves or stages was frequently found in its pure form, and was therefore obligatory, in all CNs included in this Group. Given the generic replicability, the model description in Table 3 reflects the typical move sequences or stages used in the previous - and

[10] Despite the complexity and variability of defining *communicative purpose* in genre studies (Askehave and Swales 2001), identifying the genre along its communicative purpose(s) relied on the (ESP) genre analytical framework which reveals not only the utilizable form-function correlations but also significantly the cognitive structuring of information (Bhatia 1993).

also prototypical - judgment, although in a very narrowed rhetorical configuration.

Economy of generic moves for intended purposes

As noted so far and shown in Table 3, the three-move structural model is one which captures the economy of utilizing synoptic moves in marking prior cases through a logical flow, except where the synoptic approach is reasonably done away with in Move 1, which is the normal way to briefly identify the case informatively in space constraints of the journals.

In this context, the fundamental assumption was that synoptic moves in the structured genre were designed to have an appeal particularly to practitioners (whether as legal professionals or, indeed, as students) for whom they served the ultimate purpose of providing information in the rudiments of a specific case (hence the informative purpose of the reporting genre), as well as an opportunity for them to keep abreast of the latest judicial developments. For the legal professionals (lawyers, judges), in particular, reading the important elements in a snapshot of the case may well have helped them apply those elements appropriately to later fact patterns. And the short, succinct statements listed in the narrative Facts (with no more than 3 short sentences on average) and the Decision (with no more than 4 short sentences on average), pointed to the readers as practitioners making a usable record of the prior case within an instantly informative purpose achieved in the 'commodified' publication profile of the journals.[11] Yet, implied in this purpose was that the synoptic moves may also have acted as a points-of-entry to the full judgment with which practitioners wished to become fully conversant. Where this is so, writing in the case note genre therefore allowed for the legal information to be created incrementally, by relocating the practitioners from one generic action (the rhetorically narrowed case note) to another (the rhetorically widened judgment).

However, the economy rationale of writing case notes for information purposes brings into focus some differences with other comparable genres used in the professional legal pantheon. In the earlier work of Bhatia (1993), we are informed about the communicative purpose of a similar genre labelled differently as *legal cases*. Among these:

[11] In keeping with *interdiscursivity* as part of the *colonization/commodification* process (Fairclough 1992; Bhatia 2004), I take legal discourse in the (electronic) genre product here as becoming part of the goods and, therefore, success on markets.

> "Cases, as reported in some casebooks are meant to serve as reminders to legal experts, who use them in their arguments in the classroom or in the court of law. These versions are generally very brief and contain nothing more than the essential material facts and the decision of the judge" (Bhatia 1993: 119-120).

Although 'case reports' (CRs), as descriptively labelled in my study, share similarity with Bhatia's *cases*, in terms of the focus on the essential information for legal practitioners, they still differ in terms of their publication medium (journal as opposed to casebook), and naming (case notes as opposed to *cases*). Without fussing around with labels, similarities in the summary rationale also arise between the current 'case reports' and the variously named *case reported / case summaries* prepared by the reporters of THE INCORPORATED COUNCIL OF LAW REPORTING *for England and Wales*[12], although differences are still to be found in the publication medium (journal as opposed to ICLR institutional law website), as well as the organizational structure and format of reportable cases published on this website.

Generic move and sub-move constructing information

Depending upon the communicative purpose served in the generic moves, case notes in this Group somewhat varied in the specific type of information included in the moves, as measured by the elements of *sub-moves* or *strategies* (Bhatia 1993, 2001: 86) chosen by the writers to realize the generic moves. Table 4 below shows the data results of such a variability in the move and sub-move content realizations:

[12] See the Homepage of THE INCORPORATED COUNCIL OF LAW REPORTING: <http://www.iclr.co.uk>

Moves	Information constructed in generic moves and sub-moves	NILR	ELJ
		CNs:N°	CNs:N°
1	1.1 Naming the case by partial citation: Ex: *X v Y (Court/Tribunal) / Case Concerning [specify subject] (X v Y)* *or* Naming the case by full citation:	20	
	1.2 Date hearing and judgment	20	20
	1.3 Catchwords		20
	1.4 Editor's name		20
2	2.1 Outlining the parties' contentions *Or*	9	5
	2.2 in combination with lower court/tribunal's decisions *via*	11	15
	2.3 primary sources of law	1	2
3	3.1 Outlining the ruling on a point of law *via*	20	20
	3.2 concurrences (*optional*)	6	7
	3.3 dissents (*optional*)	5	6
	3.4 primary and secondary sources of law (*optional*)	1	2
	3.5 collateral issues or any significant observation by the court/tribunal (*optional*)	3	4

Table 4. Generic move and sub-move constructing information in CNs included in Group A: occurrence frequency.

Unlike ELJ case notes, naming the case in Move 1 by full citation only, those included in NILR constantly omitted full citation in favour of naming the case by partial citation, although they named the editors as those in the other journal but did so in different positions. Factual issues in Move 2 were unevenly represented in case notes, with writers mostly opting for an outline of the parties' contentions in combination with the lower court decisions in sub-move 2.2 rather than for an outline of the parties' contentions alone (2.1), leaving the legal sources there sometimes to be moved forward from Move 3. Clearly, the three choices in such move (2.1-2.2-2.3) depended on the historical rationale of the procedural action. While all the journal case notes outlined the ruling on a point of law in sub-move 3.1, no more than a third of them added concurrences, dissents, legal sources, or collateral issues in various types of sub-move (3.2, 3.3, 3.4, 3.5), whether by sequential order or inversion, thus leaving the other two thirds and above (the large majority) of case notes to omit a similar choice of sub-moves. Where these sub-moves were omitted, the reason lay in their being optional in the rationale of the prior case, depending again upon the content requirements set by the substantive or procedural resolution of the matter in the case being reported. Under these circumstances (omitting sub-moves), writers reported a snappy two-line summary of the Decision by including the legal rule which the case established [Decision as to substantive law] followed by the disposition of the case in matters of procedure [Decision as to procedural law], as in:

> The chancellor, … /// **[Move 3]** held that those objections were not of sufficient weight to justify the refusal of the grant of a faculty. A faculty was granted. [*author's name*] ELJ 2011
> [Decision as to substantive and procedural law]

> **[Move 3]** Therefore, the Appeals Chamber held that Šljivančanin's intention to kill the prisoners could no longer be proven. The Appeals Chamber reduced Šljivančanin's sentence to 10 years' imprisonment.
> NILR 2011
> [Decision as to substantive and procedural law]

Despite some degree of *intra*generic variability in the sub-move realizations of the case notes published in both journals, writers were still observant of the essential information included in the generic move order, and therefore achieved their professional purposes or goals in the genre. By highlighting how writers constructed and interpreted the social or communicative event in the genre, this rhetorical (move) structure therefore became close to obligatory organization and depended upon the outcome of the case note genre expected by the writers and the appropriate editorial team checking and sub-editing published case material. In the set of genuinely published case notes shown immediately below, editorial intervention was evidenced by the words *Edited by* and *Name* (Managing Editor), appearing at the beginning of case notes published in ELJ or at the end of those published in NILR. It therefore suggested some kind of 'front-stage' and 'back-stage' situated roles of the editors as integral entities and vehicles for case note writing.

Move-order schematic mind: a glance

Viewed operatively, the move-order schematic mind of professional writers can be seen in the conventionalized full samples below (1-2), running along 145 and 193 words, respectively. Here, a synopsis of the material facts (i.e. those leading up to the issue) and the rationale of the church court (chancellor) and the ICTY/ICJ in arriving at its decision were succinctly given by way of 'narratives', as used here to describe the unfolding of a sequence of events and actions over time for the purpose of immediately telling what happened (hence instant recounts). This way then, narratives allowed the writers to place background information first and then relocate such information within established legal paradigms of the Decision proper:

(1)

Re St Margaret, Halliwell **[M1]**

Manchester Consistory Court: Tattersall Ch, October 2009

Confirmatory faculty – unauthorised works – costs

Edited by [name][1] and [name][2]
[1] Barrister, Deputy Chancellor of the Dioceses of Chichester and Norwich
[2] Rector of Girton, Ely Diocesan Ecumenical Officer

[M2] The priest-in-charge and a churchwarden petitioned for a faculty for roof repairs. After an oral hearing the chancellor made findings that the petitioners had authorised the undertaking of the proposed works without a faculty despite knowing that one was required and that the DAC did not support their proposal. He further found that the petitioners had completed the petition in a misleading manner and had attempted to conceal the fact that works had already been completed. ///**[M3]** He ordered that the petitioners should each personally make a contribution of £100 towards the cost of the petition to mark the gravity of their behaviour. [*author's name*]
ELJ 2010

(2)

International Criminal Tribunal for the Former Yugoslavia **[M1]**

The Prosecutor v. Šljivančanin (Appeals Chamber)

[M2] On 8 December 2010, the Appeals Chamber of the ICTY rendered its first review judgment in the case of Šljivančanin. Šljivančanin was sentenced to 17 years' imprisonment on 5 May 2009 by the Appeals Chamber of the ICTY for aiding and abetting the torture of over 200 prisoners of war after the fall of Vukovar in Croatia in November 1991 (for which he was convicted by the Trial Chamber on 27 September 2007) as well as for aiding and abetting their murder. Following new testimonial

> evidence from a former Yugoslav Army officer – Panić – the Appeals Chamber quashed Šljivančanin's conviction for aiding and abetting the murder of the prisoners. Panić testified that Šljivančanin had not been informed by Mrkšić (the former commander of all Serb forces including the Territorial Defence and paramilitary forces in the Vukovar area and sentenced to 20 years' imprisonment) about his decision to withdraw the troops who guarded the prisoners. /// [**M3**] Therefore, <u>the Appeals Chamber held that</u> Šljivančanin's intention to kill the prisoners could no longer be proven. The Appeals Chamber reduced Šljivančanin's sentence to 10 years' imprisonment. [*name*] (Managing Editor) NILR 2011

These and other examples show that the usual practice of writers was to realize their communicative purposes more effectively by relying on the distinguished (rather than embedded) syntax of the rhetorical moves. Indeed, depending on the reporting function of the genre, writers in NILR were more likely to open Move 2 with a quick foretaste of the nature of the decision, such as with the words *On 8 December 2010, the Appeals Chamber of the ICTY rendered its first review judgment*, followed by the facts in disputes in distinguished move syntax, and in any case leaving the substance of the decision to make its independent appearance in Move 3, as noted in the (<u>underlined</u>) example statements in (1) and (2) above.

Given the condensed rhetorical move sequences, however, one might expect the writers of case notes to take away the most readily attainable contents from the prior case, in ways that their case note writing would be deprived interdiscursively of the rhetorical action deriving from the judgment. Rather, by acting as 'reporters' of decided cases in the journal, writers were skillfully attentive to the reams of case material, so that the essential Issues of Fact (i.e. cause of action and issue on appeal) and Law (i.e. those required to reach a final disposition of the case) could be easily identified and linked in a concise and accurate piece of generic writing. And while this helped disciplinary readers to be instantly informed about the case in the publication medium, being heedful of the reams of case material also made a strong case for Grice's (1975) Cooperative Principle, along the potential maxims of:

- "Quantity (Make your contribution as informative as is required - Do not make your contribution more informative than is Required)"; and
- "Manner (Be brief (avoid unnecessary prolixity) - Be orderly)" (Grice 1975: 45-46).

Yet, as already seen in (1) and the qualitative/quantitative data in Table 4, a good degree of *intra*generic variability comes to surface at the rhetorical Move 1-level of case note writing, since ELJ writers widened the Move conventional boundaries by including more information than their counterparts did in NILR. In surface realizations, this widened move boundary can be seen in a lengthier ELJ case note in (3), running along 545 words:

(3)

Re St Mary Magdalene, Reigate **[M1]**

Southwark Consistory Court: Petchey Ch, September 2010

Reordering – relocation of rood screen – secular system – Bishopsgate questions
Edited by [name][1]
[1] Barrister, Deputy Chancellor of the Dioceses of Chichester and Norwich

[M2] The petitioners (the incumbent and churchwardens) sought a faculty for a major re-ordering of the grade II* listed parish church. The proposals included the relocation of the central section of the rood screen and the removal and disposal of pews. English Heritage raised no objection to the proposals. The DAC recommended the works, having consulted the (then) Council for the Care of Churches. A number of letters of objection were received from individuals. The Society for the Protection of Ancient Buildings objected to the relocation of the central section of the rood screen. The Victorian Society, in addition to objecting to that aspect of the proposals, objected to the removal of the nave pews. The local authority also objected on those two grounds. SPAB and the Victorian Society became parties opponent. The petition was determined on consideration of written representations under rule 26(1) of the Faculty Jurisdiction Rules 2000. In a judgment extending to 79 pages the chancellor carried out a thorough survey of government policy and guidance in respect of the historic environment, including in particular Planning Policy Statement 5 (2010) and what it said about to the need to recognise both that ‘heritage assets’ were a ‘non-renewable resource’ and that ‘intelligently managed change may sometimes be necessary’. The chancellor also considered the principles that lay behind the ecclesiastical exemption and, in particular, the principle that it would be operated on a basis that was ‘no less strict’ than the secular system of listed building control. ///**[M3]** <u>He concluded that</u> the principles enunciated by the ecclesiastical courts do not lead to authorisations that would not properly be available in the secular sphere. In particular, the balancing exercise enjoined by the third of the *Bishopsgate* questions involved giving greater weight to the heritage asset the more

> significant it was. The chancellor held that on the evidence the rood screen – although it had been subject to restoration in the nineteenth century – did retain a majority of original, mediaeval work and that it was 'still evidently very significant'. Applying the *Bishopsgate* questions, the chancellor held that a faculty should not be granted to permit the removal and relocation within the church of the central section of the rood screen. Having been installed in its current location in the fifteenth century, it was a 'remarkable survival' and unique within Surrey. It contributed substantially to the character of the church building and relocating its central section would destroy its integrity. The need for change that had been shown – the improvement of sight lines and the removal of a physical separation between worshippers in a large and growing church – did not outweigh the severe harm that the proposals relating to the screen would involve. The pews, by contrast, were not 'particularly special' and they could, in principle, be removed. The chancellor was not satisfied about the detail of the proposals for the chairs that would replace them. Accordingly, the chancellor made his judgment an interim judgment so that further material could be submitted to the court concerning the seating, following a meeting of interested parties. [*author's name*] ELJ 2011

For a start, the current reader will appreciate that the content in Move 2 and Move 3 above is one which frames the diverse orders of discourse through the particular modes of *intertextuality* and *interdiscursivity* noted before, and Move 3 also shows a considerable degree of argumentation or rationale from the judge which formed the basis for the reported Decision. Apart from such important observation, the above and other examples from ELJ show that writers as again made conscious choices at the service of the journal's editorial practice by including a variety of structured elements in Move 1. As I noted earlier, these elements were absent in CNs published in NILR, which only provided for a quick identification of the case by partial citation. Thus, by contrast, the ELJ writer in (3) identified the case name by full citation and provided catchwords in *italics* (i.e. *Reordering – relocation of rood screen – secular system – Bishopsgate questions*), serving up a useful strategy for the writer and the publisher to tag the subject matter of the case. The effect is that browsing through these catchwords was a quick way for the interested reader to gain an idea of the topical relevance of the case. By encapsulating the relevant legal issues with which the prior case was concerned, catchwords seemed to add yet another economical feature of marking cases in the publication profile, that is, saving the time spent on reading the judgment and writing the case note efficiently.

Aside from these information-tagging purposes, however, it is not surprising that the conventional catchwords in the current (English *loci*) 'case reports' replicate not only those used in the previous judgment but also those typically appearing in the (English *loci*) law report series published in the Weekly Law Report Daily of THE INCORPORATED COUNCIL OF LAW REPORTING *for England and Wales*.[13] The result, then, is that catchwords were not only one of the resources manifesting the kind of colonization process I referred to before (in terms of structural interpretation and description), but they also fulfilled the purpose of being eye catching and quickly read by the interested readers like newspaper headlines. Where the catchwords fitted at the top of the case note genre functioned to quickly identify the subject matter of the case presented in the published texts, the latter reasonably contributed to informing the reader about the *news value* (Berkenkotter and Huckin 1995) of reported legal developments within the journal profile.

Narrowed / widened move boundary: self-promotion and business aspects?

In this context, some implications should be drawn from the narrowed/widened Move boundary achieved through specific information in case notes published in NILR and ELJ.

On the one hand, the high informativity move-level achieved in ELJ seems to characterise a desire for self-promotion by the stakeholders concerned (writers and editors), as measured by the practice of giving prominence to their names and professional roles in 'front' and 'back-stage'. In other words, the stakeholders desire "to communicate 'private intentions' within the rhetorical context of a 'socially recognized communicative purpose'" (Bhatia 2004: 24). On the other hand, visibility given to names and roles can only contribute to building the journal's credit, and similarly add value to the publishing process through the "commodification" or "marketization" of discourse (Fairclough 1992). As with publishing in other academic domains, these strategies are pervasive in contemporary legal publishing, where the open-access (electronic) journals are competitively committed to advertising the highest quality legal research and case law developments to targeted key audiences, and in the latter commitment to keep practitioners abreast of such developments through published case notes.

By some contrast, the practice of giving prominence to writers and editors' names as well as roles was only partially featured in case notes

[13] See the Homepage of THE INCORPORATED COUNCIL OF LAW REPORTING: <http://www.iclr.co.uk>

published in NILR. Here, we have seen, the name of the Managing Editor alone was provided in 'back-stage' position to build as yet the journal's credit in marketization objectives, but with no actual writer's name. Where the writer's name is coupled with the absence of catchwords in this journal, the effect therefore seems to lower the snapshot level of move informativity already at the outset in the journal case notes.

Micro-level linguistic descriptions

Given the reporting function of the genre to provide rhetorical recounts of previous judgments, the specificity of this function was qualified by a fair degree of lexico-grammatical expressions defining the temporally sequenced information in the construction of Move 2 and Move 3. These Moves thus offered the rhetorical site where writers displayed the use of clearly identifiable strategies from an "appropriation of linguistic and discoursal resources" (Bhatia 2004: 90), as derived from the previous texts and discourses within the judgment and generally inherent in the prototypicality of such generic category.

In Move 2, whose rationale was to present the quick memo of the procedural history in the reported case, past tense forms functioned as the primary surface marker of narrative discourse (Biber 1988; Toolan 2009). The following set of extracts in (4) present a narrative focus with agency features (underlined), namely the parties' reference (and other inanimate agents), and active verbs (*italics*) in simple past tense. As noted, these features focused on the temporal sequence of events and actions borrowed from the previous case, although the tendency in NILR was to open up Move 2 with a foretaste of the Decision in the relevant court instance which prepared for the narrative focus on the parties proper:

(4)

[M2]

The priest-in-charge and a churchwarden *petitioned* for a faculty for roof repairs. ... ELJ 2010

The petitioners (the incumbent and churchwardens) *sought* a faculty for a major re-ordering of the grade II* listed parish church. The proposals *included* the relocation of the central section of the rood screen and the removal and disposal of pews. English Heritage *raised* no objection to the proposals. The DAC *recommended* the works, having consulted the (then) Council for the Care of Churches. A number of letters of objection were received from individuals. ... ELJ 2011

> The Dean of Arches *dismissed* an application for leave to appeal against the grant of a faculty by the Commissary Court of Canterbury for a major re-ordering of a grade I listed church (noted at (2010) 13 Ecc LJ 120), the proposed appeal having no real prospect of success and there being no other compelling reason why the appeal should be heard. The Commissary General *had not erred* in his approach to the *Bishopsgate* questions. ...
> ELJ 2011

> On 30 November 2010, the International Court of Justice *delivered* its judgment in the dispute between the Republic of Guinea (Guinea) and the Democratic Republic of the Congo (DRC) concerning the treatment of Mr. Diallo, a Guinean national and citizen of the DRC. Exercising its rights of diplomatic protection, Guinea *complained* about the alleged mistreatment of Mr. Diallo as a person and as an '*associe*' in his Congolese companies by the DRC at various periods in the late 1980s and mid 1990s. Mr. Diallo's mistreatment *consisted of* his arrest, detention and expulsion from the DRC and the deprivation of his right … NILR 2011

> On 8 December 2010, the Appeals Chamber of the ICTY *rendered* its first review judgment in the case of Šljivančanin. Šljivančanin was sentenced to 17 years' imprisonment on 5 May 2009 by the Appeals Chamber of the ICTY for aiding and abetting the torture of over 200 prisoners of war after the fall of Vukovar in Croatia in November 1991 (for which he was convicted by the Trial Chamber on 27 September 2007) as well as for aiding and abetting their murder. Following new testimonial evidence from a former Yugoslav Army officer – Panić – the Appeals Chamber *quashed* Šljivančanin's conviction for aiding and … NILR 2011

In these and other examples, where the use of passive verbs (e.g. *A number of letters of objection were received ... / Šljivančanin was sentenced to 17 years' imprisonment ...*) was lower in incidence than active verbs, active past tense forms alternated sometimes with the past perfect tense constructed with *had + past participle* (*The Commissary General had not erred in his approach to the Bishopsgate questions*), which thus allowed writers to report events of a 'second' or earlier past in the procedural action. As with other instances in the corpus, these examples show that writers avoided broad generalizations in Move 2 by the use of epistemic modal verbs and other (modal) lexical items.

Similarly, in Move 3, past tense forms were used to report the essentials of the rule of the case derived from the court's rationale for the Decision, and therefore qualified the reported statements around the legitimacy of such Decision. In the following extracts (5-6), for instance, writers outlined the ruling on a point of law by one or more formal pronouncements in (*that*) reported statements (underlined), which disposed of the Decision in terms of substantive law (*He concluded that ... / The chancellor held that on the evidence ... / The Court held that there were ...*) and legal procedure (*... the chancellor held that a faculty should be granted ...*):

(5)

[M3]

He concluded that the principles enunciated by the ecclesiastical courts do not lead to authorisations that would not properly be available in the secular sphere. In particular, the balancing exercise enjoined by the third of the *Bishopsgate* questions involved giving greater weight to the heritage asset the more significant it was. The chancellor held that on the evidence the rood screen – although it had been subject to restoration in the nineteenth century – did retain a majority of original, mediaeval work and that it was 'still evidently very significant'. Applying the *Bishopsgate* questions, the chancellor held that a faculty should not be granted to permit the removal and relocation within the church of the central section of the rood screen. Having been installed in its current location in the fifteenth century, it was a 'remarkable survival' and unique within Surrey. It contributed substantially to the character of the church building and relocating its central section would destroy its integrity. The need for change that had been shown – the improvement of sight lines and the removal of a physical separation between worshippers in a large and growing church – did not outweigh the severe harm that the proposals relating to the screen would involve. The pews, by contrast, were not 'particularly special' and they could, in principle, be removed. The chancellor was not satisfied about the detail of the proposals for the chairs that would replace them. Accordingly, the chancellor made his judgment an interim judgment so that further material could be submitted to the court concerning the seating, following a meeting of interested parties. [*author's name*] ELJ 2011

(6)

[M3]

The Court unanimously established the maritime delimitation by reference to Articles 74 and 83 of the United Nations Convention on the Law of the Sea and held that there were no circumstances, including the presence of the Serpents' Islands, that called for an adjustment of the provisional equidistance line for reasons of equity. [*name*] (Managing Editor)

NILR 2009

Indeed, as noted before about the criteria of move-constructing information based on the rationale of the case, the above examples illustrate that the writer in NILR (6) provided only a brief realization of the informational move by giving an outline of the Decision in a snappy one-line summary. By contrast, the writer in ELJ (5) took a more detailed approach to such a move, which was constructed by cumulative reporting of the court rulings. Of course, by meticulously reporting the Decision in past (and perfect) tense constructions, the ELJ writer above (as others in lengthier case notes there) was also concerned with the important legal standards used in the judgment, which he wrote down using (intertextually) the exact judicial words in single quotation marks (*…it was 'still evidently very significant'*) without however fully citing the relevant legal source in footnote format. While the emphasis on the actual language in the case was almost practically ignored by NILR writers (regardless of case note length), the ELJ writer above made use of information in the *em dash* (– –) punctuation mark, which was quite frequent in ELJ but absent in NILR case notes. By setting off an element in the summarised exposition of principles or reasons for the Decision, this mark was generally used to explain the preceding material (– *the improvement of sight lines …*–), also by 'conceding' the subsequent material (– <u>*although*</u> *it had been subject …*–), or sometimes digress from the main clause.

Moreover, the examples above illustrate that writers reported the act of 'deciding' by attributing the source of information to clearly identified agents in subject position (usually the chancellor of ecclesiastical court in ELJ or the international court/tribunal in NILR), although occasionally in the same text the source of information was attributed impersonally in agentless passive construction (*It was held that*) to be followed by concurrences (majority opinions):

(7)

[M3]

> *It was held that* she had not been subjected to direct or indirect discrimination contrary to the provisions of the Employment Equality (Religion or Belief) Regulations 2003. Despite evidence that another nurse had been asked to remove her cross and chain, <u>the Employment Tribunal held by a majority that</u> the other nurse had not been put at a particular disadvantage since her religious views were not so strong as to lead her to refuse to comply with the policy … . ELJ 2011

In all cases where writers reported the act of 'deciding', the declarative act was signalled by the very brief, formulaic past tense verb *held* (<u>holding</u>). Although *hold* and *rule* reporting verbs (decide) were the most frequent forms in both journals, the air of authority lent by these verb forms was replaced in some instances in ELJ by the lower authoritative tone of the *conclude/state* verb choices. Considering that, as a result of generic replicability, verbal action in case notes was relevant to keep a dialogue with judicial language, the latter also clearly emerged from other (active/passive) verb choices reporting 'matters of procedure' in the opening lines of Move 2 in both journals or the closing lines of Move 3 (disposing of the Decision in the case) in ELJ alone, as in the (underlined) examples below:

(8)

[M2]

The Dean of Arches dismissed an application for leave to appeal against the grant … ELJ

The Church of Jesus Christ of Latter-day Saints (LDS) appealed against the decision that buildings … ELJ

On 21 July 2010, the Appeals chamber partially quashed the acquittals of … NILR

The appeal was dismissed. ELJ
The appeals were allowed. ELJ

In these contexts, it should be noted that concise and impartial reporting generally did away with nominalising verbs, which occurred only occasionally in Move 2 with the verb 'find' (different from 'disposing of the case' in the usual performative verb 'find'), preparing for the rationale of 'ordering' in Move 3:

(9)
[**M2**] After an oral hearing the chancellor made findings that the petitioners had authorised the undertaking of the proposed works without a faculty despite knowing that one was required and that the DAC did not support their proposal. He further found that ... [**M3**] He ordered that the petitioners should ... . ELJ

Interestingly, however, there was only one instance in ELJ dealing with 'neglect or inefficiency of clergy discipline' shown in (10). Here, the construction of Move 2 and Move 3 was dictated by paragraphing the cumulative contents of the claims for action and ruling, using the system of lettering (i, ii) typical of legislative texts as well as judgments:

(10)
[**M2**]… diocesan secretary and the Bishop of Chester, arranged for Z to stand down temporarily as a youth worker. In March 2006, Canon

Robinson attempted to re-instate Z, having been outvoted on the matter at a meeting of the PCC. The complaint concerned:

i. Allowing Z to act as a voluntary youth worker in 2004 without first obtaining CRB clearance;
ii. After CRB disclosure was obtained, ignoring diocesan advice to terminate the appointment pending a risk assessment; and
iii. After the PCC had determined that Z should stand down pending a risk assessment, attempting to re-instate Z in March 2006 as a voluntary youth worker without obtaining a child protection risk assessment.

Each, it was alleged, amounted to neglect or inefficiency in the performance of the duties of Canon Robinson's office under section 8(1)(c) of the Clergy Discipline Measure 2003, in failing to comply with the House of Bishops' Child Protection Policy 2004, as applied in the Diocese of Chester, and not following the recommended safe recruitment practice. [**M3**] The tribunal found that:

i. Canon Robinson had failed to comply with the House of Bishops' Policy in appointing Z to start work as voluntary youth worker and that this constituted deliberate neglect in the performance of the duties of Canon Robinson's office;
ii. The deliberate conduct of Canon Robinson in allowing Z to continue to work as a youth worker following receipt of the diocesan secretary's letter constituted a failure to comply with the Policy and (by a majority of 4 to 1) that this constituted neglect in the performance of the duties of Canon Robinson's office; and
iii. Canon Robinson's attempt to re-instate Z as a youth worker constituted a failure to comply with the Policy and (again by a majority of 4 to 1) that this constituted neglect in the performance of the duties of his office.

Canon Robinson was rebuked and restrained for a period of five years from making, or sharing in the making of, any appointment involving direct or regular contact with children in respect of which enhanced or standard disclosure from the CRB is required pursuant to any relevant House of Bishops' or diocesan policy document, in any parish of which he was incumbent or priest-in-charge. [*author's name*] ELJ 2009

While the choice for the lettering system in the example potentially allowed for perusal of the contents so that the latter may be referred to easily and quickly by reducing the possibility for ambiguity, it seems that the choice was also a matter of the writer's personal style. More than that, the unique example in (10) shows that the acts of 'deciding' (substantive law) in *that*-reporting clauses in Move 3 were combined with the act of 'informing' (procedural law) by verbal report about the end-results of the incident (*Canon Robinson was rebuked ...*), provided in the closing line of the text within the purposeful activity of Move 3. Interestingly, however, the heavy tone of end-results is still unique in the current context, since it informed about the severe criticism or reproof of the *incumbent* being disposed of in that Decision.

In addition to reporting the Decision through the judicial pronouncements, writers from both journals were also concerned with majority and minority opinions, as required by the context of the prior judgment and indeed the generic prototype. As a consequence, writers added optional information in Move 3 through concurrences, dissents and collateral issues realized in the distinguished syntax of the reported sub-moves (underlined), which thus provided context for the Decision constructing-move, as in:

(11)

[M3]

> … the Employment Tribunal held by a majority that [**concurrences**] the other nurse had not been put at a particular disadvantage since her religious views were not so strong as to lead her to refuse to comply with the policy and, following *Eweida v British Airways*, concluded that the uniform policy did not 'place "persons" at a particular advantage'. The minority, by contrast, held that [**dissents**]both nurses had been placed at a disadvantage but that this was justified. [*authors' names*] ELJ
>
> The Court unanimously established ... [**concurrences**] and held that ... NILR
>
> The tribunal noted that [**collateral issue**] the case involved 'a direct conflict between the legislative protection afforded to religion or belief and the legislative protection afforded to sexual orientation'. ELJ
>
> The Appeals Chamber also observed that [**collateral issue**] the crime against the Tutsi woman was qualitatively different from the other acts of genocide … NILR

Among optional sub-moves, collateral issues (*obiter dicta*) were reported as side comments in the case notes, since they were not necessary to the court's decision but still part of the body of the court's opinion.

As with concurrences, dissents and collateral issues, a quick reminder of primary and secondary legislation was given in Move 3 in order to qualify the reported statements of the Decision in the relative optional sub-moves. Given the synoptic nature of the genre, the regular practice here was to cite primary legislation (Acts, Rules, Conventions) by their short titles and to cite secondary legislation (case law) by the name of cases outside full citation system (such as: *XvY [year] + a particular set of law reports*) although, it should be noted, the general label attached here to primary legislation became the variant for other legislation of 'internal currency' in ecclesiastical case notes (such as, Faculty Jurisdiction Rules). Citing other sources in the text (however marginal their use was in both journals) was essential only when required by the rationale of the case, since it gave support to legal principles for Decision in summary format by providing coherence to intertextual patterning (Bhatia 1993) in a variety of sources. Correspondingly, referencing was necessary to understand the Decision constructing-move in the genre, as it was in the previous judgment. Thus, in the NILR example below (12), where a two-line summary of the Decision was reported, the sequential citation of primary sources (<u>underlined</u>), using the simple preposition (*under*), was given in support of the court's reasoning (*ratio*), in ways that cited sources made the synoptic writing impressive and authoritative:

(12)

[M3]

The Court ruled that by arresting and detaining Mr. Diallo in the 1990s, the DRC had breached its obligations towards Guinea <u>under Article 9 of the International Convention on Civil and Political Rights (ICCPR), Article 6 of the African Charter on Human Rights (ACHR) as well as under Article 36 of the Vienna Convention on Consular Relations</u>. Further the Court ruled that by expelling Mr. Diallo, the DRC had breached its obligations towards Guinea <u>under Article 13 ICCPR and Article 12 ACHR</u>.

NILR 2011

Indeed, as a result of variation in move-constructing information, the writer in ELJ below (13) presented a more detailed description of the chancellor's *rationes decidendi* in the grounds of appeal via 'internal' sources and case law (<u>underlined</u>), until he outlined the ultimate Decision introduced in the past passive tense (*As no right of way had been authorised by Act, Measure or faculty, <u>it was held that no right of way existed ...</u>*):

(13)

[M3]

The chancellor rejected their objection on two grounds. First, that the objectors did not have standing to object under <u>rule 16(1) of the Faculty Jurisdiction Rules 2000</u> as they did not satisfy the definition of 'interested person' <u>in Rule 16(2)</u>: they resided primarily in the Isle of Man, did not

> appear on the parish electoral register and the freehold of the former vicarage was vested in a Manx-registered company, the objectors holding no apparent legal or beneficial interest. Second (if wrong on the issue of standing), assuming that the objectors relied upon either the rule in *Wheeldon v Burrows* or section 62 of the Law of Property Act 1925, the chancellor held that no right of way existed. Applying *Re St Peter, Bushey Heath*, which followed *St Mary Abbots, Kensington (Vicar and Churchwardens) v St Mary Abbots, Kensington (Inhabitants)*, it was impossible to create a legal estate in consecrated land except under the authority of an Act of Parliament or a Measure. Further, upon conveyance of the former vicarage, the vendor (the then incumbent) was incapable of granting such a right of way to a purchaser in the absence of the express authority of a faculty: *Re St Clement, Leigh-on-Sea* applied. As no right of way had been authorised by Act, Measure or faculty, it was held that no right of way existed; … . ELJ 2011

Further linguistic features

For the sake of complete data, other lexical (-semantic) and stylistic features of case notes in Group A are worthy of note.

Far from stating the obvious, the lexical and stylistic differences between case notes in this Group were determined by the contents of the prior judgments in the relevant law area, whether dealing with the topics of ecclesiastical and canon law (ELJ), or public and private international law (NILR). Clearly, they were also influenced by the purview of the single journals in which ecclesiastical or international case notes were published. Viewed qualitatively, the use of ecclesiastical nominal terms in ELJ such as, *chancellor*, *diocese*, *incumbent*, *Measure*, *faculty*, *Diocesan Advisory Committees*, *parish electoral register* and *vicarage*, were significant lexical features that functionally identified the law area in the rationale of the judgments reported in the case notes.[14] Of these topic-specific terms, the noun *incumbent* (i.e. a person, especially a clergyman, who holds an office or ecclesiastical benefice) was replaced by other terms of common legal currency (i.e. *appellant*, *claimant*, *complainant*, *petitioner*) under the same circumstances in which relief of some kind was sought, although unexpectedly such terms identifying the aggrieved party were never used in NILR where the party was indeed referred to by name.

---

[14] Beyond this, however, these ecclesiastical terms enable the manifestation of the past in the present since they are steeped in the English system of secular justice (in terms of processes, rules and personnel), and the ecclesiastical cases summarized in the case notes were in fact determined by both secular and church courts.

Where relief of some kind was given, the resulting (procedural) term *faculty* was given a wide coverage and, like other replaceable terms, was used instead of *authorization* (as granted by ecclesiastical authority). As judgment responsive terms in the resulting purview of the journal, these lexical features were therefore socially constructed by the limits of a particular language and discourse.

The point about common currency, therefore, brings me to the next point in this analysis: formal legal language. Here, the tendency between case notes published in both journals shows that nominals, including their appearance in a variety of collocational information, were typical of formal legal language (e.g. *judgment*, *interim judgment*, *dispute*, *application for leave to appeal*, *dismiss grounds of appeal*, *acquit of charges*, *acts of genocide*, *instigating murder*, *reverse life sentence*), and therefore the stylistic frame of case notes in both journals was essentially equal, except when foreign (French) words (... *Mr Diallo as a person and as an* '<u>*associé*</u> *in his Congolese companies* ...) sometimes appeared in NILR case notes. Under these circumstances, foreignness marked the international span of case notes in this journal, as opposed to the strictly national span of case notes in ELJ.

Group B: 'article'-like writing with intended purpose

Interestingly, case notes in Group B (ECLR, MLR) appeared under a completely different guise, revealing the preference of writers to go beyond the organizational and rhetorical confines conventionally accorded by their counterparts (Group A) writing in seemingly the same genre. A reading of case notes in Group B shows in fact that they were not only summaries of recent, topical decisions in far lengthier formats but, more importantly, were critical analyses and discussions of such decisions together with their deficiencies and likely consequences. This way then, they departed manifestly from the nutshell rhetorical structure of case notes in Group A.

Variability arising from this wider rhetorical platform thus served as a measure for the new conventional, or prototypical structure of the case note genre, defined macrostructurally by the (culturally recognized) *staged, goal-oriented social processes* of functional text organization (Martin 1984, 1992, 1998; Eggins 1994). This systemic functional approach to the case note genre allowed for the identification of its overall purpose, which this author conceived as being 'to display a critical awareness and understanding of a *significant* issue in a recent decision and its effects on the current state of law', while at the same 'alerting readers to the significance of such decision'. And while this identifiable purpose of the genre was implied in the social world projected in the text (Hyland 2004), the genre focus on the critical and close examination of one judicial opinion's reasoning and result had the consequence of advancing a particular area of legal scholarship beyond its current state (adjunct purpose).

The presentation system as the concurring criterion for 'article' generic content and purpose

Case note writers were concerned with this overall social purpose which they took up in the organization of the texts at both macro and micro levels.

At the macro level, the immediate reference was to Martin (1992: 443), who focuses on the layout of a text by suggesting that "titles, sub-titles, headings and subheadings are commonly deployed to keep track of the composition structure [of the texts]". Based on this functionality framework, the presentation system in case notes provided a useful schematic arrangement of parts or sections, which allowed the writers on the one hand to be attentive of what content went in which part/section of the case note and, on the other, to reflect their knowledge of the topic and grasp of the case they were discussing. As an important concern among writers, schematic arrangement thus allowed for the structure of case notes to have definite sections to them, namely:

- Title
- Abstract
- Introduction
- Body
- Conclusion

Functionality in the schematic arrangement of parts/sections here is in fact indicative of the *schematic structure* or *generic structure* (Martin 1984, 1992, 1998; Eggins 1994), describing the various stages through which a text unfolds in certain, generally predictable sequences to accomplish the purpose of the social genre.[15] As a result of this functionality in text

[15] Functionality of the case note genre, based on RA conventional sections (Abstract, Introduction, Conclusion), is reflected in the discussions of the three-level genre realized by *communicative purpose*, *move structure* and *rhetorical strategies* (Swales 1990, 2004; Bhatia 1993), as examined in Chapter 2. The

organization, expert case notes captured the global rhetorical structure of most legal research articles of an argumentative nature, where most of the legal topics are controversial and require the writers to be aware of all the existing aspects of the chosen topic, as well as the possible questions that need answers.

Where, in functional terms, the case note genre became similar in structure to most law research articles, differences arose from the allowable contributions made by (experimental) data-driven research articles used across the sciences as well as the social science disciplines. Unlike these articles, in fact, the assumed 'article'-like structure of case notes was devoid of the experimental Methods and Results, and therefore less frozen than the standard IMRD research articles. The reason for such destitution lay in the rationale of community writers assigning their own legitimate disciplinary practices and forms to the genre, where discussing the various aspects of the law topics along their own epistemology and legal research method meant producing arguments in contexts where writers had to form an opinion or belief about something. The idea of argumentation in case notes therefore became the activity of legal reasoning linked with problem-solving[16] in that the rule-based reasoning in the genre took place in the framework of solving a material but *significant* problem in the chosen case. And while the link between argumentation and problem, and the need for a proper reasoning (resulting from a problem), were key to justify the inapplicability of Methods and Results in the structure of the genre, the consequence was that case note writers treated the genre as a socially and rhetorically functional construct, much like the prototypical law research article genre.[17]

Exercising the solution to a problem thus allowed case note writers to emphasize the *social action* of the genre (Miller 1984; Devitt 2004; Bhatia 2004), and as a consequence support their attention to the role of law in fulfilling 'social values' or otherwise serving 'the public interest'. The assumption for such values or public interest in the genre was implied in the essence of legal rules as instruments of 'social policy' or expressions

schematic structure of the Abstract, Introduction and Conclusion rhetorical sections, it will be seen, is indicative of a text's purpose and ultimately the social expectations held for the text (Tardy and Swales 2008).

[16] In fact, the problem-solving orientation to the genre here was not dissimilar from the *problem-solution pattern* of textual organization (Hoey 2001), common in English expository-type texts, and directed towards *goal-achievement* and *knowledge-gap filling*.

[17] In fact, writers of research articles are generally committed to the solution of some formal problem in the law.

of 'public values', so that rules may be compared with the generic instrument of the ('article'-like) argumentative case note for the attainment of similar ends.

Conventional sections: *Abstract – Introduction – Body – Conclusion*

To understand how the presentation system functionally contributed to the staged organization of the content in the structure of the genre, it is important to identify and highlight the role of the conventional (or standard) sections used in case notes, where tables and graphs were absent throughout.

To begin with, the totality of *Abstracts* (A), *Introductions* (I), and the greater number of *Conclusions* (C) had their distinct functional foci (communicative purpose) in the journal case notes, where they held an independent rhetorical status. While Abstracts made their appearance in all (20) case notes included in MLR alone, where their standard content-headings (A) were omitted, Introductions appeared under the corresponding content-heading (I) in the majority of samples (MLR: 12/20 – ECLR: 8/10), or lacked such heading in the minority of samples (MLR: 8/20 – ECLR: 2/10). In the latter case, the purpose of *introducing* case analysis was rhetorically transparent, it being inferred from the specific discourse content and function of the text as well as linguistic clues. Similarly, Conclusions made their independent appearance from The Body section under the corresponding content-heading (C) in the majority of samples (MLR: 16/20 – ECLR: 6/10), or used variations to such heading in the least number of case notes (MLR: 2 – ECLR: 1) by the use of the functional headings "Implications" and "Statutory Constructive Dismissal After Buckland" (MLR) or the varied standard heading "Final Remarks" (ECLR). Here, as again, the varied theme headings functioning as Conclusion in MLR were easy to infer by the specific discourse content and clues. Only in the least occurring instances was the (C) heading missing in the case notes (MLR: 2 – ECLR: 3), where it was merged with – rather than separated from – the apparently all-inclusive Body. Under the latter circumstances, the purpose of *concluding* case analysis was still straightforward from the discourse content.

Yet, while the conventional sections described above were largely self-explanatory and readily recognizable, the *Body* of case notes (B) required a more careful reading, since it was the most important research section where legal writers examined the relationship between the decision and the existing case and/or statutory law, and discussed important issues, cases, and legislation within the issue area. Typically, the Body section was broken down into a consistent hierarchy of content headings and subheadings, which were used as signposts to inform the reader about individual aspects of the topic for the analysis of the chosen case. This, therefore, meant using as many content headings as was necessary to organize the discussion of important issues in the paper sections.

Specifically, Body sections allowed the writers to analyze the relevant Issues of Facts and Law peculiar to the court's reasoning and decision in the case (named here as Legal Background) and to critically examine *if*, *how* and *why* the court's decision and reasoning raised significant issues that influenced law and policy (named here as Author's Argument). Consequently, presenting the case in its full legal context (Legal Background) helped the writers to develop their own lines of Argument by critically examining the case and raising the significant issues involved. This organisational, rhetorical framework engaged the writers in a large amount of what can be called 'processed data', which enabled the writers to rely on the 'givens' or 'evidence' (Legal Background) to support their own Argument on the case. The following fragments in (14), typically referring to several paragraphs in a chunk and running along 11 pages of published case notes, may give a flavour of the specific content and function realized by the Body sectional headings where the emphatic order of information was located:

(14)

The Body Schematic Structure at a Glance

The internal case

A German living in Germany stripped of German nationality in a German legal process: typically an internal case, a situation in which all of the elements are enclosed in one member state, which Union law has no say in, and which must lead to the inadmissibility of the preliminary questions. However, the Court and the A.G. are of a different opinion. The A.G. reasoned as follows. Not only was *Rottmann* born an Austrian in Austria, but he had already made use of his freedom of movement as an Austrian citizen by travelling to Germany and establishing himself there. This Union citizen had thereby made use of his right of freedom of movement, and thus this was no longer a strictly internal affair. <u>The definition of the internal case is by no means an innocent one</u>. By establishing very strict criteria for the internal case – <u>only absolutely purely internal affairs can be defined as such</u> – <u>the Court is significantly stretching the boundaries of admissibility and thereby its own authority as well</u>. … <u>It seems to me that the Court is taking a different track than the 'internal case'</u>. It determines (42): It is clear that the situation of a citizen of the Union who […] is faced with a decision withdrawing his naturalization …

And despite the fact that the Court takes the original nationality of another member state into consideration … the pretext/point of departure for its ruling is first and foremost Union citizenship and its threatened loss.[4] ……

Statelessness due to loss of nationality: public international law
According to public international law, may statelessness occur when loss of nationality is entailed by the occurrence of certain legal facts? Because statelessness is regarded as a severe exclusion from the system of states with …

The preceding history
In contrast to what the A.G. claims in his introduction, cited above, this is not the first time that the question has been put before the Court of the member states' degree of latitude to organize their own laws concerning nationality as they see fit. … [***facts summary***] It started in 1982 with Micheletti, the dual national Argentine-Italian dentist who wanted to practice in Spain. Spain found – in accordance with the Spanish *Código Civil* – that the Argentine nationality was his effective nationality and therefore denied him the European rights of establishment and provision of service. The Court ruled[6] that the Spanish test of effectiveness came into conflict with European law …..

The two principles of proportionality
Which consequences does the Court now draw from the jurisprudential mantra that nationality law, to be sure, belongs to the sphere of competence of the member states according to both written and unwritten international law, but that this competence must be exercised with due regard to Union law? According to the Court (48), this is a matter of establishing …

Commentary
<u>The Court is persisting in its judicial error</u>. The question of whether the European Union has authority over the organization of the member states' nationality law not only leads to divisions in the doctrine,[11] but also among the institutions of the Union. In its interventions in the cases submitted to the Court, and again in the *Rottmann* case, the Commission has systematically taken the point of view, despite the Court's case-law, that nationality law is a matter exclusively for the member states.[12] … ECLR 2011, 7: 138-149

This writer used various content-headings at different intervals to describe the Facts controlling the critical Issues of Law in the Court and A.G.'s reasonings (Legal Background). He therefore analyzed the Law in its full context as he contended it was, and thereafter laid out the elements of his analysis (Argument) in a separate "Commentary" on the case. Correspondingly, the relationship between Legal Background and "Commentary" headings was one in which the writer drew from a synthesis of Facts and Law issues to advance his own opinions separately in the Author's Argument section ("Commentary"), which critically examined the case by raising important issues involved. Although, obviously, other Legal Background functional headings were used, such as THE STATUS OF THE ELECTION COURT AND THE JURISDICTION OF THE DIVISIONAL COURT - THE COURT'S FINDINGS (MLR); THE POLITICAL AND LEGAL CONTEXT - THE GROUNDS OF THE CHALLENGE - THE OPINION OF ADVOCATE GENERAL BOT (ECLR), separating the varied functional Legal Background headings from the author's Argument section was only observed in 6 (out of 10) samples in ECLR and 5 (out of 20) samples in MLR. Indeed, in both journals, "Commentary" (Author's Argument) was diversely labelled as "Analysis", "Discussion" or "Comment(s)", the preference for such labels however being dictated outside 'published' editorial guidelines.

Faced with this organizational system, then, it became immediately apparent that the relationship between functional headings was imperative in the organizing mind of all 'separating' writers, who wished to provide two clearly defined 'moving' processes in the Body sections of their research. Intriguingly, though, the discourse content in the fragments above shows that, even when the purpose of Legal Background sections was to provide objective descriptions of the facts and the major arguments in the judicial reasoning and decision, they equally revealed the writer's own ideas and positions interspersing with the objectivity of Facts and Law covered. This was when Background presented some inconsistency in the judicial course of action, as in (14) (underlined) or, on other occasions, presented the writer's views in support or opposition of the holding of the case, including the ratio per judge, thus forming the Author's Argument. Therefore, the relationship between the distinct functional foci became necessarily fuzzy and fluid rather than distinct throughout the Body, since it allowed Legal Background sections not only to flesh out the Issues of Facts and Law in 'discuss' type of exposition but also to create the writer's overt or covert argumentative position in recursive processes, until the writers argued *if*, *how* and *why* the court had impacted the issue area in conventionalized "Commentary" or other varied functional headings. Under these circumstances, it seemed reasonable to treat the 'moving' rhetorical processes mandated by seemingly distinct content-headings as running with unbroken continuity under a 'Discussion' section, as introduced here, and constructed around different degrees of writer's involvement and argument in the case.

I have noted the tendency in the majority (MLR: 15) and minority (ECLR: 4) of journal case notes where writers avoided attributing an independent status to their own analysis (Argument) by the corresponding section. In these instances, the result was that writers used a variety of functional content-headings and sub-headings to smoothly articulate Issues of Facts and Law (Legal Background) to their Argument within the Body sections, as measured by their discourse content and linguistic clues. The writers' rationale here was to pile up an argument almost sentence by sentence to produce a mixture of Facts and Law, which thus showed the significance of the case in relation to the critical issues. Correspondingly, the Body structure of their research paper became yet again an unfolding 'Discussion' section with the 'no bounds' rhetorical concept, where argument was continually emphasized and justifications found. The fragments below (15), referring to several paragraphs in a chunk and running along 21 pages of (MLR) published case notes, may give a taste of this 'boundless' concept:

(15)

The Body Schematic Structure at a Glance

SOLE AND COMPLETE DISCRETION AS TO DESCRIPTION

Clause 2.7(b) granted the auctioneers 'sole and complete discretion' as to the description of the property in the catalogues and other literature. That may have been designed to exclude any liability, although the granting of an unfettered power may not necessarily say anything about one's potential liability for the consequences of its exercise. But in any event sub-clause (c) is an express exclusion of liability so that braces are added to the belt. ....

THE APPROPRIATENESS OF IMPLYING A TERM AS TO *WEDNESBURY* REASONABLENESS

The argument on behalf of the claimant was that the discretion had to be exercised reasonably in an objective sense. Christie's opposed this but conceded that they were enjoined to exercise it bona fide and 'reasonably' in the sense that it must not be exercised arbitrarily, capriciously, perversely or irrationally[24]; that is to say they accepted that '*Wednesbury* reasonableness' applied by necessary implication into their agency contract to limit their discretion as to their catalogue descriptions. ....

But is this an appropriate or necessary implication in an agency contract?

In *Abu Dhabi National Tanker Company*v *Product Star Shipping limited* (*The Product Star*) (No 2)18 Leggatt LJ said:....

Should the term have been implied into this contract?

The term appears to be implied in fact rather than law, notwithstanding the general words used by Leggatt LJ: 'Where A and B contract with each other to confer a discretion on A. . .'Certainly in the *Socimer*case[25] the argument proceeded on the basis that the term was 'necessary, in the traditional sense, for the sake of business e⁄cacy'.[26] This formulation is appropriate ...

SHOULD AN INJUNCTION HAVE BEEN GRANTED: WERE DAMAGES AN INAPPROPRIATE REMEDY?
The judge granted Mr Safra an injunction restraining the sale of all 119 lots. Should the injunction have been granted or was Mr Safra adequately protected by his remedy in damages? It is well established that this question should …

The Unfair Terms in Consumer Contracts Regulations 1999
These render certain terms not binding on the ground of unfairness but they will probably not be applicable. These Regulations only apply in cases where …

The Unfair Contract Terms Act 1977
In any event, the validity of the exclusion clause could be challenged on the ground that it falls foul of the provisions of the Unfair Contract Terms Act 1977. This is not the place for a detailed examination of the issue, but exclusions of contractual liability … MLR 2010, 73(6): 1026-1047

Outside any "Comment/ary", "Analysis" or "Discussion" functional heading, this writer used the lengthy sections in the Body of research to spread out the (underlined) Issues of Facts and Law that he had collected by arguing *if*, *how* and *why* the court's decision had an effect on the issue area, while also citing legal sources to uphold his Argument. And while the argument so formed guided the reader to the important issues in the case, it was not unusual for writers to phrase such issues in terms of Questions, such as: *But is this an appropriate or necessary implication in an agency contract?*

Macro-structure

The functional use of the presentation (layout) system was therefore particularly useful in formalizing the various stages through which the case note genre unfolded in the schematic structure. As a result of this system, a five-part generic structure model, as proposed here, was identified and outlined in Table 5 for the sake of clarity and comprehensiveness.[18]

[18] In this model, I drew on Miller's (1994: 24) view of genre as a "typified social action" where *rhetorical functions* are defined by their communicative purpose.

Generic Structure	Rhetorical functions
1. Title	Identifying the topic of the case note paper together with the (cited) case being considered.
2. Abstract *optional*	Summarizing the case note paper's content.
3. Introduction	Establishing context of the case note paper and justifying the topic for discussion.
4. Discussion	Addressing the topic by: • a full description of the scenery behind the main case - i.e. analyzing Issues of Facts and Law in the court's reasoning and decision by including the wider context of case and/or statutory law (**Legal Background**); and • a critical analysis of the *significant* issue(s) arising from the court's decision and reasoning in the main case, together with the implications for the current and future state of the law and public policy (**Author's Argument**).
5. Conclusion	Summing up the author's critical arguments and positions in the paper and reinforcing the 'remarkable' aspects in the researched case.

Table 5. Five-part organizational structure model of case notes in Group B.

This standard model description expands on, and to some extent differs from, Feak et al.'s (2000) four-part structure of student-written law review notes.[19]

While rhetorical 'abstracting' did not feature in ECLR journal, where it was possibly an *optional* extra based on the editorial policy, 'abstracting' in MLR can be said to be the result of the editorial policy rather than writers' personal choices. The inclusion of the Abstract section in this generic structure model was motivated by the fact that it was part and parcel of, and therefore not a single electronically retrievable entity in, all the academic prose of case notes published in MLR. Reasonably, therefore, the fixed (obligatory) status of Abstracts in the MLR journal and its close links with the case note in such journal may assign, *mutatis mutandis*, the quality of what Swales terms a "genre set" in academic writing, which is "that part of the total genre network that a particular individual – or more usefully sometimes a class of individuals - engages in, either or both

[19] These authors outline the four-part structure as follows:
- Introduction
- Detailed discussion of a legal situation/background
- Detailed discussion of the problem
- Proposed solution and possibly evaluation (Feak et al. 2000: 201).

receptively and productively, as part of his or her normal occupational or institutional practice" (Swales 2004: 20, drawing on Devitt 1991). In terms of extra material, then, only one case note in MLR included the so-called 'Postscript' which provided additional information to what was included in the case note text and appended to the manuscript.

Apart from the Title section, the distinct stages by which case notes were organized in the above generic structure and content obviously applied to several headed paragraphs, and depended upon the amount of detailed information included in such stages. As shown quantitatively in Figure 2 below, variation in the stage length can be seen in the average word-number characterizing the various sections in the journals, where Discussion was by far the lengthier section, accounting for around 80 per cent of the average case note in both journals. It was therefore the most important rhetorical section used for exploration of the relevant law controlling the critical issue(s) in the case:

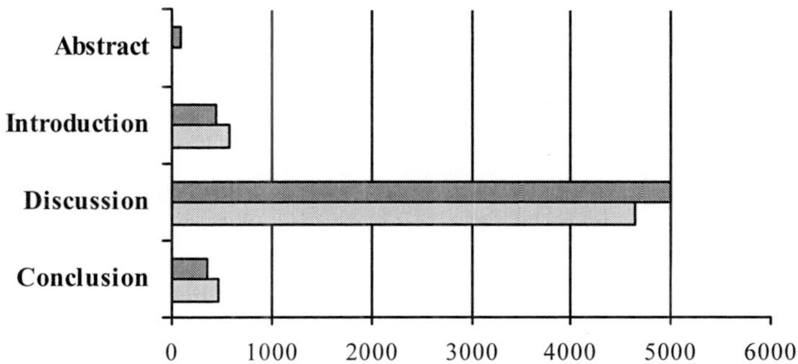

	Conclusion	Discussion	Introduction	Abstract
MLR	349,95	4998,9	442,8	79,45
ECLR	467,7	4650,2	572,7	0

Figure 2. Average word number per section in the journal case notes.

These data thus allowed the writers to produce lengthy, discursive case notes along sufficiently conventionalized and standardized communicative contexts and purposes.

Case-focused legal research articles?

We have noted that case notes, as they emerged from the (Body) Discussion section, were grounded in the analysis of the relationship between the decision in the selected case and the relevant legal context, and enmeshed in a critical evaluation of the *significant* issues involved in such case. Considering that Discussion was part of other rhetorical sections (Title, Abstracts, Introductions, Conclusions), it is not impossible that the resulting 'article'-like generic writing identified before be treated under the descriptive label of 'case-focused legal research article' genre, as introduced here, despite the conventional label of *case note* attached by the disciplinary community in the (academic) publication profile.

Of course, case notes will work best under this label if read as a 'critical reaction' or 'critical comment' genre, or similarly as a 'follow-up to reviewing' the strengths and weaknesses underlying judicial opinions and reasoning and their implications for law and policy. Whatever the label one might like to attach to the current genre, in addition to the conventional one, the consequence is that case notes will always emphasize the importance of a socially situated analysis of the genre. Given this natural consequence of the case note framework, the resulting stages in the genre offer interesting sites for descriptive analyses of language around the rhetorical features of metadiscourse (Hyland 2005a). By providing self-reflective linguistic material in the current corpus, these rhetorical features reveal the ways academic legal writers construct their disciplinary argument and knowledge, by interpersonally fulfilling the objective of the social process of the genre.

Micro-level linguistic descriptions: metadiscourse features

For the reader to have a taste of metadiscoursal argument in the disciplinary genre[20], let us have a look at the extract below:

(16) Silber J's reasoning, which is <u>in line with</u> *Williamson*but <u>incompatible</u> with *Eweida*, is <u>preferable</u> to the latter, as it captures aspects of anti-discrimination law to which the Court of Appeal paid <u>insufficient</u> attention. <u>The judgment convincingly demonstrates that</u> a belief does not need to be part of official religious dogma or accepted by the majority of a religious

[20] For detailed micro-linguistic descriptions of metadiscourse categories, see Chapter 3.

> community to be relevant for indirect discrimination purposes. What matters is whether it is a truly religious belief which relates to fundamental choices about an individual's life. A possible objection to Silbert J's reasoning is that it makes it too easy for religious individuals to overturn otherwise neutral laws and policies. That would be an exaggerated concern. The test for indirect discrimination is a two-stage test: first, we ask whether the claimant's belief which is the basis of the particular disadvantage he suffered is religious, in which case it falls within the scope of the provisions prohibiting indirect religious discrimination; then, we turn to justification. Clearly, a finding that a policy or measure has a disparate impact on people holding a particular belief does not mean that the claimant will necessarily win, as the court will examine, at the second stage of the indirect discrimination test, whether that policy or measure is justified as a proportionate means of achieving a legitimate aim.
>
> MLR 2011, 74(2): 301

Here the writer examined cases concerning indirect religious discrimination where the claimant must demonstrate that an otherwise neutral measure had caused him or her a particular disadvantage because of his/her religion. In discussing a variety of case law, the writer in particular mismatched Silbert J's reasoning in the judgment with the Court of Appeal's reasoning in *Eweida* v *British Airways*, the latter controlling the critical issue(s) in the case-focused legal research. And while the writer aligned himself with the main outcomes in Silbert's judgment, he did not hesitate to anticipate possible challenges or objections to such judgment by suggesting his different argument for a claim of indirect discrimination based on a 'two-stage test'. In this context, then, the effectiveness of the writer's argument surfaced in the text through (underlined) interactive and interactional metadiscourse devices (Hyland 2005a) – namely, the explicit use of:

- frame markers (*first*, *then*) combined with inclusive self-mentions (*we ask*, *we turn to*), allowing the writer to order the argument in the discourse;
- hedges (*possible*, *would*); and
- adjectives/adverbs in attitude markers (e.g. *convincingly*, *incompatible*, *proportionate*), helping the writer "create a convincing discourse and establish personal credibility, critical insight and disciplinary competence" (Hyland 2005a: 151).

By raising *significant issues* worthy of research, the writer thus sought to bring readers around to his forms of argument in the case-focused research, and the socio-rhetorical context of interpersonal metadiscourse was a useful rhetorical site for the writer to externalize knowledge-making inquiry in the discipline.

Group B: blending discoursal structures *in spite of* distinct generic boundaries

It becomes clear at this point that, as a result of the macro-rhetorical behaviour of Group B case notes, the writers' motivation to blend case note discoursal structure with the article generic structure made the case note genre into a far more academic legal research endeavour than otherwise observed in the synoptic approach to the 'reporting genre' (Group A). The effect is that blending in with the article made as yet another case for *colonization* in both *mixed* and *embedded* forms of *interdiscursivity* in the framework of a Critical Genre Analysis (Bhatia 2004, 2008, 2010). The fact that case notes appropriated from the formal structure of the academic article reflects the argument that "[t]he nature of genre manipulation is invariably realized within the broad limits of specific genres" (Bhatia 2004: 24-25), which in turn led community writers in the current corpus "to create new forms in order to respond to novel rhetorical contexts" (Bhatia 2004: 24). And while the resulting innovation involved "invasion of the integrity of one genre by another genre or genre convention, often leading to the creation of a hybrid form" (Bhatia 2004: 60), two basic contextual factors allowed for the identification of the generic boundaries between case notes and articles in this kind of colonization process.

Firstly, Swales' (2004: 16) argument that "[i]n academic law, the greatest kudos, still attaches to articles (often of considerable length) in the leading Law Review journals" resonated with the current corpus journals as well, where the difference between a law article and a case note was the length expected by editorial standards. In general, a glance at such standards published on the journals' webpages shows that they required articles not to exceed 12,000 words as compared to less than half (5,000) the word limit of case notes published in MLR (ECLR however being silent on this)[21], although the average word length in my MLR corpus (5,893) was almost 20 per cent over the editor's word limit. Secondly, all case notes received a dedicated section in the journal profiles, where they appeared after Research Articles which began a journal edition, and were followed by Review Articles and Book Reviews. As a matter of fact, placing articles in the front of the MLR journal allowed for case notes to

[21] See "Instructions for Authors" in ECLR journal.

stand out as a distinct generic category in its own right, as measured in particular by the breadth of the subject matter covered in both categories. A reading of such articles in the ECLR and MLR journals shows, in fact, that they analyzed case law or legislation in a conflicting or transitional area of law, or dealt with theoretical or (qualitative) empirical analyses of law by offering new legal theory or advancing empirical knowledge of some issue. Breadth, therefore, was conducive to the substantial article-length, in Swales' (2004) terms and, not least, the several part-structure as in case notes, but with extensive use of citations (whether or not footnoted), and inevitably engaged writers in a wider research process. By contrast, and despite the shared structure with articles, case notes were narrowed in breadth since, we have seen, they focused on a specific issue arising from a single judgment, and correspondingly were shorter - though still footnoted[22] – than the more extended articles. Regardless of their locations and scope in the journals concerned, both articles and case notes were written by expert legal authors alike, whether as professors, judges or lawyers. This way of contextualizing generic discourse between the article and the case note in the journal profiles and legal scholarship therefore shows that case notes were readily distinguishable from articles in nature or properties.

Yet, as an interesting aside, the argument has been made about case notes ranking lower in English legal scholarship. In that sense, the legal academic, Neil Duxbury, forcefully argues that:

> "In England the case note is commonly considered to be one of the lowliest forms of legal literature, not least because the case notes section of the law journal often provides a nursery slope for the *tyro academic* who has yet to find either the time or the confidence to engage in *more sustained research*" (Duxbury 2001: 55-56; *my emphasis*).

Although this argument for the 'lowliest' form could not be drawn from non-English case notes published in the Cambridge 'flagship' journal (ECLR), the author is silent about which academic genre is comparably the 'more sustained research' in English legal scholarship. Moreover, Duxbury's argument seems to be at odds in my data since English case notes included in MLR featured writers in their senior rather than solely junior (novice) academic positions, who demonstrated their expertise in a research area of law to those within the academy.

In light of such contextual factors defining the generic boundaries between articles and case notes in published legal scholarship, reality does

---

[22] See the analysis of Evidentials in Chapter 3.

show - in Swales' (2004) terms - that articles enjoy a commanding position in contemporary English medium law journals where they are the primary genre of the legal academy. As a consequence, they are the *primary members* of the colony influencing case notes as the *secondary members* of the genre colony, in Bhatia's (2004) terms. How far highly valued articles may be influential on legal scholars and practitioners compared to case notes, in both English and non-English speaking countries, does not fall within the scope of my discussion here. However, common practice shows that many such articles will not be published unless they exhibit legal research that is original about a 'centralized theme'. In that context, and regardless of breadth, expert-authored case notes that critically discuss a *significant* issue arising from a prior case and its implications are no less relevant to justify originality of their work around a similar 'centralized theme'. And while this is essential for the legitimation of the law discipline as a result of the role played by case notes in exhibiting original research, case notes are neither less relevant towards attention being paid among legal scholars and practitioners through the reputable English language journals. Here, the analytical and critical insights brought in by case note writing also inevitably result in advancing a particular area of law beyond its current state, as I argued before.

'Case-focused research article' in knowledge-building criteria

Where case notes imply the legitimized novelty of research and its advancement as the important criteria for a socially constructed generic discourse, the natural consequence will be for case note writers to pursue disciplinary knowledge-building criteria (Bazerman 1988, 2000; Becher 1987, 1989; Myers 1992a/b; Becher and Trowler 2001) in the context of epistemological, ontological, conventional and organizational features of their disciplinary culture (Berkenkotter and Huckin 1995; Hyland 2004; Bhatia 2004). Like most argumentative legal Research Articles in their wider rhetorical configurations, the constitutive role of case notes surfaced in the construction of "knowledge claims" (Myers 1992a) through which disciplinary writers made an attempt at claiming ownership for a new piece of knowledge and inquiry, awaiting storage in their own scientific knowledge-base. The standards for conducting knowledge-making inquiries in the case note genre were revealed (in addition to metadiscourse features) through repeated discourse strategies, which enabled the writers to maintain stability in the production of legal discourse, and therefore knowledge, by typifying or standardizing key components of the (global) rhetorical situation.[23] Thus, while the process of delivering and promoting new knowledge accounted for the case note genre to hold a less peripheral status than otherwise claimed for in the legal literature, the knowledge-making genre of case notes also acted as a stepping stone for furthering the writers' academic standing among other community peers.

Conclusion

In this analysis, I offered the classification of case note texts in terms of genre as being largely a rhetorically motivated, social phenomenon, and functionally shaped in communicative contexts and purposes of the social genre examined.

The analysis showed that a good deal of textual and generic integrity was maintained in both Group A and Group B case notes by community discourse writers, who therefore conceptualized the texts in each Group along uniform purposes or stages. Reliance on social purpose was a demonstration of (desired) membership and thus awareness of communal conventions implied in the legal discourse community. But, where as Bhatia states, "the communicative purposes of the genre-text are considerably different, requiring very different cognitive structuring" (Bhatia 1993: 22), then the analysis of the case note genre-texts in both Groups side by side revealed significant differences in the rhetorical action performed, thus showing a manifest *intra*community diversity in generic forms between writers from both Groups. In this sense, therefore, reliance on social purpose, as the main argument for communal coherence in the discourse community, concerned both (academic and professional) groupings whose text boundaries were altered in order to fulfil this purpose.

Diversity in generic forms was determined by the different perceptions and values over the rhetorical action of the case note genre among legal writers. The latter therefore gave expression to individually recognizable generic products grounded in the identities of the 'reporting genre', serving mainly as a usable record of cases in professional contexts, and the 'case-focused research article', producing and disseminating knowledge in academic contexts. And while both generic products were contextualized in terms of socially accepted situations, the broader social context suggests

[23] Typifying or standardizing key components of the (global) rhetorical situation is not new to the tradition of rhetorical genre studies (Miller 1984; Bazerman 1988; Bazerman and Russell 2003; Devitt 2004; Bazerman et al. 2009, among others).

that they were also associated with the cultural elements of disciplinary writers in the national-international divide of case note writing, as much as the organizational objectives of the journals. Diversity in generic forms therefore emphasized the complexity, dynamism and unpredictability of representing the case note genre in today's legal discourse community, as a badge of the social identity and practice of one's academic or professional identification.

This analysis therefore shows that uniformity of the case note genre exists 'in name only' and does not constitute a rhetorically single, rigid, uniform whole among 'all writers' in their membership of the legal community, which thus acquires an unstable notion in view of the genre linguistic realization taken collectively. Thus, it can only be concluded that, by holding their rhetorical membership together within each Group but still separating their rhetorical conventions and practices from another, the changing identity of disciplinary writers steered the case note genre towards a rhetorically versatile construct in law.

CHAPTER TWO

WRITING CASE NOTES FOR THE LEGAL ACADEMY: ANATOMY OF RHETORICAL SECTIONS

In the previous Chapter I revealed how rhetorical structures in each grouping of case notes published internationally create generic homogeneity among writers, but also recognized the phenomenon of *intra*-community diversity between the two case note groupings taken collectively. Diversity in the rhetorical patternings and contexts of the genre thus accounted for the complex communicative realities of disciplinary-recognized practices of academic and professional writers, who made different assumptions about the construction and use of the case note genre.

In this Chapter, I shall continue with the exploration of discursive conventions and practices that construct and reveal the social roles and identities of case note writers as community members of the disciplinary discourse. With this in mind, I will concentrate on disciplinary discourse emerging from 'academic' case note samples alone, which formed the basis for my corpus analytical data in Chapter 1. These samples are meant to complete my analysis of academic legal writing practices in the same genre.

In this Chapter, therefore, I attempt to explore how the disciplinary writing conventions are connected with the knowledge-making practices of the academic discourse community, by offering a pragmatic-level analysis of rhetorical and linguistic patterns in discourse and genre-based descriptions. I examine the rhetorical functions of the various sections characterizing the global generic structure of case notes, or 'case-focused research articles', as labelled in Chapter 1. Once again, I wish to provide the rationale of this analysis by putting it in the theoretical context of academic discourse research.

Theoretical background

The study of rhetorical sections in the pantheon of academic genres

Since Feak et al.'s (2000) valuable study of the Introduction section in (student-written) law review notes, research into the rhetorical functions performed by distinct sections in case note academic writing remains somewhat downplayed. One reason for this shortage of empirical research into these sections may be the cross-disciplinary interest shown in the global generic structure of the dominant RAs, including extensions of such structure to other academic genres, such as textbooks, book chapters, etc. For many authors, research has focused on the conventional Introduction-Method-Results-Discussion macro-structure analyses of empirical RAs[1], namely Introduction (e.g. Swales 1981, 1990; Swales and Najar 1987; Bhatia 1997b; Samraj 2002b; Ozturk 2007), Method (e.g. Bruce 2008; Kanoksilapatham 2005), Results (e.g. Thompson 1993; Bruce 2009; Lim 2010), Discussion (e.g. Hopkins and Dudley-Evans 1988; Holmes 1997; Peacock 2002); as well as micro-level analyses of linguistic features, such as citation practices of 'expert' writers (e.g. Pickard 1995) and in academic texts (e.g. Thompson 2000), extending Swales' division of citation forms (e.g. Thompson and Tribble 2001), reporting verbs (e.g. Hewings et al. 2010), hedges (e.g. Hyland 2000, 2004), and metadiscourse markers (e.g. Ädel and Mauranen 2010). Outside the formal IMRD RA structure, analytical insights have also been provided into metadiscourse interactional strategies that construct authorial identity in the Introduction section of academic law research articles (Tessuto 2008b). Allied with these analyses of the 'four' RA major sections are the studies into the generic structure of RAs (Posteguillo 1999), rhetorical functions of each section of the IMRD RA (Swales and Feak 2004), and structural patterns of RAs (Lin and Evans 2012). The list may continue but, for reasons of space available, I will stop here.

Faced with the large body of research into the IMRD model and, not least, the absence of research writing manuals and style guides accounting for rhetorical patterns of case note sections, this study aims to complete our understanding of the (macro)generic model description proposed in Chapter 1, and adds to the broader field of genre analyses. With this in

[1] In addition to the IMRD structure, and as outlined in Chapter 4, academic research has also focused on abstracts (e.g. Salager-Meyer 1990, 1992; Bondi 2004, 2005; Hyland 2000, 2004; Lorés-Sanz 2004), among other genres.

mind, I wish to provide an anatomy of the rhetorical functions performed by case note sections – namely, Title, Abstract, Introduction, Discussion and Conclusion. Regardless of the Abstract, Introduction and Conclusion sections, which may be rhetorically transparent by the conventional, standard labels attached to them in a variety of academic writing text types, the function and content of the non-conventional, non-standard 'Discussion' rhetorical section here needs to be further examined. This need arises from the rhetorical distinctiveness of the Discussion section in the generic writing conventions and practices of community writers.

Material and Method

The Corpus

As part of the larger case note corpus presented in Chapter 1, the analytical data included here were based only on 30 case notes shown in Table 1, and published in the 2009-2011 issues of *The Modern Law Review* (MLR) and *European Constitutional Law Review* (ECLR) journals.

Journal	2009	2010	2011	TOTAL
The Modern Law Review Blackwell Wiley Online	4	7	9	20
European Constitutional Law Review Cambridge Journals Online	-	7	3	10
TOTAL	4	14	12	30

Table 1. Number and publication year of case notes collected from each Journal and total number of case notes.

These case notes, labelled as **Group B** in the previous Chapter, placed writers in their 'academic' writing roles and activities, whether in national (UK: MLR) or international contexts (European: ECLR). For the sake of convenience, different quantitative data in Table 2 are reported again in each set of case note in the journals, which provided a data source of 177,570 words in the corpus of published case notes, excluding titles, footnotes and bibliography, where applicable.

	TOTAL	ECLR	MLR
Tokens	177,570	58,243	119,327
Types	9,348	4,862	7,673
Type/Token ratio (TTR)	5.39	8.57	6.57
Standardised TTR	37.27	36.38	37.70
Mean word length (in characters)	4.96	5.03	4.93
Sentences	4,536	1,596	2,940
Mean (in words)	38.26	35.53	39.74

Table 2. Different quantitative data in each set of the case notes and totals as retrieved from Scott WordSmith Tool 5.0.

As already noted, footnotes were used extensively in both journals.

Methodology

I was concerned with the conventional genre staging revealed by the rhetorical functions of case note sections (Title - Abstract – Introduction – Discussion – Conclusion), seen in their situational use of text. In order to facilitate rhetorical/linguistic descriptions of such sections, I adopted a synthetic theoretical framework which includes elements from SFL (Halliday 1994, 2004), pragmatics (Grice 1975), and discourse and genre analysis in a variety of applications (e.g. Graetz 1985; Swales 1990, 2004; Bhatia 1993, 2004; Peacock 2002; Haggan 2004; Hyland 2004; Soler 2007).

In terms of the analysis of the constituent moves in the allowable rhetorical structure of the Abstract, Introduction and Conclusion sections, the rationale for assigning discourse roles to such moves was functional – e.g. realized by clause or sentence - and formal – e.g. realized by lexico-grammatical features in text segments (Bhatia 1993, 2001; Swales 1990, 2004). However, the non-conventional 'Discussion' section was left out from the analysis of such constituents in that it appeared to be insensitive to the rhetorical move descriptions as provided in a number of genre-based studies.

Results and Discussion

In discussing the qualitative and quantitative data, I begin with a small but important rhetorical fronting device, the law title, which has received very little attention in the mainstream of academic discourse studies, whether in the RA or other genres. In what follows is therefore a thorough analysis of Title in the disciplinary academic genre.

Title

Title	Identifying the topic of the case note paper together with the (cited) case being considered.

Title appeared in the journal case notes with the (asterisked*) author's name on separate lines, his or her designation given in footnote just above the case notes. Although it is customary to indicate the name of one or more authors under the title, the habit was part of an authorship credit to the content, analysis and interpretation of the argument data presented in the case notes.

In addition to name and designation, the various informational elements included in footnotes shows that the writing of the case note was not possible unless other people, whether or not specified as academic colleagues and referees of the writers' drafts, were mentioned to support the writer's work. Concurrently, footnotes offered "a unique rhetorical space" in which writers expressed "their genuine gratitude for assistance" (Hyland and Tse 2004b: 259), and a natural propensity to the disciplinary community they served in collaborative research (Giannoni 2002). The projection of a courteous, friendly image, particularly in personal tone (*I*, *My*), was achieved in 12/20 abstracts (MLR) and 3/10 abstracts (ECLR), where THANK was the main lexical choice in the data (10 occ.) followed by DEBT, GRATEFUL and BENEFIT used only sparingly in both journals[2], as illustrated in the set of examples in (1):

[2] In addition, research programme details and disclaimers were occasionally included.

(1)

---

*Senior Lecturer in Law, University of Leicester. Thanks to (*name*) and an anonymous MLR referee for comments on earlier drafts.
MLR 2011, 74(5): 767

---

*I would like to thank (*name*) for reading over a previous draft of this note and for offering helpful comments. The usual disclaimer applies. MLR 2011, 74(1): 106

---

*Senior Lecturer, Aston Business School, Aston University. I am indebted to my colleague Professor (*name*) for her many helpful comments on an early draft of this note. MLR 2010, 73(6): 1026

---

*Professor of Public Comparative Law, The Law School of the University of Bologna. Adjunct Professor of International Law, SAIS Johns Hopkins University BC. My thanks to (*name*) for helpful discussion that helped me sort out the complex issues that emerge in this case. I am also indebted to all the participants at the Workshop on 'Constitutionalism and Secularism' held in Jerusalem on April 24th, 2010 in the frame of the International Association of Constitutional Law, and particularly to Daphne Barak-Erez.
ECLR 2010, 6: 481

As with RA abstract titles examined in Chapter 4, case note titles provided the site for the writers to gain worldwide visibility of the reported research, and the persuasive gateway for the readers to enter the research content in the genre. Although, manifestly, titles in the current texts were different in format from those examined in Group A of case notes, they were equally constrained by the space and the need to be informative in the publication profile as those in Group A. These fundamental constraints, among others, assigned generic features to case note titles here which, as a consequence, were short and condensed while containing enough information to "indicate the topic of the study" and the "scope of the study" they labelled (Swales and Feak 2004: 278). Clearly, in this context, the interactional function of focused content titles also highlighted descriptions as "condensed frames to the article" (Bush-Lauer 2000), or "the handle to the remaining of [a] paper" (Watson 2010). The focus on content so announced in the study/article/paper therefore helped to frame the readers' thinking by focusing their attention on a specific aspect of the legal issue in the case, and as a result remember the 'case-focused legal research article'.

Based on these features of case note titles, this analysis drew on the works of Anthony (2001), Haggan (2004), Soler (2007) and Wang and Bai (2007) across the academic disciplines. These authors classify titles into three/four structural categories – namely, compound titles (i.e., two-part titles separated by a colon or equivalent punctuation mark), also termed hanging titles (Day 1995) or colonic titles (Hartley 2005, 2007), nominal construction titles, full-sentence and question construction titles. Of the 30 total titles identifying the topic and scope of the study, as shown in Table 3, the most recurrent structural constructions were compound titles in both journals (13/30), although MLR made more use of such titles (11/20) than ECLR (2/10). Compound titles were followed by nominal titles in just three frequency points (10/30), although as again these titles appeared more in MLR (7/20) than in ECLR (3/10). Question titles (1/30) and full-sentence titles (2/30), although absent in some journals, were still lower in frequency. Questions also appeared with an equally lower incidence in compound constructions characterizing MLR alone (2/30), where they were used with the separating colon (:) and were therefore counted and analyzed separately from question titles:

	Compound titles	Nominal titles	Question titles	Questions in Compound titles
MLR	11/20	7/20	0/20	2/20
ECLR	2/10	3/10	1/10	0/10
TOTAL	13/30	10/30	1/30	2/30

Table 3. Structural categories of case note titles: occurrence frequency.

Despite the small number (30) of corpus titles under scrutiny, some comparative statistics can be drawn from the current data. As found also in RA abstract titles (Chapter 4), the prevalence of the compound construction titles here coincides wholly with previous findings (Haggan 2004; Hartley 2007; Soler 2007) that both humanities and social sciences researchers seem to prefer compound constructions in their RA titles. Of course, this coincidence is accounted for by the law discipline being addressed to as a social science (Harwell 2002), or as belonging to either one or the social science disciplines or to a humanities discipline (Howarth 2004).[3] While the slightly lower incidence of nominal titles was suggestive of the writers being concerned with the essence of their studies, as opposed to the writers' concern with the dual aspect of such studies in

[3] On classifying the law discipline, see Chapter 4 (Interdisciplinarity in published legal scholarship).

compound titles, the lower incidence of questions taken collectively in both journals (3/30) suggests that the writers were much less concerned with the "attention-grabbing aim" (Haggan 2004), or similarly attracting the reader's curiosity and promoting the article (Hyland 2002a). Indeed, the frequency data show that the writers further played down the aim of full sentence titles (2/30), which is "to intrigue the reader by presenting a clever, arresting title which catches the attention and acts as a lure into the article itself" (Haggan 2004: 298).

In general, therefore, the varying incidence of compound and nominal titles was useful to determine whether the text deserved further reading (e.g. Gross et al. 2002; Haggan 2004), and in this case it emphasized very concrete aspects of the text by focusing on the different levels of informativity and economy of titles (Buxton and Meadows 1977; Yitzhaki 1997; Bush-Lauer 2000). Inspired by the typology-based criteria of titles in academic writing, the analysis that follows deals with the diverse linguistic realizations of case note titles.

Compound titles

Under this construction, case note writers presented information in two-part titles separated by the colon (:), which was the most recurrent punctuation mark linking two complementary parts of information in the 13 total compound constructions. Where the colon was used, the two semantic relationships holding between the two parts of a title were typically 'Topic:Case' (3 occ.), 'Case:Topic' (2 occ.), 'Topic-Scope' (3 occ.), 'Case-Question' (1 occ.), and 'Topic-Question' (1 occ.) organizational patterns, as shown in the genuinely published title formats in (2):

(2)

Guiding Principles for Directorial Conflicts of Interests: *Re Allied Business and Financial Consultants Ltd*
[author's name]*

Topic:Case MLR

Stone & Rolls Ltd v *Moore Stephens*: An Unnecessary Tangle
[author's name]*

Case:Topic MLR

Complicating Complicity: Aiding and Abetting Causing Death by Dangerous Driving in *R* v *Martin* [author's name]*

Topic:Scope MLR

Sienkiewicz v Greif (UK) Ltd and Willmore v Knowsley Metropolitan Borough Council:
A Material Contribution to Uncertainty?
[author's name]*
Case:Question MLR

Marriage and Divorce in the Supreme Court and the Law Commission: for Love or Money?
[authors' names]*
Topic:Question MLR

The 'Topic:Case' organizational pattern above shows that the focus of the study announced in the first part before the colon tied semantically with the cited case in the second part, and the (general) topic attracted the reader's possible interest in a current disciplinary issue. This pattern was justified by the role of genre writers who were committed to bringing the expert reader's attention round to a *significant aspect* involved in the selected case for analysis, and the second information part of the title explained the coherent framework through which the (general) topic of research could be interpreted. While, seen vice versa, this pattern also naturally applied to the 'Case:Topic' organizational pattern above, it obviated the formal use of partial citation, which included the names of the disputing parties alone. As a result of this citation pattern, citing cases in manifestly 'highlights' form provided useful intertextual and interdiscursive constituents of both title and paper.

Where the 'Topic:Case' pattern was avoided in favour of the 'Topic:Scope' pattern, as shown in the above example, the 'Topic:Scope' relationships seemed to correspond more closely to Swales and Feak's (2004) identification of titles as general:specific[4], so that 'Topic:Scope' helped the writers promote an understanding of what represents a real issue in the law discipline. The fundamental assumption for this correspondence was that the topic (general) framework in the first part of the title (*Complicating ...*) added to the scope (specific) of the topic in the second part (*Aiding and Abetting ...*), and the second part of this title shows that the scope was a specific area of law in which the writers operated for their legal research. In particular, the *Complicating Complicity* title shows the expansion of the Noun Phrase in the second complementary part of information realized through post-modification by

[4] The identification of titles as general:specific is part of the authors' (2004) distinction between four types of titles with colons (problem:solution, general:specific, topic:method, major:minor).

the prepositional phrase introduced by *in* (*R* v *Martin*). Considering that this expansion was the result of the writer previewing his research framework by case 'highlights' (*R* v *Martin*), the expansion seemed to be the equivalent of a title separated by the *em dash* punctuation mark holding a third semantic relationship, in addition to the (two) parallel, symmetric relationships held by the (original) colonic title:

Complicating Complicity: Aiding and Abetting Causing Death by Dangerous Driving — *R* v *Martin*

Where this is the case, the two cohesive relationships held by 'Topic:Scope' would extend to the organizational pattern of 'Topic:Scope-Case' joining three components in the title.

Moreover, the informativeness of research aspects resulting from the general:specific relationships between the two complementary parts may explain that the above and other compound titles in 'topic:scope' were also Theme:Rheme (lexicogrammatical) structures, described as nominal groups in the titles themselves (Haggan 2004; Soler 2007; Wang and Bai 2007). In Systemic Functional Grammar (Halliday 1994, 2004), such structures can be seen again in the nominal group title already examined:

(Theme) Complicating Complicity:
(Rheme) Aiding <u>and</u> Abetting Causing Death <u>by</u> Dangerous Driving <u>in</u> *R* v *Martin*

where Theme provided the setting for the remainder of the clause – Rheme – in which Theme was developed. Still, the functional relationships between Theme and Rheme required the use of prepositions and conjunctions (*and*, *by*, *in*) to allow for the appropriate lexicogrammatical structure in the compound title, so that the nominal groups provided in themselves "the specification of the object of study" (Soler 2007: 98) necessary for the readers to gain concise information in the case note genre.

In this systemic-functional framework, there were only few instances in which nominal groups in compound title constructions addressed disciplinary terms in a given area of law, such as the pairings *Aiding and Abetting* used as near-synonyms in criminal law and *Directorial Conflicts of Interest*, as seen in the examples above. In most other cases, the specialist meanings conveyed by nominal groups in such constructions were borrowed from ordinary language (*Marriage and Divorce*), or acquired metaphorical meaning as in 'A <u>Negligent Blow</u> to Children at Risk: *MAK and RK* v *United Kingdom* (European Court of Human

Rights)'. Only in one instance of 'Topic:Scope' pattern shown in (3) below did nominal groups address the research process based on the specification of particular methodological aspects of the study:

(3)

Public or Personal Character in Election Campaigns: A Review of the Implications of the Judgment in *Watkins v Woolas*
[author's name]*
Topic:Scope (method) MLR

This pattern shows the (research process) nominal group headword *review* in the second part of the title, and the writer presented the Rheme-fronting research process term (*A Review*) by cognitively relating it to his critical estimate or correction of an important issue and results arising from the judicial decision in the (partially) cited case. While, as a result of this (research) process, the 'Topic:Scope' relationship seemed to correspond more closely to Swales and Feak's (2004) identification of titles as topic:method, the writer of the title needed again the use of prepositions and conjunctions (*or*, *of*, *in*) to concede the lexicogrammatical structure in Theme/Rheme relationships.

Indeed, the least frequent *em dash* — (4 occ.), occurring three times in both journals (MLR:2 / ECLR:1) and one time after the colon (ECLR), added to the one-only instance of the full-stop (ECLR:1). Where both punctuation marks were used to separate the two-part title, the essence of the cohesive relationship between Theme and Rheme in nominal group constructions was still observable, and the *em dashed* titles seemed to function as the substitutes for colonic titles, as in the set of examples in (4):

(4)

Interpreting the Threshold Criteria under section 31(2) of the Children Act 1989 — the House of Lords Decision in *Re B*
[authors' names]*
Topic-Case MLR

Disobedience to Law — Debbie Purdy's Case
[author's name]*
Topic-Case (party's name description) MLR

Court of Justice of the European Union
Decision of 2 March 2010, Case C-315/08
Janko Rottman v. *Freistaat Bayern*

Case Note 2
The Consequences of the *Rottmann* Judgment on Member State Autonomy — The European Court of Justice's Avant-Gardism in Nationality Matters
[authors' names]*

Topic:Scope ECLR

Unlike the ECLR title above, where the scope was presented effectively within the framework of the European Court of Justice's decision introduced in the topic, the organizational patterns of MLR titles essentially tied the (general) topic to the important cases. In these patterns, the present participle (*-ing*) was used in the first Verb Phrase part of the title to address the writer's research process, and the VP form presented the writer's distinctive personal conceptualization of his study, a legal exegesis, as part of the disciplinary specification of the topic-fronting (disciplinary) nominal group (*the Threshold Criteria under section 31(2) of the Children Act 1989*). More widely in this context, the present participle (*-ing*) used to initialize the *Interpreting* title shows that it was a useful device to increase conciseness and attractiveness (Wang and Bai 2007) of the compound (*em dashed*) title structure although, it should be noted, the VP form in the first part also functioned as a *grammatical metaphor* (Halliday 1994, 2004), which turned a verb into a noun. With the reference to cases being in focus in the second part of the above titles, however, the usual reference to *Re B* added to another opportunity available to the MLR writer, who tied the focus of his topic to the poignant case of Purdy (a terminally-ill woman) which the writer preferred to announce purposively in the context of his research paper. Interestingly, however, an exception to a two-part title arose in one isolated instance of ECLR title in (5), where the writer resorted to three parts shaped in the title by including the *em dash* after the colon:

(5)

Kücükdeveci: Mangold Revisited – Horizontal Direct Effect of a General Principle of EU Law
Court of Justice of the European Union (Grand Chamber)
Judgment of 19 January 2010, Case C-555/07,
Seda Kücükdeveci v. Swedex GmbH & Co. KG
[author's name]*

Case:Ruling (in method)-Topic ECLR

This writer linked the context of the judgment in the *Kücükdeveci* case to the relevant ruling (*Mangold*) with a separating colon, and went on by announcing the topic of his research in disciplinary content nominal construction. Although topic announcement seemed to be delayed in such organizational pattern, the writer's choice for this title format necessarily was to inform the reader first about the case 'highlights' and its results (ruling), and then the topic in third position as derived from such a ruling. More than that, and as already examined about nominal groups (in compound constructions), the second part of information after the colon (*Mangold Revisited*) presented cohesively the writer's methodological aspect of the ruling under research in past participle VP form (*Revisited*).

Where the full-stop punctuation was used to separate the two-part title, as shown in the one-only instance below (6), it seemed as yet to function as a substitute for the colonic titles:

(6)

European Court of Justice
The Legal Basis of Internal Market Measures
With a Security Dimension. <u>Comment on</u> Case C-301/06 of 10/02/2009,
Ireland v. *Parliament / Council*, nyr
[author's name]*

Topic.Scope (method) ECLR

As with the colonic title examined before (Public or Personal Character in Election Campaigns: <u>A Review of</u> the Implications of the Judgment in *Watkins v Woolas*), the ECLR title above allowed the writer to link the topic framework in the (nominal) first part to the method (critical opinion) used for the study of the case.

In general, therefore, compound titles tied two parts of information in a binary semantic realization and the use of separating punctuation marks seemed to be a matter of the writer's personal choice as well as 'unspoken' editorial policy, since the latter were unpublished in the journals concerned. Some exception to such policy was made in MLR, which 'only' provided instructions as to how best cite cases in the main text. Thus, compound construction titles presented the discussion of the topic by relating it to the relevant case in 'highlights', whether as embedded within the actual title by using either type of separating punctuation marks (MLR, ECLR), or juxtaposed in mostly sub-phrased rather than up-phrased syntax (ECLR). However, compound titles also cognitively drew the readers into an understanding of the author's argument in the paper, based on the empirical practice of discussing the nature and the central legal issue purported in the main case. And the writer's empirical experience represented the source of knowledge in case-driven legal research based on interpretable principles and disciplinary epistemology.

Nominal titles

Inquiry into case note nominal titles was enlightened by the functional-systemic perspective on nominalization (Eggins 1994; Halliday 1994, 2004), understood as a linguistic resource that allows academic writers to condense information (process/clause) into nominal group structures, while also creating cohesion. Similarly, nominal titles here, and their varying distribution in the journals (Table 3), were arranged around nominal groups also with pre/post-modifiers, and were mostly indicative of disciplinary content terms in the case-focused research paper, as in the examples set in (7):

(7)

The Strasbourg Court on the Dayton Constitution
Judgment in the case of *Sejdić and Finci v. Bosnia and Herzegovina*,
22 December 2009
[author's name]* ECLR

Court of Justice of the European Union
The Right to Family Reunification of Third-Country
Nationals under EU Law;
Decision of 4 March 2010, Case
C-578/08, *Rhimou Chakroun* v. *Minister van Buitenlandse Zaken*
[author's name]* ECLR

Extending the Confusion About Bayes
[authors' names]* MLR

Unfair Contract Terms, Unfair Prices and Bank Charges
[author's name]* MLR

European Arrest Warrant Cases and the Principles
of Non-discrimination and EU Citizenship
[author's name]* MLR

Hopes, Expectations and Revocable Promises in
Proprietary Estoppel
[author's name]* MLR

In these and other examples, the packing of lexical content in nominal group constructions provided an easy way for the writers to attract and inform the readers about the disciplinary topic, which inevitably resulted in the 'structural economy' of legal titles. Aside from nominalizations being a feature of written legal English (as well as particularly scientific English), the similarities with newspaper headlines (Huckin 2006: 102-103) were also readily apparent in the legal titles shown above. Here, the tendency to use the smallest number of words compatible with accuracy of the information enabled legal writers to present the outcome of the topic being announced by the inclusion of the relevant ideas behind the research paper. This 'relevancy' feature of condensing the main notions of the legal research also possibly reflected the practice of newspaper writers, who are engaged in providing newspaper readers with the most important, selective information and results (Bazerman 1985; Berkenkotter and Huckin 1995).

We have seen that the writers' tendency was to embed the case citation within the actual (compound) title by using either type of separating punctuation marks (MLR, ECLR), or to juxtapose case citation mostly in sub-phrased than up-phrased syntax (ECLR). Where nominal titles are concerned, the graphical formats in ECLR examples above show that case citation was juxtaposed beneath the unpunctuated nominal title (*The Strasbourg Court ...*), or the punctuated (;) nominal title (*The Right to Family ...*). These examples (with nominal titles appearing sub-phrased by case citation) seemed therefore to be the equivalent of the missing colonic titles observed before, since it was assumed that legal writers wished to specify the case to which the topic for analysis referred, and as a consequence link two complementary parts of information in the 'Topic:Case' organizational pattern.

Full-sentence (conclusive) titles

The two marginal instances of full-sentence structure titles appeared in the following graphical formats:

(8)

France
The *Conseil d'Etat* Abandons Its *Cohn Bendit* Case-Law;
Conseil d'Etat, 30 October 2009, *Mme Perreux*
[author's name]* ECLR

German Federal Constitutional Court
German Data Retention Provisions Are Unconstitutional
In Their Present Form;
Decision of 2 March 2010,

NJW 2010, p. 833.
[author's name]* ECLR

These writers used conclusive titles in a linguistically simple structure, i.e. 'Subject + (Simple Present) Verb + Complement(s)' to anticipate the conclusions and/or results of their research, which took the form of declarative (Smith 2000: 915) or informative titles (e.g. McGowan and Tugwell 2005: 83) in the underlying communicative effect. Where the semi-colon (;) was used to separate two semantic units in a relationship, the graphical formats seemed again to function as the equivalents of colonic titles holding the 'Topic:Case' relationship, where sub-phrased case citation explained the coherent framework through which the topic contained in the actual title could effectively be interpreted.

These realizations thus resulted in the titles being as concise as possible in the communicative contexts, allowing the writers to condense sufficient information in one sentence and reflect the nature of research being undertaken and the results gained. This way then, full-sentence (conclusive) titles adhered pragmatically to Grice's (1975) Cooperative Principle, along the maxims of:

- "Quantity (Make your contribution as informative as is required – Do not make your contribution more informative than is Required)";
- "Quality (Do not say what you believe to be false – Do not say that for which you lack adequate evidence)";
- "Relation (Be relevant)"; and
- "Manner (Avoid obscurity of expression – Avoid ambiguity – Be brief (avoid unnecessary prolixity) – Be orderly)" (Grice 1975: 45-46).

Questions in titles

As noted in Table 3, the use of questions in (single) question titles (1/30) and compound titles (2/30) was not as frequent as might be expected of a clear attention-attracting device in this type of academic discourse genre.

In example (9) below, showing a Double Case Note written by a different author from the other Case Note, the question made up the entire title and shaped an explicit interrogative by focusing on the topic being asked in the study:

(9)

Court of Justice of the European Union
Decision of 2 March 2010, Case C-315/08
Janko Rottman v. *Freistaat Bayern*

Case Note 1
Decoupling Nationality and Union Citizenship?
[author's name]* ECLR

While the single question title suggested the lack of definite conclusions, it indirectly let the expert readers await for an answer. Indeed, shaping an answer was less than a difficult task for such readers who may have easily attended to the accompanying abstract and/or introduction sections, which provided a useful context in which to interpret the question title under research.

Similarly, questions were placed in the second information part of the two compound structure titles:

(10)

Marriage and Divorce in the Supreme Court and the Law Commission: for Love or Money?
[authors' names]*
Topic:Question MLR

Sienkiewicz v *Greif (UK) Ltd and Willmore v Knowsley Metropolitan Borough Council*: A Material Contribution to Uncertainty?
[author's name]*
Case:Question MLR

In these examples, interpreting the question equally seemed to be less than a difficult task for the expert readers. This was justified by the longer compound structure titles including 'context-raising' 'topic' or 'case', which naturally contained more information than the single question title alone, although interpreting questions in the above compound structures may have equally been made easier by reading the answer in the Abstracts and/or Introductions.

As a result of questions being almost infrequent in titles, their use showed only a little attempt by the writers to attract the readers' curiosity and similarly engage them in the academic discourse (Hyland 2002a, 2005a).

Internal variability of the genre: combinative titles?

All of the features examined in the typology-based criteria of titles are of course treated in line with the interest of quoted researchers dealing with academic writing across the disciplines. However, in a context where case note writers were committed to construct titles by highlighting the main case to which the topic referred, the result is that case citation provides the internal variable as a function of the disciplinary genre and conventions, and the site for a wider, effective explanation of the typology-based classifications of titles in the current genre.

Unlike the graphical format of titles in MLR, providing only the parties' names in the case (rather than full citation of case) in either information part of the title, the examined title formats in ECLR usually appeared under the following different guise:

1. Court jurisdiction
2. Title of paper
3. Case (full) citation

Under this scheme, case citation was used in line with the approved form that was standard in the jurisdiction concerned, and juxtaposed beneath the actual title in sub-phrased syntax, usually by the separating semi-colon (;). The reason for supplementing the actual title with case citation underneath lay not just with the editorial guidelines of the ECLR journal, which was indeed silent about the issue, but with the expectations of the genre which required the writers to organize titles visually around the case being considered for research in precisely 'case highlights'.

Thus, where writers used sub-phrased case citations to supplement the actual titles, as examined in the typology-based criteria (i.e. compound, nominal, full sentence and question in titles), their style practice reasonably provided the notion for 'combinative types' of descriptive and informative title formats, as introduced here. This combining form between title and case citation (as an internal variable of the genre) made the title and paper not only inherently intertextual and interdiscursive in communicative function, but also obviated the communicative purpose/goal of identifying the topic in line with the function and convention of this genre. And while, as a result of such combinative types, case note titles manifestly differed from the RA abstract titles examined in Chapter 4, they shared the levels of informativeness and structural constructions characterizing RA abstract titles along the examined typology-based criteria. Locating the relevant information in variously structured titles was no less significant to recognize the writers' attempts at invoking the complexities of disciplinary notions and ideas embroiled in socio-legal relations of the current academic legal discourse.

Abstract

Abstract *optional*	Summarizing the case note paper's content.

In addition to Title, writers summarized the main content of the case note paper by including the (unheaded) Abstract rhetorical section in MLR alone. Although, as should be expected, the abstract appeared as very short textual realization in the journal, it was still an essential and inalienable part of academic legal prose here, and therefore the reflection of a "part-genre" as is traditionally of the research article (Swales and Feak 2009).

Brevity of abstracts in the journal was measured not only by their average word-length (79.45) but also by other factors, namely:

- the avoidance of redundancy through "tightly worded sentences" (Graetz 1985: 125) resulting naturally from their short length;
- the preference for nominalizations, active (rather than the usual passive) voice; and
- the avoidance of citations, except where the use of the cited source (Judgment) was necessary to introduce the general context of the legal research topic (Decision in the case), sometimes combined with other relevant professional legal source.

The inexorable effect of this was that case note abstracts gave the reader a very concise 'preview' of what was to come in the paper (Swales 1990; Bhatia 1993; Berkenkotter and Huckin 1995; Hyland 2004, Ayers 2008; Gillaerts and Van de Velde 2010). This allowed the writers, on the one hand, to go straight to the paper content by avoiding extra explanations, and the readers, on the other, to decide whether to pursue this content in the limited space available of the abstract. Succinctness, thus, accounted for abstracts to be essentially 'indicative' in character, since they served as an outline of what was presented in the case note paper, and most importantly were devoid of Methods and Results informational components typical of the 'informative' RA abstracts examined in Chapter 4.

To illustrate this in the samples below, the writers set the scene to the topic for discussion at a variously short length, and revealed a very concise, yet organizing, mind at previewing the main points of their case-focused papers:

(11)

Full text - 35 words

[**M3-S1**] The case note considers the decision in *Re B* which confirms the threshold criteria in establishing the likelihood of future harm under section 31(2) of the Children Act 1989 and clarifies the civil standard of proof. MLR 2009, 72(3): 463

Full text - 66 words

[**M3-S1**] The case note considers the impact of the Supreme Court decision in *Radmacher v Granatino* regarding prenuptial and other classes of nuptial agreement, together with recent proposals of the Law Commission for reform of the law relating to marital property agreements generally. It explores in particular the question of what, if any, core obligations of marriage cannot - or should not – be excludable by agreement.
MLR 2011, 74(3): 430

Full text - 109 words

[**M1**] In *Secretary of State for the Home Department* v *AF* (No 3), the House of Lords decided that Article 6 ECHR requires a 'core irreducible minimum' of procedural fairness such that 'the controlled person must be given sufficient information about the allegations against him to give effective instructions to the Special Advocate'. [**M3-S1**] This case-note will discuss the challenges facing Special Advocates in control order proceedings and the impact AF may have on the measure of procedural fairness owed to individuals in closed proceedings. [**M3-S1**] It will also address the judicial use of sections 2 and 3 of the Human Rights Act 1998 in arriving at the outcome in AF. MLR 2010, 73(5): 824

These and other academic writers in the journal therefore sought to provide conspectuses of their research by drawing the reader's eye on some *significant aspects* of the case under analysis, and to similarly make these *aspects* original to other disciplinary scholars and practitioners through the published papers. Despite pruning their abstracts down to size, writers were still able to promote the persuasive communicative purpose behind abstracts (Hyland 2004).

Awareness of the persuasive communicative purpose and the linguistic resources used to achieve such a purpose was displayed in the rhetorical move patterns. Applying Swales' (2004: 230-232) three-move model for RA Introductions, rhetorical moves in single abstracts were usually presented through the:

- *Establishing a territory* Move 1 (15 occ.);
- *Establishing a niche* Move 2
  by
  Indicating a Gap – Step 1A (5 occ.);
- *Presenting the Present Work* Move 3
  by
  Announcing present research descriptively and/or purposively Move 3-Step 1 (3 occ.), or
  Outlining the structure of the paper Move 3-Step 7 (1 occ.).

The paucity of move occurrences, as driven by the brevity of abstracts, shows that there were very few instances of writers constructing their abstracts around the *Announcing present research* move, as in the samples above (11), or the *Outlining structure* move, while there were many instances of writers adding the *Establishing a territory* move. Yet, signals of *Establishing a niche* were also sometimes revealed through different communicative moves. In *Presenting the Work*, however, the use of "frame markers" (Hyland 2005a) in the forms *finally, first-ly*, marked the sequence of ideas in the (M3-S7) schematic text structure, or announced discourse goals (*The/This case note/note/comment considers/will discuss*) in subject noun-phrases/verb collocations. In the latter realizations, writers drew on a predictable repertoire of (M3) purposive lexis (*case note*, *case*, *comment*, *case comment*), revealing variability in terms of naming rather than discourse function which, as I argued in Chapter 1, rested more heavily with the 'case-focused research paper' organizational structure. Finally, *I* and *We* "self mentions" (Hyland 2005a) were used only sparingly (3 abstracts) in the *I* and exclusive (co-authorship) *We* semantic roles, and as a consequence provided a very low degree of explicit author presence in the texts in favour of less-explicit author references (*This case note*) or *It* introductory subjects.

Where the *territory* combination was used, the rhetorical sequence M1+M3-S1 generally provided a fixed organizational structure of abstracts, although occasionally M1 occurred in inverted order. In this structure, writers were motivated by the need to construct *territory* around the summarised argument of the Decision in the selected case. The fundamental assumption for this opening move to take on more of a *Establishing a territory* function is that writers wished to establish the field in which they were writing, and the *territory* move represented – most reasonably - the meat and drink of case note research rather than simply the icing on the cake. In that sense, the summary of the Decision, used to inform about the rationale for the rule, served therefore to broadly outline where the subject of their case-focused paper actually fell - the 'big context' - pending of course other subsequent (move) rhetorical strategies indicating how the paper would proceed. This can be seen in the third abstract shown in (11) above, where the writer presented first a general picture of his research by placing it in the thematic context of the earlier Decision (M1), which usually made its appearance in boundedness of place deixis ('In *Secretary of State* ... v *AF*') and reproduced the original language used in such Decision through single quotation marks. This writer then proceeded directly to announcing present research (M3-S1) in two successive purposive statements to conclude the abstract, and as a consequence showed his concern with a wider (than simple Purpose) rhetorical structure of the abstract in which to present his study. As will be seen later below in the analysis of Introductions, this wider rhetorical 'abstracting' was essential for the writers to provide not only the general context for discussion but, more importantly, to state that the topic was relevant and worth investigating. This way then, the move strategy was a significant rhetorical act in the rationale of genre writers who were committed to 'abstracting' around precisely a *significant aspect* of the chosen case.

Indeed, writers were not hesitant about the need to identify how the earlier Decision selected for case note analysis created some 'niche'. In the abstract below (12), in fact, the writers in their co-authorship role proceeded from the 'big context' offered by the general subject (*Establishing a territory*) to the specificities of the subject (*Establishing a niche*), by precisely defining a case-focused research issue in the (<u>underlined</u>) gap-identifying strategies:

(12) [**M1**] In *R* v *T* [2010] EWCA Crim 2439, [2011] 1 Cr App Rep 85, the Court of Appeal indicated that 'mathematical formulae', such as likelihood ratios, should not be used by forensic scientists to analyze data where firm statistical evidence did not exist. [**M2-S1A**] <u>Unfortunately</u>, when considering the forensic scientist's evidence, <u>the judgment consistently commits a basic logical error</u>, the 'transposition of the conditional' which indicates that the Bayesian argument <u>has not been understood and extends the confusion</u> surrounding it. The judgment <u>also fails</u> to distinguish between the validity of the relationships in a formula and the precision of the data. [**M3-S1**] <u>We explain</u> why the Bayesian method is the correct logical method for analyzing forensic scientific evidence, how it works and why 'mathematical formulae' can be useful even where firm statistical data is lacking MLR 2011, 74(3): 430

While these writers were concerned with the need to situate and re-define the significance of the research field drawn from the earlier case Decision for their community peers, they also unhesitatingly reviewed professional work done by the 'apparently unquestionable' judges. As a consequence, writers exhibited the ways in which this work created the 'niche' they intended to focus on. This 'niche' was indicated lexically and grammatically by the (underlined) items which, in their textual surface, emphasized some important weaknesses arising from the judgment and further strengthened by the additive conjunct *also* (*also fails*), or some other weaknesses and inadequacies arising from the Supreme Court's decision. As should be expected, such weaknesses were drawn upon with by the writers in the rhetorically detached subjective (Author-centred) Introduction and Discussion sections.

Unpredictably, the writer in the one-only instance of 'unstructured' abstract shown in (13) below avoided properly signalled rhetorical moves, which would presumably have assisted expert readers more in previewing his research:

(13) The opinions of the minority risk creating a dangerous inroad into *Salamon* and *Caparo*. The opinions of the majority avoid that risk but reach the right result by tortuous reasoning. The answer to the case lies in a proper application of *Caparo*. MLR 2010, 73(3): 487

While the 'unstructured' realization became less than a difficult move-rhetorical reading in the next immediate Introduction section, where the writer provided all necessary move-driven information, the surface realization of the abstract shows that the writer made the content of his paper only generically identifiable by the potential audience in ways that he might also have dissuaded his audience from reading the paper.

Introduction

Introduction	Establishing context of the case note paper and justifying the topic for discussion.

The next, immediate Introduction rhetorical section was vigorously manifested in all the case notes published in both journals (MLR: 20/20 – ECLR 10/10), whether or not employing the standard heading (I), as noted. In terms of length, variability arose from the layout producing almost half to three-page Introductions in both journals, on account of the space held by the use of footnotes just above the Introduction text, which yielded an almost 30 per cent greater average word-length from one journal case note to another (ECLR: 572.7 against MLR: 442.8). Although Introductions and their preceding (Abstract) sections in MLR alone appeared to some degree to share similarities in terms of their contextual arrangements, the (length-based) textual configurations in (MLR) Introductions obviously made the major difference with those in the Abstracts, since Introductions were much wider informational accounts than the much narrower Abstracts.

With these informational accounts at work, most of the authors wrote detailed Introductions in which they reviewed items of law relevant to the case by drawing from a tangle of legal arguments in cited sources (cases, regulations, etc.). Although, intuitively, the quest for detail may have turned busy readers away, it suggests that the writers were aiming at preparing, by impressing, their informed readers for several major themes that would recur throughout their work. The effect is that detail inexorably allowed for the production of longer Introductions than one might reasonably expect from an outline of the research work. Only a tiny portion of authors from both journals produced a one or two-paragraph Introduction necessary to include a broad thumbnail sketch of their research work.

Under such textual realizations, where authors inevitably showed up as 'expanders *v* cutters', Introductions drew the reader into a variously detailed exposition of the content in the case note paper, by laying the foundation for the discussion and justification of the topic in such a paper. In general, this function was accomplished by the inclusion of different informational elements constructed at various length in the texts, and resulted in a three-move standard, organizational model proposed and outlined in Table 4:

Move	Function
1 Providing Background Information	Describing the selected case in points of facts, procedural posture and decision, together with seminal legal context (case and/or statutory law) in cited sources.
2 Identifying Research Issue(s)	Establishing the specific (*significant*) research issue(s) for its (their) inconsistencies or omissions in case-focused research gaps.
3 Outlining Research Study	Presenting the essence of the research study by descriptive purposes, research questions, or outcomes of the case note.

Table 4. Three-move rhetorical structure of case note Introductions and occurrences.

	Move 1	Move 2	Move 3
ECLR+MLR	27/30	30/30	25/30

Table 4.1. Move occurrence in ECLR and MLR Introductions: total counts.

The three-move model description above is at some variance with Feak et al's (2000: 203-209) four-move structure of (student-written) case note Introductions, where the Prefacing Move adds to the other three moves, as derived from Swales' (1990) CARS model, to provide the following rhetorical sequence: Prefacing Move - Move 1 (Establishing a research territory) - Move 2 (Establishing a legal problem or issue) - Move 3 (Addressing the legal problem and stating the nature of the argument). In addition to varying with Prefacing Move, while still being similar to the three-move structuring in the authors' findings, my model was devoid of *Hypothetical scenario* which typifies Move 1 in the authors' study.

As is clear, the structural model description in Table 4 is one in which the elements at the top, Providing Background Information (Move 1), represented the more general topic (the 'big context') for the study; they were the writers' imperative to prepare, by appealing to, the knowledgeable readers of their research study around case-focused issues via intertextual and interdiscursive features (Candlin and Maley 1997). As an important rhetorical act in the large majority of Introductions (as was in the Abstracts noted before), this scenery allowed the writer to gradually narrow down to the specific topic in the case under analysis by Identifying Research Issue(s) (Move 2). In other words, Background was necessary to more fully explain identifiable gaps arising from such case in Research Issue(s). Finally, the 'big context' allowed the writer to give a brief general account of what this analysis accomplished (Outlining Research Study – Move 3) in relation to the issue(s) identified earlier.

This way of organizing information along three Moves can be said to have affinity to Swales' (2004: 230-232) M1+M2+M3 rhetorical schema for RA Introductions, although on a broad, generalizing model and different terminology. Thus, presenting the more general topic (Background Information) for the subject under legal research took on the broad function of the *Establishing the territory* Move 1, where the significant Facts and Decision were used to provide background knowledge and establish thematic context (as was indeed the same function served by the Decision summary in the opening Move of the Abstracts)[5]; presenting the particular Research Issue(s) of the broader subject in case-focused research gaps functioned as the *Establishing a niche* Move 2 via *Indicating a Gap* (Step 1A); and finally, presenting the essence of the

---

[5] Reliance on Background information in the opening lines of case notes reflects Swales' (1990: 137) argument about RA Introductions, where "The opening paragraphs require the writer to make some decisions about the amount and type of background knowledge to be included [..], the appropriateness of the appeal to the readership, and the directness of the approach".

Research Study by explicit purposes, research questions, outcomes, or relevance, respectively functioned as the *Announcing present research descriptively and/or purposively* (M3–S1), *Presenting RQs* (M3–S2), *Announcing principal outcomes* (M3–S5), and *Stating the value of the present research* (M3–S6), in Swales' terminology.

As Table 4.1 above shows in terms of move frequency, M1 was conventionally present in 90 percent (the large majority) of journal Introductions (27/30), where it generally appeared in the opening lines of the text, or was occasionally inverted of either type of informational elements (Facts and/or Decision). When inverted, either elements appeared somewhere near or the closing lines of the text, although it was not unusual for such elements to reappear, by iteration, in M2 as well. Only in 10 percent of Introductions (3/30) were either or both informational elements omitted in M1, as in the near-opening lines below, where co-writers opted for the avoidance of Facts by inviting the reader to rely on other co-text sources:

(14) … For the facts of the *Rottmann* case we refer to the immediately preceding annotation by Jessurund'Oliveira. It would be duplication if we were to repeat a summary of those facts. … ECLR 2011, 7

While M2 was conventionally present in all journal Introductions (30/30, whether by explicitly or implicitly identifying the Research Issue(s), M3 allowed the majority of Introductions (25/30) to outline the essence of research either by purposive statements (18/30), (direct) research questions (5/30) or, in the lowest instances, by outcomes (2/30). The remainder (5/30), by contrast, failed to prepare readers for properly signalled Research Outlining statements, in which cases they left the readers with the identified Research Issue(s) alone in Move 2. Considering that prototypical schematic structure will be recognizable in terms of the most typical realization pattern, as identified by the discourse community (Swales 1990: 58), the frequency counts in Table 4.1 therefore suggest that Introductions tended in general to have a fixed rhetorical organization.

To illustrate the model description outlined in Table 4, let us now examine the following Introductions in (15), where the varying length at which they were constructed shows the writers' attempts at 'cutting' or 'expanding on' their textual configurations:

(15)

Full text 'cutter' (217 words)

INTRODUCTION

[**M1**] Proprietary estoppel has developed into one of equity's sharpest instruments in its interventions in the common law and statutory regulation of land and the distribution of assets on death. In those contexts there is a balance to be struck between the need for certainty and the need to hold people to their bargains and promises.[1] The need for certainty is usually met by imposing strict formality requirements on transactions, which in turn determine what constitutes a bargain or promise.[2][**M2**] This is not always an adequate construction of reality: bargains take place and promises are made outside of law's ordering of reality.[3] Proprietary estoppels calls into question this conception of the bargain by recognizing certain transactions that do not meet the required formalities.

[**M3**] The question is how far equity will go in giving effect to promises falling outside law's ordering of reality. What is the rationale for equitable intervention? Is equitable intervention concerned with the nature of the defendant's promise or the state of the claimant's mind? To what extent are the boundaries of equitable intervention determined by the context of the transaction? Two recent House of Lords decisions have had to grapple with these questions in the context of work undertaken in anticipation of a contract for the redevelopment of land[4] and promises to an expectant heir.[5]

(*reference to catchwords in Decisions*) MLR 2009, 72(6): 999

Full text 'expander' (841 words)

INTRODUCTION

[**M1**] On 16 December 2009, the UK Supreme Court held a state-funded Jewish school to be guilty of discrimination based on ethnic origin in the way it operated its admissions policies.[1] The Jewish Free School (JFS), one of the top-performing schools in the country, refused a place to a thirteen year old boy, M., because it did not consider him Jewish. It is a fundamental tenet of traditional Judaism that to be Jewish one must be born of Jewish mother or to a woman who converted into Judaism prior to his/her birth (*writer intrudes into the factual accounts by informing the reader about the legal foundation of Judaism*). M.'s father was Jewish by birth, but his mother, who was originally an Italian Catholic, had converted to Judaism with the criteria set by a non-orthodox branch of Judaism. The School's admissions standards only recognized orthodox criteria for conversion as valid, hence deeming neither M. nor his mother to be Jewish.[2]The Supreme Court held that the School breached section 1 of the Race Relations Act 1976[3] because its admission criteria were based on the ancestral origins of the pupil's mother, and not on his perception of himself as a Jew and on his practising of the Jewish religion. Therefore the admission test was not considered to be religious in nature, but ethnic-based. The Supreme Court instructed JFS to establish a new test that did not make determinations of Jewish identity based on ethnicity.

[**M2**] The rationale of this 5-4 decision[4] is based on three assumptions, all of which are highly problematic. The first one is that Jews constitute an 'ethnic group', at least within the scope of application of the Race Relation Act. The second assumption is the ethnic nature of the school's admission test. Given that the test mirrored the traditional rule of Jewish membership, the real question, however, is whether the latter is ultimately ethnic rather than religious. Finally, the last assumption is that denominational preference is not immunized from the application of anti-discrimination law and that the power to decide over religious membership rules might be subject to a strict scrutiny by state courts.

The case is made particularly convoluted by a number of added complexities. In the first place, the Race Relation Act is interpreted here by the Court in an inflexible, categorical way, that leaves no room for proportionality. According to the Court, direct discrimination, under British Law, can never be justified or excused, regardless of the different interests and values involved.[5]This is not the case in most jurisdictions, where non-discrimination provisions are usually subject to a proportionality analysis by courts. In the second place, the membership rule the Court focuses on is far from straightforward, because the nature of the matrilinear test is not *solely* racial. Had it been purely racial, the case would have been an easy one, although the result might still have not been desirable. The Court takes the position that distinctions made on blood relations are *prima facie* racial/ethnic. In this case, however, the ethnic origin of the mother is not decisive, or, at least, it is made less relevant by the circumstance that anybody, of whatever ethnic/racial background, can convert into Judaism, and thus acquire the same status of an 'ethnic' Jew, i.e., one born to a Jewish mother. The Court is forced to go into the analysis of what is 'ethnic' and what is 'religious', when in the case of Judaism the two partially overlap and are ultimately impossible to disentangle. Moreover, the dispute in the *JFS* case took place between two streams of Judaism, Orthodox and the Masorti, both of which believe in the matrilinear test, but disagree on the appropriate conversion standards.

The Supreme Court ended up deciding over an internal disagreement within a religious minority,[6] making a decision having to do with Jewish law and setting new criteria for admission that did not make determinations of Jewish identity based on ethnicity. The ultimate irony is that such criteria are neither the Orthodox nor the Masorti ones, but, rather, they mirror a Christian understanding of religious membership. Understandably, the United Synagogue, which represents Orthodox Jews in the UK, was 'extremely disappointed' with the ruling, which 'interfered' with the 'Torah-based imperative … to educate Jewish children, regardless of their background.'[7] The Synagogue's President, Simon Hochhauser, said:

> 'Essentially, we must now apply a non-Jewish definition of who is Jewish.'[8] (*writer reviews other items of current Decision*)
> This case raises a large, complex and intricately intertwined set of issues, including equality and non-discrimination issues, the relationship between the state and religion and diverging standards within minority groups affecting the relationship between the group and the state. It is beyond the scope of the present article to provide a comprehensive account of all of these. [**M3**] Therefore, I will concentrate my remarks on three issues, namely, the categorization of Jews in ethnic terms, the nature of the Jewish membership rule, and the justifiability of discriminatory conduct that is motivated by religion. I will do so in terms of the treatment of religious diversity in a constitutional democracy, without dealing with issues exclusively involving questions of British law, but rather those within the broader context of European constitutionalism.
>
> ECLR 2010, 6: 481-484

The different textual progression resulting from the latter ('expander') Introduction depended upon the writer's need to prepare the reader for several major review items of law relevant to the case. These were presented in case-focused research gaps by reference to a variety of (mainly professional) cited sources in footnote format, thus resulting in a detailed, descriptive Introduction.

On a comparative analysis, the writer in MLR Introduction opened the 'big context' of his research (M1) by making generalizations about the importance of the subject (*proprietary estoppel*). By emphasizing the significance of the subject in the substantive law field, the writer's statements were not even baseless since he had to provide the important disciplinary claims made within scholarship by citing the relevant sources in superscript numbers. The writer therefore left the 'big context' of the Decisions to appear in the main issues with which the two cases were concerned (catchwords) in the closing lines of the Introduction. By contrast, the writer in ECLR Introduction was motivated by the need to sketch out the 'big context' of his research (M1) around a summary of facts, procedural posture and decision. In that context, where narrative constructions in (underlined) past tense forms typified this opening move, the writer did not refrain from intruding into the historical accounts of the facts by informing the reader, presumably unfamiliar with the field, about the legal foundation of Judaism.

As is clear, the writers in both journal Introductions drew from the 'big context' to narrow down to the specific topic (Research issue) in M2, which they indicated (as in underlined items) either by asserting something contrary to disciplinary claims (counter-claim) in explicit issue-raising (MLR), or similarly by raising a number of explicit issues relevant to the case (ECLR) in identifiable research gaps. Like writers creating the (*Niche*) rhetorical move strategy in the Abstracts, writers in the Introductions were concerned to situate and re-establish the significance of the research topic drawn from academic and professional (House of Lords' Decisions) sources in MLR or from professional (Decision) source alone in ECLR, and exhibited the ways in which such disciplinary sources created inconsistencies or difficulties (gaps) the writers intended to focus on. Writers therefore moved into their lines of disciplinary (and indeed knowledge-making) inquiry by identifying how the academic and professional sites of legal discourse may be reviewed in the case-focused legal research, and the fact that they created space (by explicitly specifying the gaps) avoided the possibility that "the introduction remains flat" (Swales 1990: 158). Without neglecting that each case for gap-spotting was different and unique in its nature and features in both journals, the 'expanding' move in ECLR thus revealed an inquiring mind of the writer, allowing the informed audience to follow the highly informative topic in the corresponding move. Where the research issue was spotted in other Introductions, writers presented semantic elements of the gap-indicating strategy (underlined), as in the extracts below:

(16) Behind these simple questions (which, of course, were formulated rather less directly) lurk important matters to be resolved. The operative part of the decision of the European Court of Justice is short, sweet, and in my opinion, incorrect. ECLR

However, problems related to the use of multiple legal bases will not cease to exist. On the contrary, the new Treaty poses new ones.[14] Be as it may, the ruling which is commented on here *maintains its relevance* for appreciating the evolution of the case-law on the choice of legal basis. ECLR

Alongside the important question of exactly what the guidance given for such cases amounts to, is the question of the extent to which this guidance is applicable to cases other than those involving group violence resulting in death. MLR

What *Radmacher*does do is to invite discussion about what the fundamental obligations of marriage entail and what sort of marriage we want in English law, a discussion now being led by the Law Commission for England and Wales following the publication of its consultation paper on marital property agreements.[4] MLR

In this case the health authority in question had erred in the opposite direction as compared to the social workers in the Baby P tragedy. … This

> limb of the decision cut against the cloth of the previous House of Lords ruling in *JD*v *East Berkshire Health Authority*,[5] where … . MLR

> There are many things wrong with this ruling, but perhaps the most shocking is that … . MLR

In Outlining the Research Study (M3), writers in both Introductions proceeded along different rhetorical strategies. In MLR, the writer drew from the gap-defining strategies to present specific research issues in the form of direct questions that he intended to pursue and provide answers for in his research. As with RA abstracts examined in Chapter 4, these questions served an interactional and persuasive purpose, emphasizing the dialogic engagement of the current discourse as a social action (Bakhtin 1986; Webber 1994; Hyland 2002a, 2005a) where the reader's expectations followed the critical points in the writer's disciplinary argument. By contrast, the overt writer in ECLR announced, by explaining in (outlined) metadiscoursal "code gloss" (Hyland 2005a), the research in terms of an argumentative 'roadmap' taken in the study to achieve its objectives (*I will concentrate my remarks on three issues, namely*). And predicting arguments for the reader to preview the exact scope of the research possibly implied some 'method' (*I will do so in terms of*) that the writer wished to introduce, by re-elaboration of an established concept (*religious diversity in a constitutional democracy*), as the epistemologically adequate criterion by which to accomplish the research objective.

In other cases, the 'roadmap' served metadiscursively the purpose of previewing arguments in the schematic text structure through (underlined) frame markers, and as a consequence allowed the writers to outline the purposes of their study by explicitly sequencing arguments in the discourse:

(17) The legal issues which this note will explore are first, the scope and effect of clause 2.7 of the consignment agreement giving Christie's complete discretion as to cataloguing; second, the appropriateness of implying a term as to *Wednesbury* reasonableness into this agency contract; and finally, whether the criteria for granting an injunction restraining a breach of that term were satisfied. MLR 2010, 73(6): 1039

As with Abstracts, writers in Introductions preferred to outline their research study through a predictable repertoire of purposive lexis (*article*, *case note*, *comment*, *contribution*, *note*, *piece*) rather than announcing their goals in first person. The latter goals were achieved only in few cases by the use of *I* (ECLR: 6 – MLR: 8) and exclusive *We* (ECLR: 5 – MLR: 3) pronouns appearing in three (ECLR) or five (MLR) Introductions alone, and such cases were sufficient for (first person) writers to create a research space, in Swales' (1990) terms.

Indeed, by intuition, different rhetorical opportunities were potentially available to writers in M3. In the two-only instances below, the critical writers seemed to guide the readers towards what they achieved in the case-focused research beyond simple purposive statements, by outlining the 'scope of their argument'. The necessary assumption for this was that the writers wished to preview their own 'results' rather than 'purpose', as derived from their lines of inquiry of the issues under review:

(18) The argument presented here is that the general suspicion with which epidemiological, and by extension, scientific evidence is regarded in *Sienkiewicz* is fundamentally misguided. As Faigman has noted, 'although science can never dictate what is fair and just, it has become an indispensible tool on which the law must sometimes rely to do the fair and just thing.'[16][**solicitudes**] The general exclusionary principle advocated vis-à-vis scientific evidence in *Sienkiewicz* is a significant cause for concern and can only contribute to decision-making of uncertain scope, particularly in the context of toxic torts. MLR 2011, 74(5): 779

This comment argues that *L'Oreal*is theoretically unsound, runs counter to the thrust of the European trademark law, is difficult to reconcile with the ECJ's earlier decisions and may impact negatively on the competitiveness of the European market place. MLR 2010, 73(2): 283

While the writer's inquiry aligned with previous academic claims (*As Faigman has noted ...*), implying agreement on the issue for review from other cited sources, the presentation of argument therefore seemed to help the writers situate themselves in the *Announcing principal outcomes* move (Swales), and thereafter proceed towards the *significance* of the case qualified, as it was, for 'its state of being solicitous' in peer-disciplinary discourse.

Discussion

Discussion	Addressing the topic by: • a full description of the scenery behind the main case - i.e. analyzing Issues of Facts and Law in the court's reasoning and decision by including the wider context of case and/or statutory law (**Legal Background**); and • a critical analysis of the *significant* issue(s) arising from the court's decision and reasoning in the main case, together with the implications for the current and future state of the law and public policy (**Author's Argument**).

Discussion was the lengthier rhetorical section (ECLR: 4650.2 – MLR 4998.9) used for a systematic examination of the relevant law controlling the critical issue(s) in the case.

However, the neutral label attached to case note Discussion here should be treated cautiously in that Discussion did not attract the kind of move rhetorical patterns described of Discussions in genre-based studies of Research Articles across disciplines (e.g. Hopkins and Dudley Evans 1988; Swales 1990; Dubois 1997; Holmes 1997; Lewin et al 2001; Peacock 2002; Kanoksilapatham 2005; Basturkmen 2009, 2011). In general, these studies have described the (RA) discussion section as characterized by the presence of repeated move cycles (Swales 1990; Holmes 1997; Peacock 2002; Basturkmen 2009) organized around the findings to research questions (Hopkins & Dudley-Evans 1988; Dubois 1997; Basturkmen 2009, 2011). With a focus on move organization, Holmes (1997), for instance, provides a move model based on natural sciences to show variation in move organization in Discussions across three social science disciplines (Political Science, Sociology, History). In his large-scale study based on seven disciplines, including Law, Peacock (2002) employs Dudley-Evans's (1994) nine-move rhetorical model of RA Discussion sections in the science disciplines to similarly classify nine communicative moves in his RA Discussions:

1. *information move* (background about theory/research aims/methodology)
2. *statement of result* (either a numerical value or reference to a graph or table)
3. *finding* (same as statement of result, but without a reference to a graph or table)
4. *(un)expected outcome* (a comment on whether the result is expected or not)
5. *reference to previous research*
6. *explanation* (reasons for unexpected results)
7. *claim* (a generalisation arising from the results: contribution to research)
8. *limitation*
9. *recommendation*

Figure 2: Peacock's (2002: 481, italics in the original) nine-move model of Discussions in RAs derived from Dudley-Evans's (1994) model.

The author finds that the model is "broadly accurate overall" (Peacock 2002: 487) across the disciplines although, in terms of interdisciplinary differences, "move cycles" occur more frequently in Language and Linguistics, as well as Law (Peacock 2002: 488).

In contrast with this and other quoted studies, case note Discussions were not organized around the 'reporting of research findings' on one main account. Although case notes captured the rhetorical organization of research articles, they lacked the canonical IMRD structure and content in which to present experimental data, as I noted in Chapter 1. Allied with this rhetorical organization was that writers addressed a significant topic in the case in (qualitative) analytical research method using the layout system typical of most argumentative law research articles, as examined in the previous Chapter. In this organizational framework, writers were committed to answering a research question around this significant topic (indicated in Introduction) rather than testing a hypothesis. And, because the research question was relatively open (that is, the authors may have given multiple possible answers to the question), writers approached the case under study by addressing the theoretical and practical issues based on their own phenomenological perspectives that developed within such case. This meant observing the social and epistemological side of the law as it emerged from the Reasoning and Decision in the case. And while by so doing, Discussion writers (as those in Peacock's move 4) represented the 'outcome' of their case-focused inquiry as a 'finding' (i.e. what writers accomplished in their research paper), they still addressed or discussed the significant issue(s) in the case outside strictly reporting research methods and findings, as is customary in experimental-driven data.

These key differences thus made the identification of moves proposed in the literature inherently difficult or otherwise unrealistic in the context of case note Discussions which, as I will examine immediately below, became distinguished by the rationale of 'analysing-discussing' the various elements under case focus along the 'without-end' rhetorical framework, as I emphasized in the previous Chapter. Therefore, while the descriptive label adopted for Discussion here may conveniently describe the work done by case note writers, the 'without-end' rationale referred to also squares well with the variable methods and definitions used by genre writers in the corpus. This, then, would fit in with the view of academic genres which offer analysts distinct resources for investigating the writing conventions, social practices and values of a disciplinary research community (Bondi and Hyland 2006).

As noted, the rationale of Discussion was to put the writer's subjective and critical analysis of the significant case issue(s) and its implications for law and policy (**Author's Argument**) in its full legal context, which was presented through the objective analysis of the facts, court's reasoning and decision, as well as the wider existing law (**Legal Background**). The result was a 'chunked' composite form of Discussion represented below leading to answers for the research questions set in Introduction:

Topic(s): Analysis-Discussion
in
Legal Background + Author's Argument

Legal Background

In Legal Background, writers were elucidative of the major aspects of the judgment by giving a complete presentation of the Issues of Facts and Law in the case together with the wider legal context (case/statutory law). In other words, the 'discussion' here tracked the court's logical sequence of Law issues raised by the Facts peculiar to the case (the semiotic reality of the law) and, because these issues were often stated explicitly by the court or other judicial officers, they became reported arguments in the court/officer's reasoning and decision. In general, Issues of Facts and Law came from the party(ies) to the case, the Court/trial judge, and the relevant law, and were reported in the simple tense, with law arguments also being substantiated and referenced by a variety of legal sources cited in the footnotes. In this sense, then, Legal Background fitted in with the style of 'rewriting about cases', and became close to the rationale of Civil and Common Law judgments alike where judges conventionally rewrite questions of fact and law[6] before proceeding to their critical assessments of such questions in the "pragma-dialectical perspective" of legal argumentation (Feteris 2002, 2005).[7]

The following extracts from one case note may give a flavour of the factual and legal issues:

Legal Background

(19) THE DECISION

Case story

The judgment at hand decides an individual complaint of a German branch of the business enterprise *Honeywell* against a judgment of the German Federal Labour Court of 26 April 2006[11] in which this German court applied the *Mangold* case law of the Court of Justice. In 2003 Werner Mangold, born in February 1950, was employed for a limited period of time. German statutory law explicitly allowed for such contracts for workers older than 52. The same year, Mangold sued his employer in the

---

[6] Where Common Law Judgments are concerned, rewriting about Legal Background in the (English) MLR corpus judgments was no less significant to emphasize the "traces of orality" (Charnock 2010) in such judgments.

[7] Interestingly, Feteris (2005) offers a heuristic and critical tool for the analysis and evaluation of legal argumentation in judicial decisions by integrating insights from legal theory and legal philosophy.

> labour court of Munich. He grounded his suit in particular on the Directive 2000/78/EC, which prohibits any discrimination for the reason of age in labour relations. At the relevant moment, the Directive had not been transformed into German law. The deadline for the implementation expired a little later, in December 2003 and the European Charter of Fundamental Rights, which prohibits discrimination for the reason of age, had not yet entered into force. In answer to preliminary questions of the Munich labour court, the Court of Justice in 2005 declared the relevant rule of German statutory law to be in violation of Article 6(1) of the Directive and the general principle of anti-discrimination.[12] According to the Court of Justice, national courts were obliged to secure the implementation of the general prohibition of discrimination because of age. Even before the end of the deadline member-states were not allowed to take actions incompatible with the aims of the Directive. Though the German statute aimed at integrating older people into the workforce, an aim expressly allowed for by the Directive, the Court found in the regulation a disproportionate discrimination.
> This reasoning of the European Court of Justice is generally considered weak.[13] The Court has been accused of inventing a general principle of EU law against age discrimination and also accused of lawmaking from the bench, since such a principle existed neither in the treaties nor in the practice of most member states at that point in time. …
> *Methodology*
> Perhaps the most remarkable issue about our decision lies in its methodological approach. ….. ECLR 2011, 7: 163-164

As is clear, this writer in the *Case story* paragraph explained neutrally and briefly only those issues that had a bearing on the topic in the case. In the extracts, well-assembled Issues of Facts and Law performed a strategic staging (case scenery), since they prepared for the writer's own analysis of the critical issues in the court's decision (*This reasoning of the European Court ...*) before leading the reader into the next important issue (*Perhaps the most ...*) in 'discuss' type of exposition under a different level heading (*Methodology*). Yet, by gradually intruding into the text with his own comments, this and other writers drew from other elements in Legal Background to form their own opinions.

Much like a lawyer or judge in their (professional) generic roles, the case note (academic) writer above was a 'storyteller' of Issues of Facts and Law, and the narrative tense or narrative time determined the grammatical (past) tense of the story. The writer therefore gave such Issues the attributes of narratives based on a series of actions and events unfolding in chronological sequence. Viewed functionally, narratives emphasized the communication of "tellable" or "reportable" events (Labov 1997) in the generic writing process, even though the "reportability" dimension (in the

Labovian's model of personal narratives) was narrowed down to third-person objective narration in the current study. As shown in the *Case Story* extract above, typifying the 're-told' judgment, the preference for third-person narrative mode (as is in the prototypical judgment of Civil and Common Law jurisdictions) was in fact essential to present an 'objective', unbiased narration of law applied to facts, well outside 'subjective' narration describing participants' thoughts, opinions, or feelings. And while this mode echoed the description of Facts and Law typifying some other generic writings (such as, the Legal Memorandum in its own configured rhetorical context), it allowed for the presence of the writer as a manifestly 'inconspicuous reporter' or 'self-depersonalized narrator' of reportable actions and events. More than that, the (third-person) objective axis made its overwhelming appearance in the stretches of discourse where writers related the court's reasoning and decision by way of reported arguments, as in the extracts in (20) below:

(20) … the Court of Justice in 2005 declared the relevant rule … ECLR

… the Court of Appeal referred five questions to the ECJ … MLR

The Court found that the above statements, considered in context, were unequivocal … MLR

In the *Conseil national des barreaux* judgment rendered on 10 April 2008 the *Conseild'Etat* refined the scheme elaborated in *Arcelor*. The plaintiff pleaded that Articles 6 and 8 of the ECHR … ECLR

Still acting as impartial reporters or narrators, these writers gave accurate descriptions of substantive and procedural law arguments, but put their own spin on those arguments to form their critical analysis of the case (Argument) in recursive processes within Legal Background paragraphs, as in:

(21) [**(reported) argument in the court's reasoning**] As to the intention that the agreement should be determinative, the Court suggested that this will more readily be found from agreements concluded after its decision. [**author's argument**] *Certainly, the advice that would be given today about pre-nuptial agreements will be different, and stronger, from that previously dispensed: there is no need now to give the rather baffling advice that the agreement is formally void, but may nevertheless attract some weight, depending on the circumstances.* MLR 2011, 74(3): 436

[**(reported) argument in the court's reasoning**] Having disposed of *Hampshire Land*, Lord Phillips went on to say[13] that the courts should look

> behind the claimant company to those whose interests the relevant duty is designed to protect. **[author's argument]** *This part of the reasoning lurches perilously between the rule of attribution and the rule as to the lifting of the corporate veil.* MLR 2010, 73(3): 489

In textual realizations, therefore, the straightforward presentation of Issues of Facts and Law as narratives - 'what the party or court said/did' – held special significance throughout Legal Background (and indeed Discussion) before the author's opinions were appropriately voiced there interspersedly. Thus, it is fair to say that the significance of Issues of Facts and Law allowed Discussion writers in the genre to achieve three interrelated purposes I would like to introduce here:

(1) to represent story themes as they related to the case and to the reader's holistic goals of gaining a clear sense of the case plot;
(2) to include story in the decisional and policy-based (analogical) reasoning of the case; and
(3) to explain the legally relevant facts in the case by forming the writer's argument in such case.

Viewed functionally, therefore, the Facts and Law's underlying purposes helped to account for an 'answer' to a research issue in the academic genre of the case note in much the same way as Facts and Law account for an 'answer' to a legal dispute in the professional genre of the legal judgment. In the latter, recounting Facts and Law is important for the court to arrive at the normativity of the Decision (or Holding), and the Decision itself is the court's answer to a question presented to it for answer by the disputing parties involved, or raised by the court itself in its own reading of the case. Except where Facts and Law are enunciated in two different genres (case note v judgment), they do not seem at all to stand as polar opposites in that writers in both genres pick up Issues of Facts and Law to measure them against an articulated standard of legal argument in their own writing.

Yet, in this context, where legal disputes were objectively 're-told' in the judgment and the case note alike, the latter genre may still provide the rhetorical framework for looking at the origin and development of disputing. Following Felstiner et al. (1980-81), who write on *The Emergence and Transformation of Disputes: Naming, Blaming, Claiming* from the perspective of the sociology of law:

> "unperceived injurious experiences are - or are not – perceived (naming), do or do not become grievances (blaming) and ultimately disputes (claiming)" (Felstiner 1980-81: 631).

More specifically, in this theoretical framework, the process of disputing takes place retroactively and involves people who:

> "do - or do not - perceive an experience as an injury, blame someone else, claim redress, or get their claims accepted because of their *social* position as well as their individual characteristics" (Felstiner et al. 1980-81: 636, italics in the original).

Now, this transformation process can be seen in the *Case Story* text examined above via narration, where the injured party (Werner Mangold) recognized the 'labour discrimination for reason of age' as an injurious experience (naming), which thus became a just cause for complaint against his employer (blaming). Eventually, such complaint was voiced to the relevant legal institution, e.g. asking the labour court in Munich to make compensation for the (discrimination) wrong suffered (claiming). While this claim became a dispute in its own right, on account of the 're-told' antecedents in naming and blaming, allowing claim was then expressly voiced by the relevant Court (of Justice). By acting in its deferring institutional role in the conflict, this Court obviously required an understanding of the origin and development of the wrong as perceived by the (individual characteristics of) disputing party in the overall discourse about grievance and claim.

Author's Argument

The current reader will remember that Author's Argument was the place where writers argued on the topic in *if*, *how* and *why* analyses of the case by offering interpretations and stating implications on the identified issue(s). Writers did so by recursively drawing on descriptions of the materials given in Legal Background, as seen above, to uphold their Argument - whether or not in separating 'moving' processes. By committing themselves to an opinion, writers therefore aimed at giving convincing arguments to win the readers to their side and to adopt their points of view about the topical issue.

In drawing from a synthesis of Legal Background, writers essentially expounded on the rule or principle in the main case together with its implications for legal and policy issues. The type and extent of treatment of the rule/principle expounded on required the writers to address the legal issue in the most 'remarkable' judgment that represented a *significant* concern on several possible aspects, as when the court:

- decided the case incorrectly,
- ignored logical reasoning,
- missed some important aspects,
- departed from judicial precedent, or
- created a new area of law.

While these aspects defined the merit of the chosen judgment as a path-breaking one attracting debate, they also allowed the writers to make a variety of arguments through critical evaluation of the legal issue with which the law in the main decision was concerned, and its impact on current and future state of law and policy. Writing critically about the significant issue in the case therefore meant that writers looked for unarticulated premises, logical fallacies, manipulation of the factual record, or distortions of precedent, and entered into dialogue with their subject area through "intertextual and interdiscursive" elements (Candlin and Maley 1997). Such elements derived from the facts unravelled by parties and the legal arguments deployed by judicial officials (mainly judges), the latter however being fully substantiated and referenced with footnoted citations.

The following extracts from different case notes in the journals may give a flavour of this:

(22) **Author's Argument**

It was this aspect of the discrimination enquiry that the Court of Appeal underestimated in *Eweida*. The primary obligation not to discriminate indirectly on ground of religion in the distribution of opportunities in employment imposed by Regulation 3 and the Directive is a duty of distributive justice. MLR 2011, 74(2): 304

[deciding incorrectly: the court assigned too low a value to *discrimination* by missing the important *duty of distributive justice*]

It does not appear to me that this rule is, as has been said, founded upon principles of morality. … But I am satisfied that it might be departed from in many cases, without any fear of breach of morality, without any wrong being inflicted, and without any consciousness of wrong-doing[39].

MLR 2011, 74(4): 603

[departing from earlier precedent]

This reasoning not only rests on an unprovable assumption, but suffers from the controversial method of extrapolating downwards from high exposure population studies with the inevitable conclusion that any exposure to asbestos dust increases the risk of mesothelioma. This is not a conclusion with which all medical experts would agree.[76] Moreover, it directly contradicts the majority's obiter comments in relation to *Willmore* which imply that any exposure to asbestos no matter how insignificant is insufficient to prove causation. Lord Phillips is guilty of the very thing that he argued lay at the root of the unreliability of epidemiological evidence in mesothelioma cases.[77] MLR 2011, 74(5): 788

[showing inconsistency of reasoning and affirming the opposite of a proposition (case departure) by incorporating the court's majority 'side' (*obiter*) opinions]

The jurisprudence of the Court that is to be expected in the light of *Chakroun* is likely to have a significant impact on instances of reverse discrimination. The rights contained in Directive 2003/86/EC are explicitly not applicable to non-moving nationals of a member state and even the application to dual EU/non-EU nationals has been excluded by many member states[65]. ECLR 2010(6): 478

[emphasizing implications on matters of *reverse discrimination* drawn from the criticism of the (inapplicable) case]

Perhaps these are the wrong principles to adopt here. As we said at the outset, any interpretation of these provisions is inevitably politically controversial. The House of Lords have not done enough to outline what principles they think are relevant in interpreting the legislation. A consequence of this is that the 'test' that they propose is incoherent. MLR 2009, 72(6): 990

[emphasizing some fallacies in the (incoherent) HL judgment marked by policy-based controversies]

These critical writers defended their interpretations by showcasing the disciplinary research that they had done in an insightful investigation, and as a consequence were able to form their Argument in the case's underlying decisional rule. And while proving an argument in *if*, *how* and *why* critical evaluation had the effect of providing the widest disciplinary community with a 'fresh' look at some important issue(s) in the case, the resulting elaboration of the writer's claims and counter claims (made also with respect to literature arguments) was meant metadiscoursively[8] to persuade the audience that the writer's ideas had merit. In this sense, writing critically and persuasively reflected pragmatic dimensions of legal discourse in the Discussion section where writers' observations of the epistemic side of law in the chosen case were meant to be as accurate as possible and warranted by reasonable inferences from legally available evidence.

[8] For the (metadiscourse) micro-linguistic analysis of Discussion, see Chapter 3.

Viewed together, therefore, **Legal Background** and **Author's Argument** engaged writers with recursive processes of going back and forth between the argument elements under focus, and therefore resulted in a 'without-end' analysis-discussion section distributed across a variety of content headings. And while the mixture between Legal Background and Author's Argument defined the conventional attributes of legal discourse in Discussion section, the latter also came to describe (however broadly) the four classic rhetorical modes of discourse: *exposition, description, narration, argumentation*, or *EDNA*, in Crowley's (1990) terminology. Among these modes, for instance, the purpose of *expository* writing (accomplished through transition words, comparing and contrasting, etc.) was to inform, describe, explain, or define the writers' subject to the readers, so that expository text was meant to deposit information by preparing the reader for the writers' *argumentation*.

Beyond text-composition approaches, however, the mixture of writing modes made a strong case for the combination of rhetorical acts, or *generic values* – namely, *arguments*, *narratives*, *descriptions*, and *explanations*, in Bhatia's (2001, 2002, 2004) terms.[9] Clearly, as a result of recursive processes, the notion of *generic values* applied to Discussion outside "any specific textual sequencing, or cognitive structuring in terms of 'moves'" (Bhatia 2004: 62), in that those rhetorical acts depended upon the nature and function of the statements in the textualization process of the 'no bounds' rhetorical Discussion. As molecules in a state of matter, those rhetorical acts thus moved past one another by flowing easily to conform to the shape of an informative and evaluative Discussion section constructed objectively and subjectively.

Conclusion

5. Conclusion	Summing up the author's critical arguments and positions in the paper and reinforcing the 'remarkable' aspects in the researched case.

[9] Instead, Martin (1995) argues about *macro genre* for texts which combine a variety of *elemental genres*, such as recounts, narratives, explanations, and so forth. Still in Systemic Functional Linguistics, Paltridge (2001) is more inclined to define genre as a kind of text with related form, function and context, such as a description, procedure, or exposition. In broad terms, therefore, Paltridge's view takes the position that several aspects contribute to the identification of a communicative event as an instance of a particular genre.

As the third-shortest rhetorical section in case notes after Discussion and Introduction (see Figure 2 - Chapter 1), the Conclusion brought case notes full circle and reinforced the 'remarkable' aspects of the chosen judgment, by fulfilling the overall purpose of the social genre in the five-part rhetorical structure.

The emphasis placed on bringing the reader full circle in the notable aspects of the chosen case was not too different from other types of Conclusions used in academic writing, where writers summarize their thoughts or demonstrate the importance of the topics, among other features. In identifying and analysing the rhetorical structure of Conclusions here, reference was therefore made to the formal rhetorical descriptions of the Conclusion sections proposed by Yang and Allison (2003) for Research Article Conclusions and Bunton (2005) for PhD theses.[10] In Yang and Allison's (2003: 379) analytical model, for instance, Conclusions consist of three Moves and five Steps – namely: Move 1 (*Summarizing the study*); Move 2 (*Evaluating the study*) realized by three steps (*Indicating significance/advantage*, *Indicating limitations*, and *Evaluating methodology*); and Move 3 (*Deductions from the research*) realized by two steps (*Recommending further research*, and *Drawing pedagogic implication*). In particular, Move 1, the authors state, does not have any step to account for further realizations of the move. In Bunton's (2005) analytical model, doctoral theses consists of five Moves – namely, *Introductory restatement*, *Consolidation of research space*, *Practical implications and recommendations*, *Future research* and *Concluding restatement*. In both analytical frameworks, these authors identify a linear and cyclical rhetorical structure of the various functional moves-steps realized in Research Article and

[10] As outlined earlier in this Chapter (Theoretical Background), the Conclusion section has been considered by researchers (e.g. Hopkins and Dudley-Evans 1988; Holmes 1997; Peacock 2002) as part of the RA Discussion section within the IMRD framework. In their genre-based analysis of twenty research articles in applied linguistics, therefore, Yang and Allison (2003) focus on the Conclusion as a separate section characterizing thirteen such articles, where three moves and five steps are found. In EAP studies too, the Conclusion section has formed part of several attempts at describing specific aspects of PhD theses as a genre. In addition to the doctoral thesis Conclusion by Bunton (2005), however, other descriptions have been given of the rhetorical moves characterizing the Introduction (Bunton 2002), the Literature Review (Kwan 2006), and the organizational structure of PhD theses (Thompson 1999; Paltridge 2002). Paltridge (2002), for instance, presents an interesting analysis of fifteen doctoral theses across the disciplines. He identifies four generic thesis structures: *Traditional Simple (IMRAD: Introduction, Method, Results and Discussion)*, *Traditional Complex*, *Topic Based* and *Compilation Based*.

PhD theses Conclusions, where moves and steps are also the result of discipline-specific expectations.

While, as generally agreed in the literature, discipline specificity plays a major role in the use and construction of genres, it comes as no surprise that the linear rhetorical structure classified by the authors was not entirely revealed in the rhetorical structure realizations of Conclusions under scrutiny. A modified version of the authors' descriptive models was therefore necessary in order to categorize case note Conclusions around their typical role of *Summarizing the study*, in Yang and Allison's nomenclature. However, unlike the authors' classification of such Move accounting for no other step, the role of summarizing case notes was fleshed out in a variety of sub-move or step-outlining strategies, realized by *Indicating significance/advantage* and *Indicating limitations* (in Yang and Allison's nomenclature), and *Restating research questions, Question-raising* and *Practical implications and recommendations* (in Bunton's nomenclature). As is clear, these nomenclatures were only borrowed from the two analytical models well outside the authors' linear descriptions, and served as the starting points for the identification of functional sub-moves or steps realized in the general content and role achieved by the *Summarizing the Study* Move. However, four new sub-moves/steps were introduced whenever the case note text fulfilled different functions from those classified by the authors. These are:

(1) Indicating complexity/difficulty: *Moreover, <u>as causal questions become legally more complex</u>, it is plain that risk becomes the key element in the equation ...* MLR

(2) Indicating hypothetical scenario: *<u>And if the parties to the contract as experienced businesses do agree to exclude those in a way that is reasonable</u>, it seems inappropriate for the courts effectively to override their agreement by the grant of injunctive relief.* MLR

(3) Indicating lack of consensus: *Whether section 31(2) is the best way of expressing the threshold <u>is open to debate</u>.* ECLR

(4) Claiming by quote (mainly in superscript numbers): *For instance, it has been frequently argued that not only citizens of member states should be equipped with Union citizenship, but also third-country nationals who have established themselves in the EU.*[16] ECLR

As a result of these assumptions, the structure and content of the Conclusions, as proposed in the model outlined in Table 5, was organized into an array of sub-moves or steps which typified the overall content and role of the *Summarizing the Study* Move, and similarly gave effectiveness to wrapping up the most 'remarkable' aspects in the case:

ECLR		
Move Function	**Sub-move/step**	TOTAL
Summarizing the study and Reinforcing 'remarkable' aspects in the case	1. Indicating significance/advantage	24
	2. Restating research questions	15
	3. Indicating limitations	13
	4. Question-raising	5
	5. Indicating practical implications	21
	6. Indicating recommendations	12
	7. Indicating complexity/difficulty	7
	8. Indicating hypothetical scenario	10
	9. Indicating lack of consensus	6
	10. Claiming by quote	13
MLR		
Move Function	**Sub-move/step**	TOTAL
Summarizing the study and Reinforcing 'remarkable' aspects in the case	1. Indicating significance/advantage	36
	2. Restating research questions	29
	3. Indicating limitations	20
	4. Question-raising	9
	5. Indicating practical implications	24
	6. Indicating recommendations	10
	7. Indicating complexity/difficulty	6
	8. Indicating hypothetical scenario	12
	9. Indicating lack of consensus	5
	10. Claiming by quote	15

Table 5. Sub-moves/steps in the rhetorical structure and content of Conclusion sections in the corpus journals: occurrences.

Unlike its content, this generic model is only indicative of the organizational structure, since there was considerable variation in the sequential order of sub-moves/steps in the texts examined. As a matter of fact, writers had ample room for manoeuvre when organizing the sub-move rhetorical patterns, as they had indeed when choosing which sub-move to use in the relative organization. Such choice can, in fact, be seen in the structural results in the Table above, which reveals the different frequencies at which sub-moves made their appearances in the texts, where certain patterns (such as, *Indicating significance*, *limitations*, *implications*, *Restating research questions* and *Quoting*) also occurred in cycles. Despite the varying incidence in the chosen patterns, Table 5 shows that preference was given to summarizing around the *significance/advantage* of the work, as the most occurring (obligatory) rhetorical statement. This was not surprising since, as noted, the principle of writing in the genre was to bring the reader's attention around to some *significant* issue in the case. Apart from this, the distinct sub-moves/steps by which Conclusions were organized in their generic content and structure usually applied to one or two sentences, whether or not in embedded syntax, and this resulted in the length of Conclusions being usually kept short to half a page.

Viewed in its communicative context and purpose, therefore, the structural model description proposed above reveals the rhetorical rationale of *concluding* in the genre, where the writers' task was to summarize their ideas or arguments in the researched case, and to reinforce the most notable (case) aspects they argued for in the Discussion section through different sub-move/step-outlining strategies. And while this type of ending echoed ideas/topics presented in the Introduction section by giving the Conclusion symmetry, it also enabled the writers to come full circle in what they epistemologically achieved ('outcomes') in the research study through Discussion, as I noted before.

To illustrate this rationale, the writer in the full sample below (23) both summarized his work and strengthened the noticeable aspects in the case, and the use of various sub-move indicating strategies (**bold**) and the typical language features (underlined) contained in sub-moves contributed to making a final impression on the researched cases:

(23)

CONCLUSION

[**Indicating significance/advantage**] The cases of *Webster* and *Martin* provide an good illustration of where two questionable doctrines of criminal liability collide: constructive liability and complicity. The fact that the Court of Appeal wished to interpret the rules on complicity in such a way as to be generous to the secondary party indicates that there was an awareness that [**Indicating practical implications from Court's reasoning**] application of the law could result in over-criminalisation. [**Restating research questions**] It has been suggested that one way to justify joint enterprise inculpation could be the application of the 'change of normative position' rationale.[41] When D chooses to provide assistance or encouragement to P in a criminal activity, D crosses a moral threshold and can be held liable for the consequences. The same rationale can also be given to justify the conviction of a driver for causing the death of another. Whatever one's position on the validity of the 'change of normative position' theory and the 'pure luck' versus 'moral' luck argument,[42] [**Expressing difficulty**] it is rather more difficult to defend what becomes a double 'change of normative position' by allowing D to be convicted of

> an offence committed by P of causing death by dangerous driving. [**Indicating recommendations**] Arguably, the secondary party in such cases should be liable for dangerous driving, but his liability should stop there. MLR 2011, 74(5): 776

Among these strategies, the writer recapitulated the paper's main points without over-claiming (*Restating research questions*) and, in an attempt to show the reader how the paper's points fitted together, the writer included a provocative insight into his claims by using quotation (superscript number) from research he had conducted in the Discussion. Here, the inclusion of a brief summary of the points or themes in the middle of the Conclusion was just as important as the use of key concepts argued for in the Discussion and derived from judicial language. However, the writer did not hesitate to propose a course of action in the matter controlling the significant issue in the case (*dangerous driving*), that is, by *Indicating recommendations* for law. Suggestion for recommendation came from the use of the modal verb *should* (strong advice/necessity), which in turn allowed the statement to convey a practical solution to the researched issue. Of course, the activity of *concluding* around some practical recommendation, as solution to the case issue, was linked to the activity of legal argument and reasoning in the genre (i.e. Discussion section)[11] as problem-solving, on account of the *social action* of the genre (Miller 1984; Bhatia 2004; Devitt 2004) where writers acted as social agents within the contextual bounds of social values or public interest, as I argued in Chapter 1.[12] Given this (social) generic approach to the law field, the structure and content of case note Conclusions showed an image of *field-oriented* Conclusions in Bunton's (2005) study, where field-oriented Conclusions are often written in a *problem/solution/evaluation* type pattern.[13] Beyond this similarity, however, it is not ruled out that recommending in the above sample may have redirected the reader's thought process and helped him

---

[11] Again, see Chapter 3.

[12] Where the "social action" of the case note genre is inherent in the approach to Critical Genre Analysis (Bhatia 2004), the latter indeed shares the view of Fairclough (2003) that the analysis of language can occur as a social act - as a way to participate in the discussion and solution of social problems.

[13] Bunton (2005) distinguishes between two types of Conclusions: a thesis-oriented Conclusion is one which "focuse[s] mainly on the thesis itself; beginning with a restatement of purpose and summary findings and claims" (2005: 214-215) while a field-oriented Conclusion "focuse[s] mainly on the field and only mention[s] the thesis and its findings or contributions in the context of the whole field" (2005: 215).

or her to apply new ideas to his or her disciplinary expectations by seeing broader implications for current law.

With implications being under focus here, the writer in the sample above (23) gives an illustration of this in the textual realizations (*Indicating practical implications*), where the *that*-complementation in modalized form (*application of the law could result in over-criminalisation*) expresses the impact or effect on *over-criminalization*, as derived interpretively from the court's reasoning and decision. Unlike this modalized form and verb use in the above structure, however, other writers went for the expression of 'practical implication' statements in nominal forms, as the writer in (24) below did in the opening line (underlined) and further reiterated in the middle of his Conclusion, despite conceding the 'significance/advantage' of the evaluated material (*even though the judgment can be considered as judicial activism*):

(24) It can be concluded that *Rottmann* has potentially huge consequences and urgently requires amendments to be made with regard to several national rules governing the loss and the acquisition of nationality in order to prevent long court proceedings and preliminary ruling questions. Overall, even though the judgment can be considered as *judicial activism,* with possible far-reaching consequences with regard to the relationship between Union citizenship and member state nationality as well as for national nationality rules, … . ECLR

Still, in other instances, 'practical implications' became nominally more explicit, and involved either the current state of law evaluated in a tentatively positive way (25), or predicted the future state of law (26):

(25) Nonetheless, the establishment of the non-discrimination axiom and the very implications of the possibilities to rely on citizenship rights in the third pillar *have arguably a significantly symbolic message.* MLR

(26) Nevertheless, the implications of this judgment create a legitimate expectation that the anti-discrimination mechanism *will develop into* an independent legal instrument rather than a 'safety net' for cases that could not be applied to Article 14 of the Convention in conjunction with one of the Convention rights. ECLR

Clearly, in all such instances where implications were generalizable from the Discussion section, implying certain effects or consequences depended upon the writers observing the epistemological side of the chosen case.

With all *concluding* strategies considered, therefore, the Conclusion allowed the writers to have the final say on the case issues they had raised in the paper, to summarize their arguments, to demonstrate the notable aspects of the topics, and to incite their readers to a new view of the field in disciplinary knowledge-making inquiries.

Conclusion

In this detailed exploratory corpus study, I attempted to describe and interpret the rhetorical functions performed by the distinct sections of academic case notes, viewed in terms of their macro-organizational stages (or rhetorical structures) and the constraints on typical move structure and sequences realized in the most conventional, standard sections (Abstract, Introduction, Conclusion).

Corpus analysis reveals that case notes were based on an hourglass structure. They started with the Title (indicating content and attracting the reader's attention) and lay out the various parts/stages through Abstract (reflecting the main 'story' of the case note paper), Introduction (introducing the topic, and indicating the paper's focus and research objectives), Discussion (answering research questions/objectives in a continuous flow of Legal Background and Author's Argument), and Conclusion (wrapping up the paper's main points in notable aspects). This conventional structure allowed case notes to be read selectively for particular sections.

Where Introduction is concerned, corpus analysis reveals that genre writers thought of their Introductions as an inverted pyramid, where they began with a broad overview and then moved to the essential research problem down to the final (outline) elements of their research. This inverted triangle therefore suggests that *introducing* work in case note writing was not so different, in rhetorical function, from *introducing* the typical Research Article for publication across the disciplines, where the motivational and justificatory communicative purposes are present (Swales 1990). Although the similarities in *introducing* work between the two genres may be seen as part of the structurally wider "colonizing process" (Bhatia 2004) or hybridization investing the whole case note genre, as I argued in Chapter 1, the major difference of *introducing* between the two genres lay in the case note avoiding the Methods and Results rhetorical components typical of RAs, and revolving around some 'significant' aspect of the case under focus as substitutes for such rhetorical components. While the emphasis on the 'significant' aspects of the case provided the basis for the writer's critical argument in the Discussion and later reiterated in the Conclusion, setting the 'big context' for the research around the case Decision assigned specificity to Abstract and Introduction sections. Unlike other common labels used in academic writing, Abstracts and Introductions became less conventionalized and standardized in content and function, on account of the disciplinary expectations shaped in the communal conventions of the genre. As such, the focus on 'big context' became part of the writers' choice for move patterns and functions in the Abstracts and Introductions, where a certain degree of homogeneity in move strategies was revealed among corpus writers, except for those realizing move strategies in Conclusions.

In particular, functional and rhetorical distinctiveness emerged from the analysis of the Discussion section, which differed overtly from the conventionalized and standardized Discussion section of experimental RAs, on account of genre-specific conventions governing objective (Legal Background) and subjective modes of argument (Author's Argument) in a 'boundless' rhetorical concept. The specific rhetorical function of the Discussion revealed the need for genre writers to make their critical analysis clear, by balancing objective statements with statements that rested on such objectivity to form their own (subjective) argument. And while balancing between objective and subjective statements was necessary for the disciplinary reader to understand the significance of the topic(s) in the case, the rhetorical idiosyncracy of the complex, yet intriguing, Discussion texts revealed the culturally and socially situated practices of genre writers committed to a systematic pursuit of knowledge-making inquiries for such reader.

CHAPTER THREE

METADISCOURSE IN THE CASE NOTE *DISCUSSION* SECTION

In the previous Chapter I focused on the rhetorical contexts and functions of case note sections, responding to perceived schematic structures or stages in the global organization of the genre. The important feature emerging from the user-friendly schematic structure was that the various sections allowed for legal research to be organized incrementally and progressively, and as a consequence provided the source of useful information about the ways texts are constructed and the rhetorical contexts in which they are used. Analysis of the rhetorical sections therefore proved an invaluable way of looking at the texts as the writers' response to the social context and practice of the genre.

In this Chapter, which concludes my research 'excavation' into the case note genre, I shall continue with the exploration of discursive and social practices shaped in case note texts. To do so, I will focus my attention on the use of interpersonal metadiscourse rhetorical strategies employed in the *Discussion* section of case notes. This section is a good example of academic legal writing as a social and communicative engagement between writer and reader, and provides the generic and discoursal construction of disciplinary practices based on evaluating, persuading and negotiating appropriate participant relationships. First, however, it is useful to outline briefly the theoretical context of my research study.

Theoretical background

An important feature of many recent studies across the disciplines has been the growing interest in the interpersonal dimensions of academic discourse. Attempts have been made to emphasize the dialogical framework of academic writing (e.g. Hyland 2005a/b; Thompson 2001), by acknowledging the *stance* and *engagement* framework, which has been described in terms of *stance* (Biber and Finegan 1989; Biber 2006)[1], *evaluation* (Hunston 1993, 1994; Thompson and Hunston 2000), *appraisal* - identified as *graduation of attitudes* and *engagement* (Martin 2000; Martin and Rose 2003; Martin and White 2005), and *metadiscourse* (Hyland and Tse 2004a, Hyland 2005a/b).[2] Although these conceptual frameworks emphasize overlapping areas such as emotion, modality, politeness, value, and so on, they have significant implications for the interpersonal nature of academic discourse, which involves interaction between the writer's authorial persona and the reader, and relates to the social constructionist theories behind expressions of interpersonal meaning.

In this context, extensive research has been conducted into the use of interpersonal rhetorical strategies employed in a variety of academic genres (including academic articles), such as engagement markers (e.g. Hyland 2001b, 2002a/b; Giltrow 2005), evaluative markers (e.g. Swales and Burke 2003), writer presence (e.g. Vassileva 1998; Kuo 1999; Hyland 2001a; Harwood 2005a/b), hedging (e.g. Salager-Meyer 1994; Crompton 1997; Hyland 1998), and mitigation in teacher written feedback (Hyland and Hyland 2001), to mention only a few.

The need to interpersonally negotiate participant relationships in academic discourse is one which also brings into focus the social dependence of genre practices upon variation in the communicative contexts and purposes achieved in a variety of academic genres. While, methodologically, generic variation accounts for a number of *metaphors* (Swales 2004) or *colony* (Bhatia 2004) as implied in the nature of genre, it is also a question of the dynamic configuration of genres in today's complex organizational activity of the academia and the professions. In this framework, interpersonal generic resources come to the fore to reflect the academic purposes of writers in their own contexts and purposes, and provide the input to understand the different ideas the writers represent to their audiences and the different interactions they create with their readers.

---

[1] In the earlier (1989) work, for instance, Biber and Finegan describe the *stance* framework as the lexical expression of attitudes, feelings and judgments with regard to the propositional content of the message.

[2] Hyland's (2005a) framework of metadiscourse moves away from previous classifications of metadiscourse, which generally organise the linguistic units under the functional headings of textual and interpersonal metadiscourse (e.g. Vande Kopple 1985; Crismore 1989; Crismore et al., 1993; Mauranen 1993; Hyland 1998), towards a model of metadiscourse which "offers a way of understanding the interpersonal resources writers use to organize texts coherently and to convey their personality, credibility, reader sensitivity and relationship to the message" (2005a: 59).

With interpersonality features of academic texts in mind, I document and analyze the use of metadiscourse rhetorical patterns which help academic writers in the Discussion section of the case note genre to construct appropriate writer-reader relationships, while connecting discourse features with disciplinary practices in academic legal writing. As such, this study seeks to contribute to the present body of research into metadiscourse studies applied to the law discipline.

Material and Method

The Corpus

As part of the larger case note corpus presented in Chapters 1 and 2, the analytical data included here were based on a set of 20 texts published in the 2009-2011 issues of MLR journal and 10 texts published in the same year issues of the ECLR journal, totalling a set of 30 case note Discussion sections. Figure 2 in Chapter 1 has shown the average word number in the Discussion (ECLR: 4650.2 / MLR: 4998.9) being far higher than other sections.

Methodology

The Discussion rhetorical section was chosen from among other sections because it was the lengthier but also intricate section, consisting of interwoven parts (Legal Background + Author's Argument), where objective and subjective analyses-discussions were revealed, respectively.[3] Allied with such intricacy was the suggestion that Discussion was the section where the writers' research mostly paid off, since writers took the existing rules, explained them, and applied them to the material facts as they were argued in the case by telling the readers which side they were on. This way then, Discussion writers engaged with the concept of Argument

[3] Obviously, other sections (Abstracts, Introductions and Conclusions) may also have formed the subject of the (metadiscourse) analysis here since, as Hyland (2005b: 190) argues in his Conclusion on stance and engagement in research articles, "[e]ven the most rhetorically innocent sections reveal writers' efforts to persuade their audience to their claim". However, the quantitative data (unreported here) obtained from these sections only revealed the paucity of metadiscourse resources employed there. This, as a consequence, allowed me to confine the analytical accounts of these sections to the rhetorical/linguistic descriptions presented in Chapter 2.

as a process, which involved aspects of persuasion and reasoning of where the weight lay in the factual and legal data available in the case.

In the rhetorically subjective part of Author's Argument, therefore, Discussion was micro-anchored in the dialogical framework of academic writing, involving interaction between the writer's authorial persona and the reader. Here, Hyland's (2005a) metadiscourse analytical model was chosen from among the various theoretical frameworks of interpersonal meaning I outlined in Theoretical Background before. Specifically, my research questions were twofold:

1. To what extent Hyland's metadiscourse framework is applicable to the Discussion section of the legal case note genre?
2. How do Discussion writers convey their personality, credibility, and evaluation of research material, and interact with their readers?

In the absence of comparable (metadiscourse) studies into case notes, answers to these questions will be provided outside statistical analyses applied to the frequency counts. The reason for this being the purpose of the corpus study, which was to provide a descriptively linguistic account of this neglected genre and, in particular, to establish broad distributional patterns of metadiscourse in the Discussion section.

The choice for the metadiscourse analytical procedure in this study brings me to outline first the conceptualization of metadiscourse. Hyland (2005a: 37) defines metadiscourse as ''the cover term for the self-reflective expressions used to negotiate interactional meanings in a text, assist the writer (or speaker) to express a viewpoint and engage with readers as members of a particular community". The key feature of this functional model is explicitness, since it is "related to the author's awareness of both self and audience" (Hyland 2005a: 58) and designed to create a particular discoursal effect. Hence, the three key principles are that metadiscourse "is distinct from propositional aspects of discourse", "refers to aspects of the text that embody writer-reader interactions", and "refers only to relations which are internal to the discourse" (Hyland 2005a: 38). Hyland justifies the interaction function of his model along the *interactive* and *interactional* dimensions, by providing a classification of the functional resources that are necessary to enact these dimensions in text.[4]

[4] However, the author is careful to acknowledge the limits of his model description in that the "imposition of discrete categories on the fluidity of actual language use inevitably conceals its multifunctionality, blurring simultaneous meanings in an

In keeping to the principle that metadiscourse categories are intrinsically interpersonal and ultimately aim to persuade the reader (with propositional aspects that serve to guide to the world beyond text), I therefore looked at the *interactive* and *interactional* resources employed by Discussion writers in the corpus journals. Specifically here, *interactive* resources "organize propositional information in ways that a projected target audience is likely to find coherent and convincing" (Hyland 2005a: 50), while *interactional* resources "involve readers and open opportunities for them to contribute to the discourse by alerting them to the author's perspective towards both propositional information and readers themselves" (Hyland 2005a: 52).

The search inventory of such resources included metadiscourse items listed by Hyland (2005a), who provides a comprehensive taxonomy for the current analysis. These resources were computer screened and manually analyzed to ensure that the items performed a metadiscoursal role. Manual analysis was the most appropriate procedure to follow on account of the propensity for natural language use to have different functions in text. Such was, for instance, *and/or* conjunctions used in legally established binomial phrases (e.g. *a person committing <u>or</u> preparing an act of terrorism*), or those used in the citation of cases (e.g. *Powell <u>and</u> English*) or parliamentary acts (e.g. *Accessories <u>and</u> Abettors Act 1861*). Correspondingly, these items were not counted as metadiscourse tokens in the Discussion texts. Given the typicality of academic legal writing in the genre prompt, however, additional insights were provided into *if*-conditionals and the citation system based on "superscript numbers", the latter replacing "integral citations" (Swales 1990) in the main text of corpus Discussions. The greater analytical focus on such resources was dictated by the specificity of the disciplinary genre, and as a consequence were seen as integrative frameworks for the metadiscourse analysis here.

Results and Discussion

In Chapter 2, covering the analysis of the Discussion section, we noted that writers drew from the scenery behind the main case (Legal Background) to provide a critical evaluation of the significant issue(s) in such a case (Author's Argument). Here, therefore, writing descriptively and critically meant expressing a variety of rhetorical functions in the text,

---

'all-or-nothing' interpretation of how particular devices are used" (Hyland 2005a: 59). He therefore concludes: "I hope the model described here overcomes many of these limitations and offers a comprehensive and pragmatically grounded means of investigating the interpersonal resources in texts" (Hyland 2005a: 59).

such as expressing cause-effect relationships, comparing and contrasting ideas, indicating the strength of claims, supporting claims by cited sources in order to determine one's views, and so on. These and other (interpersonal) functions provided the linguistic material for a distributional account of interactive and interactional metadiscourse uses in the academic writing of the texts. In Hyland's (2005a: 49) taxonomy, then, interactive resources "help to guide the reader through the text" while interactional resources "involve the reader in the text".

Table 1 reports the total frequency counts of interactive and interactional metadiscourse categories and the total tokens in the comparable corpora of the Discussion section:

Metadiscourse category	***Interactive*** ***N° & %***	***Interactional*** ***N° & %***
ECLR Discussion (Total Tokens: 4650.2)	2010 – 57.7%	1472 – 42.3%
MLR Discussion (Total Tokens: 4998.9)	4117 – 48.6%	4352 – 51.4%
TOTAL	6127 – 51.3%	5824 – 48.7%

Table 1. Total frequency of interactive and interactional metadiscourse categories and total tokens in the comparable corpora.

Viewed collectively in both journals, quantitative results show that writers were slightly more interactive (51.3%) than interactional (48.7%) in the comparable corpora, thus revealing a tendency for the guidance of readers through the text rather than their involvement in the text. Viewed, individually, however, non-native (European) writers in ECLR tended to favour more interactive (57.7%) than interactional resources (42.3%), while native (English) writers in MLR tended towards the opposite by favouring interactional resources (51.4%), although in frequency terms the difference was not so marked among MLR writers. In terms of frequencies, therefore, the interpersonal orientation of the metadiscourse categories allowed ECLR Discussion writers to assign a purely textual role for metadiscourse, as compared to MLR Discussion writers, who assigned a purely evaluative and engaging role for metadiscourse where epistemic judgements controlled the writer-reader disciplinary interaction in the text.

Qualitative findings of the various metadiscourse devices used in each category and their total frequency counts can best be appreciated in Table 2 below:

ECLR					
Interactive	***N°***	*%*	***Interactional***	***N°***	*%*
Transition markers	1389	39.9	Hedges	589	16.9
Frame markers	51	1.4	Boosters	352	10.1
Endophoric markers	12	0.3	Attitude markers	314	9.1
Evidentials	430	12.4	Self mentions (*exclusive*)	31	0.9
Code glosses	128	3.7	Engagement markers	186	5.3
TOTAL	2010	57.7	TOTAL	1472	42.3
MLR					
Interactive	***N°***	*%*	***Interactional***	***N°***	*%*
Transition markers	2866	33.8	Hedges	2127	25.1
Frame markers	155	1.8	Boosters	1055	12.5
Endophoric markers	68	0.9	Attitude markers	616	7.3
Evidentials	597	7.1	Self mentions (*exclusive*)	55	0.6
Code glosses	431	5	Engagement markers	499	5.9
TOTAL	4117	48.6	TOTAL	4352	51.4

Table 2. Number of metadiscourse items (interactive and interactional) in ECLR and MLR Discussions.

On the one hand, the broad distributional patterns of metadiscourse resources in the Table indicate that transition markers, evidentials and code glosses were the most frequent interactive devices among ECLR and MLR Discussion writers alike. On the other hand, interactional metadiscourse was best reflected through the use of hedges, boosters, attitude markers and engagement markers among the same group of writers. Choices of interactive and interactional metadiscourse devices thus allowed legal writers to guide readers through the argumentative nature of the Discussion, and to call on the shared understandings of the academic legal community by assigning the reader the role of informed participant in the development of discourse.

In what follows is the analysis and discussion of metadiscourse linguistic realizations in both categories.

Transition markers

Computer readable data show that transition markers were the most frequent interactive resources among writers in both corpora (ECLR: 1389 / MLR: 2866), where transitions run the gamut from a total of 35 forms surveyed in the corpora. Of these forms, Table 3 illustrates the five-top linguistic realizations.

Transition markers: forms			
ECLR		MLR	
	N°		*N°*
And	586	And	995
Or	166	But	330
But	105	Or	328
However	82	However	136
Therefore	51	Also	128

Table 3. Five-top transition forms: occurrences.

The use of the standard co-ordinating conjunctions (or *conjunctives*)[5], especially *and*, *but*, *or*, came naturally for writers who presented:

- a non-contrasting idea (*and*):

(1) The Court has been accused of inventing a general principle of EU law against age discrimination <u>and</u> also accused of lawmaking from the bench … . MLR

- a contrast by setting up explicit opposition (*but*)[6]:

(2) … the German court engages with the political organs of the EU, <u>but</u> not with its courts… . ECLR

- a contrast by 'strengthening' that one thing was not true but a different thing was true with more reason, logic or other justification in the '*not…but rather*' structure:

(3) Mr Cobbe's expectation <u>was not</u> that he would be entitled to a certain interest in land, <u>but rather</u> that the parties' would negotiate a contract.[11] MLR

- a choice or possibility (*or*):

---

[5] The term *conjunctives* is derived from Halliday and Hasan's (1976) category of connectives, which have additive, causal, adversative and temporal relations.
[6] All the accounts of the standard ('contrast') meaning of *but* clause, as in the current example, did not include discourse-initial *But*.

(4) One cannot underscore member states' autonomy to organize their own nationality law and at the same time grant Union law influence <u>or</u> something like indirect influence on this reserved domain.[16] ECLR

- a choice or possibility in indirect questions with *whether* by introducing alternative possibilities:

(5) It makes a difference, according to the Court, whether someone was already an Union citizen, such as Rottmann, <u>or</u> whether on the other hand someone like Ms. Kaur could not be deprived of her Union citizenship … . ECLR

Particularly in example (5), where the conjunction *whether* is used (instead of *if*) to introduce alternative possibilities (neither of which is a condition), disciplinary writers revealed genre-specific forms of argumentation constructed around reasoning in the alternative, and therefore gave a vivid picture of their own discourse practices.

In the use of the top-occurring additive conjunction (*and*), in particular, various possible functions were conveyed (<u>result</u>, <u>'pure' addition</u>, <u>comment</u>) through pragmatic connections between ideas and issues, as illustrated in the following set of examples in (6):

(6) In the *English* appeal (which considered the 'fundamental difference' rule) the House of Lords held that D was not guilty of murder <u>and</u> allowed the appeal. MLR

[<u>result</u>: 2nd clause (decision as to law procedure) results from the 1st clause (decision as to substantive law)]

English courts apply the *lex fori* to matrimonial cases, <u>and</u> so it is necessary to determine what impact the pre-nuptial agreement would have in English law … MLR

[<u>result</u>: 2nd clause results from the 1st clause]

In *Fairchild*,[17] the House of Lords modified <u>and</u> significantly relaxed the legal rules relating to causation … MLR

[<u>'pure' addition</u>]

<u>And</u> that brings us to the appeal to the instant case <u>and</u> the decision of the Supreme Court. MLR

[<u>initial *And*</u> as a useful device to the writer as <u>the argument continued</u>]

[2nd clause <u>adds</u> to the 1st clause]

> This naturally confused the courts as they could not see how to combine this probability with the other evidence in the case – and indeed there is no proper way of doing so. MLR
> [comment: 2nd clause (as a code gloss) comments on or explains the 1st clause]

Clearly, in these and other instances, writers considered the available material in previous texts and discourses with a view to raising relevant issues for legal argument construction. Consequently, establishing which types of links in Discussion also revealed the writers' understanding of the nature and significance of the case issue(s), and similarly their comprehension of the problem-solving task in hand.

As Table 3 shows, however, other items were used to link information in different ways. Such were the conjunctive adverb *however* ('by contrast/on the other hand', 'to whatever means or degree', 'nevertheless/yet'), additive *also*, and *therefore* ('consequence/as a result' marking an inference on the speaker's part as 'thus'), as in:

(7) In all other cases, the expert could say simply that one cannot exclude the possibility that the two marks were made by the same shoe. This, however, does not convey any evidential value. MLR
['by contrast' – contrastive connective]

> The EAW permits exceptions for statutory limitation only if the Member States have made such a declaration in accordance with Article 4(7) EAW. However, there is no reason why a state's own nationals should be treated more favourably than non-nationals in this regard either. MLR
> ['nevertheless/yet' – concessive connective]

> The PTA 2005 specifically provides that the Special Advocate is 'not to be responsible to the person whose interests he is appointed to represent'.[19] Therefore, the normal lawyer-client relationship does not obtain. MLR
> ['consequence/as a result']

> The father had also claimed the infringement of his Article 3 right to protection against 'inhuman and degrading treatment', though this claim was swiftly dispatched … . MLR
> ['adding more information to what was already there']

Among the varied examples above, expressing different meanings, the conjunctive adverb *however* was mostly associated with 'contrast' rather than 'concession'[7] and, as a contrastive (or adversative) connective, it was the preferred form to express interpersonally the writer's negative judgement of the material in the opposing statement. Clearly, contrasting statements with the conjunct *however* added to other such statements marked with the (contrastive) connective *but* [8], or other parallel forms, such as *by contrast/on the other hand/rather*, whether in 1st or 2nd clause position.

In addition to the five-top occurring connectives reported in Table 3, transitioning smoothly between issues to assure logical flow was also apparent in the use of common subordinating conjuncts occurring at different frequencies – namely: *because* (ECLR: 49 / MLR: 80), *since* (ECLR: 32 / MLR: 58), *even if* (ECLR: 10 / MLR: 52), *although* (ECLR: 13 / MLR: 60), *though* (ECLR: 5 / MLR: 39), *even though* (ECLR: 18 / MLR: 19), and *while* (ECLR: 23 / MLR: 58). These 'subordinators' introduced either reason clauses (*because*, *since*):

(8) She invoked Article 10 of the Directive of 27 November 2000 because she wanted a reversal of the burden of proof to be applied … ECLR

[2nd clause defines a logical reason for the action in the 1st clause by explaining it]

or concessive clauses (*even if, although*, *though, even though, while*):

(9) In terms of political accountability, it seems worrying that although section 3 interpretations may result in a 'rewriting' of the relevant statutory provision, the Government can still claim such decisions as human rights victories. MLR

[conceding the action in the main clause which is unexpected under the circumstances]

The referring court considered that paragraph 622 of the BGB contains a difference of treatment directly linked to age, and, while it is not convinced that it is unconstitutional, it regards its compatibility with European Union law as doubtful. ECLR

[conceding the action]

---

[7] In reverse, Szczyrbak (2009) analyses concession in judicial discourse (European Court of Justice judgments) and reveals that *however* (and *although*) are the most frequent markers of concession.

[8] As noted, the connective *but* occurred only as a signal of 'contrast' in the current data. This contrasts with research by Barth-Weingarten (2003) who finds that *but* is the most frequent 'concessive' marker in spoken interaction. In my data, it was extremely difficult to interpret the use of this conjunction as 'concessive', because intuitively writers did not present any information to concede on.

These *dicta* suggest that even if the UK Supreme Court thinks that a Strasbourg decision is wrong, it may have no option but to submit to it.
[concessive conditional] MLR

The methodical reading of the texts in (9) and elsewhere in Discussion shows that these subordinators were the primary exponents of 'concession'[9], and made their appearance in initial, medial, or final position clause, serving 'to concede' a certain part of an argument before proceeding to question the validity of the point under discussion. The example above in (9), using the *although* clause, shows in particular that conceding involved an element of 'surprise' or 'unexpectedness' in the relations holding between clauses (Quirk et al 1972, 1985; Hultman 2003: 190)[10], in ways that that concessive *although* also possibly involved an element of 'incongruity' in the information presented, as in:

(10) Thus, there may be scope for future election court findings to be challenged on that basis, although it is not alien to English law for factual findings to be immune from review. MLR
[conceding the action in the main clause which is incongruous under the circumstances]

From the perspective of interpersonal metadiscourse, concessive uses of conjuncts went beyond text relation[11] "by demonstrating a sensitivity to

---

[9] Various terminological classifications have been given to such conjunctions as *although* or *even though/even if*. Reference is made to *although* as a "subordinating conjunction" (Quirk and Greenbaum 1973), or as a "concessive connective" (Kőnig 1988), implying that the references are not mutually exclusive despite the fact that their meanings change in such classifications. In particular, Kőnig (1986: 234) notes three typical forms of conditionals: *Conditionals* (if p, (then) q), *Concessive (irrelevance) conditionals* (Even if p, q), and *Concessives* (even though / although p, q.). Besides the treatment of concessive conjuncts in Quirk et al.'s (1972: 674) classification, or as markers of the concessive clause group in Svartvik and Sager's (1996: 340) classification, other discourse coherence relations have been advanced around 'concession' (e.g. Halliday and Hasan 1976; Mann and Thompson 1992; Grote et al. 1997; Crevels 2000; Barth-Weingarten 2003). These varied taxonomies show that 'concession' or 'concessivity' is not a straightforward definition.

[10] According to Quirk et al. (1972: 674), "[c]oncessive conjuncts signal the unexpected, surprising nature of what is being said in view of what was said before that".

[11] However, from the perspective of Rhetorical Structure Theory, where Concession is a discourse phenomenon, all instances of concessive uses identified text relation, by connecting clauses as well as larger units in discourse when the "speaker

audience understandings and explicitly attempting to engage with these" (Hyland 2005a: 42). In this context, therefore, concessive conjuncts contributed to a positioning of the writers on the relevant arguments (facts and rules) controlling the issues in the case, and were important interpersonal rhetorical strategies in the legal argument construction of Discussion. Here, in fact, writers frequently confronted and assessed the merits of different arguments recovered from Legal Background, which had to be understood and accepted by the widest readership. The effect of this dynamic act of arguing can therefore be described as a careful journey through various propositions made in the case, each of them however building up its own argument with the writer's reasons.

Beyond pure exponents of concession, the connective subordinating item *then* was also recorded in the corpora (ECLR: 21 / MLR: 88), where it was used in different structures and functions, such as expressing temporal sequence (ECLR: 6 / MLR: 32), adding by contrasting with a preceding argument in (*but*) *then* adverbial structure (ECLR: 4 / MLR: 15), and expressing logical condition in (*if*) *then* structure (ECLR: 9 / MLR: 16), among others. These structures and functions created complex relationships between ideas, as shown in the following set of examples:

(11) The company obtained payments under letters of credit by presenting to banks false documents in relation to fictitious commodity trading; it then paid the money out to other participants in the fraud.[2] MLR
['subsequently/soon afterward': event/temporal sequence]

This necessarily implies that revocation of nationality due to fraud in the naturalisation procedure can be in conformity with Union law, even if that brings loss of Union citizenship with it; but then a second proportionality test must be applied regarding this loss of the fundamental status of Union citizen. ECLR
[contrastive: 'from another viewpoint']

After all, if the court thinks that the material is necessary to enable the controlled person to answer the case against them, then the decision will be flawed and the order may have to be quashed.[29] MLR
[logical condition expressed by the (if p, then q) argumentative frame]

---

acknowledges the apparently contrary information but then advances the nucleus anyway" (Mann and Thompson 1992: 39). In Rhetorical Structure Theory, in fact, texts are assumed to consist of (at least) two spans, linked by a particular discourse relation. In Mann and Thompson's (1992: 36-37) distinction, there are two types of spans: the *nucleus* (more essential to the speaker's purpose and more independent than the other), and the *satellite*, as the dependent type of span.

Following Hyland's (2005a: 45-48) distinction between "internal and external' reference" conveyed by connective items, it is clear that the external relation of temporal conjunction *then* (*it then paid*) differed from the logical relations that are internal to the writer's argument (*but then* / *if* ... *then*), so that the internal/external distinction was important to characterize the metadiscoursal values performed by such connective item. In general, therefore, the pragmatic characterization of the different connective devices used in the corpus meant utilizing appropriate rhetorical strategies that revealed semantic relationships between stretches of discourse in cohesive ways, and similarly enabled the writers to activate cognitive and discourse perspectives in the discipline.

With our focus still being on the 'if p, then p' syntactic frame, however, the central issue in the direct conditional clause in the example in (11) was clearly the relationship between the main clause (apodosis) and the subordinate clause (protasis), since the former expresses a situation that is contingent on a situation expressed by the latter (Quirk et al. 1985). In this context, and as Dancygier and Sweetser (1997) argue, the compositional relevance of *then* is one which emphasizes a strong dependency relation between the two clauses, since the item deictically relates to the writer's cognitive space and becomes exclusive by its reference to the situation described in the protasis. The item thus excludes the tentativeness usually associated with the *if*-clause.[12] The effect, as Dancygier and Sweetser (1997) argue, is that the 'if p, then q' frame marks a more categorical tone and more authoritarian writer stance than the simple 'if p, q' frame. Regardless of a categorical stance interpretation suggested by the authors, the properties of the entire conditional sentence in the corpus were, in general, determined by the properties of the protasis (factual/predictive and hypothetical degrees conveyed by verb tenses), so that conditional sentences discussed factual or hypothetical situations and their consequences. In this framework, the logicality relation between the two clauses also allowed natural language conditionals to involve Idealized Cognitive Models-ICMs (Lakoff 1987), where mental spaces are structured by the activation of schematic conceptualizations, inference and reasoning processes for categorizing reality.

---

[12] In this context, therefore, the *then* exclusive reference to the situation described in the *if*-clause (protasis) is different from the *even if*-concessive conditional seen above in example (9), where the apodosis is asserted independently of the protasis which is constructed as a concessive conditional. As shown in example (9) above, this means that a state of events described in the apodosis took place regardless of the situation in the protasis being the case.

The important role of *if*-conditionals in the genre's argument and reasoning

The emphasis placed on conditional sentences in the 'if p, then q' and 'if p, q' frames is meant to go to the quick of the matter, which is about the important role of conditional argumentation and reasoning in the current study.

Although, as it seems, the *if* token is not treated in Hyland's (2005a) taxonomy of metadiscourse resources[13], its relevance here lies not only in the rhetorical specificity of the case note genre[14], but also in one of the basic axioms in genre analysis that the communicative contexts and purposes of a given discourse are influenced by the lexico-grammatical and textual strategies employed by the writers. This means that disregarding the discipline-specific feature of legal argumentation and reasoning[15] in the current analysis would diminish the image of the

---

[13] In explaining the use of metadiscourse in writer-reader interactions and (distinction of) external and internal relations, Hyland provides the following examples: "If it is said that the individual constituent should dominate over the social one, then the desirable political arrangements will be those …" (2005a: 42, underlined in the original) and "If you link the swipe card to your mobile number then you can use it at any one of over 60,000 TopUp points where …" (2005a: 46, underlined in the original). The examples suggest that the emphasis is on the interactive metadiscourse use of the (underlined) logical connective *then* alone, conveying the writer's (internal) logical argument, as shown in the corpus extracts above (11). Where interactive metadiscourse here is sufficient to influence the propositional content, the logicality of the writer's argument is necessarily realized by the compositional contribution of the conditional subordinator *if*. The latter contributes to the proposition expressed in the utterance containing the logical connective *then*, and similarly discusses the situations or implications and the consequences in the entire *if*-conditional sentence.

[14] Conditionals are a key part of other forms of legal writing, such as academic Legal Problem Question Answer writing (Tessuto 2011a), professional (Barrister's) Opinion writing (Tessuto 2006), or professional (legislative) writing. In the latter, conditional clauses are formal features of the syntactic expression of normative or regulatory provisions (Bhatia 1993).

[15] Argumentation is inherent in human communication, verbal and visual, oral and written, monologic and dialogic. Legal argumentation, in particular, is a multidisciplinary field of inquiry, drawing its assumptions and methods from disciplines such as legal theory, legal philosophy, logic, rhetoric, linguistics, sociology, and artificial intelligence. The model for the analysis of argumentation in general, as developed by Van Eemeren and Grootendorst (1992), has led other scholars such as Feteris (1990, 1993, 2002, 2005) to provide a normative theoretical model for the description of relevant features of legal argumentation.

discourse practices and conventions shaped by the community writers in the genre based, as it is, on its contextual, purposeful activity. Also on this point, Hyland (2005a: 138-141) draws attention to the importance of *situational context* in his discussion of community, and states that metadiscourse, which is always situated, "must be analysed as part of a community's practices, values and beliefs" (Hyland 2005a: 37). Consequently, the formal role and function of the subordinating conjunction *if* realized in different conditional constructions may serve to integrate the metadiscourse analytical approach taken in this study, in addition to concessive uses and other subordinating conjunctions examined before.

As a highly valuable linguistic resource in the current genre, *if*-conditionals accounted for a total of 203 occurrences in the corpora (ECLR: 54 / MLR: 149), including the lower occurrences of *if-then* clauses examined above.[16] The most frequent (clause-order) patterns with comma were:

- 'if p, q' frame:

(12) If the Directive does not include unconditionality and precisely phrased provisions, the implementing degree may be tested against the Constitution. ECLR

If the Court were to say that the expert was not to use a logical procedure, rather than a 'mathematical formula', the flaw in its reasoning would be obvious. MLR

and 'q, if p' frame:

---

[16] Many systematic studies carried out by linguists from different theoretical perspectives have shown the importance of *if*-constructions in academic discourse. Among these studies, the focus has been on a detailed typology of conditionals (Quirk et al. 1985); clause ordering (Ford and Thompson 1986); cognitive domains in which content, epistemic and speech act conditionals take place in direct causal manifestations (Sweetser 1990); the role of hypothetical conditionals, course-of-events conditionals and pragmatic conditionals (Athanasiadou and Dirven 1997); the presence of *if* as a marker of non-assertiveness and space builder and as a connector in the p, q syntactic frame (Dancygier 1998); the typical non-assertiveness of conditional clauses used for hypothesizing and hedging, conceding points of view, and envisaging alternatives (Declerck and Reed 2001; Carter-Thomas 2007); and the presence of *if*-conditionals in the genre-sensitive analysis of legal texts (Facchinetti 2001).

(13) The proportionality principle which takes a central place in the *Rottmann* case could prove to be relevant, if an application for naturalization is rejected because …. ECLR

It implies that D would probably have committed the crime himself if he had been the one to confront the victim, … MLR

In these clause-orders, the conditional subordinator also appeared in medial position:

(14) It is surely a feature of a logical, balanced or robust approach that <u>if one applies it to different figures</u> it will produce different results. MLR

and in questions, usually constructed in 'if p, q?' frame:

(15) <u>If property is the label given to that which the law protects, why should we concede property in reputation in the first place?</u> Here powerful rhetorical devices … are to be treated with considerable care. MLR

Only in much lower instances did *if*-conditionals appear in elliptical forms (*if so*, *if applied*), or as constructional variants of the *if* lexical token (*only if*), which had restrictive meaning by excluding all other conditions (*liability arises <u>only if</u> the customer chooses*).

In the above and other instances, writers had to carefully specify the conditions under which the case-focused research issues were carried out, and the *if* operator allowed the writers to manoeuvre the discussion of the legal issues in some kind of conjectural, speculative space. Consequently, the typical non-assertive value of the *if* operator, introducing p and q parameters in the particular cognitive domains (Dencygier 1998), signalled to a large extent the category of hypothetical conditionals proposed in the literature (Athanasiadou and Dirven 1997; Declerck and Reed 2001), since q and q parameters came to bear upon the contingencies with which the relations between protasis and apodosis confronted Discussion writers in the genre. In this kind of dialectical argument and reasoning, *if*-conditionals were often anchored in the 'Present+Modal', 'Past+Modal', and Past Perfect+Conditional Perfect' verb sequences expressing various degrees of hypotheticality, and the q clause included mostly the following modal verb forms: *would, would have, will, may*, *may have*, *might*, *might have*, *could*, *could have*, and *can*.

As a consistency of approach most valued by the writers, hypothesizing in the contingency was closely related to the argumentative nature and objectives of the Discussion in the genre, where the evidence (arguments in Legal Background) had to be carefully weighed for the writers to make their own claims (Author's Argument). In other words, Discussion writers needed to assess the merit of controversial issues by adopting a problem-solving approach to such issues, and *if*-clauses enabled the writers to speculate on possible solutions in the interpretative, hypothetical space opened by such clauses. And while the hypothetical *if*-clause allows the proposition to be presented with a low level of writer commitment (stance) to its epistemological status, the *if*-conditional sentence was also therefore opened to "hedging" effect.[17] Hedging, after all, is not new to academic or professional legal writing where, in addition to establishing conditions, it is also a matter of establishing qualifications or exceptions to an assertion. In the examples presented above (12-14), in fact, the hypotheticality encoded in the *if*-clause treats the relative content as provisional, pending the reader's acceptance of the situation described in the q clause, and as a consequence was used for conceding points of view, or envisaging alternatives (Declerck and Reed 2001; Carter-Thomas 2007).

It follows that conceding viewpoints or envisaging alternatives coincided with the interpersonal function of the *if*-clause, used as a rhetorical device for establishing interpersonal relations in the disciplinary discourse here and creating conditions by which the writer's claim could be favourably welcomed by the reader. [18] The interpersonal/dialogic perspective of the *if*-clauses therefore acted as the driving force for establishing consensus of the conditional claims between writer and reader.

Frame markers

Of the total frequency of frame markers reported in Table 2 (ECLR: 51 / MLR: 155), the most frequently used devices shown in Table 4 were those which:

- guided the reader in the presentation of different arguments in a particular order (*First/ly*, *Second/ly*, *Finally*),
- listed items in a sequence (*a,b, / i, ii*),
- or announced discourse goals (*I will argue*).

---

[17] Salager-Meyer (1994) and Hyland (1994, 1998) identify *if*-clauses as part of a variety of hedging devices in academic writing. The essence of hedging (as an epistemic modality category) is that "academics are crucially concerned with varieties of cognition, and cognition is inevitably 'hedged'" (Hyland 1994: 240).

[18] Obviously, creating conditions for the acceptance or non-acceptance of claims is a key rhetorical aspect of (interpersonal) academic written communication.

Frame markers: forms			
ECLR		MLR	
	N°		*N°*
First/ly	18	Second/ly	53
Finally	14	First/ly	39
Secondly	13	Final/ly	19
		Listing (a,b / i, ii)	11
		Numbering (1, 2)	10
		I will argue / I will now turn / I consider below / …	9

Table 4. Most frequent forms of frame markers: occurrences.

Presenting the order of arguments can be seen in the example below:

(16) First, discrimination on account of a person's ethnic origin is a form of racial discrimination, which follows from established definitions in international law. Secondly, racial discrimination is a particularly egregious kind of discrimination, requiring from the authorities special vigilance and a vigorous reaction.[69] ECLR

Other forms occurred only in isolated instances, such as *in sum*, *to conclude* (labelling stages), *lastly* (sequencing), and *in this article/paper/ case note/note/comment* (announcing goals). Overall, then, writers in both journals did not seem to be concerned with a wider and richer repertoire of frame markers.

Endophoric markers

Endophoric markers were lower in frequency than frame markers, and made their appearance in the linguistic forms shown in Table 5, equalling the total incidence of such forms (ECLR: 12 / MLR: 68).

Endophoric markers: forms			
ECLR		MLR	
	N°		*N°*
-as was mentioned before -in the previous section	9	-as noted above -as has been/was noted above -described above	29
-as has been noted -as noted above	3	-see below	18
		-referred to above	14
		-discussed below	7

Table 5. Forms of endophoric markers: total occurrences.

Endophoric devices referred readers to other parts of the text by recapturing, extending or summarizing an argument, as in:

(17) As noted above, an employer is entitled to argue that its actions in constructively dismissing an employee fell within the range of reasonable responses … MLR

By acting intratextually, many such devices were closely linked to the persuasive use of citations (evidentials) discussed immediately below.

Evidentials

It is well known that citation plays a key role in academic legal writing, showing how a cited work is grounded in the current state of disciplinary knowledge. Table 6 reports the total frequency of evidentials in the corpora, where they were extensively realized by the well-established culture of superscript numbers to mark the footnoting citation style.

Evidentials: forms			
ECLR		MLR	
	N°		*N°*
superscript numbers	430	superscript numbers	597

Table 6. Forms of evidentials: total occurrences.

The overwhelming use of superscript numbers (e.g. [12, 13, 14]) throughout the main text referred the readers to the corresponding footnotes, which gave the source detail or other information at the bottom of each page. In this "non integral" (Swales 1990) citation device, 15 to 60 citation numbers in Discussion sections (with 2 to 14 corresponding footnotes at the bottom of the page) show that they were an essential element in demonstrating the amount of research performed on the topic, as well as the writer's understanding of the relative importance of the issues and related areas of law involved in the case. This was vital for the reader to gauge the strength and validity of the referenced material by contributing to the writer's academic credibility.

The citation style in the Discussion section (and indeed in Introductions and Conclusions) consisted of two elements:

(a) citation notes in the main text using superscript numbers placed at the end of the quoted statement, clause or phrase;

(b) footnotes for all citations.

In (a), superscript numbers allowed writers to engage with critical discussion of the legal arguments made in a variety of sources (legislation, cases, reviews, reports, etc.) by including them in the reported information (whether or not in *that*-clause), and cited sources were therefore acknowledged in the text and detailed in footnotes.[19] In the set of extracts below, for instance, writers summarized (often) from a case by citing the judge(s) from whose judgment they had taken the quote:

(18)

> The Court does not start with an analysis of the objective and content of the contested measure, as one might have expected. It refers to the 'tobacco advertising II case'[58] judgment and holds that Article 95 enables the Community to act either to strike down existing and future obstacles to the functioning of the internal market, on the condition that the latter are likely to arise.[59]
>
> [58] Case C-380/03 *Germany* v. *Parliament/Council* [2006] *ECR* I-11573.
> [59] Par. 64. ECLR 2010: 147

> However, it is obviously right that in general the claim should be brought by in the name of the company, as was held by Moore-Bick LJ in *Man Nutzfarhzeuge AG*v *Freightliner*.[37]
>
> [37] [2005] EWHC 2347 at [324]-[327].The decision was upheld on appeal at [2008] PNLR 5, but this point did not arise. MLR 2010: 493

> In its *Societé KPMG* judgment of 24 March 2006,[32] the highest administrative French court established the principle of legal security as a 'principe général du droit'.
>
> [32] Conseil d'Etat Ass. 24 March 2006, petition No 288460 (*Société KPMG*). ECLR 2010: 129

[19] As noted in Chapter 2, discussing arguments meant that writers referred to other subjects (judges or other judicial officials) in the cited sources by summarizing or paraphrasing the reported information.

> First instance judges found the principles enunciated in MB difficult to apply in practice.[37]
>
> [37] For an account of the ambiguities and difficulties arising from MB, see Lord Phillips in AF n 9 above at [8]-[21]. MLR 2010: 840

> … the Court held that 'although . . . Parliament intended that a lawful decision of the election court must be final', one made 'on a wrong interpretation of the law' was not made immune from challenge.[4]
>
> [4]n 2 above at [47].MLR 2011: 609

In these instances, where the superscript number was placed at the end of the portion of text to which the corresponding note referred, writers in essence summarized the main ideas and 'findings' from the cited sources by incorporating them into their own arguments. Similarly, writers used single quotation marks (usually fewer than five lines) in the text to mark the source's original language, leaving longer quotations to be indented as separate paragraphs outside (direct) quotation marks. While ellipsis occurred only sparingly in a series of three full stops ('…'), reporting other subjects' ideas and arguments also concerned the use of the adjunct agent structure *According to* in subject position, followed by replication of the original language used in the case through direct quotations in the superscripted clause:

(19)

> According to Lord Hoffmann, in a passage which proved pivotal to the outcome in Sienkiewicz, 'it should be irrelevant whether the other exposure was tortious or non-tortious, by natural causes or human agency or by the claimant himself.'[29]
>
> [29]Barker n 12 above at [17]. MLR 2011: 781

This way of engaging with another cited source was therefore typical of 'writing about legal cases', and marking the source's exact language and meaning by single quotation marks was essential for the writers to focus on the particular phrasing in the quoted source in order to support their arguments in the text. From the reader's point of view, the recurrent use of quote-worthy language was essential to understand the writer's arguments about a cutting edge issue in the case. Quoting the original words thus suggested that the way the source packages its message could not be brought to a simpler or reduced form in the superscripted statement.

In (b), footnotes for all citations not only detailed the cited sources but also provided other information that was regarded as inappropriate for inclusion in the main text. The full examples below (20-21) demonstrate how a series of footnotes might look, and include sequentially numbered citations in a variety of legal sources:

(20)

Footnotes

---

[20] Art. 13(1)d.
[21] Art. 15(1).
[22] Conclusions of 20/09/2001.
[23]The Council was requested to put forward proposals for measures on data retention by service providers. *See* declaration on combating terrorism of 25/03/2004.
[24]The need to swiftly adopt common rules in the area of data retention was emphasized in the Council declaration of 13/07/2005.
[25]The legal bases were Art. 31(1)c and 34(2)b. *See* Council document 8958/04 of 28/04/2004, available at the Council's register.
[26] Ibid.
[27]Art. 5.
[28]For example, as a result of consumers' requests for flat-rate services, the need to store traffic data was decreasing to the extent that it was becoming superfluous for companies to retain traffic data. *See* Council document 8958/04, *supra* n. 25.
[29] COM (2005) 438 final. ECLR 2010: 141

(21)

Footnotes

---

[26]Brussels II *bis*: Council Regulation (EC) No 2201/2003 concerning jurisdiction and the recognition and enforcement of judgments in matrimonial matters and matters of parental responsibility.
[27]See the principles articulated in *Miller, McFarlane*n 21 above and developed in subsequent Court of Appeal authorities: S. Harris-Short and J. Miles, *Family Law: Text, Cases, and Materials*(Oxford: OUP, 2nd ed, 2011, forthcoming) ch 7. As Lady Hale notes ([2010] UKSC 42 at [186]), the fact that the wife's wealth derived principally from family gifts would probably have justified some departure from equal sharing in this case, even without the agreement, given the relatively modest length of the marriage.
[28]See J. Scherpe and A. Dutta,'Cross-border enforcement of English ancillary relief orders: Fog in the channel - Europe cut off?' (2010) 40 *Fam Law*385.
[29][2008] EWHC1532 at [137]
[30]*ibid* at [89]-[93]. MLR 2011: 433

Extensive footnoting, as it appears above, allowed writers not only to detail sources in bibliographic citation by referring to, say, a Case ([2008] EWHC1532 at [137]) in (21), but also to provide extra information by carrying on the legal arguments from the main text and similarly enter more into the stream of discussion. As shown in the examples above, carrying on arguments relied on a number of 'tags' (*see*, *ibid*, *cf.*, *above*) to help supplement, explain, or differentiate information in the cited sources, although *but see* (contradicting between two cited propositions), *contra* (contradicting between the original and subsequent proposition in the cited sources) and *compare with* (literally comparing between two or more sources) were other common citation signals. In (20), for instance, the use of the extra material contained in the citation note[28] ('For example, as a result of consumers' requests …') was explanatory of the argument made in the text, and the endophoric items (*See*, *supra*) referred the reader to an earlier document in the footnote. Alternatively, the choice was to acknowledge previous statements in non-reporting *that*-clause, as in the example (21) with footnote[27] ('As Lady Hale notes ([2010] UKSC 42 at [186]), the fact that …'), showing that the writer wished to supplement the other author's argument, regarded as relevant rather than incidental to the subject under discussion. In this instance, the effect was that the statement looked like a 'textual footnote' – a textual sentence that supplemented an argument made within the text. Moreover, writers were not hesitant to engage with academically cited sources, as shown in (21) with footnote[27] ('S. Harris-Short and J. Miles, *Family Law* ...'), the reason for their use being the value of academic claims which add credit to the legal arguments made in the professional (especially judicial) sources of law. By so doing, community writers manifested the important dialogue between two related but also conflicting worlds of intra-disciplinary legal discourse: the academy and the profession.

In this framework, it becomes clear that the use of superscript numbers and corresponding footnotes shed a considerable light on the analysis and discussion of the controlling issue in the case. Although, perhaps, superscripts carried a different rhetorical effect from traditional in-text citations, footnoting showed that the writers had properly researched and critically understood the particular area of law. As an important criterion against which the writers judged the relevance of the researched issue in the epistemological discursive framework of the law, the high number of footnoted citations therefore provided the evidence for the writer's disciplinary argument constructed through "intertextual and interdiscursive" elements (Candlin and Maley 1997) necessary for the communal activity of legal knowledge-making in the discourse community. In constructing knowledge, merit-granting (Davenport and Cronin 2000) and persuasion (Case and Higgins 2000) became the ultimate motivating factors in citation in ways that "[n]ew work has to be embedded in the literature of the community to demonstrate its relevance, importance and the credentials of the writers" (Hyland 2005a: 158).

Beyond these purposes and values of citation, however, the preference for the footnoting pattern[20] was clearly the result of the legal journals in the corpus creating published style guides, which were then acted upon or adapted by case note writers.[21] Although the publication of such style guides may render citation analysis here unproblematic and perhaps result in this author's analytical efforts being irrelevant, it remains that the footnoting practices in the disciplinary culture of law have until now been left unreported in discourse and genre-based research studies.

Code glosses

Of the total incidence of code glosses (ECLR: 128 / MLR: 431), Table 7 shows the five preferred forms of code glosses used to explain or expand the writers' arguments, and which had their parallel meanings to other forms.

Endophoric markers: forms			
ECLR		MLR	
	N°		*N*°
( )	27	( )	146
such as	26	such as	58
- -	14	that is (to say)	54
e.g.	13	for example	42
i.e.	13	i.e.	40

Table 7. Five-top code glosses: occurrences.

[20] Disciplinary similarity in the abundant use of footnoting system can be discerned between the law and the sciences. In his study of evidentials in science research articles (Physics and Engineering), Hyland (2005a) in fact argues for "the predominance of non-integral structures" which "explains the overwhelming use of the footnote format in the sciences" (2005a: 159).

[21] Specific formats for citations in the case note corpora reflected most common styles used in research papers – namely, the *American Psychological Association* style (used in the social sciences), the *Chicago Manual of Style* (used in business communication, economics, and social sciences), and the *Modern Language Association* style (used in the humanities).

Code glosses occurred either within parentheses ( ) or outside them, and in both cases the use of *such as* had its parallel forms to *e.g.*, *for example*, *for instance*, *As an illustration*, and *by way of illustration*. Similarly, *that is* had its parallel forms to the abbreviations *i.e.* and *viz* and the adverbs *namely* and *specifically*, leaving the adverb *in other words* to have its parallel to the adverbial form *put differently* in marginal instances. In the same vein, the dash – punctuation mark functioned as an alternative form to parenthetical remarks ( ), and the latter form also marked off interactional personal asides in relatively few instances, as will be seen later in this analysis.

Where code glosses came into play to set out the writers' arguments, they usually provided "explanation" or "specification" of information, as part of Hyland's (2007: 274) "two discourse functions of reformulations" in the unfolding text. In the first two examples illustrated in the set below (22), for instance, reformulating the material allowed the writers to explain, by gloss, the particular institutional tasks involved in the presidency or the legal concept involved in property law (as used again in the court's actual language), thus making the gloss user-friendly for the widest readership:

(22) The Presidency can be seen as both a collective head of state and head of the executive branch. It performs some of the typical tasks of a head of state, <u>such as appointing ambassadors and international representatives</u>.
ECLR 2010: 313

This is particularly so where the agreement deals with known circumstances, or <u>for example</u> preserves specific 'non-matrimonial property', <u>such as an inheritance</u>, from the ex propriatory effect of the equal sharing principle.[70] MLR 2011: 438

The Court started by noting that the preamble of the EAW <u>(unlike the instrument itself, it could be added)</u> allows for some consideration of safeguards for the individual in criminal law proceedings under the law of mutual recognition. MLR 2010, 73(5): 829

This is not quite how the defendant's had put their case at trial. Rather, the defendants had argued that if the relative risk was less than two, then the deceased's mesothelioma may well have been idiopathic; <u>that is to say, of unknown cause</u>. MLR 2011: 783

Parenthetical reformulation ( ) was most common for glossing where a variety of explanatory items occurred, as in:

(23) Although it is true that a statistical association is not the same as causality, epidemiological evidence is routinely used in the non-legal world (e.g., as a matter of public health policy) in discussions and decisions about causation of disease … MLR 2011: 788-89

Since the shoe type concerned seems to be favoured by suspects (viz its relatively common appearance in the FSS database), this, in the present case, produced … MLR 2011: 451

Special difficulties may arise with regard to cases of so-called 'identity fraud' (submission of false personal data, like a false name, age or place of birth) during the naturalisation procedure. ECLR 2011: 156

or where the bracketed material was consequentially explanatory of the hypothetical condition, as in:

(24) If the courts are unable to provide straightforward directions to jurors in cases of murder (hence 15 appeals in 11 years), how can they be expected to do any better in relation to other offences? MLR 2010: 254

In other instances, such as in (25), parenthetical reformulation served to further specify the disciplinary concept in line with the conventional expectations of the professional (judicial) community:

(25) … and the media offering varying assessments about whether English law now recognizes 'binding' pre-nuptial agreements (or 'ante-nuptial' agreements, as the Supreme Court appears to prefer). MLR 2011: 432

and, in the connective (*or*) context shown in the example, reformulation seemed to be "a pragmatic or discoursal equivalence rather than a strictly logical or propositional one" (Hyland 2007: 277).

By the same token, reformulation served a number of jobs. It helped the writers:

to specify (by distinguishing between) the name of different cases on the list using the short citation system (to be then detailed in footnote):

(26) This question has arisen in two recent cases in relation to consumer bank charges: the first was decided by the UK Supreme Court in agreed test case proceedings brought by the Office of Fair Trading (the Bank Charges case)[1]; the second … MLR 2009: 654

to refer to the case as a shorthand device in the discussion of the reported argument:

(27) It was submitted that Mr Barker's case was no different from *Wilsher* v *Essex Area Health Authority*[26] (*Wilsher*) where young Martin Wilsher failed to establish … . MLR 2011: 780

to determine the topic of the judgment by adding further 'things said by the way' (obiter) in the source work:

(28) The majority judgment set up a new framework within which to address the relevance of pre-nuptial (and, obiter, postnuptial) agreements to the exercise of the court's discretion to grant ancillary relief. MLR 2011: 434

to spell out the justice's refusal to concur with the opinion of a majority:

(29) By a majority of 8:1 (Lord Hoffmann dissenting), the House of Lords in *AF* supported the idea of a 'core irreducible minimum' of procedural protection … . MLR 2010 841

or to state legislation specifically by re-naming articles:

(30) In that case, if the constitutional provision … the *Conseil d'Etat* will examine the complaint under the conditions of Article 234 CE (presently Article 267 TFEU), with due regard to the Court of Justice's *Foto Frost* case-law. [39] ECLR 2010: 130

While writers went more for explanations rather than specifications in their parenthetical remarks, the insertions of some verbal unit in the *em dash* (-) punctuation mark seemed to be an alternative to, or a more relaxed form than, the parenthesis mark of punctuation ( ), and possibly stronger than a comma (,). This can be seen in (31), where dashes were used to set off part of the writer's argument in explanatory verbal unit:

(31) Does Community law preclude loss of Union citizenship due to the lawful – by internal law – revocation of the nationality of a member state with statelessness as a consequence? ECLR 2011: 139

Spain found – in accordance with the Spanish *Código Civil* – that the Argentine nationality was his effective nationality, and therefore denied him the European rights … ECLR 2011: 142

In a context where reformulations disambiguated parts of legal arguments by reinforcing their rhetorical connections, code glossing therefore helped "contribute to the creation of coherent, reader-friendly prose, while conveying the writer's audience-sensitivity and relationship to the message" (Hyland 2007: 266).

Hedges

Of the total frequency of hedges interactional resources (ECLR: 589 / MLR: 2127), writers from both journals revealed the use of the top-six linguistic forms reported in Table 8.

Hedges: forms			
ECLR		MLR	
	N°		*N*°
Can	94	Would	282
Would	74	May	244
Could	64	Could	176
May	49	Can	154
Possible	33	Might	147
general(ly)	32	Reasonable	95

Table 8. Six-top hedges: occurrences.

Computer readable data show that these preferred forms were part of a total of eighteen and twenty-five different forms of hedges in ECLR and MLR corpora, respectively, where adverbial, adjectival, nominal and verbal forms were used (e.g. *assumption*, *certain x*,*be/leave open to*, *likely*, *little*, *often*, *reasonable*, *partially*, *probability*, *questionable*, *rather x*, *seem*, *suggest*). These varieties included instances of phrases where writers combined several hedges by linking a modal auxiliary verb with a lexical verb with hedging content (e.g. *it would appear that*), or a lexical verb followed by an adverb or adjective with a hedging content, where the latter item reinforced the hedging effect inherent in the lexical verb (e.g. *it seems reasonable that*). All these realizations show that hedging was epistemologically related to modality, dealing with the relativity of a particular truth or knowledge.[22]

[22] In this sense, reference is to the category of epistemic modality which concerns "the degree of commitment by the speaker to what he/she is saying" (Palmer 2001: 51; Larreya 2009: 13, among others). Hyland (1994, 1996, 1998) and Kranich (2011), among others, have shown that epistemic modal markers are used either to express the speaker's uncertainty (content-oriented mitigation), or to leave room for other opinions by avoiding categorical statements (addressee-oriented mitigation).

Where modality defined the major characteristic of hedging in Discussion, the data in Table 8 therefore show that there was a considerably higher incidence of hedges realized through the preferred forms of modal auxiliary verbs with epistemic use, which were used at the expense of other (lexical) means of epistemic modal marking. Yet, the tendency to construct sentences with epistemic modal auxiliaries interacted with the use of non-modalized declarative sentences, where writers were fully committed to the utterance made.

The set of examples below (32) gives an overall picture of the varied forms of hedges, including cases where writers weakened the degree of commitment by modalizing the statements in some way, namely with a modal auxiliary such as *could*, *may* or *would*:

(32) One could therefore argue that there is no need to refer to Article 47 EU, and that a reference to Article 10 EC and the principle of loyal cooperation would have been more appropriate. MLR 2010, 73(5): 828

Instead, as we shall see below, the agreement may now be treated as determinative unless it would be unfair to do so. MLR 2011, 74(3): 436

Furthermore, companies nowadays are likely to have either unlimited capacity, pursuant to section 31(1)'s removal of the requirement for an objects clause, or else a very broadly drafted general objects clause providing a close equivalent to unrestricted capacity.
MLR 2011, 74(4): 601

Ultimately, it may be impossible to come to a satisfactory conclusion in a causing death by driving case. MLR 2011, 74(5): 776

A possible explanation for this contrast is that the Court carries out a legal basis test that is different depending on the nature of the contested act (i.e., an EC act concluding an international agreement or an EC measure).
ECLR 2010, 6: 154

That nationality law is thereby made dependent on Union law to a certain extent, while Union citizenship is precisely presented by the Treaty as being a dependent variable of the possession of the nationality of a member state. ECLR 2011, 7: 147

In these and other instances, where legal argument construction required extension of the factual and legal issues, hedges revealed the "writer's plausible reasoning rather than certain knowledge", and emphasized "the subjectivity of a position by allowing information to be presented as an opinion rather than a fact and therefore open that position to negotiation"

(Hyland 2005a: 52). The use of these strategies therefore indicated that disciplinary writers were regulated by specific epistemological norms, which expected them to make disciplinary hypotheses by explaining 'possible' arguments that arose from a set of different case-focused issues. Given these norms, writers thus weakened the certainty of their propositions through such hypotheses, and hedges were important rhetorical strategies to win the acceptance of the readers towards the writers' arguments in interpersonal discourse. Where the important metadiscourse role of hedges implied lack of certainty through hypotheses in order to conduct disciplinary inquiries, the equally important argumentative role of *if*-conditionals in which hedges also occurred (especially through epistemic modal verbs) contributed indeed to this hypothetical, plausible world of the writers' non-assertive arguments.

Boosters

Of the total frequency of boosters (ECLR: 352 / MLR: 1055), Table 9 reports the top-five linguistic forms of such resources.

Boosters: forms			
ECLR		MLR	
	N°		*N°*
will	51	will (not)	211
certain(ly)	33	clear(ly)	90
established	21	very	70
precise(ly)	18	cannot	67
clearly	13	certain(ly-ty)	59

Table 9. Five-top boosters: occurrences.

Although the top-five boosters occurred out of a total of fourteen and twenty different forms (e.g. *doubtless*, *entirely*, *in fact*, *fully*, *impossible*, *indeed*, *never*, *obvious, plain, really*, *sure, true*, *unequivocal*) in both corpora, Table 9 shows that the modal auxiliary *will* accounted for the largest percentage of all the boosters found in the corpora, where its use was to a large extent conventional in the generic discourse. Despite the proportionally higher incidence of the modal, all boosters allowed the writers to present their case-focused research with "certainty and construct rapport by marking involvement with the topic and solidarity with an audience" (Hyland 2005a: 53).

In the set of examples (33) below, we can appreciate the value of such boosting devices used to amplify the strength of the writers' arguments, in terms of the propositional information and the interaction with the reader:

(33) While successful navigation of these issues will not render the agreement prima facie binding on the court (because of *Hyman*), it will bring the parties within reach of the Supreme Court's key proposition,...
MLR 2011, 74(3): 437

This was not an issue in *Begum* itself, as the claimant's view that she had to wear a coat-like garment known as jilbab at school was clearly one shared by other (but not all) Muslims. MLR 2011, 74(2): 294

Certainly, member states no longer need to take annulment actions against Community acts in order to safeguard the Union's powers since the Community was superseded by the Union and now we only have Union acts. ECLR 2010, 6: 139

The reason, in short, is that as a matter of law, *Fairchild* applies. On the face of it, this is very odd because the concept of risk that is central to the test is ultimately rooted in statistics. MLR 2011, 74(5): 789

Burton J's conclusion that a philosophical belief does not need to be comprehensive or shared by others to fall within the ambit of anti-discrimination legislation cannot be reconciled with the reasoning in *Eweida* which focuses on social doctrine and widespread acceptance of the particular religious viewpoint. MLR 2011, 74(2): 302

Here, the modal auxiliary verbs (positive/negative) played a similar role to other boosting expressions, by talking about the present/future with certainty through *will not/will* (to express the writer's reference to a 'general rule'), or by talking about that 'something was impossible' through *cannot*. Both epistemic modal expressions, in fact, were inherent in deductive argument where significant issues in the case were extracted for the first time and their inferences presented with assurance. The writer in the Burton example above, for instance, presented his disciplinary argument by feeling sure that the judge's conclusion 'was not possible or realistic' in the comparable (*Eweida*) judicial decision. Therefore, boosting by the positive or negative form of a modal verb served to indicate the level of confidence in the proposition by relying on the objective status of the information.

Attitude markers

Of the total frequency of attitude markers (ECLR: 314 / MLR: 616), writers from both journals revealed the top-ten forms of such resources (Table 10) realized essentially through attitudinal adjectives.

Attitude markers: forms			
ECLR		MLR	
	N°		*N°*
relevant	30	relevant	85
necessary	29	necessary	48
important	25	difficult	40
essential	20	proper	40
significant	19	appropriate	38
appropriate	18	important	35
difficult	15	significant	31
crucial	15	legitimate	23
concrete	12	interesting	20
interesting	12	correct	19

Table 10. Top-ten forms of attitude markers: occurrences.

These preferred forms occurred in a total of fifteen and nineteen different expressions in ECLR and MLR, respectively, where adjectival and adverbial forms were commonly used (e.g. *(in)correct(ly), depressing, good, importantly, interestingly, legitimate, problematic, remarkable, surprising(ly), unfortunately, straightforward, unusual, worrying*), together with sparingly used attitudinal verbs in the *I/We agree/disagree* realizations. According to Hyland (2005a: 53), attitude markers "indicate the writer's affective, rather than epistemic, attitude to propositions. Instead of commenting on the status of information, its probable relevance, reliability or truth, attitude markers convey surprise, agreement, importance, obligation, frustration, and so on". Thus, by using words and expressions such as *important*, *necessary*, *surprisingly relevant*, *I find it interesting*, *the judgment fails to explain*, *it is alarming that*, *it is difficult to see that*, etc., writers inevitably expressed their attitude to what they said in a variety of ways, and the words or expressions used similarly appeared with a positive meaning (e.g. *interesting*, *relevant*, *significant*) or negative meaning (e.g. *difficult*, *incorrect(ly)*, *problematic*). The interpersonal use of attitude markers therefore allowed the readers to understand the writers' personal judgments within their texts through different expressions of evaluative meaning.

Computer readable data show that attitude markers made their appearance under four main formal categories:

1 adjectives as pronominal modifiers;
2 adjectives as subjective complement;
3 adverbs as adverbial sentences; and
4 nouns and verbs with specific semantic content.

In category 1, where linguistic realizations of attitude markers were more commonly identified, the following set of examples (34) shows that adjectives as attitude markers functioned, for instance, as noun premodifiers (e.g. *relevant decision*), or occurred in comparative forms (e.g. *less relevant*), indicating a particular position from which items were viewed:

(34) In this landscape, categorizing the opportunity as one which the company would be interested in or capable of taking advantage of is not relevant.
MLR 2011, 74(4): 606

The second relevant decision makes the picture considerably more complicated. ECLR 2011 (7): 162

…the position of the Court on the importance of the body's role in the overall legislative process is less relevant when it comes to the constitutional orders of the states parties to the Convention.[105]
ECLR 2010 (6): 330

… the Strasbourg court did not consider all the relevant arguments,[91] gave insufficient weight to important considerations[92] or had not 'received all the help which was needed to form a conclusion'.[93] MLR 2010, 73(4): 543

However, as shown in (35), adjectives were also used predicatively (subjective complements), and the writer's value judgment of the material in the proposition was also often pre-modified by the adverb *highly*, functioning as a booster:

(35) The rationale of this 5-4 decision[4] is based on three assumptions, all of which are highly problematic. ECLR 2010, 6: 482

In addition to expressing personal judgments of 'difficulty' (*problematic*), as above, signalling attitudes and reactions to the evaluated material also allowed the writers to make interpretive statements of 'inconsistency' (*illogical*) and 'incompatibility' (*inappropriate*) along negative parameters of the propositions, whether or not in pronominal modifiers, as in (36):

(36) But this legal fiction plugged directly into conventional legal doctrine relating to causation and created a virtual legal but illogical equivalence with *Bonnington Castings Ltd* v *Wardlaw*[24] … MLR 2011, 74(5): 780

The fact that the fight against crime and terrorism was a determining factor in adopting the Directive rendered Article 95 inappropriate.[50] The reference to the investigation, detection and prosecution of serious crime in Article 1(1) of Directive 2006/24 only served to indicate the legitimate objective of the restrictions imposed on the rights of individuals.[51]
ECLR 2010, 6: 144

In category 2, adjectives functioned as subjective complements in sentences with expletive *it* structures, as the example (37) below illustrates:

(37) When we then combine these two areas of law it becomes difficult to see the rationale behind punishing a supervisory driver, sitting in the driving seat, who has little control over the manner in which the car is being driven …It is alarming that the appellant in *Martin* had been charged with, tried for and convicted of an offence that simply did not exist.
MLR 2011, 74(5):776

The co-writers in (37) were concerned about the intractable issue in the rationale of the case at hand, and expressed a particularly worrisome predicament which heightened the negative rhetorical effect. Although these writers hid behind a manifestly objective formulation of their argument in 'it is (that)' structure, this metaphorical objectification device was highly useful in the genre since it allowed Discussion writers to present objective, measured evidence of the facts, in addition to the subjective construal of their arguments through explicit authorial presence (self-mentions), as examined immediately below.

In category 3, adverbs functioned as sentence adverbials and the few linguistic items recorded helped the writers to express their value judgments of the material, as in:

(38) Unfortunately, as we can see from R v T, courts came to expect experts to give evidence in the form of a conclusion about whether two marks had a common source.[8] MLR 2011, 74(3): 446

Importantly, such grounds might be found in circumstances less serious than those which would vitiate the agreement as a matter of contract law: undue pressure falling short of duress, … MLR 2011, 74(3): 431

Interestingly, he also stated that since the very notion of rehabilitation cannot adequately be dealt with on an *ad hoc* basis, there is therefore no reason why a national with no link to the Member State …
MLR 2010, 73(5): 828

Not surprisingly, these conditions are also found in the case-law of the Court of Justice and as such are not problematic. ECLR 2010 (6): 128

Interestingly, at this point, the Court came back to the link between electronic data retention as such, prescribed by European law, and … ECLR 2010 (6): 516

Under these circumstances, there were few opportunities where adverbs were also modified by superlatives (*More importantly, however, ...*), or hedged by other adverbs (*The decision, quite extraordinarily, invoked ...*).

Finally, in category 4, writers expressed their attitude to the propositional content by using nouns and verbs in various constructions, and marked their negative tone in the utterances as illustrated below:

(39) The difficulty in explaining this also stems from the way fingerprint evidence has classically been given. MLR 2011, 74(3): 448

The danger of doing so is illustrated by this very judgment in which the Court has proceeded from several demonstrably false premises. MLR 2011, 74(3): 455

… it is difficult to understand why this should be the case given the lack of knowledge about causal mechanisms … MLR 2011, 74(5): 774

As an admission by the court, this not only represents a failure to decide the matter for the parties, it also represents an admission that …
MLR 2010, 73(6): 203

The judgment fails to explain how reasoned judgments are to be arrived at when several factors are involved, other than by appeals to 'experience' and 'judgment'- black boxes the Court would apparently prefer to remain unanalyzed. MLR 2011, 74(3): 454

Hence, the limitation of the scope of application of Directive 2000/78 would only remain relevant with regard to the provisions that go beyond expressing the general principle. ECLR 2011 (5): 450

> This is reflected in the lack of provisions adequately addressing the situation of family members of TCNs who are moving to another member state. ECLR 2010 (6): 470

It becomes clear that, by emphasizing the writers' evaluative viewpoints on the research material in the case, the use of different attitude markers was significant to impart the 'personal' impression of the writers, in terms of what they deemed *appropriate*, *difficult*, *interesting*, *logical*, or some other way for their interpretive statements. This way then, Discussion writers were able to exercise some kind of influence over the readers' interpretation of the evaluated content, and direct the readers to an appropriate understanding of their statements in persuasive criteria.

Self mention

In the use of self mentions realized by personal pronouns (e.g. Biber et al. 1999; Kuo 1999; Tang and Jon 1999; Harwood 2005a/b)[23], Table 11 shows that the subjective *I* pronoun ranked higher than the possessive *my* and objective *me* forms of the pronoun. Much lower in this rank was the exclusive function of first-person plural pronoun *We* recorded in one journal alone.

Self mention: forms			
ECLR		MLR	
	N°		*N*°
I	22	I	38
We (*exclusive*)	-	We (*exclusive*)	4
My	6	My	8
Me	3	Me	5
TOTAL	31	TOTAL	55

Table 11. Total occurrences of self mentions.

[23] In academic writing, the use of personal pronouns may be considered as the resultant of the writers' efforts to order things in the real world, which is reproduced through language. The discursive world is thus ordered by institutional norms that are deeply rooted in specific community practices (Swales 1990, 2004; Fairclough 2003; Hyland 2005a; Ädel 2006). In addition, contrastive studies into English as a Lingua Franca of academic communication show substantial differences between native and non-native writers of English in the use of personal pronouns in (international) research articles (e.g. Candlin and Gotti 2004; Lorés 2004; Mur 2007).

Aware of the ambiguity typical of the exclusive/inclusive (pronominal) *We* divide, the exclusive function of the pronouns *I* and *We* was essentially determined by the single and joint nature of authorship in the corpora, where single-authored case notes made their major appearance (i.e. nine single-authored and one co-authored case notes in ECLR as opposed to fifteen single-authored and five co-authored case notes in MLR). Despite the higher frequency of the exclusive *I*, however, not all writers in the journals were prepared to use it in their Discussions, since the pronoun appeared only in five (out of ten) texts in ECLR and thirteen (out of twenty) such texts in MLR. In these journals, moreover, the pronoun *I* spread out differently by one to four such instances in individual Discussions.

Overall, all forms of the pronouns in Table 11 allowed the writers to intrude into the text and signal their overt presence, but the writer visibility in the text depended upon the discourse function performed by such pronouns in particular contexts. In the majority of instances, exclusive *I* enabled the writers to organize the text and guide the readers through the course of their case-focused research. This can be seen in the set of examples (40) below:

(40) Their Lordships' *dicta* on the binding nature of the decision in *A* v *UK* give rise to important constitutional questions about the meaning an implications of section 2 of the HRA. It is to this question that <u>I will now turn</u>.
MLR 2010, 73(5): 843

It does seem surprising that an issue of this kind should be raised for the first time in the House of Lords. <u>I proceed on the facts as assumed by all the other judges</u>.
MLR 2010, 73(3): 488

This subverts the basic principle in *Caparo*, <u>which I consider below</u>.
MLR 2010, 73(3): 491

Secondly, only precisely and unconditionally phrased provisions of a Directive can be applied instead of national law. This latter condition happened not to be fulfilled in *Mme Perreux*, <u>as I will explain later</u>.
ECLR 2010, 6: 128

In such instances of authorial textual intervention, the signposting function of the pronoun became close to a low-risk "I as guide" category (Tang and John 1999), and made the discourse more vivid while also catching the attention of disciplinary readers.

In the minority of instances, exclusive *I* provided the rhetorical opportunity to present the writers' orientation to their arguments, as in:

(41) There is generally agreement though that the EAW does not offer any grounds for refusal based on a need to respect proportionality and that such an assessment may only be made by the competent judicial authority of the issuing Member State.[26]I disagree with this. MLR 2010, 73(5): 832

Prior to the Supreme Court hearing, I argued that Smith LJ's interpretation of section 3 of the Compensation Act 2006 was flawed.[41]
MLR 2011, 74(5): 784

Thus, other than A.G. Poiares Maduro, I am of the opinion that the nationality law of the member states occupies a privileged position with regard to delineating the powers of the EU and the member states, including in cases that cannot be seen as purely internal.
ECLR 2011, 7: 148

Here, the evaluative options offered by the pronoun and verb collocates reveal the critical perspective from which the writers' statements should be interpreted, as well as the contribution the writers made to the discipline through the presentation of research material. Expressing a critical attitude to the statements was vital for the genre writers who, as noted in Chapters 1 and 2, were committed to identifying logical fallacies, unarticulated premises, and other features in the case's underlying decisional rule. Personal reference in these and other similar instances therefore suggested that writers were establishing their authorial presence in the most possible degrees of "I as originator" and "I as opinion-holder" – namely, "showing that they perceive themselves as people who have the *right* and the *ability* to originate new ideas (Tang and John 1999: S29, italics in the original).[24]And while exclusive *I* was a risky choice in the interactive Discussion (because *I* is the most powerful authorial presence in Tang and John's classification), presenting new ideas with conviction was implied in the essence of case note writing, which required genre writers to offer a 'fresh' look at some *significant* issue(s) in the case by forming a critical (expert) opinion and argument.

Outside exclusive *I*-persona, critical opinion was equally expressed through the marginally occurring exclusive *We* pronoun, as in (42), where co-writers projected themselves in the *We* for *I* construction:

[24] Where the emphasis on *new ideas* in Tang and John's (1999) taxonomy is sufficient to warrant reporting in the media, the personal pronoun *I* (and *We*) in published academic writing become *self-promotional* in function, where they create a *picture of noteworthiness and uniqueness* in Harwood's (2005a/b) parlance.

(42) Section 58 is in no way unique in giving the courts an extensive role in fundamentally shaping the contours of the criminal law. If they are to take on that role, something about which we will express doubts in a moment, it is vitally important that principles are outlined for interpretation in these non-ideal circumstances. MLR 2009, 72(6): 986

But given the scope of the *actus reus*we take it that this is uncommon in this context. MLR 2009, 72(6): 991

Few other opportunities arose in the corpora by omitting arguments introduced with the pronoun *I*. Where this occurred, writers replaced the pronoun with such (exclusive) lexical phrases: *In my opinion*, *In my view*, *My view*, *My own position*. As substitutes of the "I as originator" and "I as opinion-holder" categories, such lexical phrases personalized writers' arguments as critical opinions and standpoints that evolved in the disciplinary discussion:

(43) In my view, it means that the UK courts are not bound to follow all Strasbourg decisions in every single case, no matter what the circumstances.[87] MLR 2010, 73(5): 845

In my opinion, the contested Directive could indeed be validly enacted under Article 95, although it is acknowledged that … ECLR 2010, 6: 150

The cases of the first-person pronoun in the possessive form (*my*), as illustrated in (43), show the tendency of writers to avoid moving from exclusive to inclusive uses of pronouns in the same sentence. Yet, there were very few instances where they did not do so. This can be seen in the single-authored example (44) below, where the exclusive phrase (*in my view*) was juxtaposed with an unambiguously inclusive *we* pronoun in conditional clause to invite the reader and other community members to participate in an interactive discussion:

(44) The reason, therefore, why it is not natural to view any liability in a customer … is that the customer makes no firm commitment to pay them at all on concluding the contract. This can be seen, in my view, if we were to adopt the common law terminology of consideration used by Lord Walker, for a promise to pay money if the promisor chooses to do … .
MLR 2011, 74(1): 117

Admittedly, this moving strategy has a particular rhetorical effect since the inclusive (*we*) writer wished to make the reader apprehend his claim more quickly, and to gradually bring the reader around to the acceptance of his conditional argument. This strategy now brings me to consider inclusive *we* as part of engagement markers below.

Engagement markers

In the use of engagement markers, Table 12 shows that the writers explicitly addressed the readers in the text through inclusive *we* pronoun, directives, questions, and personal asides, used at varying distributional degrees.

Engagement markers: forms			
ECLR		MLR	
	N°		*N*°
We (*inclusive*)	18	We (*inclusive*)	94
Us	12	Our	22
Our	2	Us	25
Directives	119	Directives	205
Questions	35	Questions	128
		Personal asides	25
TOTAL	186	TOTAL	499

Table 12. Total occurrences of engagement markers.

Like the exclusive *I* pronoun failing to appear in all Discussions, as noted, inclusive *We* pronoun made its appearance in seven (out of ten) ECLR texts and eighteen (out of twenty) MLR texts. In terms of the occurrence frequencies, the stance projected by Discussion writers in *I* and *We*-persona depended, in general, on how they wished to relate their arguments to the readership in its community-based expectation.

An orientation to an interactive discussion with the reader and other members of the legal community can first be seen by the use of inclusive *we* in the single and co-authored examples (45) below:

(45) It is against this background that we must read *Cobbe* and *Thorner*, and in which we can understand the assertion that *Cobbe* marked the 'death of proprietary estoppel'.[93]MLR 2009, 72(6): 1009

What can an expert say about whether the suspect's shoe left the footwear mark at the scene? To answer this question we have to go back to basics. The need to do so is illustrated by the judgment … MLR 2011, 74(3): 445

Whereas widespread possession of knives substantially erodes security against being stabbed,[22] we might doubt that widespread possession of information that anyone can get hold of at any time substantially erodes security against terrorist attacks. MLR 2009, 72(6): 989

When the latter objective is at stake, the threshold, triggering the adoption of EC legislation, was set at a very low level, as we know from the most recent 'tobacco products' case-law,[112] .... ECLR 2010, 6: 157

In providing a systematic examination of the relevant law controlling the critical issue(s) in the case, these writers stood out as knowledgeable 'researchers' of those issues, and drew the audience into the understanding and elaboration of their arguments by expressly instructing the audience how to interpret the 'soft' data. And while elaborating arguments was meant to raise interestingness and novelty of the researched topic arising from the noteworthy case, inclusive *we* helped the writers to persuade the audience that their arguments were correct, thus creating solidarity in the disciplinary community.

Creating interestingness and novelty in the inclusive prose can also be seen in examples (46-47) below, however with different rhetorical effect. Here, inclusive *we* pronoun allowed the writers to refer forward or back to topics in order to draw the audience into their arguments:

(46) Instead, as we shall see below, the agreement may now be treated as determinative unless it would be unfair to do so. MLR 2011, 74(3): 436

As we have seen, the application of the general principle amounts to a *de facto* application of Directive 2000/78. ECLR 2010, 6: 308

or to sum up issues already covered:

(47) What we can see from this is that relatively little progress has been made in specifying the kind of information that falls within section 58(1). MLR 2009, 72(6): 988

Directives were the most frequent engagement devices after questions, and were used "to see things in a way determined by the writer", or similarly "to guide readers' reasoning" (Hyland 2005a: 154), thus securing the rhetorical objectives of the writers in their case-focused research. Directives were mostly signalled by obligation modals (e.g. *must*, *should*, *ought*), and less so by predicative adjectives with modal ('necessity') meaning and imperatives (e.g. *Assume that*, *let us*). By way of examples:

(48) It must be emphasised that the new tort has not been expunged from the armoury of precedent where it sits uneasily next to *Gregg* v *Scott*[34] and *Hotson* v *East Berkshire AHA*[35] in which the House of Lords … .
MLR 2011, 74(5): 781

… one should have regard to both the scope of the director's duties and the scope of the company's business. MLR 2011, 74(4): 600

The crux of this section is the prohibition on publishing a false statement of fact that relates to the candidate's 'personal character or conduct'. This should be distinguished from statements relating to the candidate 'public' character. MLR 2011, 74(4): 610

(49) In grasping the full dimension of these matters it is necessary to clarify some broader points about the nature of EU criminal law cooperation and the function of mutual recognition more generally. MLR 2010, 73(5): 832

To illustrate what an expert can say about evidence let us use the example of paternity evidence. MLR 2011, 74(3): 445

That element can, of course, already be included in the proportionality test by national law, but to the extent that that is not the case, it must be examined separately. ECLR 2011, 7: 144

One must take into consideration that rights connected to Union citizenship, such as the right of petition, can be exercised from the member state of which a person is a national without that person ever having made use of … ECLR 2011, 7: 147

However, a general judicial protection against arbitrariness implies that it must be possible to argue in court that the answer given on the question was (also) correct, … ECLR 2011, 7: 159

First, it should be noted that when the member states, among them France, accepted the Treaty of the European Union and … . ECLR 2010, 6: 125

Questions were preeminently "the strategy of dialogic involvement, inviting engagement and bringing the interlocutor into an arena where they can be led to the writer's viewpoint" (Hyland 2005a: 153). As shown in the set of examples (50) below, this kind of rhetorical strategy allowed the writers to go on to answer the question in the text, and the concrete or measurable answer to the controlling issue(s) in the case was therefore opinion-based:

(50) Where they are not in a position to know the truth of such allegations, can they really be said to be the 'sovereign' arbiters of such a campaign? Unfortunate though it is, wherever the courts are obliged to interfere in democratic politics, there is no other way of protecting the integrity of an election. MLR 2011, 74(4): 614

Does *Radmacher* deliver a devastating blow? We may start by noting that English law does not create any community of property or joint ownership of assets *during* marriage, … . MLR 2011, 74(3): 441

This in turn raises two questions: (a) should there be a threshold at all and, if so, (b) is its formulation in the Children Act 1989 the right one? We have no doubt that a threshold is needed. It would simply not be human rights compliant to base intervention solely on the welfare principle.
MLR 2009 72(3): 474

What about the employers Mr. Helm and the company Swedex? Their legal position is negatively affected as a result of the invocation of the Union general principle of non- discrimination based on age. Mr Helm faces the invalidity of his contract … . ECLR 2010, 6: 307

The question remains: which practical implications could the decision have? One answer might be: the decision tries to make the ECJ be more sensitive to member-states' constitutional grievances. ECLR 2011, 7: 166

While in these cases the interpersonal nature of the texts was enhanced by question raising, the dialogic use of inclusive *we* pronoun in answer-giving was still crucial to enhance such interpersonality. Yet, there were very few instances where questions were used in subheaded titles appearing in **bold** face, and helped to position the writer in relation to other (often judicial officers') arguments, and thereafter to be answered throughout, as in:

(51) But is this an appropriate or necessary implication in an agency contract?

In *Abu Dhabi National Tanker Company* v *Product Star Shipping limited (The Product Star) (No 2)*[18] Leggatt LJ said:
'For the purposes of judicial review … .' MLR 2010, 73(6): 1040

Personal asides were observed in MLR alone, where they appeared as parenthetical remarks ( ) in rather few cases. While, in general, personal asides were interruptions in text where the writers gave (parenthetical) departures or digressions, the metadiscoursal use of asides allowed for "a relationship between participants which does not depend on an assessment of what content needs to be made explicit: they are interventions simply to connect" (Hyland 2005a: 153). By way of examples:

(52) Though MAK argued that his membership of a tight-knit Muslim community and the widespread knowledge of his accusations (apparently reaching all the way to India) provided such an element, these aggravating factors were not deemed severe enough. MLR 2010, 73(6): 1030

Regardless of whether we approve of these minority views (and these examples must be among the least sympathetic), why should they not be part of democratic debate? MLR 2009 72(3): 482

Conclusion

In this descriptive study, I have sought to offer a comprehensive and pragmatically grounded analysis of metadiscourse in the Discussion section of the expert case note genre, by demonstrating how the use of metadiscourse resources facilitates interpersonal relationships in disciplinary academic writing.

Overall data show that there were not substantial variations in the use of interactive and interactional categories of metadiscourse between the ECLR and MLR Discussion corpus, where such categories were only accounted for by the tenuously more interactive uses when setting out an argument. The ECLR corpus, however, contained more interactive resources which allowed the writers to refer more heavily to textual features than in the MLR corpus, where writers indeed employed slightly more interactional resources to engage the readers into more discursively detailed arguments and perspectives. Although these varying distributions across interactive and interactional forms may partly be attributable to the MLR Discussion sections being slightly longer than the ECLR Discussion sections, it is argued that they were dependent on the preferences that the journal writers accorded to the particular socio-rhetorical activity of metadiscourse.

In the interactive uses of metadiscourse, writers were more concerned with semantic and pragmatic relations between ideas by the use of transitions, but were still cautious to contextualize their case-focused research by attributing borrowed material from legal sources (evidential) and explaining or specifying information (code glosses). In the interactional uses, however, writers were more concerned with the degree of commitment to their claims and evaluative viewpoints by hedges than by boosters, and the varying incidence of such devices depended upon the rationale of content when constructing the same material in the epistemology of case-focused legal research. Both hedging and boosting were important communicative resources by which the writers acknowledged the potential viewpoints of readers, and similarly construed and achieved persuasion in interpersonal discourse. While interpersonal relations in the examined data were also established by the important *if*-conditionals, as hypotheticality functional resources with hedging effect, deciding whether an argument was weak (hedging) or strong (boosting) demonstrated that academic evaluation cannot be solely guided by established 'rules' arising from the investigated case. Ultimately, evaluation depends upon the writer's 'personal' ability to see similar rules in order to solve some contestations in the chosen case, and needs to incorporate the voices of different participants in respect of the disciplinary content formed in Discussion, where the collaborative, yet indeed competing, worlds of the legal academy and the profession often come into play. Given this content, writers took up different positions by expressing their positive or negative attitude to propositional information (attitude markers) and building a relationship with disciplinary readers (engagement markers), and decided to adopt an exclusive or inclusive authorial presence as the context of their research required.

On the whole, interpersonal metadiscourse features were crucial for community writers to construct a competent critical argument in Discussion texts, and to present effective, consistent prose based on factual and legal analyses of evidence and inference from the chosen case. The fact that Discussion writers were engaged with case note inquiries by expressing critical positions about noteworthy issues in the case meant that metadiscourse strategies were important to promote and advance disciplinary knowledge around these issues. Case note-driven inquiries created new ideas and interpretations in the disciplinary forum by locating writers in their own epistemological, ontological and ideological sites of culturally-shared writing practices. And while shared knowledge practices were rooted in the very social activity of the case note genre, writing metadiscoursively defined the ways in which Discussion writers conveyed their personality, credibility, and evaluation of legal research material in appropriate interaction with the reader.

PART II:

ABSTRACTING LEGAL RESEARCH

CHAPTER FOUR

LAW RESEARCH ARTICLE ABSTRACTS: RHETORICAL MOVE-STRUCTURE AND LINGUISTIC REALIZATIONS

In the previous Chapters I focused at length on Case Notes as the least researched genre in the applied linguistic landscape. Now I wish to concentrate my attention on the Law Research Article Abstract, one of the most researched genres among applied linguists within and across disciplines.

It is hard to disbelieve that the academic law abstract is often in the public view and creates an impression of the writer's research work around various parts: motivation, problem statement, approach, results, and conclusions. Despite the fact that these parts result in the brevity of the abstract, they must do almost as much work as the multi-page paper that follows the abstract, and similarly increase the chance of people taking the time to obtain and read the paper. Relevance of 'abstracting' thus becomes the source of inspiration for the current analysis. But while much has been said about 'abstracting', little knowledge exists about the rhetorical and linguistic realizations of 'abstracting' in the law discipline.

In this Chapter, therefore, I briefly outline the existing literature and indicate the importance of law abstract writing together with the focus of my research objectives. I then present the empirical material and the research methodology, and finally discuss the impact of material and method on the findings and draw some tentative conclusions.

Literature Review

The genre of the RA abstract and its variation across disciplines and cultures has formed the subject of much academic discourse research over the last two decades (e.g. Salager-Meyer 1990, 1992; Tibbo 1992; Bhatia 1993; Ventola 1994; Santos 1996; Melander et al. 1997; Huckin 2001; Martín-Martín 2002; Samraj 2002a, 2005; Dahl 2004; Hyland 2004; Bondi 2004, 2005; Bondi and Silver 2004; Bondi and Cavalieri 2012; Lorés 2004; Stotesbury 2003, 2005, 2006a/b; Bonn and Swales 2007; Breeze

2009; Bellés-Fortuño and Querol-Julían 2010; Burgess and Martín-Martín 2010). These descriptive studies identify the characteristic rhetorical organization and the various formal features realizing the abstract moves, including explicit evaluative language from a cross-cultural perspective. The multifaceted research emerging from these invaluable studies provides evidence of the academic abstract as an important "part-genre" in the research article (Swales 2004: 239), on account of the tons of published research articles where abstracts are crucial for helping readers locate specific research in the academic landscape. And while the argument has been made for research article abstracts to be necessarily different from research articles in terms of function, rhetorical structure and linguistic realizations (Lorés 2004), article abstracts are no less relevant than other article sections, such as the introductions (Swales and Najar 1987; Swales 1990, 2004). Rhetorical descriptions of introductions, in fact, have also been shown to form generic interrelations with those of the research abstracts (Samraj 2005) and, despite similar interrelations, both academic abstracts and introductions remain somehow controversial, in terms of the different macro-organizations which fulfil different communicative purposes (Bhatia 1993: 76-93).

Research abstract in academic legal scholarship

Despite the many invaluable studies of the part-genre in the research article across the academic disciplines, the abstract genre in the discipline of Law has remained largely neglected among academic discourse and genre scholars. Little in fact is known about the macro and micro structures of law abstracts, which are part of the large amount of published law research articles.

The important role of the legal abstract genre in legal scholarship is led by the international community of legal scholars, who constantly report a considerable amount of research in major English medium international language journals dealing with current legal issues. In general, analysing such issues means reporting new and original research results or reviewing existing results, and this kind of academic work usually relies on the publication of the scholarly abstract and the accompanying article. These kinds of publications therefore allow the law journals to be an excellent resource for distributing academic research output and scholarship, and the formally published academic works inevitably become the sources for contributing to knowledge in the law field, in the same way as publishing in other academic fields contributes to *disciplinary knowledge* (Hyland and Bondi 2006). In this process, where the international community of scholars is involved, it is no surprise that English stands as "a genuine *lingua franca*" (Swales 2004: 43, italics in the original), or has a global function (Flowerdew and Gotti 2006) facilitating academic exchange in such journals (Wood 2001), and as a consequence boosts a globalised orientation to academic legal research. [1] This is illustrated by the proliferation of law journals with 'global' or 'international' in their titles, where re-elaborations of national, international or comparative law fields are significantly introduced for the worldwide audience. In other words, a global(ised) picture of legal research here brings into focus discussions about 'global law' or 'global legal culture' that transcends the national legal boundaries. [2] The results of such denationalised boundaries are useful not only because they set the context for a more global discipline of the law concerned with all levels of legal relations, but also because they allow English to be the *de facto* global language of scholarly legal communication where a plurality of legal paradigms are increasingly blended together.

However, in the current age of massive information, the law abstract becomes even greater in importance if we attend to the availability of disciplinary e-journals, which provide easier access to legal scholarship in a variety of law areas. As a matter of fact, electronic access enables the readers to browse through the research abstract in order to quickly obtain the information they want, and to identify the research articles they are mostly interested in. By acting as a point-of-entry for any one research paper in the discipline, the abstract therefore enables the widest readership to decide quickly whether or not to pursue the full content of the legal research article, as noted in several studies across the disciplines. Clearly, the writers' chances of their research article being selected for reading will depend on the strategic use of structural features in the abstract, since a well-organized abstract can attract more readers and make them want to learn more about the research project. Where the abstract is expected to give a good snapshot of the academic value in the law article, the close relationship between the two writing systems will obviously provide the tool for any individual scholar to further the progress of legal scholarship

[1] In this context, the global function of the English language is part of the more general phenomenon of 'English as an international language' (EIL) or 'World Englishes' (e.g. McArthur 1998; Jenkins 2003), along with 'English as a global language' (e.g. Crystal 2003), among other labels.

[2] Viewed from different law areas, the global phenomenon of legal research issues is already clear by transnational fields of study, such as environmental law, family law, public international law, internet law, international criminal law, international crime, transitional justice, and so on.

in their specific research topic. And this, in turn, allows for the new and relevant ideas and arguments developed not to be impervious to the newsworthy information, as is traditionally of the scientific journal article (Berkenkotter and Huckin 1995; Melander et al. 1997).

Realistically, open access publishing through e-journals are a good fit for furthering such progress and projecting newsworthy information[3], since the publication of abstracts and accompanying articles in online repositories not only ensures quick dissemination of legal scholarship, but also increases the authors' visibility and strategies in the advancement of legal research and, in general, the academic value system. And while the commitment to such a value carries with it a responsibility by all participants in the scholarly communication process, whether as academics (authors) or institutions (journals), the availability of e-journals provides ways for strengthening the academic legal community by enhancing communication for the widest readership, whether between legal scholars, between legal scholars and practitioners (attorneys, judges, lawyers), and the wider public, across national and international barriers. This way then, electronic publishing ensures the public's right of access to community scholarship, where legal knowledge is foregrounded in the research abstract and detailed in the research article.

In this study, I wish to contribute to analytical research studies conducted so far, by investigating how the academic community of legal scholars 'abstract' their research article publications. The purpose of this study will therefore be twofold: firstly, to explore the organizational (move-based) patterns of discourse which shape the construction and use of this genre among disciplinary writers and, secondly, to examine the main lexico-grammatical features that realize the generic moves across legal research article abstracts. As again, I shall look for significant features of variability or standardization in the writing of the genre.

[3] Yet, as I footnoted in Chapter 1, a robust account of open (electronic) access publishing is also given by (expert) live-blogging (UKSCblog), used mainly for talking about the law of practice in professional legal discourse. While this internet-based venue equally serves to project newsworthy information about important topics raised in a particular field of law through Case Comments, it also provides the vehicle for focused discussion of a particular idea or point of view between legal practitioners and scholars. For scholars, therefore, the digitally-based venue provides an opportunity to broaden the academic legal discourse beyond law practitioners' blogs.

Data and Method

Text corpus

As shown in Table 1, a total (synchronic) corpus of 150 electronically retrieved, peer-reviewed (single and co-authored) RA abstracts were randomly selected in a set of 30 samples from each of the five academic Oxford University Press Journals published online in the 2007-2011 issues – namely, *British Journal of Criminology: An International Review of Crime and Society* (BJC), *Oxford Journal of Legal Studies* (OJLS), *Industrial Law Journal* (ILJ), *International Journal of Transitional Justice* (IJTJ), and *Journal of International Economic Law* (JIEL).

OUP Journal	2007	2008	2009	2010	2011	TOTAL
British Journal of Criminology	6	2	4	8	10	30
Oxford Journal of Legal Studies	6	5	6	3	10	30
Industrial Law Journal	5	5	6	9	5	30
International Journal of Transitional Justice	-	6	8	10	6	30
Journal of International Economic Law	-	7	8	11	4	30
TOTAL	17	25	32	41	35	150

Table 1. Number and publication year of abstracts collected from each OUP Journal and total number of abstracts.

As with Case Notes examined before, the method for corpus selection reflects the highly reputable journals which provide the English language medium for publication in a wide range of topics for a variety of international focused readers, whether as academics, researchers, lawyers, or government officials. As a result of the impact of technology, allowing many reputable publishers to move towards electronic (rather than solely paper-bound) publishing, law journals afforded much useful information by allowing the Title, Abstract, Keywords and Article to be electronically filed and stored. Based on the affordances of searchability, portability and accessibility, the academic legal literature in the e-journal database used the abstract as a stand-alone entity, which thus resulted in being dynamic and user-responsive for the current study.

Due to the different material falling within the purview of the journals, abstract authors were encouraged to include interdisciplinary material in areas of relevance for their research submission. Interdisciplinary approaches to law, in particular, may be seen in the JIEL journal where a broad range of subjects concerned the relation of law to international economic activity. Other journals, such as OJLS and BJC, generally focused on questions of legal interest, but were still sensitive to the issues arising from the relationship of law to other disciplines. Thus, for instance, BJC invited authors to focus on jurisprudential, sociological, psychological, political or other perspectives in order to account for the interface between crime and society as a topic of socio-legal interest.

In the journals, more than half of selected abstracts were written by English native authors affiliated mostly to academic law institutions in the UK, USA, Australia and Canada. Their Anglophone status was controlled by author names and supported by personal e-mail communication with respective journal boards. The remaining abstracts were mostly written by US or European-based authors whose names connoted non-Anglophone status, as supported again by personal e-mail communication. These 'non-native' authors underwent language editing before submission, in a context where abstracting services were not provided to either (native/non-native) category of author. The majority of native and non-native authors held senior academic status while the minority had junior academic roles.

Based on these criteria and requirements for corpus building, different quantitative data were obtained in each set of the journal abstracts, as shown in Table 2. The main data source for this study was a 23,545 word corpus which covered a total of 829 sentences based on a total average of 28.21 words per sentence. A list of abstract titles and journal source is provided in Appendixes.

	TOTAL	BJC	ILJ	JIEL	OJLS	IJTJ
Tokens	23,545	4,129	3,991	5,392	5,132	4,901
Types	4,173	1,378	1,224	1,468	1,524	1,484
Type/Token ratio (TTR)	17.84	33.71	31.10	27.36	29.75	30.43
Standardised TTR	50.01	41.05	42.82	46.28	45.87	42.76
Mean word length (in characters)	5.48	5.61	5.38	5.52	5.31	5.58
Sentences	829	152	137	187	175	178
Mean (in words)	28.21	26.89	28.73	28.69	29.27	27.39

Table 2. Different quantitative data in each set of the abstracts and totals as retrieved from Scott WordSmith Tool 5.0

Law research article abstracts: definition and purpose

The various sources used for data analysis were associated with conventional definitions and purpose of the representative texts.

It has been argued that the abstract is a "description or factual summary of the much longer report" (Bhatia 1993: 78), a summary of the salient points of the article (Berkenkotter and Huckin 1995), or a "selective representation" of the article content (Hyland 2004: 64). Besides these established definitions, it has been argued that abstracts "have both a more modest and more urgent purpose: to persuade readers that the article is worth reading" (Hyland 2004: 64)[4], and persuasion is achieved by elements of "promotion" in abstracts (Hyland 2004: 75-78). In addition to persuasion, then, the argument is made that abstracts need to project "a convincing and authoritative image" of the work summarized by the writers (Swales and Feak 2003: 39).

Based on these theoretical understandings, and far from stating the obvious, law abstracts were no different from other disciplines since they were concise, factual previews of the article content by depicting the writer's cultural know-how pursued in the article. As such, law abstracts were important instruments of scholarly legal communication where writers sought to convince the academic readership of the importance and validity of their research. In general, the characteristic features of a valid and convincing research previewed in the abstracts were fact-finding (i.e. to describe and to interpret what the law is on a particular subject), fact-systematizing, and describing legal policy and trends the writers were constantly engaged in their empirical or theoretical research articles. Given these features, the informative purpose of law abstracts not only helped to disseminate and promote the writers' research work around the various rhetorical parts, but the possibilities inherent in the electronically published abstracts and accompanying articles paved the way for the open access to disciplinary knowledge which, in turn, accelerated the process of scholarly legal communication.

[4] This argument is made as part of the distinction between the abstract and the article. According to Hyland (2004: 64), "[t]he research article is a codification of disciplinary knowledge, where writers seek to persuade their communities to accept their claims and certify them as recognized and legitimate knowledge".

The epistemology of published legal scholarship

Prior to reporting the analytical data in the chosen genre, it is important to familiarize the reader with the actual nature of legal research (or legal scholarship) carried out by academic legal authors in the current corpus.

The immediate procedure for identifying the research styles was to attend to the content of the law research articles by reading the journal articles. Here, authors made a clear-cut distinction between research undertaken for a prevailingly academic readership and applied research designed for the needs of practitioners and policy-makers and, in such distinctions, authors were clearly concerned with "an original elaboration of disciplinary knowledge" (Bondi 2006: 57). Based on such distinctions, and as law faculty informants also made it explicit, two available modes of inquiry were identified in the research journals: theoretical (doctrinal) and empirical research methodologies.[5]

On the (meta) theoretical side of the enquiry, authors analyzed and expounded the law on particular issues with reference to primary (legislation) and secondary sources (case law), while also presenting new methodological approaches for addressing such issues. In these approaches, theoretical research focused on the doctrinal analysis of law (i.e. the formulation of legal doctrines) through the analysis of legal rules which, in Anglo-American (Common Law) territorial jurisdictions, are commonly known to be rooted in statutes and cases. Characterized by the study of legal texts in those sources of law, the methodology of doctrinal research came to describe the "black-letter law" tradition of legal exegesis in legal parlance (Arthurs 1983; Card 2002). Yet, doctrinal research was also driven by policy considerations about the political, economic or social implications for law reform, legislation, or case-law in the current state of the law. Epistemologically, then, theoretical investigators provided an answer to their policy research question by offering interpretive, qualitative analyses required by doctrinal research – whether by means of

[5] Apart from the identification of the research method(s) by reading the journal articles, other relevant data were identified in the journal articles. Here, in general, discourse tended to be epistemically grounded (that is, concerned with the production of knowledge and the different knowledge claims) and presented linguistically by nominalizations, agentless passive constructions, and almost plain syntax. Graphs or other visual aids were used only sparingly (that is, when required by the subjects covered) to convey stylistic and rhetorical features in the texts. Extensive use of "integral" and "non-integral" (Swales 1990) citations in a variety of sources (academic and professional) added to the discourse style in the law journal articles.

legislation or judicial development through the relevant courts. The current reader may catch a glimpse of this later in this analysis through some theoretical abstracts, which inquired into the 'doctrine of reportage' (within the law of tort) or the 'Default Retirement Age', where authors applied the relevant legal rules to the peculiar facts of the situation in order to find and develop legal doctrines.

On the empirical side of the enquiry, by contrast, authors (re-)examined empirical research in the light of observations, experience, or experiments, and rhetorically used a set of contemporary quantitative, qualitative as well as comparative research in real-world data. Typically, quantitative and qualitative research involved case studies, control groups, surveys, interviews and participant observation, used as empirical methods to generate quantitative as well as qualitative data. Unlike traditional doctrinal analysis of law, the epistemological nature of legal research placed more emphasis on the understanding of law as a social phenomenon.[6] As a matter of fact, this form of legal research is often described as *law in context* or *socio-legal research* in legal parlance (e.g. Cownie 2004) to emphasize the important distinction between the doctrinal research (rarely used for law practicality) and the law in context, which thus embraces the broader social, economic and political context.[7] Reasonably, therefore, the stronger tendency towards the observation of law and legal institutions as social entities among Anglo-American legal authors in the abstracts suggested a proper notion of empirical legal research 'in action'. This not only allowed for wider intellectual debates about law and its social goals but, most importantly, enriched the interpretation and application of law in different areas by giving rise to an evolving area of knowledge and expertise. As a result of the importance of empirical scholarship in accounting for the relationship between law and society, authors produced more empirically than theoretically grounded

[6] Support to this understanding of legal research also comes from a number of legal commentators (see Osborn 2001; Greenfield and Osborn 2006, among others). By challenging the traditional hegemony of doctrinal legal analysis (the "black-letter law"), these authors argue for broader, social approaches to the agenda of law (as well as to legal curricula) in Anglo-American contexts, where socio-legal empirical research tends to be the dominant approach to legal scholarship.

[7] Not coincidentally, the broader scope of Anglo-speaking legal studies, including empirical legal research in its wider social, economic and political context, has formed the subject of the (*UK*) *Nuffield Inquiry on Empirical Legal Research* (2006), which focuses on "how legal processes, outcomes and structures operate in the 'real world'" (2006: 1, The Inquiry - <http://www.ucl.ac..uk/laws/socio-legal/ empirical>).

research articles, and the methodological distinction was reflected in the accompanying abstracts.

In this context where, as noted, both modes of enquiry were also typically driven by the purview of the journals for submission, the result was that theoretical and empirical enquiries often tended towards descriptive and normative forms of legal research (as faculty informants also made this explicit), although sometimes the two forms overlapped in the same journal article and resulting abstract. In the descriptive approach, authors aimed primarily at gathering knowledge (i.e. descriptions and explanations) about the object of study in an attempt to find out ‘how things are’. In the normative approach, on the other hand, authors aimed to define ‘how things should be’, as in Kelsen’s (1976) normative nature of legal rules. In this framework, therefore, theoretical and empirical approaches provided the argumentative tools for authors to demonstrate knowledge of the researchable issues, and the degree to which their articles, as summarized in the abstracts, systematically contributed new scholarly knowledge in the law discipline.

Interdisciplinarity in published legal scholarship

The notion of a legal research ‘in action’ can best be understood by its interdisciplinary goals pursued through a range of neighbouring disciplines.

In this respect, the debate over which particular discipline the law may fall under has led legal commentators to commonly address the law as a social science (Harwell 2002), or as belonging to one of the social science disciplines or to a humanities discipline (Howarth 2004). Rather similarly, the debate raised in the context of academic writing for different disciplines has been to address the law as an academic knowledge continuum of applied disciplines, such as business studies, health and social welfare (Coffin et al. 2003: 66-67), which “rest on science, social science or humanities foundations” (Coffin et al. 2003: 48).

These arguments show that it is rather difficult to categorize the discipline of academic law in terms of a monolithic entity in that the law disciplinarity emerges as one which crosses the boundaries between the sciences, social sciences and the humanities. Such leaky boundaries therefore provide an interdisciplinary understanding of law where the model of boundary work operates in such a way as to take account of a range of contributing disciplines that produce a common, yet indeed unifying whole of, legal research despite those disciplinary differences. The result of this interdisciplinary process is one which emphasizes a pragmatically collaborative engagement, based on the dialectics of multi-modal law necessary for socio-legal research. Such engagement was reflected in the methods of scholarly enquiry used in the abstracts and associated articles, where the writers drew on other disciplinary processes and procedures to accommodate their own intradisciplinary content, purpose, and texts based on the proclaimed objectives of legal norms. Clearly, this multi-modal approach was a matter of epistemology and practice conceived in the context of the law disciplinary culture, which then allowed the writers to engage in an evolving area of collaborative knowledge and expertise. Allied with the culture framework was the drive towards interdisciplinarity in Law (as reflected indeed in the journal policy), which required knowledgeable writers to discuss emerging law issues by useful and important references to other disciplines, such as Economics, Sociology, Political Science, Psychology, Philosophy, Ethics, and so on. These references were vital to conduct a wider contextual work about law and other social formations with which the legal inquiry interacted, and as a consequence served to establish productive (and hence collaborative) relations with other disciplinary concepts, theories, and values. As such, interdisciplinary work testified to the variety of scholarly endeavours in fostering new, wider avenues of legal research, which were represented in the broader social context of human action. By providing collaborative ways of thinking and writing at various levels of legal inquiry, interdisciplinarity also became the necessary interdiscursive engagement, offering a consistent and compatible methodology for the description, interpretation, and explanation of law in published legal scholarship.

Methodology

Corpus abstracts were manually analysed for their rhetorical move structure, and computer screened for other formal (micro) linguistic patterns realized in the generic moves. Specific lexical features in less-explicit authorial references were however analysed through a concordance software, Scott WordSmith Tools 5.0, used to run the frequency word counts on the corpus.

The analysis of the rhetorical organization was carried out using primarily the macrostructure of the research article (IMRD – Introduction, Methods, Results, Discussion), as often proposed in the literature (e.g. Nwogu 1990; Swales 1990; Bhatia 1993; Ventola 1994; Martín-Martín 2002), and resulting in four Moves: Purpose, Methods, Results and Conclusions (Bhatia 1993: 78-79). This analytical tool was integrated by other rhetorical move strategies employed in the Swalesian's (2004) revised CARS model for introductions. The reason for the integrated tools was to accommodate the writer's individual choice in producing the abstracts, and therefore to present a fuller picture of the structure of the rhetorical moves employed in the collected abstracts. Considering that abstracts were presented in a limited rhetorical space, the importance attached to different moves and steps by the authors in the corpus was inferred by their recurrence in the abstracts. In this study, moves and steps, viewed as "rhetorical instruments that realize a sub-set of specific communicative purposes associated with a genre" (Bhatia, 2001: 84), formed the units of analysis. The rationale for assigning discourse roles to rhetorical moves and steps was functional, realized by clause or sentence, although it was possible to identify their functions also through a variety of grammatical and lexical features in a text segment (Bhatia 1993: 87; Swales 1990, 2004: 229).

The analysis of the linguistic patterns realized in generic moves was carried out by a combination of theoretical tools for authorial presence and agency (e.g. Ivanič 1998; Hinkel 2001; Hewings and Hewings 2002; Hyland 1999b, 2004, 2005a/b; Hyland and Tse 2005).

Results and Discussion

In this section, I discuss the most salient results and hypotheses from the quantitative and qualitative analyses of the corpus abstracts.

The macrostructure of abstracts: move frequency

Firstly, the frequency of moves was explored in the journal abstracts, yielding the raw data reported in Table 3:

	BJC	ILJ	JIEL	OJLS	IJTJ	Total
Establishing a territory Move 1	14	10	16	14	19	73
Establishing a niche Move 2	5	2	2	5	7	21
Introduction / Purpose	39	49	51	36	42	217
Method	33	16	14	15	31	109
Results	27	19	21	22	26	115
Discussion / Conclusion	21	12	19	13	18	83
TOTAL	139	108	123	105	143	618

Table 3. Move frequency in the corpus: occurrences.

Of the total moves occurring in the corpus (618), Introduction/Purpose was the most frequently occurring move (217) followed by Results (115), Method (109), Discussion/Conclusion (83) and *Establishing a territory* move (73), down to *Establishing a niche* move (21).

Leaving aside Move 1 and Move 2, as they will be dealt with later in this analysis, I begin with an illustration of the Introduction/Purpose-Method-Results-Discussion/Conclusion moves, as derived from Bhatia's (1993: 78-79) formal descriptions of abstract patterns, and integrated with further linguistic elements characterising such moves in the corpus.

Moves: linguistic signals

Introduction/Purpose Move: the author's intentions, theses or hypotheses as well as goals of the legal research were generally signalled in syntax and lexis in present tense, and the lexical signals of verbs functioned to explain the rhetorical element of the Purpose move. Purpose elements were often indicated by subject noun-phrases/verb collocations, as in the sets of examples in (1), and less so by copulative complements in 'identifying be' clauses, as in (2), where the noun phrase also typically drew on a predictable repertoire of 'purposive' lexis:

(1) *This article examines* legal and geopolitical aspects of the China-Taiwan Economic Cooperation Framework Agreement (ECFA). ... IJEL

This article examines <u>whether</u> prisoners' children have more adult convictions than children whose parents were convicted but not imprisoned . ... BJC

This paper pursues a line of enquiry regarding employment laws which promulgate standards (rather than rules), the legitimacy of which is premised on the need to scrutinize managerial autonomy pursuant to a norm-setting, rather than norm-reflecting agenda. ... ILJ

(2) *The aim of this article is to* examine the relationship between trust, testimony and truth recovery processes as part of post-conflict transition. ... IJTJ

The purpose of this study is to better understand the crime-commission process of clandestine drug laboratories and identify significant points for intervention by using crime scripts. ... BJC

Method Move: the author's methodology was indicated by the main procedures, criteria or conditions used in the empirical legal research. Expressing *how* (the *means*), the author was able to carry out his/her research presented in typical language features, namely: the preference for present tense verbs rather than past passive verbs, inanimate nouns (e.g. *article, study, analysis*) with active present verbs, and sometimes *I/we* present tense constructions. Linguistic signals of *means* used to achieve research goals included participial phrases and prepositional structures (e.g. *drawing, by+, on+, with+, by using/the use of*):

(3) ... *Drawing on 37 life-history interviews conducted in 2006*, we find that *gacaca* reinforces a particular version of postgenocide justice that renders the average Rwandan citizen largely powerless over individual processes of reconciliation while serving to maintain a climate of fear and insecurity in their everyday lives. ... IJTJ

... The article broadens our understanding of precarious work *by offering the term 'multiple work relationships' as a prism through which to look at various situations where employing and working functions are distributed among several people or entities. ...* ILJ

... *Taking advantage of a unique set of homicide narratives drawn from court and police records in the Udmurt Republic*, this study examines stability and change in the distribution of Russian homicide victim, offender, and incident characteristics before and after the fall of the Soviet Union. ... BJC

This article describes the various provisions of REACH *by comparing REACH to the prevailing chemicals management regime in the world's second major importer of chemicals, the United States*. It finds that REACH reverses the burden of proof ... . JIEL

By contrast, the author's methodology in theoretical research was indicated by the general reference to the legal works and/or analytical methods of other scholars. Referencing, however, lacked in the parenthetical form, such as by citing Author, Year, Page, and appeared as: *Drawing on Daly's work on familial justice, this paper investigates the role of the family ...* . (OJLS). In this system, the general reference to other theoretical works was sufficient to indicate an interpersonal dimension in relation to the rhetorical tenor of the text (Hyland 1999a; Thompson 2005), and to be constitutive of the academic knowledge exchange in the disciplinary community being invoked. Although found only in few cases (15 theoretical abstracts), general references to academic sources allowed the authors in 3 abstracts to follow on previous methods, theories or studies as in the *Daly's work* referencing example above, or to criticize and reject such methods, models or theories in 9 abstracts through grammatically or semantically negative lexis (such as: *I argue that Murphy's moral argument yields relatively limited results, and that his epistemological arguments do not succeed in showing that ... / In this article, I critically evaluate the positions of Professors Jeremy Waldron and ... / I argue that NJT is true under none of these interpretations*). Only in 3 abstracts did authors indicate cognitive gaps in previous research (such as: *This article fills a gap in the literature ...*).[8]

Results Move: the author's summary of findings drawn from purpose or method was indicated in the research being reported and appeared mainly in present tense, with past tense however occurring only occasionally (*The evaluation found that the sites had a number of impacts on the young people who visited them, ...*). While the verb form *find* generally distinguished this move, signalling results was also presented in the form of an argument with the verb choice *argue* in the reporting of empirical and theoretical research.[9] This can be seen in the *italicised* set of examples below:

(4) ... *We argue that international investment law is, in the short term due to legal and extra-legal factors, more likely than any other area of international economic law to give rise to initiation of legal action and examine the most probable substantive norms likely to be violated.* IJEL

... This article describes and critiques the 14 individual opinions expressed to-date; discusses related legal issues; and compares the position in other international courts. *It argues that the WTO strikes a balance by permitting*

---

[8] In this study, I draw on the terminology used in Stotesbury's (2003, 2006a) analyses of negative evaluation in research article abstracts, defining five different critical speech acts – namely, cognitive gaps, criticism of previous research, criticism of a previous theory/model/method, criticism in the discussion/conclusions, and innovation in the field. Only cognitive gaps, criticism of previous research, and criticism of a previous theory/model/method were identified in my corpus.

[9] On this point, I follow Hyland's (2004) description of the "Product" move in research abstracts. According to Hyland (2004: 69), "Essentially a product is an outcome, or what the paper achieves. In the soft disciplines this is often an argument, where writers discuss or address a topic rather than report research findings".

individual opinions, if in the report and anonymous; but that 10 of the 14 were incorrect or unnecessary, and the others avoidable. ... IJEL

... This article explores the development of victim rights in sentencing through a comparative analysis of the rights of family victims in homicide sentencing proceedings across Australia, the United States, England and Wales and Canada. *Of the various rights afforded to victims of crime, the use of family victim impact evidence in the sentencing of homicide offenders proves most contentious, ...* OJLS

... Unlike prior research on race/ethnicity in which minority offenders are often found to be more harshly treated by sentencing courts, *we find that Indigenous status has no direct effect on the decision to imprison, after adjusting for other sentencing factors (especially past and current criminality). ...* BJC

We find that there is a high failure rate of complainants' cases, that success rates vary across types of representation and that a disproportionate number of claimants are from the public sector. ILJ

Discussion/Conclusion Move: the authors drew conclusions from their findings by commenting or interpreting results in present tense claims. Here, authors tended to narrow down or widen out the findings to the scope of the research by including explicit announcements of discussion/conclusion (*are discussed / The authors conclude*) also in the form of a final argument (*It argues that*), signals of implication (*The major implications for*), recommendation (*The findings emphasize the need for / evaluations should proceed*), suggestion (*Suggestions are made*), gap issues for current research (*It remains to be seen*), or expressing doubtful speculation (*The article questions how*), as in:

(5) ... The implications of these findings are discussed in the context of recent policy developments. BJC

… The authors conclude by welcoming the draft recommendations from the Council of Europe's Parliamentary Assembly to draw up a set of guidelines for the protection of whistle blowers and consider drafting a framework convention. ILJ

... The article concludes with a syncretist view – that interpretive, ideal-based evaluations should proceed alongside positivist impact assessments. IJTJ

... The findings emphasize the need for rigorous, ongoing evaluation of transitional justice processes to appreciate properly the complex and dynamic nature of individual attitudes and the influence of emergent events. IJTJ

... The major implications for accessing employment rights are considered and the article concludes by making a series of recommendations for reform. ILJ

... It remains to be seen, however, whether the participants in the bargaining process have the commitment and capacity to enable the legislation to re-collectivise the labour market in any significant way. ILJ

... Suggestions are made for either adjusting the facilitative mediation model or seeking an alternative that complements existing dispute resolution services, particularly those provided by ACAS. ILJ

... The article questions how such impacts relate to wider social processes (for example, human rights reform, violence prevention and transitional justice) and how social and political processes ... It argues that transitional processes can make better use of the specific resources memorial sites have to offer. IJTJ

While logical connectors (e.g. *however, thus*) occurred only sparingly in this move, and general knowledge claims through epistemic modality markers (e.g. *may*, *possible*, *suggest*) occurred when so required by the context, authors sometimes tended to conclude by evaluating the efficiency of their research through lexical items such as *valuable, new, important*. While these items functioned as attitude markers, conveying positive evaluation (Thompson and Hunston 2000) and similarly projecting a positive image of the researcher, they also served as "promotional" (Berkenkotter and Huckin 1995) tools in the news value of research:

(6) ... Finally, the article evaluates China's assertive legalism strategy that enhances its recent participation in WTO rule-making and disputes against the US and the European Union. This research, therefore, provides a *valuable case study* for other emerging economies and the multilateral trading system. IJEL

... The article raises *important considerations* for China as it finalizes its telecommunications law, which has been in the drafting stages for many years. IJEL

> ... This paper understands the role of issuer liability in a broader context as a 'corporate governance' device, and from this starting point, develops a *new approach* to the legal problem of cross-border securities liability.
> OJLS

> ... Yet, rather than representing the end of 'marketization', debates concerning the organization of forensic science have entered a new phase. These hold *significant implications* for understanding the relationship between crime, science and advanced liberal governance. BJC

Under these circumstances, Discussion/Conclusion sections came to reflect Santos' (1996) Move 5 pattern (Discussing the research), categorized as Submove 1 (Drawing conclusions) and Submove 2 (Giving recommendations) to varying degrees.

Recycling and embedding moves

In addition to the move linguistic realizations, move frequency was also related to the space devoted to particular moves throughout the abstract. To this end, the noticeable incidence of Introduction (I)/Purpose (P), Method (M) and Results (R) moves reported in Table 3 shows that authors also opted for them as recurrent moves, thus accounting for a varying incidence in individual abstracts, as illustrated in Table 4 and Figure 1 below:

BJC	I: 9/30	M: 6/30	R: 4/30
ILJ	I: 16/30	M: 3/30	R: 3/30
JIEL	I: 15/30	M: 4/30	R: 3/30
OJLS	I: 8/30	M: 2/30	R: 1/30
IJTJ	I: 9/30	M: 3/30	R: 1/30
TOTAL	57/150	18/150	12/150

Table 4. Recurrent moves in journal abstracts and totals.

	BJC	ILJ	JIEL	OJLS	IJTJ
I	9	16	15	8	9
M	6	3	4	2	3
R	4	3	3	1	1

Figure 1. Recurrent moves in journal abstracts.

Overall, both the Table and the Figure show that just over one third of the total abstracts in the corpus (57/150) devoted space to recycled Purpose, while only a small proportion of them devoted space to recycled Method (18/150) and Results (12/150). Although in all such cases authors invariably indicated the importance attached to recycling particular moves, which required more emphasis and explanation in the writing of informative and indicative abstracts, the wider space conventionally given to Purpose was mostly determined by the authors framing their indicative abstracts in simply purposive announcements outside the IMRD structuring.

To illustrate this in the abstracts reporting empirical work, the tendency to repeat move cycles led the authors to emphasise different elements of their research in a closely syntactic space, as in the set of excerpts in (7), or otherwise to move from general to more specific elements of their research, as in (8):

(7) **[P]** The research described in this article investigates the extent to which witnesses who testified in the Special Court for Sierra Leone (SCSL) report the experience as positive or negative. **[P]** It also seeks to identify the factors that contribute to these evaluations. ... IJTJ

... **[R]** The results show that incidents vary according to dimensions of victim targeting. For assassinations, these dimensions are proximity and specificity, whilst bombings vary in the level of 'intent to harm' and the type of victim. **[R]** Correlational analysis reveals that the group goes through periods of increased and decreased activity involving all forms of action, rather than displaying a substitution effect between different method. BJC

... **[R]** It argues that the WTO strikes a balance by permitting individual opinions, if in the report and anonymous; but that 10 of the 14 were incorrect or unnecessary, and the others avoidable. **[R]** It further argues that different views are adequately recorded in the summary of the parties' arguments or the Dispute Settlement Body (DSB) minutes; and that ... . JIEL

… **[M]** In-depth interviews of the two groups were conducted in the Israeli prisons in which they served their sentences **[M]** Prison personnel were also interviewed and court and prison files examined to validate the women's background and criminal history. … BJC

(8) ... **[P]** This paper provides an overview of the most relevant anthropological evidence on patterns of violence in non-state societies. **[P]** Specifically, trends and overall levels of violence, age and sex patterns as well as social and environmental factors are reviewed in order to determine whether contemporary concepts and patterns of violence are universal or culturally specific. ... BJC

Clearly, recycling also occurred in a relatively more distant space throughout the abstract, such as when Purpose (underlined) recurred after Method in the P-P/M-P-R rhetorical and other sequences. While this tendency showed the author's attempt to claim the significance of the topic in Purpose, which prepared for the equally significant Method and Results, it also implied the notion that rhetorical moves do not appear solely in standard order but in recurring patterns (Swales 1990).[10] In general, therefore, recycling move patterns was a means for the authors to gain reader interest in the legal research being reported, and to similarly enhance the persuasive objective of the abstract based on promoting the scholarly work. Cycle patterns, therefore, brought into focus the ways legal authors claimed knowledge and established links with other community members.

In this context, the general tendency in the abstracts was to keep the rhetorical moves distinguished in the relative syntax, as seen above. However, as Table 5 below shows, exceptions to this arose overall in half of the abstracts (74/150) where the general tendency was to embed two types of moves from Introduction, Results and Method within the same

[10] In this context, several studies across academic disciplines (e.g. Hopkins and Dudley-Evans 1988; Kanoksilapatham 2005) have focused on the notion of recurring patterns.

sentence, although embedding Conclusion with either Purpose or Method also occurred marginally.

BJC	M/P: 8/30	P/M: 7/30	M/R: 7/30	P/R: 1/30	P/C: 1/30	-	-
ILJ	-	P/M: 8/30	M/R: 4/30	-	-	-	-
JIEL	M/P: 3/30	P/M: 3/30	M/R: 1/30	P/R: 2/30	P/C: 1/30	-	-
OJLS	M/P: 1/30	P/M: 6/30	M/R: 1/30	P/R: 1/30	-	R/M: 1/30	-
IJTJ	M/P: 9/30	P/M: 4/30	M/R: 6/30	P/R: 2/30	-	-	M/C: 1/30
TOTAL	21/120	28/150	19/150	6/120	2/60	1/30	1/30
OVERALL	74/150						

Table 5. Embedded moves in journal abstracts and totals

In line with Bhatia's (1993, 1995) argument for "move mixing", the tendency to squeeze information in a single sentence among corpus writers was quite normal, since syntax allowed the writers to incorporate two moves in the same sentence. And while, beyond syntactic units (i.e. sentences), the analysis of moves meant analyzing the rhetorical values of discourse, the tendency to move embedding was also, as Hyland (2004: 73) argues, "a rational response to the space constraints of the abstract".

To illustrate this in surface realizations, the empirical excerpt in (9) presented one embedded case of Purpose/Method moves, and the Method used to achieve the research goal received further treatment of the material, by recycling it in the proximate sentence:

(9) … **[P]** The purpose of this study is to better understand the crime-commission process of clandestine drug laboratories and identify significant points for intervention **[M]** by using crime scripts. **[M]** This objective is achieved through a qualitative content analysis of 25 court cases in which a crime script comprising seven stages is identified... .

BJC

Similarly, the excerpts in (10) presented one embedded case of Method/Results move pairs, while the excerpts in (11) presented two embedded cases of Method/Purpose move cycles using participial phrases (underlined):

(10) ... **[M]** Using a comparative approach, **[R]** this article shows that the contract of employment in South Africa is in a relative state of unification. ILJ

… **[M]** A matched analysis of the outcomes from 116 mediated cases, relative to an unmediated control group, **[R]** found no significant impact of early resolution attributable to judicial mediation. … ILJ

… **[M]** This article uses the case of Serbia **[R]** to show that the EU has not been a consistent 'surrogate enforcer' for the tribunal. … IJTJ

(11) … **[M]** Drawing on relevant literature in the forensic and legal areas, **[P]** the article provides a brief outline of the legal context created by the ECCC and examines various projects that have recorded evidence relating to the mass graves. **[M]** Employing an analysis of semi-structured, in-depth interviews with forensic and legal experts as well as representatives from the ECCC and the Documentation Center of Cambodia (DC-Cam), **[P]** the article explores the value of forensic science for the ECCC, including its impact on humanitarian issues in Cambodia. IJTJ

In a different syntax, though, the excerpts in (12) show that embedding was realized through non-finite 'to+infinitive' clauses:

(12) **[M]** A unique set of homicide narratives drawn from court and police records are used **[P]** *to examine stability and change in the distribution of Russian homicide victim, offender, and incident characteristics before and after the fall of the Soviet Union.* BJC

[M] Case law from fiscal and company law as well as employment law is drawn on **[P]** *to illustrate some of the problems for law and policy of complex employment relationships.* ILJ

In these and other similar examples, embedding two moves within one sentence can also be seen by the method of legal research. Concretely, this method focused on real-world data (e.g. case studies, control groups, interviews), which were verifiable or provable by means of observation, experience or experiment in the law, but invariably dependent upon the space constraints in the corpus journals.

Interestingly, however, there were occasions (9 occ.) when authors used explanatory statements to form, most possibly, part of the Purpose clause or Method clause. In example (13) below, where the author stated the main purpose of the research **[P]** and potentially 'how' **[M]** the research accomplished its purpose in embedded form, the use of explanatory material helped the author to better instruct or inform the reader about the ethnographic data elements used in the Method clause:

(13) ... **[P]** This article focuses on Guatemala's National Reparations Program (PNR) **[M]** as critically viewed by Mayan Q'eqchi' victims. **[Explanatory material]** *The Q'eqchi' are the second-largest Mayan group in the country and among the most severely affected by the internal armed conflict of 1960 to 1996. In Guatemala, the dominant culture is non-indigenous, although the majority of the population is indigenous Maya. This raises the complex issue of the actual and potential role of cultural context in dealing with grave human rights violations.* **[R]** The results ... . IJTJ (my italics)

The macrostructure of abstracts: move sequences

Despite the fact that all moves were represented across the abstracts, the data in Tables 6 and 6.1 below indicate that variability was significant in single abstracts with regard to the IMRD rhetorical structure. Overall figures in Table 6 show that only a handful of abstracts in the corpus (23/150) contained the I-M-R-D sequence in combination with background Moves 1 and 2 of the CARS model (Swales 2004), which I will discussed later in this Chapter.

	I-M-R-D pattern	**Combined patterns**	TOTAL
BJC	I-M-R-D:6/30	1-I-M-R-D:2/30 2-I-M-R-D:2/30	10/30
ILJ	I-M-R-D:2/30	-	2/30
JIEL	-	1-I-M-R-D:1/30 1-2-I-M-R-D:1/30	2/30
OJLS	I-M-R-D:1/30	2-I-M-R-D:1/30	2/30
IJTJ	I-M-R-D:5/30	1-I-M-R-D:1/30 2-I-M-R-D:1/30	7/30
TOTAL	14/150	9/150	23/150

Table 6. Frequency of IMRD move sequences and combined patterns (CARS moves) and total figures.

By contrast, overall figures reported (for reasons of space) in Figure 2 at the end of this Chapter, and partially shown in Table 6.1, illustrate that an astonishingly large majority of abstracts were at variance (127/150), since they omitted one or two moves in this sequence (78/150) or changed the order of moves in such a sequence (49/150), whether or not still in combination with the CARS moves. In these cases, abstracts were also often presented in metatextual previews, including sometimes direct questions (Qs) placed at the beginning or middle of the abstracts:

	Varied rhetorical patterns: omission	Total
BJC	I-M-R:1/30; I-R-D:1/30; 1-I-M-R:2/30; 1-I-M-D:1/30; 1-M-R-D:1/30; 2-1-I-M-D:1/30; 1-2-I-R:1/30	8/30
	Varied rhetorical patterns: changing order	Total
BJC	1-M-I-M:1/30; M-I-R-D:1/30; 2-M-I-R-D:1/30; M-I:1/30; 1-M-I-R:1/30; I-R-I-D:1/30; 1-I-M-I-R:1/30; 1-I-M-I-M-R-D:1/30; I-M-I-M-D-M:1/30; I-M-R-I-M-R-D:1/30; 1-M-I-R-I-D:1/30; 1-M-I-I-R-D:1/30	12/30

Table 6.1. Frequency of IMRD variations and total figures.

The omitted moves category included abstracts that presented recurrent (cyclical) patterns of Purpose, Method and Results in a closely syntactic space, such as the I-M-M-R-D sequence, or otherwise presented one or more purposive announcements, such as the 1-I or I-I-I-I sequences, which usually functioned as previews. The changing order category included abstracts that reversed the conventional position of moves and similarly presented recurrent patterns, occurring this time in a relatively more distant space from a given move, such as the (underlined) I-R-I-D or 1-I/M-R-M/R-I-D sequences. The different data provide the criteria for introducing here the phenomena of 'less-structured' abstracts produced by the authors in the corpus, as opposed to the strictly-structured phenomena of abstracts based on the more informative IMRD structure. In other words, the criteria mean that the move sequences were highly unpredictable in the corpus. As a result of the higher incidence of less-structured documents, then, legal authors showed a preference for "indicative" rather than "informative" (Ventola 1994; Lorés 2004) versions of their abstracts.

In this context, results data confirm other studies (e.g. Melander et al. 1997; Lorés 2004; Huckin 2006; Belotti 2008, 2012) dealing with move structure variation in abstracts within and across the social science and humanities disciplines, and imply that authors abstained from useful abstract-writing manuals offering advice on drafting 'well-structured' abstracts that would cover all the essential academic elements of the full-length paper. In this study, the authors' abstracting practice affected not only empirical research (which is usually previewed according to the IMRD standard structure across the disciplines), but also theoretical work which, as Swales (2004: 207-208) argues, is less standardized than the experimental work based on the (IMRD) standard structure. Despite this argument, and in the absence of manuals providing formal descriptions of theoretical research abstracting in the law, attempts were made to adapt as much of the IMRD rhetorical elements as possible to theoretical abstracts in the corpus, by relying on their grammatical and discourse functions.

IMRD sequence

To account for the various rhetorical opportunities available to legal authors, let us begin with the empirically grounded abstracts in (14) and (15). In these examples, authors extracted all the key informational points from the article by following a recognized and established Purpose-Method-Results-Conclusion pattern in the texts. These points, however, were only formal rather than substantial in the surface realizations of the abstracts, since they did not serve as highly aggregated substitutes for the accompanying articles. Except for the commonly used Introduction and Conclusions sections, Method and Results sections were in fact formally absent from these and other few articles with which the abstracts were associated. Despite the relative absence of these formal descriptions in the accompanying articles, authors potentially went for the "informative" (Ventola 1994: 335; Lorés 2004: 281-282) types of strictly-structured abstracts:

(14) **[P]** This article examines attitudes among soldiers in the Armed Forces of Bosnia and Herzegovina – many of whom stood on opposing sides of the war front over a decade ago – toward the International Criminal Tribunal for the former Yugoslavia. **[M]** It is based on an anonymous survey of 463 soldiers conducted in five Bosnian cities: Sarajevo, Mostar, Tuzla, Banja Luka and Bijeljina. **[R]** The author finds that soldiers believe the Court has made some successes toward its extended mandate, in particular in its contribution to various aspects of democratization. Court architects hoped war crimes trials would bolster the prospects for long-term peace and stability in the country. **[C]** In conclusion, this article addresses a segment of society not often given voice in scholarly studies of transitional justice and adds to the growing scholarship on former combatants. IJTJ

(15) **[P]** This paper applies the concept of 'new visibility' to recent developments around policing, particularly the prevalence of mobile phone cameras in the wider community and the capacity via video-sharing platforms such as YouTube, and social networking sites like Facebook, to share images of apparent police misconduct with mass audiences and to

mobilize groups into taking action of some kind. **[M]** Two case studies, the Ian Tomlinson case in London in April 2009 and the Robert Dziekanski case in Vancouver in October 2007, are used **[R]** to show the unprecedented power of this new capability and the challenges that it poses for police image management. **[D/C]** The implications for police legitimacy and accountability of these developments are discussed. BJC

By introducing the reader to the scope elements of the research that they wished to tackle in purpose statements, these authors focused on measurable results by relying on (quantitative and qualitative) methods in real-world observations and experience noted before (i.e. survey and case studies describing actual interventions in the field), and then drew conclusions from their "results-driven" study (Swales and Feak 2004) in detailed and factual rhetorical formats. Clearly, these formats are not new to contemporary law since the latter is increasingly infused with data-gathering methodology, such as in the field of criminal law and criminology reported in the abstracts above (14-15). However, as a result of the neighbouring disciplines I referred to before, the experimental, objective methods used to substantiate the validity of the findings in the IMRD formats above provided the authors with guideposts for data analysis in the sciences, where "new knowledge is accepted on the basis of often quantifiable experimental proof" (Coffin et al. 2003: 48) in aptly standard IMRD formats. The empirical formats mirrored the methods most commonly relied on in the social science disciplines, such as Economics and Sociology, which have partly borrowed methods from the sciences, in Coffin et al. (2003) terms, or appeared to be more expressly interpretive (as in the humanities) of the methods applied to empirical data. Following these empirical-data formats, then, the author in (14), on the one hand, presented a clearly marked conclusion statement (*In conclusion*), offering a specificity and an answer to the research issue by considering how the research had an influence on the studies in transnational justice. The author in (15), on the other, was concerned with the implications of the current study (Discussion/Conclusion) by considering how the research had an impact upon police (mal-)practice and responsibility. This way then, the empirical formats come to the fore as collaborative results of the interdisciplinary understanding of the problems where the cross-boundary work was both a matter of method generated by interested disciplines and of socio-legal research. This understanding reconciled methodological boundaries through a wider disciplinary space and generated new knowledge of law disciplinarity as an evolving legal research 'in action', where individual and societal interests in the research process were accounted for by the contingencies arising from the wider, practical context of law in its interaction with society.

Similarly, regularities in the IMRD sequence were revealed in empirical abstracts from other journals, where authors described a single topic area of the law (*employment contract*) on which empirical work was based by observation. In the empirical abstract in (16), for instance, the author provided sufficient key information of the legal research in the Purpose-Method-Results-Conclusion pattern, although he stated the basic findings first and then elaborated or qualified them in a recycled Results move:

(16) **[P]** This article explores the evolution of the contract of employment as well as the development of the employee/independent contract or dichotomy in South Africa with reference to six broad themes: the Master and Servant laws, social welfare legislation, the control test, Roman-Dutch law, tax legislation and industrial relations legislation. **[M]** Using a comparative approach, **[R]** this article shows that the contract of employment in South Africa is in a relative state of unification. **[R]** This article further shows that some of the assumptions about the historical evolution of the contract of employment and the influence of Roman and Roman-Dutch law are overstated and that more recent developments, such as tax legislation, arguably had a greater influence on the dichotomising of labour law. **[C]** Finally, the article asks whether this state of unification is not responsible for the processes, such as casualisation and externalisation, that alienate employees from statutory protection. ILJ

Swalesian CARS model forming a compound in move sequences

In Table 6 we have seen that only 14 abstracts were selective in the formal use of the IMRD move sequence. Against this selective pattern, the general tendency among authors was to adopt an expansive rhetorical approach, by locating additional moves on the IMRD sequence (9/150) or its varied rhetorical patterns. In such cases, it was clear that authors wished to provide not only enough background information to enable the readers to follow description and motivation of their research in a persuasive framework, but also to accommodate their research to other members in the discipline by relying on a shared knowledge. [11] Thus, in the Swalesian's (2004) CARS model for RA introductions reported in Table 7,

[11] Though by different terminology, providing background information reflected Santos' (1996) Move 1 pattern (Situating the research).

these authors chose to locate particular segments appearing before Introduction/Purpose, and realized through Establishing a territory (Move 1) and Establishing a niche (Move 2) rhetorical strategies.

Move 1 – *Establishing a territory* (citation required)
via
Topic generalizations of increasing specificity

Move 2 – *Establishing a niche* (citations possible)
via

Step 1A	Indicating a gap
	or
Step 1B	Adding to what is known
Step 2 (optional)	Presenting positive justification

Move 3 – *Presenting the Present Work* (citations possible)
via

Step 1 (obligatory)	Announcing present research descriptively and/or purposively
Step 2* (optional)	Presenting research questions or hypotheses
Step 3 (optional)	Definitional clarifications
Step 4 (optional)	Summarizing methods
Step 5 (PISF**)	Announcing principal outcomes
Step 6 (PISF)	Stating the value of the present research
Step 7 (PISF)	Outlining the structure of the paper

Notes: "possible recycling of increasingly specific topics" [from Move 1 to Move 2-1A or B]; "*Steps 2-4 are not only optional but less fixed in their order of occurrence that the others"; "**PISF: Probable in some fields, but unlikely in others" (from Swales 2004: 230, 232)

Table 7. Swales' (2004: 228-233) revised CARS model for RA Introductions.

Following this model, and as shown by the varying frequency of these Moves in Table 3, authors in the abstracts were far more concerned with *Establishing a territory* (73 occ.) by "Topic generalisations of increasing specificity" in Move 1 than *Establishing a niche* for their research study (21 occ.) by "Indicating a gap" in Move 2-Step 1A (16 occ.), or "Adding to what is known" in Move 2-Step 1B (5 occ.). On the basis that Swales' revised model allows for Move 1 to consist of one single step ("Topic generalizations of increasing specificity"), on account of the difficulties encountered by researchers "in operationalizing the 1990 distinction between Move1-Step1 (*claiming centrality*) and Move 1-Step 2 (*making topic generalizations*)" (Swales 2004: 227, italics in the original), merging the two procedural steps in Move 1 was, as Swales (2004: 227) himself concedes, almost a regular procedure in the current corpus. This meant that legal writers made "research-world" statements by expressing the significance of their study to other researchers (Swales 1990; Samraj 2002a/b), or made *centrality claims* as "appeals to the discourse community whereby members are asked to accept that the research about to be reported is part of a lively, significant or well-established research area" (Swales 1990: 144). Indeed, the possibility of legal writers making centrality claims to "real-world" issues (Samraj 2002a/b, 2005; Breeze 2009) was not ruled out in the current corpus. Although, in responding to Samraj's (2002a/b) suggestion for "real-world" claims, Swales (2004: 228) maintains that "such claims can just as easily be situated in the research world", evidence from the written data in the corpus suggests that legal writers were also anxious about some real and pressing issue in the world of legal order, which required them to establish the significance of their research in scholarly writing. Where the nature of the real-world claim did emerge, the effect was a wider discoursal value being added to the writers' legal discussion, which thus provided support for centrality claims or topic generalizations in the disciplinary culture and practice of law.

In addition to these operationalizing features, no use was made of citation in the parenthetical form (Author, year, page) in either type of Moves, and the corpus revealed that only the Steps 1A-1B in Move 2 were selected. These steps often appeared in combination with Move 1 (i.e. 1-2 as in Tables 6 and 6.1), thus leaving the Step 2 (Presenting positive justification) in Move 2 to be virtually absent from the corpus. Indeed, there were marginal cases (2 occ.) in which providing background information via Move 1 and Move 2 also included the "Counterclaiming" strategy (Move 2-Step 1A) in Swales' (1990) model, as shown below:

(17) **[M1]** Scholars and layman alike have long assumed that the Nazi regime kept the German people in line by employing heavy doses of coercion involving arbitrary justice and lethal repression meted out by dreaded organizations of the Nazi criminal justice system such as the Gestapo and so-called Special Courts. **[Counterclaiming]** Between the late 1980s and early 2000s, this view <u>was challenged</u> by a number of scholars who gained access to and analysed previously unavailable archival evidence and who became convinced that the Nazis did not rule primarily through coercion; rather, the Nazi regime was popular with most Germans who gave the regime their voluntary consent. ... BJC

In general, locating Move 1 and Move 2 on the IMRD and/or its varied rhetorical patterns confirm Lorés' (2004) findings of "combinatory type" abstracts in her wider analysis of the IMRD sequence and the whole CARS models.

Move 1 / Move 2 compounding IMRD

To illustrate the Swalesian's combinations in the empirically grounded abstracts below, the author in (18) outlined first what is currently known or is common practice within the legal field of study. He therefore defined the term or process (*tied aid*) to explicitly orient the readers in the discipline. The author then justified the relevance of his research by demonstrating a deficiency in current knowledge, as signalled by the (underlined) semantic elements achieving the gap-indicating strategy. In this case, the abstract potentially proceeded from Move 1-2 to an I-M-R-D move pattern:

(18) **[M1]**'Tied aid' refers to aid granted by one country or countries to another on condition that the goods or services acquired are purchased from the donor(s). Despite the fact that tying aid seems contrary to the World Trade Organization's (WTO) basic principles of free trade and is an important issue for developing countries, **[M2–S1A]** it has received little attention from scholars or practitioners, even during the current 'development round' of negotiations. **[P]** *This article fills a gap in the literature* **[M]** by elaborating the way in which tied aid in relation to goods is affected by WTO rules. **[R]** The analysis reveals that the WTO Agreements give little specific attention to the issue and that practices relating to tied aid are either outside the WTO rules or covered only in a limited or uncertain way such that the rules have little practical impact. **[D/C]** Given the importance of tied aid for trade and for the WTO's development agenda, the analysis thus indicates that tied aid is an area requiring future consideration in the WTO. The analysis also serves to elucidate the complex legal architecture of the WTO Agreements as they relate to tied aid, which is important for any future efforts to address this subject. JIEL

The aim of research here was implied in the background Moves and signalled by the clause (*This article fills a gap in the literature*), exposing an unsolved problem in knowledge. In this pattern, then, the author narrowed the legal topic down from the wider world emphasised through specific topic generalizations to a specific study in the discipline. By contrast, the author widened out the research focus in Discussion, relating deeper findings of the current study to the real-world problem, and evaluating the results in terms of their relevance for future research and relationship with WTO.

Interestingly, however, there were occasions outside the gap-indicating strategy when authors allowed themselves the freedom to present centrality claims or topic generalizations of disciplinary empirical work in fact-narrating scheme, as in:

(19) **[M1]** The system of conciliation and arbitration established under the Conciliation and Arbitration Act 1904 was both highly collectivised and highly centralised in character. It was often assumed to be inimical to collective bargaining, although there was in fact a great deal of collective bargaining, both inside and outside the formal system. Starting in the early 1990s, there was a shift away from the traditional emphasis on conciliation and arbitration in favour of formal recognition of collective bargaining at enterprise level. In 1996, a new element was introduced in the form of individual statutory agreements (Australian workplace agreements (AWAs) which prevailed over, and had the capacity entirely to displace, otherwise applicable collective instruments. Public concern at these developments played a major role in the defeat of the (conservative) Howard Government in 2007. The Labor Government that replaced it was committed to the 're-collectivisation' of the system, and to the abolition of AWAs. This second commitment was honoured in 2008, and a new bargaining regime was put in place by the Fair Work Act 2009. **[P]** This article examines <u>that</u> new system. **[R]** It finds that the techniques adopted by the 2009 Act are more sophisticated and nuanced than those that have been adopted in jurisdictions such as the USA, Canada and the UK, and as such seem to avoid many of the pitfalls that have thwarted attempts to promote collective bargaining in those countries. **[C]** It remains to be seen, however, whether the participants in the bargaining process have the commitment and capacity to enable the legislation to re-collectivize the labour market in any significant way. ILJ

The surface realization shows, on the one hand, the author's decision to produce a lengthy and detailed account of the facts (173 words) in Move 1 and, on the other, to present a very concise purpose statement using *that* discourse deixis to refer to a prior portion of discourse realized in Move 1 (i.e.: *... and a new bargaining regime was put in place by the Fair Work Act 2009*). The Purpose move was a summary of the article introduction (Swales' three moves, 2004), though often realized by Move 3 of the (Swales') Introduction, as in most cases of the corpus here. With Method being omitted in the surface realization, this author was therefore mainly concerned with the presentation of the findings from which to deduce conclusions based on gap issues about the current research, and thus wrote his abstract along a Move 1-I-R-C rhetorical sequence.

Where arguing for topic generalizations was explicitly avoided in the surface realizations, authors of empirical works as in (20) and (21) below justified the relevance of their contributions in the IMRD (20) or IMR (21) structures, by immediately presenting a negative evaluation of some feature of the research 'territory', as signalled again by the (underlined) semantic elements achieving the gap-indicating strategy:

(20) **[M2–S1A]** Research into emotion, crime and anti-social behaviour has lacked psychological input and rarely considered the multi-directional associations between emotion, crime and morality. **[P]** We present a study analysing audio recordings of two community groups meeting in a deprived inner-city area with high rates of crime, **[M]** using conversation analytic and discursive psychological techniques to conduct an affective–textual analysis that draws out aspects of participants' moral reasoning and identifies its emotional dimensions. **[R]** We found that moral reasoning around crime and anti-social behaviour took three forms (invoking moral categories, developing moral hierarchies, invoking vulnerable others) and was bound up with a wide range of emotional enactments and emotion displays. **[D/C]** Findings are discussed in relation to contemporary government policy and possible future research. BJC

(21) **[M2–S1A]** Little in-depth research has been conducted on or attention paid to the experience and opinions of survivors regarding issues such as reparation, justice, reconciliation and truth in dealing with the aftermath of atrocities. Less still has been said of the way in which victims' identities impact on these views or are considered in the design of programs aimed at redress for past violations. **[P]** This article focuses on Guatemala's National Reparations Program (PNR) **[M]** as critically viewed by Mayan Q'eqchi' victims. **[Explanatory material]***The Q'eqchi' are the second-largest Mayan group in the country and among the most severely affected by the internal armed conflict of 1960 to 1996. In Guatemala, the dominant culture is non-indigenous, although the majority of the population is indigenous Maya. This raises the complex issue of the actual and potential role of cultural context in dealing with grave human rights violations.* **[R]** The results of extensive ethnographic field research conducted between 2006 and 2009 reveal the need for a locally rooted and culturally sensitive PNR. IJTJ

Indeed, in (21), which provides the full abstract already noted in example (13) above, justifying the research in the chosen rhetorical structure meant the use of some explanatory material (my italics). This was necessary for the reader to understand the ethnographic data-gathering criteria outlined only cursorily in the Method clause from which to achieve the findings of one's own research.

Still, in other instances, such as in (22), the choice was to open the abstract with a specific topic generalization followed by *Adding to what is known* (Move 2-Step 1B) marginally occurring strategy. This introduced the reader to the relevance of the ongoing contribution by recycling Purpose move in order to detail the research elements announced in the previous, more general purpose statement. The result was a Move 1-2(1B)-I-I-R rhetorical sequence achieved in the empirically grounded abstract:

(22) **[M1]** Anthropological sources on non-state, tribal societies offer a wealth of evidence on violence that can expand the spatial and temporal gaze of criminological research. **[M2-S1B]** Reviewing this literature allows for a more comparative analysis of patterns of violence and challenges contemporary notions of social change and order. **[P]** This paper provides an overview of the most relevant anthropological evidence on patterns of violence in non-state societies. **[P]** Specifically, trends and overall levels of violence, age and sex patterns as well as social and environmental factors are reviewed in order to determine whether contemporary concepts and patterns of violence are universal or culturally specific. **[R]** The findings presented here indicate that violence in non-state societies is a ubiquitous but culturally varying phenomenon used by males and may be related to interdependent social organizations and networks of exchange. BJC

These and other examples, where the CARS move segments (Move 1 – Move 2) appeared before the IMRD structure or its variations, indicated that authors introduced their research purpose in the abstract where authors writing article introductions will have announced their research descriptively and/or purposively via Move 3-Step 1 in Swales' (2004) revised CARS model. As I already noted in example (19) above, therefore, the reporting practices in (22) brought us round to the argument made by Bhatia (1993: 82) that "the article introduction ends where the abstract begins", by admitting that "the two seemingly similar genres are very different in their communicative purposes, and, hence, are instances of different genres" (Bhatia 1993: 76).

Yet, as argued before, the need to establish the significance of their legal study did not preclude the authors from grounding their centrality claims within the topicality of real-world issues, such as those in examples (23), (24) and (25) below, or claims within scholarship, such as those describing Raz's theory of authority (26), theories of authority and remedial regime in contract breaching (27), or scholarship in transitional justice (28):

(23) **[M1]** China joined the World Trade Organization (WTO) in 2001 after almost 15 years of negotiations, making extensive commitments to open its markets to foreign investment and liberalize trade in goods and services. China represents a huge potential market for foreign telecommunications service providers; **[M2-S1A]** yet, in practice, foreign involvement in this market is extremely limited. **[P]** This article identifies key commercial and legal barriers ... . JIEL

(24) **[M1]** The European Community (EC) is currently negotiating Economic Partnership Agreements (EPAs) with several groups of developing countries. An element which the EC Commission likes to highlight is the objective of sustainable development. **[P]** This article analyses the potential of this 'presiding principle' of sustainable development as a treaty objective—in the EPAs and other treaties in international economic law. **[M]** Defining parameters are ... . IJEL

(25) **[M1]** In 2006, the Special Court for Sierra Leone arrested former Liberian President Charles Taylor for war crimes and crimes against humanity. The trial is currently underway in The Hague, but human rights observers have questioned the relevance of a trial held such a distance from Sierra Leone. **[P]** This article examines the tensions inherent in communicating justice from within international courts; in particular, how various judicial prohibitions challenge transparency and the public's right to know. **[M]** Based on empirical evidence gathered by the author while producing video outreach documentaries for the Special Court press office, **[C]** this article seeks to contribute to research on mechanisms of both justice and communication. IJTJ

(26) **[M1]** Joseph Raz's famous theory of authority is grounded in three claims about the nature and justification of authority. According to the Preemption Thesis, authoritative directives purport to replace the subject's judgments about what she should do. According to the Dependence Thesis, authoritative directives should be based on reasons that actually apply to the subjects of the directive. According to the Normal Justification Thesis (NJT), authority is justified to the extent that subjects are more likely to comply with right reason by following the authority's directives than by following their own judgments about what right reason requires. **[P]** In this article, I consider a number of ways in which NJT might be construed as a justification for authority. ... OJLS

(27) **[M1]** Following the recognition by the House of Lords in *AG v Blake* of the gain-based remedy of an account of profits in a contractual context, an increasing number of commentators have argued that the English remedial regime for breach of contract should be further reinforced by the introduction of punitive damages **[M2-S1A]**. **[P]**This article considers whether there may be a role for punitive awards in contract law. ... BJC

(28) **[M1]** Transitional justice appears to be an established field of scholarship connected to a field of practice on how to deal with past human rights abuses in societies in transition. The original focus of transitional justice discourse was that human rights law requires accountability in transitions, rooted in the discipline of law. Over time, this focus has been expanded to include a much broader range of mechanisms, goals and inquiries across a range of disciplines. In order to probe the current state of the field, **[P]** this article argues against the current conception of transitional justice as a praxis-based interdisciplinary field. ... IJTJ

The almost equal tendency to both claiming strategies in the corpus positioned legal authors in ways that they classified statements of legal significance along different discoursal values and, more importantly, emphasised the circulation of systemic problems and possible solutions in the scientific field, where interdisciplinarity of legal inquiry also played a major role. By providing support for the introduction of centrality claims or topic generalizations in the law inquiry, discoursal values therefore helped the writers operate within and across different academic, professional and institutional levels of legal discourse. Among these levels, for instance, the author in (27) felt the need to present a general picture of the academic research by placing it in the professional discourse (thematic) context of their Lordships' Decision (*AG v Blake*), and quickly moved to the specificities of the field of study (*introduction of punitive damages in contractual context*) by showing how, in the eyes of the discourse community, this Decision had missed the 'niche' the writer intended to concentrate on. The author, then, proceeded from a more general account of the 'territory' towards 'establishing a niche', and concluded with a (hypothetical) purposive announcement of the present research. Of course, this and other discourse-level strategies served to establish a persuasive framework for the acceptance of the ongoing research as being "important, central, interesting, problematic, or relevant" (Swales and Feak 2004: 244), and to demonstrate the authors' credibility in the discipline. However, the different levels of legal discourse in the examples above were important to emphasize interactive patterns of *interdiscursivity* (Bhatia 2004, 2008, 2010) "exploited for the construction and interpretation of discursive as well as disciplinary practices" (Bhatia 2010: 34) in the production of the academic abstract genre. And these interactive patterns of *interdiscursivity*, in particular, were held accountable to an explicitly defined series of rules, court decisions, agreements, treaties, doctrines and procedures represented in a manner established by the law disciplinarity and tradition.

Other rhetorical opportunities

Other rhetorical opportunities arose from theoretical as well as empirical research materials. In the theoretical abstract shown in (29), for instance, the author made specific topic generalizations concerning the previous state of knowledge within the research field (*protective labour law*), and introduced his solution to the problem described in Move 1 by outlining the main purpose or aims in the final (fifty-five word) sentence. Although, at first sight, this sentence may suggest the primary objectives of the research outlined in one-only purposive statement, it reasonably turned out to compress Purpose, Method and Discussion into just one-sentence summary:

(29) **[M1]** Historically, protective labour law pushed back against capitalist labour markets by facilitating workers' collective action and setting minimum employment standards based on social norms. Although the possibilities, limits and desirability of such a project were viewed differently in classical, Marxist and pluralist political economy, each perspective understood that the pursuit of protective labour law would produce recurring regulatory dilemmas requiring trade-offs between efficiency, equity and voice and/or between workers' and employers' interests. **[P]** This article reviews the concept of regulatory dilemmas as formulated in the three major traditions of labour law scholarship, **[M]** methodologically assesses recent work by Deakin and Wilkinson and by Hyde, that proposes to reform labour law and overcomes regulatory dilemmas, **[D]** and discusses an alternative approach to understanding regulatory dilemmas based on the work of Wright. ILJ

Where the author's choice for compression may be explained by space constraints in the abstract, it also clearly achieved the move-embedding effect on the surface of the text. In this context, it should be admitted that the author did not go for detailed and specific information about the substance of the article, as a handful of others at least did in the corpus by producing informative abstracts. As a result, the organizational structure of the abstract in (29) potentially was a Move 1-Purpose-Method-Discussion rhetorical sequence, stating the goals of the research and the way the facts were treated and discussed in the paper by means of an "indicative" version of the abstract (Ventola 1994; Lorés 2004). As is clear, this and other similar abstracts positioned the author's ideas within a broad context of related theories in which the important criteria were the relevance of theoretical content to disciplinary researchers and/or practitioners. Moreover, this and other similar abstracts described a novel method for use in academic and professional settings in ways that the conceptual contribution of the accompanying articles was more important than providing experimental details in the Results move which, as a matter of fact, was omitted in (29).

Outside of squeezing moves into one sentence, reporting theoretical research in an increased length of the moves can be seen in the abstract below (30), where the author (in first person) opted for the more informative IMRD move structuring in separate sentences, while also embedding Method/Results in one sentence. Here, the conceptual contribution of the study allowed the author to give only as much detail as was necessary to understand the value of his critical and deconstructive interpretation outlined in the Method clause. The author therefore introduced, by recycling, new disciplinary concepts (underlined), as part of his methodological criteria used to create the findings in the current research, so that the rhetorical structure was one of P-M/R-M-C move sequence:

(30) **[P]** In this article, I analyze the conceptualization of transitional justice underwriting Slavenka Drakulić's book, *They Would Never Hurt a Fly*, on the trials at the International Criminal Tribunal for the Former Yugoslavia (ICTY) in The Hague. **[M]** I adopt a critical and deconstructive strategy of interpretation **[R]** that reveals Drakulić's idea of 'justice for the Balkans' as not only internally incoherent and fractured but also politically problematic. **[M]** I introduce two concepts as central to Drakulić's storytelling about transitional justice in the former Yugoslavia: (i) the idea of a 'broken time' and (ii) the idea of a 'razed home.' **[C]** I conclude that Drakulić's narratives of justice are aimed at repairing broken time and rebuilding the razed home in a way that reveals the author's redemptive, rather than political, thinking about transitional justice. IJTJ

In other cases, such as in (31), reporting theoretical research, the author combined the Purpose move with an explanatory statement (*The doctrine of reportage provides protection ... public interest*), informing the widest readership about the research question stated in Purpose. This time, however, he omitted the method statement as well as the background (CARS) moves, thus showing as yet an unpredictable case of varied rhetorical move pattern:

(31) **[P]** This paper examines the 'doctrine of reportage'—a particular application of the *Reynolds* qualified privilege defence to defamation recognized by the House of Lords in *Reynolds v Times Newspapers Ltd*. **[Explanatory Purpose elements]** The doctrine of reportage provides protection for the neutral reporting (republication) of defamatory allegations made by others in the context of a dispute or controversy of

public interest. **[R]** It is argued in this paper, however, that this emerging defence is doctrinally distinct from the privilege recognized in *Reynolds* and that its jurisprudential basis needs to be reconsidered. Moreover, the development of the defence under the guise of *Reynolds* privilege has led to confusion, both by courts and by commentators, as to its potential breadth. **[D]** It is suggested that the public interest justifications underpinning the reportage defence need to be explicitly re-examined by the courts in order to define its proper scope. Following an examination of these public interest justifications, it is argued that a broad interpretation of the defence should be rejected. OJLS

Considering, in functional terms, that the Purpose move provided the context for the study of the disciplinary issue, *the doctrine of reportage*, followed by what the study achieved, the conceptual contribution of the research helped the author to achieve Results by presenting them in the form of an argument (*It is argued*), followed by suggestions and interpretations for the study in the Discussion move. The assumption that findings were linked to relevant academic argument among this and other argumentative authors was suggested by the participatory and interactive mechanism of academic discourse, which "involve writers in discoursal practices that are largely *argumentative* and competitive" (Hyland 2004: 18, my emphasis in italics). As a result, the author in (31) was able to conduct policy research on the legal topic (*doctrine of reportage*), as derived from the facts in case-law (*Reynolds v Times Newspaper Ltd*), and to construct his 'normative' arguments about these facts in order to show the relevant effects on the current system of law.

Yet, the IMRD move structuring became even less predictable in other theoretical as well as empirical materials. In the theoretical abstract shown in (32), for instance, the author (appearing again in first person) potentially guided the reader towards what he himself accomplished in the study of legal philosophy:

(32) **[Move 1]** Mark Murphy contends that, whatever the merits of any philosophical argument for anarchism, most people are obligated to obey the law. Murphy defends a moral argument designed to show that most people in reasonably just political communities are obligated to obey the law. And he advances epistemological arguments calculated to support two key claims. First, people who believe they are obligated to obey the law are entitled to retain their belief in the face of anarchist criticism. Second, a credible account of political obligation can accommodate the concerns that drive anarchist arguments in such a way that no anarchist argument against political obligation could, in principle, be successful. **[R]** I argue that Murphy's moral argument yields relatively limited results, and that his

epistemological arguments do not succeed in showing that anarchists could not convict folk-believers in political obligation of unreasonableness.
OJLS

Specifically, this author used topic generalizations concerning the current state of knowledge in legal scholarship to introduce the reader to his counterclaims in the research area covered although, following Swales' (1990) earlier CARS model (Move 1-Step 3), this author seemed to be equally concerned with reviewing items of previous research by relating '*what* has been claimed with *who* has claimed it'. As a consequence, the roadmap statement beginning with *I argue* suggested not just a preview of the study in purposive announcement, but rather a preview of one's own results derived from comparisons to pre-existing literature. By describing the theoretical outcome of his article, as supported by the background context, the author therefore went for a less-structured type of indicative-descriptive abstract.

On three occasions, however, the corresponding noun (*argument*) was used in place of the *argue* lemma in other theoretical abstracts, as below:

(33) **[P]** This paper seeks to contribute to the field of transitional justice by adding new insights about the role that trials of victimizers can play within democratization processes. **[R]** <u>The main argument</u> is that criminal proceedings affirming the value of equal respect and concern for both victims and abusers can contribute to the socialization of citizens' politically relevant emotions. More precisely, using law constructively to engage public resentment and indignation can be successful to the extent that legality is not sacrificed. **[Continuing a tradition]** In order to locate this argument within the rich literature on the pedagogical functions of transitional trials, this paper enters a dialogue with three emblematic texts. Lawrence Douglas's narrative jurisprudence approach, Judith Shklar's critique of the limits of legalism, and Marc Osiel's interest in 'discursive solidarity' represent starting points for a more complex conceptualization of the relationship between democracy, law and emotional education within transformational periods. OJLS

In this rhetorical format, the author described Purpose elements of the study first and there again what his own research essentially achieved in victim and perpetrator studies applied to the growing field of transitional justice (*The main argument ... / More precisely, ...*). But, as a result of the corpus abstracts being highly unpredictable in the rhetorical sequences, the remaining two sentences were functionally interpreted as "Continuing a tradition" (Move 2-Step 1D, Swales 1990), since they expanded on the law topic in the current research and similarly created the final (theoretical) outcome of the research being reported. Whether this was the case, the 'continuing-a-tradition' reading amounted to only an isolated instance in the corpus.

Unpredictability in the move structure also emerged in other cases of less-structured theoretical abstracts, as shown below (34-36). Here, one-sentence summaries resulted in the authors focusing perhaps too narrowly in the reported research:

(34) **[P]** This essay examines the contractual analysis of retirement and the potential influence of past judicial approaches in the new era of statutory prohibition on age discrimination. ILJ

(35) **[P]** This article further develops the concept of the 'contract for intermittent employment' set out by Freedland in *The Personal Employment Contract*, and explores its potential to alleviate the plight of casual workers in today's labour market. ILJ

(36) **[P]** This article describes developments that have modified the at-will doctrine in the United States. **[R]** It argues that the courts are evolving a hybrid type of employment contract which is neither strictly at-will nor a general form of dismissal protection. ILJ

The surface realizations show that the author in (34) went for a very terse abstract (twenty-six word length), by compressing the space left to other moves in favour of one-only purpose statement, as did the author in (35) producing a thirty-six word abstract. By some contrast, the author in (36), though still keeping to a compressed abstract length (thirty-nine words), went beyond his peers' realizations in the same journal, and showed his readers that he had at least an idea of what the research would lead to, and therefore appeared to be more cautiously attentive of his readers to understand the outcome [R] of his research goal [P]. While in all three such cases[12] the authors yet again went for indicative-descriptive versions of the abstracts, it is likely that their choice was influenced by the (ILJ) journal's submission guidelines providing no minimum word-length for acceptable abstracts, except for the vague word-length requirements set by the journal ('Articles must be accompanied by an abstract of up to 200 words'). Whatever the reason, tersely telling the reader in (34-35) what original observations the articles were trying to offer proved adequate in the circumstances, not only because the abstracts were published but also

[12] Interestingly, the word length of these abstracts was in contrast with the general tendency of abstracts in the corpus responding in length to publisher requirements, which were set in the maximum of 120, 150 or 200 words.

because they were meant to quickly capture the essence of the value added by the articles. On the other hand, it is not unlikely that the authors' terse writing may have left the unsophisticated reader to meander through simply purposive announcements well outside some other key informational components.

Where indeed authors from the same or other journals allowed themselves more space in their abstracts, as shown in the one-hundred two word abstract in (37) and the two-hundred word abstract in (38), there was often an attempt to outline the main goals of their theoretical research in multiple purpose statements, serving as yet as indicative-descriptive types of abstracts. To illustrate this, the author in (37) presented his policy research on the *Default Retirement Age* regulations and case-law to outline the scope of his study, and potentially allowed the inexperienced reader to understand the complexity of the research subject (*default retirement age*) set out in the initial purpose statement, by distinguishing it from its departure principle (*equal treatment*) set out in the adjacent explanatory statement:

(37) **[P]** This article considers the <u>default retirement age</u> adopted in the UK in 2006. **[Explanatory Purpose elements]** It is an exception to the <u>principle of equal treatment</u> and requires an objective justification as a legitimate aim with appropriate and necessary means to achieving that aim. **[P]** Reasons why a traditional retirement age existed are considered together with a consideration of the development of government policy in this regard. **[Explanatory Purpose elements]** Government policy has largely followed that of employers' wishes. **[P]** Judgments of the European Court of Justice in relation to proportionality and age discrimination are examined and the case brought by Age UK against the government is looked at in more detail. ILJ

(38) **[P]** This article discusses the significance of the landmark decision of the European Court of Human Rights (ECtHR) in *Demir and Baykarav Turkey*, **[Explanatory Purpose elements]** which reversed earlier jurisprudence to hold (i) that the right to collective bargaining is 'an essential element' of the right to freedom of association in Article 11 of the European Convention on Human Rights and Fundamental Freedoms (ECHR) and (ii) embedded the jurisprudence of the International Labour Organisation and the European Social Charter into that right. **[P]** The authors examine the ECtHR's extension of the *Demirand Baykara* principle to include collective action and review the Strasbourg court's jurisprudence generally on the right to strike. **[P]** Full consideration is given to (i) the treatment of these developments by the English courts in *Metrobus Ltdv UNITE the Union* and *EDF Energy Powerlink Ltd v RMT* and (ii) their wider implications not only for British but also for European

Union (EU) labour law. **[P]** The authors consider the apparent collision between the trade union rights established under the ECHR in *Demir and Baykara* and the trade union liabilities introduced under EU law by the *Viking* and *Laval* judgments of the European Court of Justice, taking into account some significant issues that arose in the BALPA v British Airways litigation in 2008. ILJ

Similarly, the mindful author in (38) used an explanatory statement to inform the naive reader about the judicial Decision presented in summary (snapshot) style. Clearly, this Decision formed the subject of his policy research question based, as it was, on the implications for case-law in current legal understandings. He then went on to outline purposive statements that captured interdiscursively what judges as a community 'do' and 'say' in their institutional and professional practice. In particular, the lettering system (i) (ii) in (38) showed the quickly inspecting reader how the purpose statements were structured and what the various elements of the research framework were in preview format.

Unlike in (38), the author's decision in (39) resulted in the case-law explanatory elements being distinguished in the relative syntax (*In these cases, ... in the exercise of that right*), which in themselves reported the main points (summary) of the judicial Decisions. Explanatory elements were followed by the more specific elements of the research stated, by recycling, in the Purpose move from which to deduce some implications (Conclusion) in the embedded syntax:

(39) **[P]** This article analyses the judgements of the European Court of Justice (ECJ) in Case C-438/05 *International Transport Workers' Federation and Finnish Seamen's Union v Viking Line* (Judgement 11 December 2007) and Case C-341/05 *Laval v Svenska Byggnadsarbetareförbundet* (Judgement 18 December 2007). **[Explanatory Purpose elements]** In these cases, the ECJ held that where industrial action infringes an employer's free movement rights under Article 43 EC (freedom of establishment) and Article 49 EC (freedom to provide services), respectively, these Treaty provisions can have horizontal direct effect against the unions organizing the action. Unions may defend themselves against these claims by asserting a right to strike (which the Court recognized as a fundamental right within Community law) but only where they are acting proportionately in the exercise of that right. **[P]** The article explores the key elements of the ECJ's decisions on direct effect, fundamental rights and proportionality, **[C]** and draws out some of the implications of these cases for English law. ILJ

In these cases, we can still appreciate the different academic, professional and institutional levels of discourse being constructed in the abstracts interdiscursively, as I argued before. As a result of these interdiscursive levels, the reference to *regulations* in (37) and the (national and European) *case-law* in (37-39), as professional and institutional genres, suggested in particular that the abstracts functioned as (loosely defined) 'informative' documents of regulatory and judicial practices, which prepared for the descriptive, explicative and normative types of authors' research, well outside strictly-doctrinal work.

Interestingly, however, the phenomena of less-structured abstracts became even more unpredictable in the one-only instance of empirical abstract shown below:

(40) **[-]** One of the most important challenges facing the international investment law regime today is how to strike a balance between principles regarding the protection and promotion of foreign investment on the one hand and principles regarding the protection of society and the environment on the other. **[-]** A number of states have made significant progress towards meeting that challenge by adding interpretive provisions, general exceptions clauses and new preambular language to a new-generation of international investment agreements (IIAs). **[-]** If the serious substantive and procedural questions they raise can be answered satisfactorily, these new treaties may go a long way towards saving the international investment law from the legitimacy crisis it is currently experiencing. JIEL

Arguably, this author allowed himself the space to make the topic under investigation only generically identifiable by the widest readership, and failed to even provide a clearly signalled purposive statement for such readership to meander through. Although some move signal in either Purpose or Results/Discussion types may have assisted a casually browsing lay-reader, the rhetorical rationale of the abstract seemed to accommodate only the technically sophisticated reader. Thus, as a result of any move signal lacking in the surface realizations [-], the rhetorical format above was labelled as an instance of 'unstructured' abstract. Beyond this, however, an intuitive reading may suggest the three sentences to achieve different argumentative purposes, as summarised below:

- 1st + 2nd sentence: presents specific topic generalizations (Move 1) of the research by providing a concrete illustration of the international investment challenge met by the states;
- 3rd sentence: presents the article's claim in conditionality form.

In addition, other rhetorical opportunities were available to authors who presented their empirical and theoretical abstracts in text-organizing metatext, with the preview category of metatext (Mauranen 1993) describing what was about to follow between sections of the text (e.g. *Section III reviews ...*). This textual function, as found in 16 abstracts, was usually performed in a paragraph of the abstract which previewed the entire structure of the article, and corresponded more closely to Swales' (2004) *Outlining the structure of the paper* (Move 3-Step 7). Here, it seemed reasonable to extend metatextual elements to metadiscourse elements in cases where "frame markers" (e.g. *First*, *Secondly*, *then* etc.), in Hyland's (2005a) terminology, were also used to serve the purpose of previewing textual organization of the article. In this context, authors tended to indicate the structure of their article by opening it first with Topic generalizations (41), or Purpose (42) and, only marginally (2 occ.) with direct questions as in (43), placed in the opening lines of the abstracts to frame the text in previews. In (43), in particular, the author presented the 'text as actor' (*Section II argues*, *Section III reviews*, *Section IV argues*, *Section V concludes*), as opposed to other alternative structures in the corpus presenting the 'author as actor' (e.g. *In Part I ... / In Section III we describe ...*), or the 'content as subject' (e.g. *In Section II, the framework is described ...*). In all the examples shown below (41-43), where the elements in the Purpose, Results and Conclusion moves were also revealed, the text-organizing metatext/metadiscourse previewed the rhetorical acts in the indicative version of the abstracts by informing the readers of how the article unfolded in the global organization:

(41) **[M1]** The Lindsey Oil Refinery dispute in the early Spring and Summer of 2009 raised issues about the posting of European Union workers to the UK to fulfil a contract on a multi-employer construction site at a time of high levels of unemployment in the UK construction industry and deepening recession. According to press reports, the dispute was resolved only with an agreement to hire at least 100 'British' workers at the site. This raises questions as to the compatibility of the deal with Community law. **[P]** This article looks <u>first</u> at the dispute at the Lindsey Oil Refinery and the legal issues raised. **[P]** It <u>then</u> takes a step back to consider the broader question of the extent to which local hiring clauses can legitimately be included in procurement contracts. ILJ

(42) **[P]** This article analyses the Treaty of Lisbon, a Treaty whose fate hangs in the balance following the Irish 'no' in June 2008. <u>It is structured as follows</u>. **[P]** <u>First</u>, the processes leading to the adoption and ratification of the Treaty are examined. **[P]** <u>Second</u>, the structure of the Treaty and the institutional framework are explained, together with changes to the social

provisions. **[P]** Third, the possible impact which the Treaty, if ratified, would have on labour law is discussed. Particular attention is devoted to the changes in the values, aims and objectives of the Union and to the European Union's proposed accession to the European Convention for the Protection of Human Rights and Fundamental Freedoms. **[R]** It is argued that these changes may influence the internal market case law of the Court of Justice, which, as the *Viking*, *Laval* and *Rüffert* cases demonstrate, represents a significant threat to national labour laws and practices. ILJ

(43) **[Question]** Is ineffective protection of international public goods, and thereby also of interrelated national public goods, the inevitable fate of humanity? **[P]** The negative answer to this question in Section II argues that ineffective protection of public goods is mainly due to a lack of adequate theories, rules, and institutions for overcoming the *collective action problems* in multilevel governance of interdependent public goods. **[P]** Section III reviews the competing conceptions of 'international economic law' (IEL) such as public international law approaches, multilevel economic law approaches, 'global administrative law' (GAL) approaches, 'conflicts law approaches', and 'multilevel constitutional approaches'. **[P]** Section IV argues that—similar to the experience that 'national public goods' can be supplied democratically only in a framework of constitutional, legislative, administrative, and judicial rules and procedures supported by domestic citizens—multilevel governance of 'international public goods' requires a multilevel constitutional framework for multilevel rule-making and judicial protection of rule of law and constitutional rights supported by domestic citizens as 'primary' legal subjects of IEL. **[C]** Section V concludes that multilevel governance of interdependent public goods must no longer be designed only as 'foreign policy', but also as part of 'multilevel constitutionalism' necessary for protecting common, reasonable self-interests of all citizens and states. JIEL

Questions in titles and abstracts

Questions also contributed to varying the rhetorical patterns of the abstracts and naturally depended on the authors' perceptions of the rhetorical context. Table 8 shows that very little effort was made by the authors in using questions, since the latter occurred only in few instances across the corpus abstracts (14/150), while being twice as frequent in titles (29/150).

	Questions in titles	Questions in abstracts
IJTJ	5	1
BJC	5	-
JIEL	8	8
OJLS	3	4
ILJ	8	1
TOTAL	29	14

Table 8: Occurrence frequency of questions in titles and abstracts.

Despite the paucity in using questions in titles and abstracts, authors exploited the interactivity of questions to serve an "attention-grabbing aim" (Haggan 2004) or to attract the reader's curiosity and promoting the article (Hyland 2002a)[13]. This took place in a context where obviously abstract titles allowed the writers to gain worldwide visibility of their research (Hyland 2009; Swales 2004), and provided the persuasive gateway for the readers to enter the research content in the genre (Haggan 2004).

In order to understand the use of questions in titles, it may be useful to have a glance at the title constructions in the corpus, where only compound, nominal and question titles were used by the authors.[14] As Table 9 shows, compound titles were by far the most recurrent structural constructions (90/150), followed in incidence by nominal titles (57/150), down to the least-common question titles (3/150), and the preponderance of the compound constructions concurred on previous findings of RA titles in both humanities and social sciences (Haggan 2004; Soler 2007). Apart from questions making up an entire title (single question title), however, questions also appeared as the first or second part of the compound title (26/150), where they were separated mostly by the colon (:) and only occasionally by the hyphen (-); in these cases questions were counted as part of compound constructions.

[13] In addition, see Sala (2010) on interrogative forms in legal research articles.

[14] In this analysis, reference is to the works of Haggan (2004), Soler (2007) and Wang and Bai (2007).

	Compound titles	Nominal titles	Question titles	Questions in Compound titles
BJC	17/30	13/30	-	5/30
ILJ	19/30	11/30	-	8/30
IJTJ	22/30	7/30	1/30	4/30
JIEL	20/30	9/30	1/30	7/30
OJLS	12/30	17/30	1/30	2/30
TOTAL	90/150	57/150	3/150	26/150

Table 9. Structural categories of abstract titles: occurrence frequency.

In the set of compound construction titles shown in (44), containing the legal problems under investigation, questions enticed readers into pursuing the full content of the article, and similarly drew them into an understanding of the empirical or theoretical issue:

(44) MFN-based Jurisdiction in Investor-State Arbitration: Is There Any Hope for a Consistent Approach? JIEL

Classifying Employment Relationships – More Sliding Doors or a Better Regulatory Framework? ILJ

Watching a Bargain Unravel? A Panel Study of Victims' Attitudes about Transitional Justice in Cape Town, South Africa IJTJ

Stop and Search in England: A Reformed Tactic or Business as Usual? BJC

Like the majority of compound titles, titles in nominal structure labelled current disciplinary issues in a string of nominal groups to summarize the article, as in (45):

(45) Transitional Justice and Peace-building after Mass Violence IJTJ

Governance Processes, Labour–Management Partnership and Employee Voice in the Construction of Heathrow Terminal 5 ILJ

Family-Based Justice in the Sentencing of Domestic Violence BJC

The Dramatic Implications of *Demir and Baykara* ILJ

While compound and nominal titles contained enough information about the topic they labelled in the study, it was not unusual for authors to announce the topic by citing cases, as in 'The Dramatic Implications of Demir and Baykara' in (45). As noted about case note titles in Chapter 2, announcing the topic by partial case citation was a means for selectively focusing on the significance of a landmark Decision. Announcing the main topic of the article, while also capturing the reader's interest, can be seen in the three marginal instances of question titles below:

(46) What is a Crime?
OJLS

Does the WTO Need a Permanent Body of Panelists?
JIEL

A Truth Commission for Northern Ireland?
IJTJ

By constructing current disciplinary issues in synoptic formats for the readers to possibly respond to, question titles above and those placed within a two-part (compound) title therefore emphasized the (writer-reader) dialogic engagement (Haggan 2004; Hyland 2002a, 2005a/b; Soler 2007).

Where questions occurred in the abstracts, their low incidence (14) was due to their uneven spread in the abstracts where they appeared mostly in WH forms than in *yes/no* polar questions. Within the WH group, 'How' and 'What' question forms were featured in the abstracts in which they were used for different argumentative functions: framing purpose, organizing discourse, defining a 'niche' and anticipating a response. In the empirical abstract below (47), appearing in one instance alone in the corpus, four direct WH questions presented the specific research issues the author intended to pursue and provide answers for in his research, and added to two (underlined) polar questions:

(47) **[P]** This article analyzes several unresolved issues in World Trade Organization (WTO) law that may affect the WTO-consistency of measures that are likely to be taken to address climate change. **[WH questions]** *How should the WTO deal with environmental subsidies under the General Agreement on Tariffs and Trade (GATT), the Agreement on Agriculture and the Subsidies and Countervailing Measures (SCM) Agreement?* Can the general exceptions in GATT Article XX be applied to other agreements in Annex 1A? Are processing and production methods relevant to determining the issue of 'like products' in GATT Articles I and

> III, the SCM Agreement and the Antidumping Agreement and the TBT Agreement? *What is the scope of paragraphs b and g in GATT Article XX and the relationship between these two paragraphs? What is the relationship between GATT Article XX and multilateral environmental agreements in the context of climate change? How should Article 2 of the TBT Agreement be interpreted and applied in the context of climate change?* **[P]** The article explores these issues. JIEL

As an effective strategy, questions created concept mapping by helping the readers to begin their thinking about the research issues and decide in which direction to steer their reading. Viewing the discourse in the genre as interactive and persuasive with the reader, questions implied a "dialogic involvement" (Hyland 2002a; 2005a: 153) in ways that they "create anticipation, arouse interest, challenge the reader into thinking about the topic of the text" (Webber 1994: 266). Thus, the use of questions above appeared to serve largely two textual functions: setting out the author's research purpose by posing questions and structuring the reader's responses to them by organizing the discourse (Webber 1994).

Given the ubiquity of rhetorical questions in academic writing, the author's priority in the theoretical abstract in (48) seemed indeed to manage a 'response' to a question by placing it in the next utterance (*In Australia one influential view on this issue was by Sir Owen Dixon when he called for a 'strict and complete legalism' for judges*), and thereafter to manage his own 'response' in the form of a counterclaim (*Dixon's strict legalism no longer commands the respect that it once did ... when they decide cases*):

(48) **[WH questions]** *How do judges decide cases?* **[Polar]** *Are judges controlled by rules, principles and professional standards of reasoning or do they decide as politicians, using the law as an instrument to achieve predetermined goals?* In Australia one influential view on this issue was expressed by Sir Owen Dixon when he called for a 'strict and complete legalism' for judges. Dixon's strict legalism no longer commands the respect that it once did and his view is now commonly seen as naïve or as a noble lie intended to hide the freedom open to judges when they decide cases. **[P]** This article examines first Dixon's understanding of strict legalism. **[R]** It will argue that Dixon understood it as a form of practice and not as a rigorous scholarly system. **[P]** Secondly, it will analyse *Wilson v Darling Island Stevedoring* to see whether the leading judgment of Fullagar J is in accord with Dixon's judicial method. In *Wilson* the High Court was presented with a persistent legal problem — **[polar]** *could stevedores claim the benefits of exemption and limitation clauses that commonly featured in bills of lading arising from the transport of goods*

and people?[**P**] <u>The third section of the article will consider</u> the obvious belief of many of the judges in the authorities examined that the commercial inconvenience of not protecting stevedores was too great to ignore. These judges were willing to grant stevedores the protection of exemption clauses in contracts of carriage, a trend that continued, indeed accelerated, after *Wilson*. So, even if Fullagar J did judge as a strict legalist, **[polar]** *does this perceived commercial imperative raise doubts about the appropriateness of this style of judging?*[**C**] <u>In conclusion, the article will consider</u> the implications of showing that the reasoning in *Wilson* displayed a fidelity to Dixon's notion of strict and complete legalism. OJLS

While initial questioning potentially served as a lead-in strategy, informing the reader of how the text unfolds in the preview sequential structure of the article, the author's priority in using the remaining two questions (*could stevedores claim the benefits ... / does this perceived commercial imperative ...*) seemed to functionally define a gap (Swales 2004: 230)[15] in the doctrinal analysis of Dixonian strict legalism as applied in the unsolved judicial methods.

Rather similarly, other authors used questions in the opening lines to frame the text in previews, as in (49), or to anticipate a response to an open question by placing it again in the next utterance (<u>underlined</u>), as in (50) and, in both cases, authors invariably showed their commitment to engaging the potential reader in the discursive framework of the research:

(49) **[WH question]** *How should citizens evaluate the ever more important case law of international economic courts and their sometimes inadequate responses (e.g. by investor-state arbitration) to 'the governance gaps created by globalization (which) provide the permissive environment for wrongful acts by companies of all kinds without adequate sanctioning or reparation'?*[**P**] <u>Section I recalls</u> that the customary law requirement (as codified in the Vienna Convention on the Law of Treaties) of settling 'disputes concerning treaties, like other international disputes, in conformity with the principles of justice and international law', including 'universal respect for, and observance of, human rights and fundamental freedoms for all' (Preamble VCLT), reflects the constitutional functions of courts to interpret and apply law in conformity with 'rule of law', justice and human rights as constitutional restraints on the 'rule of men' and their

[15] In discussing *Later Parts of Introductions* in the research article, Swales (2004: 230, italics in the original) states that "… most studies of introductions show that "indicating a gap" is by far the most common option. More important, the rarer other options of "counterclaiming" or "question-raising" may not *functionally* be very different from gap-indication".

'rule by law'. **[P]** Section II explains why some of the governance problems of the World Trade Organization (WTO) are due to power ... .
JIEL

(50) **[M1]** In June 2007, the Supreme Court of Canada expressly overruled 20 years of jurisprudence that interpreted the freedom of association as excluding collective bargaining. This about-face by the Supreme Court was unexpected. **[WH question]** *What gave rise to this remarkable decision and what does it portend for the role of the courts in labour relations in Canada and beyond?* The recent successes before the courts have led some observers to suggest that it may now be a propitious time for a coordinated and proactive litigation strategy to vindicate labour's collective rights.**[P]** This article offers some preliminary answers to these broader questions and issues **[M]** by focussing on the Supreme Court's decision in the *Health Services and Support* case. ILJ

In (50), where the use of question followed a topic generalization and provided a well-defined research "niche" (Swales 1990), the strategy seemed to depend as yet on 'answering' the question raised in the form of a centrality claim, albeit hedged.

In addition, indirect questions were recorded in the corpus where they occurred twice as much (30 times) as direct questions. Being introduced more by 'Whether' in open-ended questions than by 'How', indirect questions were used mainly in purpose statements, whether or not recycled or introduced by topic generalizations, to present hypotheses behind the intention of the paper, and occasionally in conclusion statements, as in:

(51) **[P]** The objective of the article is to examine whether the new text has indeed delivered on its promise, namely to improve the existing agreement and to eliminate any remaining discriminatory measures and practices. ...
IJEL

(52) **[M1]** The implied obligation of mutual trust and confidence has assumed, in a short space of time, considerable significance within the law of the employment contract. The decision of the House of Lords in *Johnson v Unisys* [2003] 1 AC 518 demonstrates that statute may serve to constrain its growth. **[P]** This article explores whether other statutory rights are likely to have a similar impact upon the implied term. **[P]** The article goes on to explore whether the influence of public law values will constrain mutual trust's capacity to regulate an employer's discretionary powers. **[C]** The article concludes by asking whether mutual trust's future development may be influenced by the standards and ethics of Human Resource Management. ILJ

Where indirect questions were avoided, the preference was to convert them into noun phrases.

The microstructure of abstract moves: linguistic realizations

Distribution patterns of various linguistic features in the generic moves of abstracts were investigated through use of personal and impersonal forms projecting authorial presence in various ways.

Personal forms

Personal forms were examined through the metadiscourse (interactional) resources of self-mentions (Hyland 2005a) by the use of first-person pronouns, including the subjective, objective and possessive cases (*I, my, we, our, us*). In this study, the analytical focus on first-person markers was taken as a key element in establishing the individual stance and identity of the author, as noted in the literature (e.g. Ivanic 1998; Kuo 1999; Tang and John 1999; Hinkel 2001; Hyland 2001a, 2004, 2005a/b; Bondi 2005; Harwood 2005a/b)[16], although in socio-rhetorical works focusing on the broad notion of voice the labels have been attached to *community identities* or *disciplinary identities* (Medway 2002; Dressen-Hammouda 2008), *disciplinary voices* (Matsuda and Tardy 2008), or *academic tribes and territories* (Becher and Trowler 2001).

A glance at the paucity of frequencies in Table 10 shows that authorial presence through self-mentions was not a predominant feature of abstract writing in the law corpus.[17]

[16] These authors provide taxonomies for the pragmatic functions of personal pronoun that revolve around the issue of authorial presence and the relationship of the author with the reader and the academic community. Among them, Tang and John (1999) analyze the students' use of pronouns by focusing on the degree of authorial presence in their writings. The discourse functions they identify range from the least face-threatening "I as representative" to the most powerful "I as originator". Harwood (2005b), who elaborates on the pronominal functions advanced in earlier studies, identifies the rhetorical effects created by the academic writer, such as: "describing and/or critiquing common disciplinary practices", "elaborating arguments on behalf of the community".

[17] As no exception to this feature, Biber et at. (1999: 235) argue that first person pronouns are meager resources in academic writing.

Self-mentions	*I*	*My*	*We*	*Our*	*Us*
BJC	3	0	14	2	0
ILJ	4	0	4	1	0
JIEL	2	0	6	2	1
OJLS	18	2	1	0	0
IJTJ	9	0	5	0	1
TOTAL	36	2	30	5	2

	I	*We*	**Absence of self-mentions**
BJC	1[R]; 2[D]	7[I]; 1[M];3[R];3[D]	13/30
ILJ	1[I]; 3[R]	2[I]; 1[R]; 1[D]	16/30
JIEL	1[I]; 1[R]	3[I]; 3[R]	17/30
OJLS	8[I]; 4[M]; 4[R]; 2[D]	1[D]	13/30
IJTJ	1[I]; 4[M]; 2[R]; 2[D]	1[I]; 1[R]; 3[D]	13/30

Table 10. Occurrence frequency and absence of self-mentions across the journal abstracts, and their distribution across the abstract moves.

Except for the first-person pronouns *I* and *we* mainly controlling the rhetorical situation in 9 abstracts across BJC (*We*: 14) and OJLS (*I*: 18) and slightly less so in 5 abstracts across IJTJ (*I*: 9) and JIEL (*We*: 6), self-mentions were only very loosely distributed across the remaining journals, and were absent in more than half of the corpus journals in favour of impersonality forms examined later in this Chapter. Faced with such a disproportion in explicit author presence, the total incidence of self-mentions in Table 10 shows that the pronoun *I* ranked relatively higher (36) than the pronoun *we* (30), leaving other self mentions to occur only rarely across the journal abstracts. Where first person pronouns did occur, however, they allowed thematization of the rhetorical elements of the moves in the abstracts by performing three main discourse functions in Hyland's (1999b: 118) terms: to organize their arguments, to introduce their research activities, and to show their positions. While these functions also involved challenging other researchers' interpretations and/or methods, or providing evaluations and/or suggestions for the current or future research, they were also performed through impersonal constructions.

Aware of self-representation in writing being a subtle and complex multidimensional phenomenon (Cherry 1998), the higher incidence of the (exclusive) first-person pronouns *I*/*We* in the current corpus seemed to be determined by the writers' experience and confidence in the researchable topic, although the rhetorical site of abstracts (acting as points-of-entry for the legal research) was also clearly suggestive of the writers wishing to show and promote the importance of their legal scholarship along the various move patterns. Whatever the inference, the decision to intrude into the texts largely through the *I* and *We* pronouns gave writers maximum visibility in the research process, and responded to the rhetorical and social awareness of knowledge advancement by synthesizing the resulting knowledge in the writers' own inquiries. As will be seen in move-based transitions, knowledge-building criteria were channelled through the various possible degrees and (exclusive) roles of "I as guide", "I as architect" and "I as recounter of research process" in Tang and John's (1999) categories, which in themselves characterized low-risk textual authorial intervention.

Verb forms co-occurring with *I*, *We*, *The author* in different structures

As shown in Table 11, the nature of authorial presence in *I/we* person themes and other items of explicit author reference was also analyzed by the choice of verb forms realized in the moves, whether or not occurring in "evaluative *that*-clause" structure (Hyland and Tse 2005):

Verbs co-occurring with *I/we/the author* 'subject case+main verb' or 'subject case+"evaluative *that*-clause"' structure						
	BJC	ILJ	JIEL	OJLS	IJTJ	TOTAL
Argue	1	1	2	9	5	18
Find	4	1	2	-	2	9
Examine	2	2	-	2	2	8
Suggest	1	3	-	-	1	5
Evaluate	-	-	-	4	-	4
Consider	-	1	1	1	-	3
Conclude	1	1	-	-	1	3
Discuss	1	-	-	1	-	2
Analyse	1	-	-	-	1	2
Assess	1	-	1	-	-	2

Table 11. Top-ten forms of reporting verbs in the journal abstracts and abstract moves: occurrence frequency

The data in this Table show that different verb forms were employed with the verb *argue* as the most popular choice (18), followed by *find* (9) and *examine* (8) and other verbs in the corpus.

I/*We* and verb forms realizing different rhetorical move structures

In this section, I examine how self-mentions used in conjunction with verb categories to refer to the writers' types of activity contributed to the realization of different rhetorical moves.

Table 10 has shown that the first-person singular pronoun *I* ranked higher in OJLS theoretical journal alone, where it occurred twice as much in the Purpose move (8[I]) than in the Method (4[M]) and Results alone (4[R]), and usually combined with the "discourse" (*argue*) and "research" (*examine/evaluate*) verbs.[18] To illustrate this in OJLS, let us consider the theoretical excerpts below (53-54), where a doctrinal theory and policy analysis of the law were provided. The author in (53) was more likely to present the goal of the article by offering a central argument or thesis in the Purpose elements of the research, as he was with the examination or evaluation goals using *examine* and *evaluate* verbs in (53-54). Here, the use of an *I* pronoun and co-occurring verbs enabled both authors to organize the text (*First I* ... *then* ... / *I end* ...) and direct the reader to the material by focusing on their research and discourse activities:

(53) **[P]** I argue that there is methodological space for a functional explanation of the nature of law that does not commit the theorist to a view about the value of that function for society, nor whether law is the best means of accomplishing it. **[P]** *First* I examine the proper role for function in a theory of law **[R]** and *then* argue for a neutral functional theory, addressing issues raised by Leslie Green, Stephen Perry, Michael Moore and John Finnis. OJLS

(54) **[P]** In this article, I critically evaluate the positions of Professors Jeremy Waldron and W.J. Waluchow on the right-based merits of entrenched constitutions and strong judicial review. ...**[R]** I argue that the anticonstitutionalist approach to the 'dead hand of the past' is self-refuting, and that it is simply another constraint on autonomy. **[C]** I end by expressing serious concerns … . OJLS

The author in (53) displayed explicit authorial argument and provided an evaluation of the purpose elements in "evaluative *that*-clause" (Hyland and Tse 2005) through discoursal verb *argue*, while the author in (54) exploited the evaluative potential of self-projection by adopting an

[18] These verbs are derived from Hyland's (2004: 27) taxonomy based on the type of activity.

explicitly critical stance to the source authors through the modifying adverb *critically*. Like any theoretical article substantiating the positions put forward with evidence from a discussion of the topic, the potential result statements using *argue* helped the authors to present the outcome of their important research.

Similarly, the text-organizing function of the *I* pronoun guided the reader through the argument in the theoretical abstract below:

(55) **[M1]** Joseph Raz's famous theory of authority is grounded in three claims about the nature and justification of authority. According to the Preemption Thesis, authoritative directives purport to replace the subject's judgments about what she should do. According to the Dependence Thesis, authoritative directives should be based on reasons that actually apply to the subjects of the directive. According to the Normal Justification Thesis (NJT), authority is justified to the extent that subjects are more likely to comply with right reason by following the authority's directives than by following their own judgments about what right reason requires. **[P]** In this article, I consider a number of ways in which NJT might be construed as a justification for authority. **[P]** *First*, I evaluate NJT construed as a principle that would provide a practical justification for an individual to accept or recognize a particular person or persons as a preemptive authority. **[P]** *Second*, I evaluate NJT construed as a principle that describes the conditions under which a state or legal system is morally legitimate. **[R]** I argue that NJT is true under none of these interpretations. OJLS

In addition to stating the scope of the research in the Purpose elements, the author was concerned with the presentation of the global structure of his article, until possibly deducing the main results, which then challenged other scholars' interpretation (*I argue that NJT is true under none of these interpretations*). Reasonably, by using the verb *argue* in the reporting of theoretical research, the author only considered the "knowledge claim" (Myers 1992a) or "field-central claim" (Bloor and Bloor 1993) to be a (theoretical) argument rather than a fact, since the author offered his own position on the construction and deconstruction of theoretical issues based on the doctrinal interpretation of law. The preview sequential structure, using "frame markers" (Hyland 2005a), was a useful strategy to inform the readers of how the article unfolds in the global organization.

Unlike writers in theoretical OJLS extending their authorial presence (*I*) to all moves, those in BJC empirical journal narrowed their authorial presence to abstract moves, as shown in Table 10. The sample in (56) shows that the *I* pronoun linked the researcher to his results and inferable conclusions, in addition to his methodological procedure (embedded in the textual realization) that made importance to such results:

(56) **[P]** This paper addresses the effects of recent political and economic trends on the construction of forensic science in England and Wales. **[M]** Using documentary sources and fieldwork, **[R]** I show that neo-liberal initiatives have differentially reconstructed relationships between forensic scientists and the police. **[C]** I argue that this stems from contested interpretations of scientific integration that have selectively appropriated elements of neo-liberalism. Neo-liberal reform of forensic science has, however, exposed actors to new risks, culminating in the UK Government's announcement to close the Forensic Science Service. Yet, rather than representing the end of 'marketization', debates concerning the organization of forensic science have entered a new phase. These hold significant implications for understanding the relationship between crime, science and advanced liberal governance. BJC

In constructing conclusion, this writer widened out the focus of his findings by including important implications in the study, and similarly reminded readers of the relevance of the research to real problems.

In the case of *We*, ranking higher in BJC journal (Table 10), the pronoun helped the writers in their largely exclusive role to perform pragmatic acts across the moves at a varying incidence. The exclusive semantic reference of the pronoun was determined by the co-authored nature of the research work figuring out in twenty-eight abstracts, although reasonably the exclusive reference also bound the author to the reader for persuasive objectives. In this form of semantic reference, and as shown in Table 11, authors writing for other empirical abstracts were more inclined to use the verb *find* (9) than *argue* to report their findings in the Results moves using data-gathering procedures (such as case studies and interviews). Therefore, they presented the nature of their research activities as being related to real-world claims. While other verbs (e.g. *examine*) were also relatively used in the rhetorical moves other than Results, the set of examples below (57) illustrate the exclusive *we* pronoun and the co-occurring verb *find* fronting the writers' competence and merit of the research outcomes (Results) to the discipline's collective knowledge:

(57) … **[M]** Comparing the Russian data with research, conducted in England and Wales and other countries in which a more punitive response has been adopted in recent years, **[R]** we find unexpected similarities, and contrasting attitudes, and a strong welfare orientation among the Russian public. BJC

[M2] Internationally, sentencing research has largely neglected the impact of Indigeneity on sentencing outcomes. **[M]** Using data from Western Australia's higher courts for the years 2003–05, **[P]** we investigate the direct and interactive effects of Indigenous status on the judicial decision to imprison. **[R]** Unlike prior research on race/ethnicity in which minority offenders are often found to be more harshly treated by sentencing courts, we find that Indigenous status has no direct effect on the decision to imprison, after adjusting for other sentencing factors (especially past and current criminality). ... BJC

[P] This paper seeks to identify, for the first time, trends in claimant use of the Irish Employment Equality Acts 1998–2008. **[P]** Specifically, we examine types of claimant representation, the sectoral origin of claims and the outcomes of equality cases. **[M]** Our findings are based on an analysis of 434 employment equality cases decided by the Equality Tribunal in the seven-year period 2001–07 and interviews with key informants from equality bodies and trade unions. **[R]** We find that there is a high failure rate of complainants' cases, that success rates vary across types of representation and that a disproportionate number of claimants are from the public sector. ILJ

[P] In this article, we untangle the relationships among law, power and justice as they impact on the lives of ordinary Rwandans brought into contact with the state and local officials through the *gacaca* process. **[M]** Drawing on 37 life-history interviews conducted in 2006, **[R]** we find that *gacaca* reinforces a particular version of postgenocide justice that renders the average Rwandan citizen largely powerless over individual processes of reconciliation while serving to maintain a climate of fear and insecurity in their everyday lives. ... IJTJ

... **[R]** We find that the MPA has not been more widely adopted since the completion of T5 which is indicative of institutional constraints on labour–management partnerships in Britain. … IJTJ

The types of activity carried out in verb forms by exclusive pronoun were reflected in the specific communicative purposes of the writers in certain moves.

By contrast, there were only two single-authored abstracts shown in (58) and (59) in which the semantic reference of the pronoun *we* was typically inclusive - i.e. used instead of *I*. In these isolated instances, the pronoun occurred in clearly marked discussion/conclusion statements, where the writer offered a generalization and/or implications of the research question (58), or offered an interpretation and/or application of the results to answer the stated research question (59). Here, the type of activity referred to by the authors favoured as yet research verbs (*evaluate/conclude*), also in modalized form (*we can evaluate*), and discoursal verb (*discuss*):

(58) ... **[C]** To conclude, in general, this risk can only be averted by the more stringent version of the rule, as it is only by preventing the fiduciary from ever considering the legitimacy of a specific conflict of interest that we can evaluate the process of reflection which is so prone to being subverted by self-deception. OJLS

(59) ... **[D/C]** We discuss the potential mechanisms through which the structural and cultural shifts are resulting in these changes and conclude that the ongoing transition is largely responsible for the changing nature of homicide in Russia. BJC

In these instances, shifting position from an exclusive to inclusive authorial *we* pronoun seemed to have the rhetorical effect of persuading the readership about the legal topic to be tackled. And while the persuasive effect sought to invite the readers into the authors' important arguments by treating them as disciplinary equals, it also served to plug a knowledge gap in the discipline.

Although, as Table 11 shows, the verb *examine* was the third most frequently occurring verb (8) after *argue* and *find*, and was used to refer to research procedures in purpose and method statements, other verbs used in combination with *I/we* pronouns had very few token number indeed. Among these, *analyse* (2) and *show* (2) allowed the authors to focus on research activities and procedures in purpose and results statements, respectively, while the cognitive verb *suggest* (5) was a conscious strategy to hedge the strength of the claim in results and discussion statements, as opposed to *look at* (1) and *provide* (1), as used in purpose statements, and *use* (2) in method statements, being neutral verb forms.

Other evidence of authorial reference

In addition to *I/we* self-mentions, other less frequently occurring items of explicit author reference in the third person were found in two journals (*the author*: 1 - *the authors*: 6):

Authorial reference	*The author*	*The authors*
BJC	0	0
ILJ	0	3
JIEL	0	0
OJLS	0	0
IJTJ	1	3
TOTAL	1	6

The authors:2 [I] *The authors*:1 [D]	*The authors*:1 [I] *The authors*:1 [R] *The authors*:1 [D] *The author*:1 [R]
ILJ	IJTJ

Table 12. Occurrence frequency of other explicit authorial references in the corpus and their distribution across the abstract moves.

Like the explicit *I/we* theme choices being given their special focus, these items also syntactically foregrounded the participants in the process of legal research production, and characterized Purpose, Results and Discussion moves in various verb forms (*argue, consider, examine, find, conclude*), whether or not in (evaluative) *that* structure. In the three instances alone of "evaluative *that*-clause" (Hyland and Tse 2005) found in the same journal (IJTJ), the items foregrounded the authors' main findings and discussion through discoursal and research verbs in the *argue* and *find* forms, thus "pointing directly to the implications of the findings in the projected clause" (Hyland and Tse 2005: 131):

(60) … **[P]** The authors examine the ECtHR's extension of the *Demirand Baykara* principle to include collective action and review the Strasbourg court's jurisprudence generally on the right to strike … ILJ

(61) …**[C]** The authors conclude the article by welcoming the draft recommendations from the Council of Europe's Parliamentary Assembly to draw up a set of guidelines for the protection of whistle blowers and consider drafting a framework convention.ILJ

(62) ... **[M]** Using the political conflict in Peru as a case study, **[R]** the author argues that the thesis that rape is a weapon of war obscures other rape regimes during political conflict. These include rape ... JITJ

[D] ... The authors argue that special protection measures, land deeds for women and better access to justice must be included in transitional justice processes as a means of fostering gender-equitable development. IJTJ

... In promoting truth-telling initiatives and confronting the past, memorializing the departed and burying the dead, and resolving ongoing or recent community conflicts, **[R]** the authors find that local-level programs have distinct advantages. IJTJ

Other less-explicit items of author presence

However, self-referential items noted above related to other less-explicit items projecting authorial presence through use of the nouns ARTICLE, ESSAY, PAPER and STUDY, as shown in Table 13:

Less-explicit authorial items	*N°*	*%*	IJTJ	OJLS	JIEL	ILJ	BJC
PAPER	35	0.15	3	5	1	5	21
STUDY	23	0.10	4	1	4	1	13
ESSAY	2	0.01	-	-	-	2	-
ARTICLE	188	0.80	46	37	59	39	7

Table 13. Concordance data of less explicit authorial references using WordSmith Tools 5.

The concordance-based analysis of these items reveals that ARTICLE was the preferred expression in the corpus, followed in far lower incidence by PAPER, STUDY and ESSAY. The preference for ARTICLE seemed therefore to emphasize the broader research area of the discipline. The following are common concordance lines from the corpus:

N	Concordance – ARTICLE – 188 occ. – 0.80%	CORPUS
1	ble democratic transition, **the article argues that** these eff	IJTJ
2	left an ambiguous legacy. **This article uses** the IER – a trut	IJTJ
3	tice after mass violence. **This article uses** lessons from pra	IJTJ
4	come-generating component. **The article reviews** this and oth	IJTJ
5	former Yugoslavia (ICTY). **The article provides** a theoretica	IJTJ
6	sitional justice paradigm. **The article explores** the potential	IJTJ
7	human rights violations. **This article critically examines** t	OJLS
8	rrent state of the field, **this article argues against** the cu	OJLS
9	deeply divided societies. **This article discusses** the advance	ILJ
28	communication. **The aim of this article is to examine** the rel	JIEL
29	ecial Court press office, **this article seeks to contribute** t	JIEL

N	Concordance – PAPER – 35 occ. – 0.15%	CORPUS
1	post-conflict transition. **The paper uses** the case study of	IJTJ
2	creditation' of testimony. **This paper suggests** such distrust	IJTJ
3	covery adopted. Ultimately, **the paper argues for** a holistic,	IJTJ
4	traint or 'deference'. **In this paper, I seek to demonstrate**	ILJ
5	ng drug treatment courts, **this paper explores** the relationsh	BJC
6	f lawmaking in this area. **This paper presents** a quantitative	BJC
14	des towards crime issues. **This paper will explore** these issu	BJC
15	ng conventional legality, **this paper draws on** legal conscious	BJC
16	ldstein 1985). **The aim of this paper is to examine** the valid	OJLS

By constantly making the ARTICLE or other nouns the subjects of active clauses (Theme) and leaving the rest of the clauses to focus on the Rheme of the clauses, these items included deictic forms (*this article, this paper*) and functioned metadiscoursively to announce the elements of the research particularly in the Purpose and Conclusion moves. In addition to being expressed in the dominant present tense form, as noted before, and only in four instances in the future form (*will*) to predict the research question, these items co-occurred with quite a large set of variously frequent verbs that are of a wide currency across various disciplines, as shown in Table 14.

Verbs	Occ.
Examine	26
Explore	20
Conclude	16
Argue	14
Analyse	11
Consider	9
Provide	8
Focus	8
Present	8
seek to	7
Discuss	6
Use	6
Offer	6
Review	5
Describe	5
Show	5
Contribute	4
Address	3
draw on/upon	3
Suggest	3
Find	3
Apply	2
Demonstrate	2
Investigate	2
Reveal	2
Develop	2
Distinguish	2
Proceed	2
Aim	1
Broaden	1
Contend	1
Comment	1
Contextualize	1
Categorize	1
to be concerned with	1
Identify	1
Introduce	1
Evaluate	1
Highlight	1
Employ	1
look at	1
Question	1
Explain	1
Understand	1
Pursue	1
Raise	1
Recall	1

Table 14. Frequency of verbs co-occuring with ARTICLE, ESSAY, PAPER, STUDY.

Where these items occurred in purpose statements, in subject noun phrase / verb collocations or in copulative complements in 'identifying be' clauses, as noted before, the aims of the research were thus described in terms of the written product, so that the concordance items objectivised the abstracts by making them appear impersonal in the readers' hand. And this kind of impersonality and objectivity added to the noticeable frequency of agentless constructions discussed in the next section.

To further illustrate how the most frequently occurring noun ARTICLE collocates in the corpus via visual devices, the following word cloud was obtained from WordSmith Tools - Word Cloud 6 by selecting the statistical measure "log-likelihood" (Dunning 1993) scores. The font sizes of the words collocating with ARTICLE in the word cloud below show the strength of log-likelihood relations:

Impersonal forms

A good starting point for impersonality here is to consider the conventions proposed in most manuals and textbooks, where "[e]radication of the self ... allows the research to speak directly to the reader in an unmediated way" (Hyland 2001a: 208). Actually, guidelines for writing abstracts across the disciplines often advise on the use of passive voice and other impersonal constructions, despite the fact that avoidance of the self will produce 'lifeless' prose in the formal realizations. In contrast to the general assumption that abstracts rely on objective and impersonal style in the narrow sense, this analysis suggests that a degree of authorial involvement (stance) is portrayed in legal abstracts when certain evaluative material serves to distance the authors from their research activities outside the greater responsibility of *I/We* authorial stance.[1]

In the majority of abstracts in the corpus, impersonal forms of discourse were realized by the use of the passive voice, anticipatory *it* subject, or by attributing agency to inanimate subjects. Table 15 shows the distribution of such patterns across the journals, where they accounted for a substantially high total frequency of 143 occurrences of all such cases.

Impersonal forms	*N°*	*%*	IJTJ	OJLS	JIEL	ILJ	BJC
Passive voice	37	25.87	9	6	7	8	7
Anticipatory *it* subject[2]	26	18.19	3	8	3	6	6
Inanimate subjects[3]	80	55.94	22	7	20	11	20
TOTAL	143	100	34	21	30	25	33

Table 15. Occurrence frequency of impersonal forms and percentages in single journals and totals.

The passive voice category (25.87%), including either the phenomenon as subject of a passive verb plus any other complementary material, was used predominantly in simple present and only rarely in simple past to variously present purpose, method and discussion statements, as in:

(63) **[P]** Therefore, social capital is proposed. / **[D]** Findings are discussed in relation to contemporary government policy and possible future research … BJC

[1] Indeed, the view that academic writing is not entirely devoid of the writer's presence has been acknowledged in several studies (e.g. Swales 1990; Ivanič 1998; Kuo 1999; Hyland 2001a, 2004). As a consequence, a variety of linguistic features such as anticipatory *it* subjects (Hewings and Hewings 2002) or evaluative *that*-clauses (Hyland and Tse 2005), to mention only a few, have been studied for the persuasive criteria pursued in (socially-situated) academic texts.

[2] Example realisations: *it is argued that / it is shown that / it is demonstrated that / it is suggested that / it is concluded that.*

[3] Example realisations: *This/The article argues/contends that / The findings are that / The analysis reveals/demonstrates that / The paper argues that / The /study/results show that / The article concludes that / The evaluation found that.*

[M] In this paper, the DCFR is measured against the criteria of internal consistency and systematic integrity (Part 4). OJLS

[P] Full consideration is given to (i) the treatement of these developments by the English courts in *Metrobus v UNITE the Union* ... . ILJ

[D] The argument is advanced that a by-product of the common law and statutory policy initiatives lying at the heart of the regulation of managerial autonomy has been .... . ILJ

[D] Suggestions are made for either adjusting the facilitative mediation model or seeking an alternative that .... . ILJ

[P] Specifically, trends and overall levels of violence, age and sex patterns as well as social and environmental factors are reviewed in order to determine whether contemporary concepts and patterns of violence are universal or culturally specific... . BJC

Where clauses with anticipatory *it* subject did occur (18.19%), they functioned to "both express opinions and to comment on and evaluate propositions in a way that allows the writer to remain in the background" (Hewings and Hewings 2002: 368). By presenting the rhetorical elements of the various moves, these clauses enabled the authors to engage in the evaluating process of the research usually through a small set of research and discoursal verbs (*argue*, *conclude*, *suggest*, *show*, *demonstrate*, *discover*), as in:

(64) [R] It is shown that his explanation of legal authority depends not only upon familiar jurisprudential notions ... OJLS

[R] It is demonstrated that the authority of a legal system depends very much on its ability to negotiate and accommodate struggles based upon feelings of right—struggles between citizens, between citizens and State, and between States. [R] It is also argued that the manner in which Jhering relies on the idea of *Rechtsgefühl* undermines the received wisdom that he was an interest theorist. OJLS

[M] Using two case studies, [R] it was discovered that the triad leaders converted the social capital they developed into mainland China into economic capital through … . BJC

[D] It is argued that these changes may influence the internal market case law of the Court of Justice ... ILJ

[D] While there is an isolated indication that the Appellate Body is edging closer to a re-interpretation of the provision, it is suggested that the dispute settlement process could be modestly simplified with some amendments to the DSU. IJEL

In the empirical excerpts above, reporting the findings through research verbs *demonstrate* and *show* signalled a strong commitment to the evidence shown by the authors. By a similar token, the choice of *argue* helped self-assured authors to evaluate their own findings in the Results move, or to present an interpretation and/or implications of the results drawn on in their research in the Discussion move. In these and other instances, therefore, authors concealed their interpretive research activities and reporting practices behind objectivity and impersonality features, cut loose from the responsibility implied by the very subjective *I/we* authorial presence.[4]

Where authors attributed agency to inanimate subjects in a comparably higher incidence (55.94%) of nouns (e.g. ARTICLE, STUDY, FINDINGS), including sometimes anaphoric reference made to them (*it*), objectivity was presented essentially in the elements of Results and Discussion moves:

(65) **[R]** The results show that incidents may vary according to dimensions of victim targeting… . BJC

[R] The analyses reveal that all types of violence combined account for about 22 per cent of all deaths... . BJC

[D] This article seeks to demonstrate that the adoption of punitive damages, without wider reform of the existing remedial regime, may lead to inconsistencies… . OJLS

[R] The article finds that while such incentive projects receive limited attention and funding, they have achieved successes in repairing social relationships, addressing poverty and strengthening communities in Bosnia… . IJTJ

---

[4] The use of the first personal pronouns in combination with knowledge claims and beliefs provides the context for Ivanič's (1988) argument about the writer's responsibility. While the author recognizes that claims made outside explicit subjectivity are interpreted to be made by the writer, she maintains that by avoiding *I* the writer withdraws from his or her responsibility for the assertions made (Ivanič 1998: 306).

> **[R]** The data analysis shows that approval of the unique conditional amnesty offered by the TRC was at first surprisingly high, with many respondents acknowledging its practical rationale, but it fell dramatically by 2008. … IJTJ

> **[R]** The main findings are that a sustainable development treaty objective is one of many legal tools to achieve an integration of economic, environmental and social interests… . IJEL

> **[D]** The analysis suggests a need for legislative intervention which, it is argued, should entail innovation in remedial design, to better translate the standards set into changes in workplace conduct. ILJ

These examples show that the *that*-complementizer, common to English academic prose, was generally kept in the formal realizations of mainly the Result move, while it was removed only in few instances (as in *The analysis suggests ...*) where it equally occurred in the Result or Discussion moves. While the preponderance of *that*-clauses in Results coincides with Hyland and Tse's (2005) analysis of Results found in their evaluative *that*-clause constructions, removing the more authorial stance from such constructions allowed the authors to achieve "the level of generality they appealed to" (Hylands and Tse 2005: 133) in the research elements of the moves, and to similarly convey "the objectivity of the findings and the effectiveness of the techniques used" (Hyland and Tse 2005: 133). Even by objectifying research elements, evaluative *that* was important to evaluate the author's action as a researcher who promoted his argument convincingly and therefore encouraged further reading of the whole article. In addition to *that*-constructions, however, the noticeable incidence of hedges (Hyland 2005a/b) through epistemic adverbs (e.g. *likely*, *some*, *generally*: 1.05%), modal verbs (*may/might*, *could*, *would*: 0.41%), and lexical verbs (*seem*, *suggest*: 0.16 %), contributed to withholding complete commitment to a claim in the various move sections outside more authorial *I/we*. Hedges, therefore, suggested another way of hiding authorial presence in the abstracts, and dropped a hint at authorial evaluation on account of the backgrounded author.

Conclusion

The data analysis reported in this study was designed to be illustrative of the diversified types of rhetorical move patterns that shaped the construction and use of the legal abstract genre. Although the purpose of this study was not to suggest a definitive description of such patterns, as further analysis may be needed into the rhetorical and linguistic realizations of law abstracts, the study sought to widen the knowledge of the disciplinary genre by systematic corpus insights.

On the level of rhetorical organization, the findings in this study suggest that legal authors used the abstract genre by responding to recurring and new rhetorical move patterns of different types. Findings indicate that only the very low minority of authors wrote strictly-structured (informative) abstracts in the standard IMRD format typical of the research article, while the very large majority stepped out of this format by writing differently less-structured (indicative) abstracts, whether in empirically or theoretically grounded materials. Whatever the optional structure, the majority of authors tended to motivate the inter/disciplinary research question by integrating IMRD and its varied rhetorical patterns with the moves that are typical of the revised CARS rhetorical strategies. Although, in all these strategies, move patternings revealed the inherently complex summarizing task of abstract writing and how the authors thought they could best rhetorically orient, by persuading, the readers in the presentation of their published research, the patternings were also obviously a matter of individual choice. Choosing or selecting parts that created an impression of the writers' research work – motivation, problem statement, approach, results, and conclusions, provided the framework for the varied or standardized practices of genre writers, who were motivated by their diverse needs, priorities, values, methods of inquiry, and cultural backgrounds and, not least, expected knowledge of readers. And while personal choices legitimized the community writers' new inter/disciplinary research projects in the context of their epistemology, practice and culture of academic law, they also accounted for the more complex, dynamic forms of the genre (Bhatia 2004; Swales 2004), and similarly the "very unpredictability of the discursive realities of the world" (Bhatia 2004: 113).

On the level of (micro)linguistic realizations, variability in the genre played only a marginal role, since authors made the abstracts appear as an impersonal rather than personal linguistic choice. Explicit *I/we* self-mentions in the rhetorical move elements enabled the authors to frame research claims by emphasizing the validity of their contributions to the scholarly debate. Discoursal self was essential to synthetise a persuasive research model necessary for the advancement of knowledge-building inquiries in the law discipline. Where explicit authorial presence was heavily reduced in the abstracts in favour of impersonal forms, authors presented their research activities in independent and objective criteria to the scholarly debate. Objectivity features of abstracting was a consequence of the authors wishing to distance themselves from matters of research methods, findings, and interpretations in an attempt to set up a kind of 'firewall' against attack. Although, by keeping themselves out of the line of fire, as it were, writers let the studies speak for themselves at least to some degree, they were still able to promote an evaluative and interpersonal view of academic legal discourse in the genre based on a persuasive endeavour between writer and reader.

	Varied rhetorical patterns: omission	TOTAL
BJC	I-M-R:1/30; I-R-D:1/30; 1-I-M-R:2/30; 1-I-M-D:1/30; 1-M-R-D:1/30; 2-1-I-M-D:1/30; 1-2-I-R:1/30	8/30
ILJ	I-M-R:2/30; I-M:1/30; I-R:3/30; I-D:1/30; I:7/30; 1-I-R-D:1/30; 1-I-R:1/30; 1-I-M:3/30; 1-I-D:1/30; 1-2-I-M-D:1/30; 1-I:2/30	22/30
JIEL	I-M-R:2/30; I-R-D:2/30; Q-I-R-D:2/30; I-D:5/30; 1-I-M-R:1/30; 1-I-R-D:2/30; 1-I-M-D:2/30; 1-I-R:2/30; 1-I:1/30	19/30
OJLS	I-M-R:1/30; I-R-D:3/30; I-M:2/30; I-R:2/30; I-D:1/30; 1-I-R-D:3/30; 1-I-R:2/30; 1-I:2/30; 1-R:1/30; 1-2-I-M:1/30; 1-2-I:1/30; 2-I-D:1/30	20/30
IJTJ	I-D:1/30; 1-I-M-D:1/30; 1-I-R-D:2/30; 1-I-R:1/30; 1-I-D:1/30; 2-I-M-R:1/30; 1-2-I-R-D:2/30	9/30
TOTAL		78/150
	Varied rhetorical patterns: changing order	TOTAL
BJC	1-M-I-M:1/30; M-I-R-D:1/30; 2-M-I-R-D:1/30; M-I:1/30; 1-M-I-R:1/30; I-R-I-D:1/30; 1-I-M-I-R:1/30; 1-I-M-I-M-R-D:1/30; I-M-I-M-D-M:1/30; I-M-R-I-M-R-D:1/30; 1-M-I-R-I-D:1/30; 1-M-I-I-R-D:1/30	12/30
ILJ	I-M-I-I-M-R-D:1/30; 1-2-I-M-R-I-D:1/30; I-R-I-D:1/30; 1-I-M-R-M-R-I-D:1/30; I-I-M-I-R:1/30; I-M-I-R-D:1/30	6/30
JIEL	1-I-R-I-D:1/30; 1-I-D-M-R-D:1/30; 1-R-M-I-I:1/30; 1-I-R-D-R:1/30; 1-2-I-M-I-R:1/30; 1-M-I-R-M-R-D:1/30; M-I-M-I-R:1/30; I-Qs-I:1/30; 'unstructured' 1/30	9/30
OJLS	I-M-R-I-M:1/30; 1-2-I-M-I-M-I:1/30; I-R-M-D:1/30; I-M-I-R:1/30; 1-R-M:1/30; 1-I-M-I:1/30; 1-I-R-M-D:1/30; Q-I-R-I-Q-I-Q-D:1/30	8/30
IJTJ	I-M-I-I-R-D:1/30; 1-M-R-I:1/30; 1-M-I-R-D:1/30; 1-I-M-I-R-D:1/30; 1-M-I-R:1/30; 1-I-M-R-I-D:1/30; 1-M-R-I-D:1/30; 1-M-I-M-M-M-M-M:1/30; 1-2-M-I-R:1/30; 2-I-M-I-M-I-R:1/30; 1-I-R-M-I:1/30; 1-M-I-I-R-D-R:1/30; I-M-R-M-D:1/30; 1-2-I-M-I-M-I;1/30	14/30
TOTAL		49/150
TOTAL		127/150

Figure 2. Frequency of IMRD variations and total figures.

PART III:

ASSESSING AND KEEPING FACE IN LEGAL RESEARCH

CHAPTER FIVE

EVALUATION AND POLITENESS IN LAW BOOK REVIEWS

In the previous Chapters I focused on the least or most notable and overt genres (Case Note, RA Abstracts) of the legal academy and profession, by recognizing that the law disciplinarity involves an understanding of the writers' discoursal practices. In the generic writings examined until now, this means that texts are not only socially constitutive of the disciplinary community practices and culture, but also of individual standing and power resulting from epistemological principles of the discipline. Together these features influence or control the actions of genre writers in their efforts to guide readers into disciplinary knowledge inquiries as licensed in such practices.

In this framework, however, the revolution in legal research provides as yet exciting challenges for those writing about legal scholarship, and burdensome book reviews are a case in point. As with other disciplines, book reviews in the law are not only descriptions of the book's purpose, content, and authority, but also 'reaction' papers where strengths and weaknesses of the academic material are evaluated. And while there seems to be no right way to write a book review, analysing the "genre-text in a situational context" (Bhatia 2004: 164) provides an interesting site in which the complex communicative realities of published legal scholarship are involved. Although the genre of Book Reviews occupies a wide research landscape across the disciplines as the genre of Research Article Abstracts, little is known about Book Reviews in the law discipline. This Chapter, which concludes my journey into academic and professional legal genres, provides an understanding of the ways in which academic legal writers evaluate the books they are reviewing, and adds to the academic discourse literature.

In this Chapter, I first outline the existing literature and indicate the focus of my research objectives, and then present the empirical material and the research methodology. In presenting the analytical procedures, I describe some of the methods or theories of linguistics, discourse and genre analysis which are relevant for the analytical goals and scope of this exploratory study. Finally, I discuss the impact of material and method on the findings and draw some conclusions.

Literature Review

Book Reviews have formed the subject of several invaluable studies by linguists and applied linguists, dealing with the academic genre from different research perspectives. These studies have mostly noted that book reviews vary according to time (Salager-Meyer and Zambrano 2001; Salager-Meyer et al. 2003; Salager-Meyer and Alcaraz Ariza 2004; Salager-Meyer et al. 2007) and disciplines (Lindholm-Romantschuk 1998; Hyland 2004), and have included individual and edited studies of intercultural and interdisciplinary variations on the topics of academic evaluation and identity from different theoretical perspectives (e.g. Salager-Meyer et al. 2003; Del Lungo Camiciotti and Tognini Bonelli 2004; Salager-Meyer et al. 2005; Tognini Bonelli and Del Lungo Camiciotti 2005; Giannoni 2006; Bondi 2009; Hyland and Diani 2009; Tse and Hyland 2008; D'Angelo 2008, 2010). In a context where two major functions, informative and evaluative, have been identified of book reviews (e.g. Gea Valor 2000, 2010; Hyland 2004; Salager-Meyer et al. 2005), analytical studies on the book review genre across the disciplines have also shown that they share a number of rhetorical moves (Motta-Roth 1996, 1998; Moreno and Suaréz 2006, 2009, 2010), or reveal additional move sub-functions (Nicolaisen 2002). In addition, research has shown that book reviewing "is built in terms of the characteristic ways of arguing in the discipline for the acceptance of new published material" (Motta-Roth 1996: 115).

In these studies, however, book reviews from the law discipline seem to remain largely under-investigated, despite the fact that they occupy as great a proportion of the law journal space as peer review articles and other genres. The writing of law book reviews emphasizes the practice of journal editors as *gatekeepers* (in Swales's (2004) terms) who increasingly report new scholarly contributions in line with the subject matter charter of their journals and regardless of the researchers and reviewers' backgrounds. As with the electronic availability of Abstracts in the research article journals seen in the previous Chapter, today's access to reviewed contributions is made easier by online law journals supporting rapid publication ahead of the print issue.

In a context where the intent of book reviewing in the law discipline ensures suitability and editorial quality in international academic communication, the analytical focus on the social practices of the disciplinary community in the genre becomes even more necessary. The book review genre is basically a critical evaluation of different aspects of a scholarly book, and plays a vital role in "the manufacture of knowledge" (Hyland 2004: 43) of other scholars' research within the disciplinary area. Given this role in the academic community, book reviews "offer a direct, public, and often critical, encounter with a particular text, and therefore of its author" (Hyland 2004: 41), and as a consequence provide an interesting and stimulating site in which to investigate the pragmatic, interpersonal level of academic discourse in the law discipline.

In this evaluative context, a number of previous studies have focused on criticism in written genres by dealing with the influential models of politeness (e.g. Brown and Levinson 1987, 2009; Holmes 1988, 1995; Myers 1989; Hyland 2004) and the ways in which patterns of linguistic activities are carried out in culturally different speech communities (Brown and Levinson 1987; Blum-Kulka et al. 1989). Outside the realm of contrastive pragmatics in cross-cultural inquiries of politeness strategies, linguistic activities in (English single-culture) book reviews are in fact a classic example of politeness realizations which in themselves constitute "Face-Threatening Acts/FTAs" (Brown and Levinson 1987), and reviewers seek to use strategies to maintain a positive interpersonal relationship by mitigating criticism at the global and local levels.

The importance of politeness can also be seen outside the current academic genre and discipline. A number of investigators, in fact, have focused on communicative practices within health care settings (e.g. Myers 2003; Iedema et al. 2006; Sarangi 2006), and similarly advanced the field of politeness research in the workplace by addressing "the issue of what constitutes polite (and impolite) behaviour in specific workplace settings" (Bargiela-Chiappini and Harris 2006: 27). Interestingly, here, discussion of relevant aspects relating to linguistic and non-linguistic phenomena of politeness in various disciplinary studies (e.g. business studies, sociolinguistics, cultural studies, foreign language teaching, among others) has culminated in the publication of the *Journal of Politeness Research. Language, Behaviour, Culture*.

In an attempt to contribute to the existing studies in the field, I examine the expression of positive and negative evaluations by framing them within the evaluative speech acts of *praise* and *criticism* (Hyland 2004) and the *politeness* rhetorical strategies (Brown and Levinson 1987). These taxonomies shape the interpersonal relationship between the writer and the audience in the academic genre. The most significant micro-level results are discussed and conclusions drawn regarding the main purpose/function of the book review genre, in light of epistemological and social factors that construct the contemporary discourse practices of book reviewers in the law.

Material and Method

The Corpus

This study examined a synchronic corpus of 30 electronically-retrieved academic reviews, consisting of single and co-authored law books published in two randomized sets of 2007-2010 issues of the Cambridge University Press Journals, namely 15 book reviews from *The Cambridge Law Journal* (CLJ) and 15 from *The International Journal of Law in Context* (IJLC), as provided by the Cambridge Journal On-Line Service in the Book Review Section. These reputable journals provide the English language medium for publication in a wide range of legal topics for a variety of international focused readers, whether as academics, practitioners, judges, administrators, or students. Each issue of the journals contained a rather extensive section of book reviews and different material fell within the purview of such journals. As well as emphasizing all aspects of law, including jurisprudence and legal history, CLJ in particular pursued contemporary developments of the law. By contrast, IJLC was an interdisciplinary exercise in legal studies and critical research, with law interfacing between other disciplines such as science, literature, humanities, sociology, psychology, geography, and so on. A list of book review titles and journal source is provided in Appendixes.

In these journals, the majority of reviewers (22) were native (CLJ: 12 / IJLC: 10 – Tot. 22), being mostly UK-based with academic status in British institutions, and their name sometimes appeared under different book reviews. Only in the lower minority of book reviews (CLJ: 5 / IJLC: 3 – Tot: 8)[1] was the native status of reviewers difficult to establish. In both cases, e-mail communications with the Review Editor of the journals informed this author that book reviews underwent regular editing work particularly in terms of format, with some reviews however undergoing more editing than others when needed. The large majority of reviewers dealt with single or co-authored books, while only one of them (IJLC) simultaneously dealt with two books. The reason for this joint review was to establish strengths and weaknesses between the published works

[1] These reviewers were institutionally based outside English-speaking countries (i.e. Germany, France, Israel).

dealing with a similar topic. Therefore, their assembled texts were left unmodified in the corpus.

Based on these criteria for corpus building, Table 1 below provides different quantitative data retrieved from WordSmith Tool 5.0 resulting in a 48,863 word corpus.

	CLJ	IJLC	OVERALL
Number of BRs	15	15	30
Years	2007-2010	2007-2010	
Total number of words	16,838	32,025	48,863
Total number of citations	0	96	96
Average length per text	1,126	2,144	1,635
Sentences	503	1,054	1,557
Sentence length	30.80	30.27	30.44
Average word length	5.17	5.01	5.02

Table 1. Size of the law BR corpus: number and publication year of BRs including citations and average length per text

In addition to the data in Table 1, there were differences with the corpora since some book reviews in IJLC were three times as much in word length (3,230 max), as compared to CLJ (1,395 max). In this study, the reviewed book author's name was kept anonymous as (Author) while the reviewed book title was left undisguised (*italics*).

Methodological procedure

This study examined the frequency and use of reviewers' positive and negative evaluations realized in the review texts.

Aware of evaluation as being a broad cover term[2], this study associated reviewers' positive and negative evaluations to the evaluative speech acts of praise (positive) and criticism (negative) as semantic units, derived from Hyland's (2004) study of book reviews. According to Hyland (2004),

[2] In their seminal work, Thompson and Hunston (2000: 5) define evaluation as "[…] expression of the speaker or writer's attitude or stance towards, viewpoint on, or feelings about the entities or propositions that he or she is talking about". In Speech Act Theory, Austin (1962) stated that language has illocutionary force which expresses the speaker's intention. As such, speech acts have been claimed to operate by universal pragmatic principles (Austin 1962; Searle 1975; Brown and Levinson 1987), or to vary in conceptualization and verbalization across cultures and languages (Wong 1994).

praise is defined as "an act which attributes credit to another for some characteristic, attribute, skill, etc., which is positively valued by the writer", while criticism is "the expression of dissatisfaction or negative comment on the volume" (2004: 44). This approach to categorizing positive and negative evaluations was integrated by politeness phenomena described in Brown and Levinson's (1987, 2009) theory, which addresses positive and negative face for both writers and readers in various "face-threatening acts" (FTAs), and by elements of self-representation (e.g. Tang and John 1999; Hyland 2005a) and genre theory (Swales 1990).

Brown and Levinson's (1987) theory, in particular, lies on three basic notions: face (derived from Goffman 1967), face-threatening acts (FTAs), and politeness strategies. According to Brown and Levinson (1987: 13), face consists of "two specific kinds of desire ('face-wants') attributed by interactants to one another: the desire to be unimpeded in one's actions (negative face), and the desire (in some respects) to be approved of (positive face)". During interaction, either or both of these face aspects can be threatened to varying degrees, giving rise to the notion of face-threatening acts (FTAs). Such acts "run contrary to the addressee's and/or the speaker's positive and/or negative 'face'" (1987: 65), and therefore require the use of politeness strategies to maintain face and harmony in social interaction. Positive politeness strategies (oriented to the hearer's positive face) and negative politeness strategies (oriented to the hearer's negative face) are therefore developed for the purpose of dealing with these FTAs. Brown and Levinson (1987: 92) identify different strategies for performing FTAs ranked in descending order of politeness: bald-on-record, off-record, on-record, and with redress.[3]

[3] More recently, however, attempting to save face for another has led some authors to describe politeness as the "expression of the speakers' intention to mitigate face threats carried by certain face threatening acts toward another" (Mills 2003: 6), or as "a set of norms or values that crucially influences the volitional and strategic action of individuals ... [and] reflects in verbal and nonverbal behaviour something of the deep-seated values of individual cultures" (Bargiela-Chiappini and Harris 2006: 12). However, as speech acts and politeness are some of the main areas of interest in pragmatics, evidence of a variety of such communicative phenomena has also been the focus of cross-cultural comparisons in different languages (de Zarobe and de Zarobe 2012).

By close analytical reading of the texts, evaluative items were tagged inductively by a combination of various lexico-grammatical or discourse units (e.g. adjectives, nouns, verb phrase)[4] in their context/co-text, and interpreted in their propositional and metadiscoursive content (Hyland and Tse 2004a; Hyland 2005a: 21-22). Under this procedure, positive and negative evaluations were counted and analyzed separately, by identifying whether they occurred as explicitly positive or negative comments in entire sentences, and in combination with mitigation devices used to soften the blow of the criticism. Below are the instances of positive and negative evaluations in entire sentences, where positive semantic units, as in (1), contrasted with negative ones, as in (2), or were combined in mitigated criticisms (MCs), as in (3-4):

(1) (Author)'s grasp of the subject is clearly superior(+), as he explores cost-benefit analysis, incentivization and the Coase Theorem in depth(+). CLJ

(2) (Author) fails to take economic facts into account(-). IJLC

(3) Comprehensive and analytical(+), if at times disorganized(-), *Economics of the Law* is a gratifying addition(+) to the growing scholarship on law and economics. CLJ

(4) Whilst the useful concluding sections of each chapter aim to address these questions(+), the authors make no real attempt (-) to extend this evaluation outside the courtroom or the statute book, ignoring the evidence(-) produced by the British Institute of Human Rights and others… IJLC

Drawing on Hyland's analysis of criticism in the book review genre, three main categories of mitigation strategies were identified in the corpus - namely, "praise-criticism pairs", "hedges", and "other attribution" (Hyland 2004: 55). Further strategies that fell outside such categories were labelled as OTHERS.

The aspects of positive and negative evaluative acts in the corpus were then coded in most of Hyland's (2004: 47) "general" and "specific" categories of evaluation (Table 2), and did not include the specific content categories of "publishing", "tasks", and "exercises", on account of their absence from the current corpus.

[4] The combination of these evaluative items in the genre also reflects the writers' overt positioning in academic prose, which is linguistically enacted by "the use of an evaluative lexical item, usually an adjective, main verb, or noun" (Biber et al. 1999: 968).

Focus	Description
Content	
(i) General	Overall discussion: e.g. coverage, approach, interest, currency, quality
(ii) Specific	Argument: e.g. insight, coherence, explanatory or descriptive value
Style	Exposition: clarity, organization, conciseness, difficulty, readability and editorial judgments
Readership	Value or relevance for a particular readership, purpose or discipline
Text	Extent, relevance and currency of references, the number, usefulness and quality of diagrams Index items, tasks and exercises
Author	Writer's experience, reputation, qualifications or previous publications
Publishing	Price, quality and production standards of the book

Table 2. Categories of evaluation in book reviews, as adapted from Hyland (2004: 47).

Results and Discussion

In this section, the most salient results and hypotheses are presented from the quantitative and qualitative analysis emerging from the various book sections.

Positive, negative and mitigated evaluations: frequency distribution

I explored the total frequency distribution of explicitly positive, negative, and mitigated evaluations across the various book sections, yielding the data reported in Table 3 and Figure 1.

	Positive		Negative		Mitigated		TOTAL	
	N°	*%*	*N°*	*%*	*N°*	*%*	*N°*	*%*
CLJ	188	59.9	18	5.7	108	34.4	314	49.3
IJLC	113	35	30	9.3	180	55.7	323	50.7
TOTAL	301	47.3	48	7.5	288	45.2	637	100

Table 3. Positive, negative and mitigated evaluations in the corpus: figures, percentages and totals.

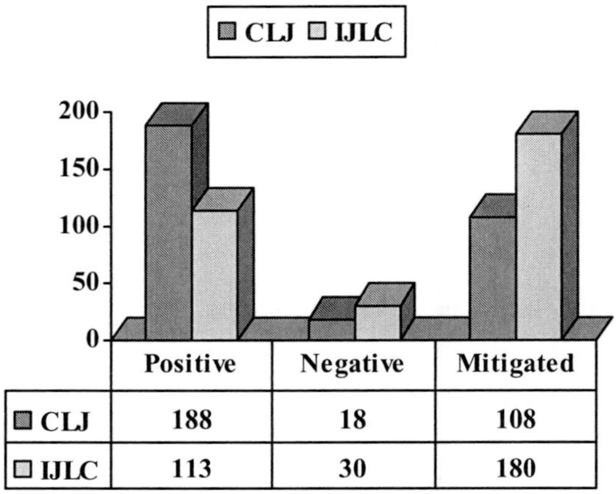

Figure 1. Positive, negative and mitigated evaluations in the corpus.

Table 3 shows that a total of 637 explicitly positive, negative, and mitigated evaluative acts were detected in the corpus journals, divided almost evenly in incidence between the two journals (CLJ: 49.3% - IJLC: 50.7%). Where negative evaluations are ignored, accounting for only 7.5% of the total incidence of evaluative acts, the corpus turned out overall to be slightly more positive (47.3%) than mitigative (45.2%) in evaluations. If the corpus is broken down into single journals, then, Table 3 shows that reviewers in CLJ tended to be more positive (59.9%), while reviewers in IJLC tended to be more mitigatively negative (55.7%) in their evaluations.

However, the frequencies of explicitly positive and negative evaluations as well as mitigated criticisms varied across the 30 book reviews. In CLJ, positive evaluations ranged from 6 to 26 instances, while negative evaluations ranged from 0 to 8. The frequencies of mitigated criticisms ranged from 3 to 14. In IJLC, the range was 3 to 14 for positive, 0 to 9 for negative, and 2 to 25 for mitigated criticisms. The frequency range of negative evaluations shows that they were statistically marginal, since in CLJ more than two thirds of book reviews did not contain any such comments, as compared to almost half of book reviews in IJLC. Thus, leaving aside negligible negative comments, all but 1 book review in CLJ may be considered 'positive reviews' while almost two thirds of book reviews in IJLC (9 BRs) may be considered 'mitigative reviews'.

Positive evaluations across book review sections

Reviewers in both journals explicitly expressed **positive comments** in the **opening**, **intermediate** and **closing sections** of the books in positive politeness strategies. Such strategies were addressed towards the author's positive face, by attending to the hearer's wants and desires to be approved by others in B&L's model.[5] In the opening (reader-oriented) sections, in particular, commenting positively served as an effective global strategy "to convey overall impressions within a restricted space", and consequently "to limit the scope of negative comment" (Hyland 2004: 48) in the intermediate and closing sections.

Opening sections

In the opening sections (introducing the book in its general context of research), positive evaluations were often concerned with general content focus regarding coverage, interest, currency, and quality, and sometimes with author focus regarding experience and reputation. Here, the rationale of the positive comments often required attitudinal markers (adjectives and adverbs), addressing positive face in variously used AFFECT (Martin 2000)[6] emotional responses and dispositions to the book description and evaluation, with such expressions as *excellent*, *candidly acknowledging*, *admirably researched*, *clearly superior*, *the best available*. These expressions therefore intensified the reviewer's reaction and involvement in the evaluated material. Of course, reviewers were considerate about many such positive expressions being used in a sentence, which could have made it look like an adjective positive list. By describing such

---

[5] In terms of B&L's model, positive politeness in the current data functions by implicating solidarity or closeness with the hearer (author), and is consistent with Goffman (1967) presentation rituals.

[6] In Martin's (2000: 147) APPRAISAL theory, the three groups labeled AFFECT, JUDGMENT and APPRECIATION are ways of thinking about attitude which involves positive or negative feeling, and JUDGMENT and APPRECIATION are interpreted as institutionalizations of AFFECT.

qualities with little backing evidence already at the start of reviewing, the perception was that reviewers wished to convey a marketing campaign exercised to the benefit of the media institution, namely the Cambridge University Press Journals which employed the reviewers. This perception was gained not only linguistically by the use of such expressions, but was also reinforced extralinguistically by the institution pursuing the business commitment on the global market, with the CUP website indeed spelling out that "the Press operates with keen commercial awareness" (Cambridge Journals: "About Us: Capabilities and Culture").

With a publicity attitude at work, therefore, most reviewers were often positive in the opening lines of the book, as in (5):

(5) This excellent book explores the protection of personal identity and freedom through human rights law. It opens with a powerful statement of the importance of a sense of self and the challenges to that sense of self posed by modern life:

> 'A sense of one's own personal identity is crucial to human beings. Without a sense of identity the sense can disintegrate, …' IJLC

This is a wide-ranging, thoughtful book from which I have learnt a lot. It joins a number of debates ongoing for a generation about law and its impact upon gender relations (for example, Smart, 1989). IJLC

or delayed their positivity in the first few lines of the book, as in (6), where they resorted to the rhetorical move types and steps of the CARS model (Swales 1990) for the RA introduction:

(6) MONOGRAPHS ABOUT TORT LAW seem never to have been in short supply. Occasionally, authors produce theoretical books that deal with the subject as a whole. Yet much more common are those that examine some particular aspect or area of tort law, such as negligence, nuisance, product liability, defamation, or the economic torts **[Establishing a territory-Move 1: Step 1+2]**. Until recently, one such book has been conspicuous by its absence [**Move 2: Indicating a gap-Step 1B**]; but (authors) have now plugged that gap by rising to the most unenviable challenge in tort law scholarship and writing *The Tort of Conversion*. CLJ

On some occasions, such as in (7), commenting positively on the currency and quality of the book in the opening lines also allowed reviewers to tentatively relate to, and thereafter point out a specific gap in, other books on a similar topic, thus commending what the book under review attempted to cover in the disciplinary community of scholars:

(7) IN TIMES WHERE the European Commission's "more economic approach" to competition policy often is accepted as the new and only standard for competition policy without any questions asked about other, non-economic objectives, (author)'s book refreshingly goes against this trend as it examines the relevance of non-economic goals in contemporary EC competition policy. This task is very much to be lauded as his work fills in a gap in the English speaking academic literature which, up to this point, does not appear to have attempted an in-depth analysis of this important topic in a comprehensive manner [**Move 2: Indicating a gap-Step 1B**]. Until now, the works which are probably closest to (author)'s book insofar that they might be considered as having (at least partially) examined similar points are D. Schmidtchen, M. Albert and S. Voigt (eds.), *The More Economic Approach to European Competition Law* (Tübingen 2007), and A. Künzler, *Effizienz oder Wettbewerbsfreiheit?* (Tübingen 2008) [**tentatively relating to other books on the topic**]. However, neither of these books deals exclusively with the question of the importance of public policy considerations in competition policy concerning Article 81 EC [**pointing out a specific gap in books**]. In other words, (author) has written a much needed book. CLJ

Only in lower instances in the corpus (5 occ.) did writers delay further their opening positivity by resorting again to CARS rhetorical move types and steps constructed in the initial paragraph, as in:

(8) The cross-border trafficking of women for the purposes of sexual exploitation has been the focus of considerable attention in recent years. Though far from a new phenomenon, the scale of its contemporary manifestation, its apparent connection to networks of organised crime and state corruption, its intersection with heated debates over divergent models for the regulation of prostitution, and its situation within broader contexts of globalisation, socioeconomic displacement and migration control have ensured its status as a 'high priority' in policy discussions nationally, regionally and internationally. Official statements condemning this criminal activity have proliferated and national laws have been developed in which the components of this offence are set out alongside options for the punishment of its perpetrators and the recompense of its victims [**Establishing a territory-Move 1: Step 1+2**]. But while much ink has been devoted to the topic of sex trafficking in the past decade, there has been a lack (until recently at least) of sustained academic engagement with the theoretical constructs that underpin these responses, and an absence of literature that has sought critically to reflect upon the motivations and merits of these policy initiatives by – amongst other things – interrogating its foundational concepts of 'exploitation', 'migration', 'vulnerability' and 'choice', as well as its preoccupation with prostitution over other forms of

domestic or labour servitude [**Establishing a niche-Move 2 > Indicating a gap-Step 1B**].

It is against this backdrop that (author)'s recent book makes such a valuable contribution. Focusing specifically upon anti-trafficking initiatives at the European level, and candidly acknowledging its restricted coverage in terms of the class of trafficked person (women) and the purpose for which they are trafficked (sexual exploitation), the book offers impressive and careful coverage of this fast-moving and challenging subject matter. ... . IJLC

This reviewer introduced the general topic of the research (*Establishing a territory*-Move 1) by making a centrality claim of the topic (Step 1-Move 1) and making topic generalizations as neutral kind of general statements about phenomena (Step 2-Move 1), thus raising the interest and importance of the topic among readers. He then went on to show some limitations in the literature manifested in *Indicating a gap* (Step 1B) in *Establishing a niche* (Move 2) for the research under review until he shifted to a new paragraph where the book was introduced by positive descriptions of general content aspects relating to coverage, interest and currency of the book. While, in the excerpts above (6-8), the reviewers used the *Indicating a gap* strategies as their first negative evaluative comment (by showing incompleteness or lack of knowledge of the topic among disciplinary scholars), their positive comments served indeed to bridge the identified gaps by acknowledging a scholarly work's uses and contributions. The result was that the books were often explicitly commended for being *analytical*, *comprehensive*, *excellent*, *insightful*, *readable*, and *valuable*, as the most frequently used adjectival evaluations implying marketing-oriented objectives.

Intermediate sections

In the intermediate sections, outlining the organization of the book, positive comments focused on specific aspects of the book related to argument (insight), style (clarity, organisation) and text (extent, relevance and currency of references, index items). While these aspects were also intensified by superlatives, adjectives and adverbs (as was particularly among CLJ reviewers), they were presented this time in focused evaluation and drawn upon with more backing evidence of the positive quality descriptions than in the opening sections. This can be seen in the set of extracts (9) below:

(9) The ensuing analysis is as readable as it is erudite and comprehensive, encompassing the substantive, theoretical and practical questions that one would expect to find in a learned treatise on the subject – and more. CLJ

These subjects represent the most exciting developments in the field of law and economics. The chapter on the law and economics of the public sector is the strongest component of the book and one that makes (author)'s work worthy of recommendation on its own. CLJ

(Author)'s is a strongly argued piece, with detailed analysis of what the ECJ says as well as what it does. CLJ

(Author)'s recurrent criticism of the neoliberal regime and the corresponding need for governmental intervention in markets is undeniably prescient. CLJ

Thus (author)'s draft Constitution covers most topical constitutional issues. The draft proposes solutions to each of these, with reasoned explanations. It therefore provides a useful focus not only for public and political discussion, but also for the teaching of British constitutional law and politics at many levels. IJLC

Other chapters present forceful arguments which are wholly convincing. The re-imagining of the deference debate as really all being about weight in chapter 5 makes not only the terminology better, but also more readily enables the argument about what types of reasons for giving weight are good and bad. CLJ

There is also a very useful section on the less well-explored area of horizontal rights, or the extent that the HRA applies to infringements between private parties. IJLC

(Author) offers a new approach to the analysis of the cinematic experience of crime. The theoretical tools are put forth in the first two chapters and then applied eminently to cinematic treatment of revenge and rape (chapter three: *Sudden Impact* – Clint Eastwood, 1983; ... . IJLC

The issues (author) addresses at this point connect fruitfully with the work of such philosophers as Alasdair MacIntyre (1981, ch. 14) and Joseph Raz (2003), ... IJLC

These examples show the typically rhetorical organizations of the intermediate sections, where the greater reliance on the backing evidence enabled positive reviewers to confidently express objective judgments of the book in Present Simple tense. Without exception, these reviewers were aware of the interpersonal implications that their cognitive judgments would carry on the credibility of the reviewed author and on the readers alike.

However, there were cases where the objective descriptions of the book became more personal in these sections and highlighted the strengths of the book. The positive reviewer in (10), for instance, exploited the reported argument of the reviewed author to create a “niche” (Swales 1990) for his own claim on the topic through the possessive pronoun *my*, so that overtly claiming common view with what was reported had a significant role in highlighting the achievements of the book:

(10) The authors conclude, *rightly in my view*, that the courts’ obligation could ‘arguably be satisfied by considering the Strasburg authority put before it’, so that ‘having taken the decision into account they would not be obliged to follow or apply its reasoning’ (p. 53). ... The authors are right to warn that as the HRA approaches its tenth birthday its future is uncertain. IJLC

Closing sections

In the closing sections, different tendencies were observed. Reviewers from almost half of the journals (14 BRs) provided a closing positive evaluation of the book by explicitly offering credit to the content and value of the work and its author(s), as well as recommending the book to the widest disciplinary readership, as in:

(11) ... The law and Shakespeare make uneasy bedfellows as this thought-provoking collection demonstrates time and again. IJLC

By contrast, only three reviewers in IJLC foregrounded such credit in the opening sections of their books. In this share (14 BRs), reviewers tended to lavishly endorse the objective features of the book by intensifying their certainty of the reliability and significance of the work with the predictive modal *will* (22 occ.), or otherwise combining the proximity of *will*, *cannot* (8 occ.) and *should* (10 occ.) modalized sentences with Present Simple tense (38 occ.), leaving the reader in no doubt of their final assessment of the material:

(12) Many of the chapters in this volume will incite further debate, and none of them can be accused of simply rehearsing old arguments. The book is an invaluable resource for scholars, graduate students and able undergraduates. CLJ

In sum, this book is an encouraging addition to the literature on corporate governance. The academic writing considered is diverse, and the text is enlivened by diagrams, graphs, tables, and statistical comparisons from other economic studies. Equally impressive are the comparative and historical perspectives employed by the writers. CLJ

This admirably researched and well written book is one of the most significant legal contributions to current debates on poverty, human rights an global justice. It should command the attention of students, scholars and activists in the field of international law and beyond. CLJ

(Author)'s knowledge of both cinema and law give her the tools as well as the authority to discuss the effects of image on movie-goers. Her work is very well documented, her analysis pertinent and refined. Her contribution to the field of law and image cannot be contested. *The Scene of Violence* is above all a good read. The general public will appreciate her study of films they already know and will undoubtedly be interested in her particular analysis. Law and film scholars will find thought-provoking ideas to apply to other cinematic works. At the beginning of this book, the author sets out a series of questions she promises to deal with: How does the spectator enter into dialogue with crime images? How is his imagination set to work? What do these films suggest about the law and the legal system? *Her promises are kept.* JILC

Where modal verbs did occur for persuasive objectives in the genre, there was obviously an awareness among these reviewers of the interpersonal implications of the modal meanings lent to their positive comments and, in particular, the presence of the modal *should* and the suasive verb *command* (Biber's Dimension 4, 1988) conveyed the reviewer's judgment of the book as being advisable for the identified users.

Yet, the tendency to reiterate certainty about the scholarly value of the book and its author, led one reviewer in (13) below also to include editors' positive judgments based on the particular scholarly approach taken in the book:

(13) In summary, this slim volume is a fascinating collection of papers, each of which reflects well the overall theme of the work. Those interested in the specific issues covered will no doubt find much to explore. *The editors note that* the relationship between law and medicine (each understood intellectually, professionally and institutionally) in the context of law making is a much under researched topic and should be justly proud that their work presents a collection that breaks much new ground in this area. As such it will be of interest to those working in both the fields of legal and

medical history along with socio-legal scholars interested in these interfaces between law and medicine. CLJ

Although, in these cases, endorsing the qualities of the books still sounded like a marketing campaign for the benefit of the media institution, reviewers in the other share (12 BRs) of the journals however continued to endorse the book, despite expressing some criticism through a variety of mitigating rhetorical strategies discussed later below.

Negative evaluations across book review sections

Where, as a result of the weaknesses identified, **negative comments** became the evaluative focus of the books in negative politeness strategies (i.e. addressed towards the author's negative face)[7], they were found to occur mostly in the **intermediate** parts of the book, and only relatively so in the **opening** and **closing sections**.

As shown by the frequencies in Table 3, and discussed later in detail, in all these sections the very large majority of negative comments were structured in various mitigation devices to soften the full effect of the FTA-criticism (CLJ: 34.4% - IJLC: 55.7%), and addressed general and specific content aspects of the books in addition to style and text.[8] Obviously, mitigated criticisms meant that critical reviewers were not fully rejective of the book aspects under assessment.

By contrast, only in the very low minority of cases in both journals (CLJ: 5.7% - IJLC: 9.3%) were negative comments **unmitigated** in the act, and allowed reviewers to make **bald criticisms** about such aspects of the book, as in the set of extracts in (14), or otherwise to justify similar criticisms in belittling comments, as in (15), by adding emotionally-charged intensifiers such as *turgidly incomprehensible*, *most irritatingly*, etc. to convey the reviewer's depreciative involvement:

(14) However, <u>it lacks clarity</u>, devoting too much time to an explanation of the origins of the theories rather than their meanings. CLJ

---

[7] As its term implies, negative politeness avoids the positively polite assumption of solidarity, a feature that is derived from Goffman's (1967) avoidance rituals.

[8] Although the current data confirm Hyland's (2004) analysis of book reviews where praise is often global, the focus on general aspects characterizing intermediate sections in the current data adds to the author's suggestion that criticism is often directed at "specific content and textual features" (Hyland 2004: 48-49.

Inconsistencies in style that range from playfully simple (establishing a market for a fictitious beverage) to turgidly incomprehensible (Coasian externalities regarding pollution from a mill) will leave readers with a vague impression as to both the intended audience as well as the inherent complexity of the subject matter. IJLC

(Author) later states that proportionality is a standard of legality and not just a standard of review (p. 292). Again, this cannot be so obvious. Under the HRA the standard of legality is set by s.6 and the standard of review is proportionality. IJLC

Thus, the chapter does not take into consideration, for example, the (lack of) follow-up to the recommendations issued by De Mistura's Commission,[2] implementation of the EU Directives and the recent measures on security (i.e. extension of the maximum period for pre-removal detention to six months). IJLC

What (author) does not make clear, however, is the fact that Teubner, following Luhmann, is not involved in the game of providing … . IJLC

(Author) does not deal with the questions of what Cs should justify the application of labour laws or … . IJLC

Exploitation is another of those politically charged issues whose complexities the book oversimplifies. IJLC

(15) Before a more considered look at the content is taken, three tedious complaints need to be made. First, there are too many typographical errors, usually of names. This is highly distracting Secondly, the book has an unhappy aversion to neutral citations, which is unhelpful for people wishing to rely on the book's research because they will have to look up the neutral reference themselves, and entirely awkward when a case has only been reported in a specialist set of reports. Thirdly, and most irritatingly, the table of cases adopts a bizarre dislike of cases in which the first party is named only as A. This means that anyone wishing to see which pages discuss the *Belmarsh Detainees* case will not find it listed anywhere under "A" and will have to persevere to the "S" section to find it. Alongside that case is *Secretary of State for the Home Department* v. *AF (No 3)* [2009] UKHL 28; [2009] 3 W.L.R. 74, which is listed under "A" as well (with the parties reversed), only with more page references in its first appearance.

CLJ

There is a salient inconsistency in the author's argument because ... .

IJLC

As is clear from the above surface realizations, these reviewers did not feel obliged to defend the poor books for their faultless clarity, inconsistent style, typographical errors, etc, nor did they stretch to play up faults in such books. These blunt (unmitigated) criticisms therefore seemed to address (author's) negative face wants clearly, unambiguously and in the most direct manner, and consequently were categorized as performing the FTAs bald-on record, in terms of B&L's model. The most commonly used impersonal rhetorical strategies to convey unmitigated criticisms included:

- 'there-be' structure
- 'author/book+negative verb' in subject position
- agentless passive
- use of verbs indicating negative evaluation of the action (e.g. *ignore, lack*)
- negatives (e.g. *no, not, neither ... nor ...*)
- negative adjectives (e.g. *difficult, unfortunate*) in anticipatory *it* clause

Taking overt personal responsibility for the criticism

The preference for the impersonal rather than more personal expression of criticism suggested that the reviewer's explicit presence in the texts might constitute the most face-threatening act in the interpersonal genre, by impinging more upon the author's freedom of choice and action in terms of the B&L's politeness model.[9] Based on this perception, the most face-threatening categories in my corpus were exclusive *I* personal pronoun and *my* possessive pronoun, as derived from Tang and John's (1999) analysis of "I as opinion-holder" and "I as originator".[10] Tang and

[9] In this context of most FTAs by the more explicit author's presence, Myers (1989), for instance, states that "the making of a claim threatens the general scientific audience because it is a demand for communally granted credit" (1989: 5). Other scholars, such as Markkanen and Schröder (1992), suggest that an FTA can be mitigated by the use of the exclusive pronoun *I* with a hedging effect (see, for instance, Salager-Meyer 1994, 1997 and Hyland 1998 on hedges), and argue that the use of the pronoun is a useful strategy for the writer to be persuaded of his/her opinion (such as, in 'I feel …' / 'I think …' structures) and for the reader to decide whether or not the claim is justified.

[10] At a discourse level, Tang and John's first person functional taxonomy goes from the least powerful authorial presence (with 'I' as representative, 'I' as guide, 'I' as architect, 'I' as recounter of research process) to the most powerful authorial presence (with 'I' as opinion-holder and 'I' as originator). In 'I' as originator

John argue for the most powerful (face-threatening) category of the first person in that:

> "the writers 'claim authority' and exhibit some form of ownership of the content of their writing, showing that they perceive themselves as people who have the *right* and the *ability* to originate new ideas" (Tang and John 1999: S29, italics in the original).

Table 4 shows the totals of stance self-mention (Hyland 1999b, 2005a) examined in various contexts of use outside quotes.

Self-mentions			
	CLJ	IJLC	TOTAL
I	1	27	28
My	1	15	16
We (mitigative)	2	13	15
We (non-mitigative)	3	81	84
Our	4	15	19
Us	4	32	36
TOTAL	15	183	198

Table 4. Self-mentions: occurrences and totals in the corpus.

Thus, where reviewers claimed authority of the evaluative content using the personal pronoun *I* (18 occ. out of 28 totals) and the possessive pronoun *my* (16 occ.), they seemed to increase the negative force of the criticism by marking "an overt acceptance of personal responsibility" (Hyland 2005a: 79), and similarly a "contextually situated authorial identity" (Hyland 2005a: 53). By adopting a more threatening voice in author's face-harm, reviewers in these categories usually expressed dissatisfaction, controversy or debate on specific aspects of the book.

With this in mind, let us consider the final two-sentence critiques in (16):

(16) (Author) claims that he has developed a novel approach to unresolved legal issues concerning property in the body, one rooted in the law of equity in England and Wales. He argues that equity possesses the flexibility to deal with the manifest inadequacy of the traditional common-law approach to property in tissue excised from the body – essentially, that there is no such

category, in particular, the authors state that the pronoun "calls for the writer to present or signal these [ideas or knowledge claims] as *new*" (Tang and John 1999: S29, italics in the original).

thing, and therefore no legal protection for tissue donors in such cases as *Moore*[1] and *Greenberg*.[2] *I yield to none in my indignation at these injustices, but I fail to see that (author)'s elaboration of the concept of equity – only delivered in the final chapter, at the abbreviated length of four pages – provides more than a superficial 'solution'. Instead, once again this book left me feeling frustrated by its tendency to skate over complex arguments.* (my italics) IJLC

This reviewer made his entrance into the critiques by first declaring his unequivocal stance towards the injustice issue (*I yield to none*) and, once there, he went on to criticize the author for glossing over a complex matter of textual style (*I fail to see*). In the latter criticism, the reviewer himself ('I' as originator) performed a bald-on record act, since he did nothing to minimize threats to the author's face, although he minimally sought to avoid the plain (bald) FTA by going with an off-record criticism juxtaposed by "irony" (Brown and Levinson 1987: 211) in quotations to suggest sharp incongruity beyond the simple and evident action of the author.[11] His unambiguous, direct (bald) criticism was then followed by the reviewer's negative emotional response to the evaluated book, as measured by the emotional adjective *frustrated*.[12]

Still, there were cases such as those in (17) in *I* pronoun co-occurring with *my* in variously structured attitude markers, where claiming authority of the content projected the bluntly critical reviewer as an opinion-holder:

(17) In particular, *I anticipate that a non-urgent review of the constitution would generate calls for abolition of the monarchy and disestablishment of the Church of England*, which would cause far more heated public and press controversy than, say, the introduction of PR for elections to the House of Commons, reform (or abolition) of the House of Lords, or a new British Bill of Rights. *These three are, in my view, far more important and urgent than questions to do with the monarchy and the Church of England.* ... If a 'We the People' Constitution were adopted, would the government, the press and the public be content for a court to strike down the offending provision on the new ground that it was contrary to the Constitution? *I very much doubt it.* An alternative constitutional narrative, *and one which to my*

---

[11] Quirk et al.(1985) refer to irony as an implicit device to express disagreement, disbelief, and criticism.

[12] The reviewer's negative response and disposition through the identified adjective follows Martin's (e.g. 2000) three basic semantic categories of evaluation: emotional (evaluations expressed as a mental state of the evaluator), aesthetic (evaluations targeted at the work of the person being evaluated), and behavioral or judgment (evaluations targeted at the behavior or character of the person being evaluated).

> mind *is closer to reflecting the mentality of the British or English*, is that the terms on which the people ... . (my italics) IJLC

> On this, there are schools of thought. One argues that the incremental approach is appropriate, that old patterns of behaviour cannot be broken and new ones instituted overnight. The opposite view is taken by those who press for rapid change to minimise the capacity for resistance to the mooted new pattern. It seems that the first view – arguing for change in the long term – is the dominant approach in Africa. And this does not seem to be (author)'s view. On the contrary, *I favour the view that change has to be swiftly implemented.* (my italics) IJLC

In the excerpts, the critical reviewers realized certain circumstances beforehand and intervened into the discourse by expressing future challenges, reservations and/or refutation as "expert knowledge holders" (Hemais 2001: 57). These knowledgeable reviewers had no qualms about disclaiming the issue of the *'We the People' Constitution* in the book, and therefore increased the potential imposition on, and face-threat to, the author. Although in these and other similar instances the reviewer's explicit presence created "a personal *ethos* of competence and authority" (Hyland 2005a: 79) in the discourse, the presence however did not avoid the obstruction of the author's freedom of choice and action in the genre. It therefore seemed to have the opposite effect to politeness – that of providing the potential source for conflict with the author.[13]

Taking no personal responsibility for the criticism

Interestingly, there was one book review shown in (18) below, where the pronoun *I* occurred repeatedly in one paragraph (7 occ.) outside the negative face-harm of the book's author, and addressed the disciplinary dialectics behind the logical argument in the book as a method familiar to readers:

(18) A sceptical response to this part of the argument about the PGC is: so what? Why does it matter that the PGC guarantees all agents the generic conditions of agency? Besides being interesting in and of itself, the PGC is significant because of the structure of the argument that supports it. The argument is necessary, which means in part that it is an argument that anyone who regards themselves as an agent must accept on pain of contradiction. If I regard myself as an agent, then I must accept that I need

[13] It is worth noting that the personal responsibility frame of criticising adversely in *I*/*my* pronouns was a rhetorical strategy found particularly in IJLC.

the generic conditions of agency. Must I also accept that other agents need these conditions and should be guaranteed them? Yes, say (authors). This answer rests on this argument: I must hold that I have the generic rights for the self-sufficient reason that I am an agent. But it follows purely logically from "the fact that I am an agent is by itself sufficient for me to have the generic rights" that "the fact that X is an agent is by itself sufficient for X to have the generic rights." (p. 43).[4] Its rational power is one reason why (authors') argument matters and what makes it salient in contemporary moral philosophy. IJLC

This isolated pronominal usage was defined as *I* generic subject, referring to the generality of people familiar with the dialectics, and therefore functioned as the "plural *we*" in Tang and John's (1999) taxonomy, replaceable by the generic *we* 'as a proxy for a larger group of people' (Tang and John 1999: 27) in the discipline.

In addition, the unique status of the *I* pronoun was recorded in two other marginal instances in 2 book reviews (3 occ.), where it functioned as a "frame marker" (Hyland 2005a: 51) to organise evaluative discourse, whether or not led by an apology clause:

(19) *Since it would be neither possible nor helpful to summarise the argument of the entire book*, I will concentrate on the general analysis of the first three chapters, an analysis which underpins the book as a whole. IJLC (my italics)

Mitigating negative evaluations: opening, intermediate and closing sections

As reported in Table 5, mainly eleven rhetorical strategies for **mitigating negative evaluations** were identified in the **opening**, **intermediate** and **closing book sections**. Although, as I noted before, these strategies abounded heavily in the intermediate sections, they highlighted "a careful balancing act which reflects both ideational and interpersonal orientations" (Hyland 2004: 42) across the various book sections. These strategies were therefore redressive of the negative comments made in the genre, where they counterbalanced the disruptive effect of face-threatening acts for both reviewer and reviewee, in terms of B&L's model.

The data in both journals show that hedges rhetorical strategy ranked much higher in incidence (39.3%), followed by questions in IJLC alone (17.5%) down to praise-criticism patterns (15.2%) and other rhetorical strategies:

Mitigation rhetorical strategies in opening, intermediate and closing sections	CLJ		IJLC		TOTAL	
	N°	*%*	*N°*	*%*	*N°*	*%*
Praise-criticism / Criticism-praise + other patterns	20	6.9	24	8.3	44	15.2
Hedges	53	18.4	60	20.8	113	39.3
Other attribution:						
General reader	3	1	2	0.7	5	1.7
Specific reader	2	0.7	1	0.3	3	1
Author	4	1.4	8	2.8	12	4.2
Future researcher	2	0.7	4	1.4	6	2
OTHERS						
Inclusive *we*	2	0.7	13	4.5	15	5.2
Indefinite generic subject *one*	13	4.5	11	3.8	24	8.4
Questions	1	0.3	49	17	50	17.5
Apology	4	1.4	1	0.3	5	1.7
Suggestion	4	1.4	7	2.4	11	3.8
TOTAL	108	37.5	180	62.5	288	100%

Table 5. Rhetorical strategies for mitigating negative comments across the various book sections: occurrences, percentages and totals.

Opening sections

Bearing in mind the relative incidence of negative comments in the openings, the excerpt below best illustrates the commonly used mitigating rhetorical strategies employed in the opening paragraph of a book review:

(20) I found this book frustrating and disappointing, much as I wanted to like it. The topic is unimpeachably important, and some good things were promised by (author)'s conference papers on two European Commission projects in which I also took part. *Unfortunately, that promise has failed to materialise in this book*. While I am sympathetic to (author)'s overall argument that we need to afford some form of property rights in tissue, once it has left the body, to those who donate the tissue as well as those who use it subsequently, I do not feel that he has made a coherent case. (my italics) IJLC

In the four-sentence critiques, the hostile reviewer foregrounded his discredit of the book by criticizing it for being *frustrating and disappointing*, although he never dismissed the book in the closings. He therefore went bald-on record with critical judgment showing how emotional his criticism was, as measured by the negative adjectives of emotion (Martin 2000). The reviewer seemed to impose upon the author's freedom of action by also positioning himself in the author's research community but, as a result of the author incurring debt, his negative face was threatened in the act revealing emotional reactions of the reviewer towards the state of affairs, as signalled by the attitudinal sentence adverb *Unfortunately*, used eight times in the corpus. While the 'failure-persona' construction of the author also implied the reviewer to address his own face concerns, the polar comments in the final sentence softened the blow of the criticism triggered by highly charged feelings towards the book in negative politeness strategies.

Intermediate sections
Praise-criticism / criticism-praise and other patterns

The use of polar comments in the praise-criticism pattern suggested in Hyland's (2004: 55-56) analysis added to criticism-praise and other patterns arising in the intermediate sections. In these evaluative patterns, a comment of one type was syntactically joined but subordinated to another type in various mitigating devices:

- a contrastive structure introduced by a concessive subordinator, such as *although, despite* and *while*;
- an adversative coordinator, such as *but*; or
- an adverbial concessive conjunct, such as *however* and *nonetheless*.[14]

These patterns are exemplified in the following mitigated criticisms addressing general and specific aspects of the book:

(21) This expansive approach is not directly criticised, <u>but</u> there is a call for outer limits to be set out. CLJ

He stops short of a firm conclusion that the law intervenes in such circumstances as a general rule outside as well as inside property law, <u>but</u> contemplates that possibility. CLJ

[14] On the many taxonomies of 'concession' in the literature, see Quirk et al. (1985), Mann and Thompson (1992), Rudolph (1996), Crevels (2000), and Hultman (2003), among others.

> While it may seem rather ambitious to seek to cover an area as large as "the common law world", (author) ably demonstrates that there is much common ground on this issue among the common law jurisdictions. CLJ

> Chapter 4 relies on an interesting split between standards of legality and standards of review. However, the argument that *Wednesbury* is a standard of review and not a standard of legality (p. 102) cannot be sustained. CLJ

> Although it is probably debatable whether or not "economic efficiency" can easily qualify as a public policy, (author) nonetheless makes a strong case for the need of the (continuing) recognition of public policy in EC competition analysis. CLJ

> (Author) describes himself and his approach as falling within the amber light category of public law scholarship (pp. 2–3). Unfortunately, the amber light is not mentioned again and so precisely what this category means is not fully developed, but attempts to find coherent, principled and rational middle ground solutions is something seen regularly throughout *Public Law*. IJLC

> Despite its considerable antiquity, conversion remains an important modern-day tort as *OBG* and the protracted *Kuwait Airways* v. *Iraqi Airways* litigation amply demonstrate. IJLC

> While the restriction upon both women and sex trafficking is justified – not least on the premise that this is the formulation of contemporary people trafficking that has most extensively captured the political and public imagination – one consequence of this approach is that it, somewhat inevitably, leaves certain important questions unaddressed. IJLC

> Furthermore, while it is beyond doubt that the ''right to development'' does hold much transformative promise, this reviewer wonders whether (author) invests too much in the emancipatory potential of this particular norm. Indeed, she herself admits that the right to development ''lacks a certain conceptual clarity, and is so far void of empirical application'' that might help refine its meaning (p. 52). IJLC

In these and other examples, reviewers counterbalanced a positive comment with a negative comment in the sentence and vice-versa, and this usually appeared in combination with contrastive connectives in the two-part structure of presenting counterclaims, such as 'Although/Despite/ While [in front position]' contrasting with information in the second clause, as seen above, or other combinations such as 'Of course/Granted [in front position]' … 'but', or 'Even if/Perhaps [in front position]' … 'however'. No doubt, these (contrastive) types of connective expressions in claim statements marked the writers' awareness of the genre as an inherently threatening act in interaction[15], and the reviewers' expressions of mitigation had an important interpersonal role of anticipating responses from reviewed authors and readers as members of a shared academic discourse community. Although, in general, criticism is highly valued in academic writing, mitigated two-part structures were an effective politeness strategy to soften the blow of a specific FTA-criticism through a "more balanced comment" (Hyland 2004: 54), and consequently allowed reviewers to address the social face-concern of the authors and readers in the disciplinary forum.

Indeed, there were occasions in which the rationale of the paired comment required certain concessive subordinators, such as *while*, to be located somewhere in the middle of the overall evaluation, so that the pattern was a negative-positive-negative-positive evaluation structure unit:

(22) *The heavy, often clouded emphasis on constitutional theory*[-], while instructive for its contextualization of the roots of expropriation in international law (ch. 2)[+], *detracts from*[-] the much more focused material on the international investment disputes brought under the North American Free Trade Agreement ("NAFTA") and the fair and equitable treatment standard which (author) analyses with considerable vigour (ch. 3)[+]. CLJ

Similarly, there were occasions in which reviewers resorted to the '*if +adjective* (with no verb)' structure by 'conceding' the importance of the contrast referred to in the evaluation with a similar meaning to *(al)though*:

(23) Comprehensive and analytical[+], if at times disorganized[-], *Economics of the Law* is a gratifying addition to the growing scholarship on law and economics[+]. CLJ

Where the medial (position) *if* structure did occur, the result was to reverse the order to a positive-negative-positive evaluative unit.

---

[15] The significant role of 'contrasting' has been noted by several authors in different academic genres. Barton (1993), for instance, argues for the importance of 'contrast' in emphasizing 'problems' that typify introductions to argumentative essays, while Swales (1990) emphasizes the important role of 'contrast' in *Establishing* and *Occupying a Niche* in research article introductions.

Hedges

As noted, the use of hedges held the lion's share across mitigation strategies. Hedges mainly comprised the epistemic modal verbs (*may, might, could, would*), the lexical verbs (*appear, attempt, seem, suggest*), and the range of tentative items (e.g. *fairly, generally, largely, likely, a little, most, often, perhaps, sometimes, unclear, usually*), as the defining features of "epistemic and affective function in knowledge-making genres" (Hyland 2004: 56). Indeed, the semantic operation of hedging in the current data was also achieved by Questions, as argued by B&Levinson, who treat them as types of hedge. Beyond Hyland's (2004) analysis of criticism, therefore, these additional textualizations were treated separately here under the label of OTHERS.

As shown in the list of excerpts in (24), hedges were used in evaluations of general and specific content aspects of the book:

(24) Their opening claim, that such a book is "long overdue" (p. 1) would scarcely be doubted by academics or practitioners. But can just one book meet the needs of both? After all, most practitioners are likely to want a reliable, comprehensive, expository guide to the law (with occasional critique of controversial or errant judgments) while academics interested in conversion are more likely to be drawn to the fascinating peculiarities of the this tort's evolution, ... CLJ

For all that it may be a fairly slender volume, *The Tort of Conversion* is packed with learning, … . CLJ

While it may seem rather ambitious to seek to cover an area as large as "the common law world" ... . CLJ

The circumstances that may require a judge or other judicial officer to engage in some soul-searching regarding his so-called "duty to sit" and his obligation to "recuse himself" when possibly compromised are so varied that it would take a brave person to attempt to tackle the topic of judicial recusals as a whole. CLJ

Given the timing of the conference, a few years before the Lisbon Treaty was brought into force, one might think that the work has missed out a little. CLJ

At the same time, though, there is a sense in which, perhaps, (author)'s deconstruction does not go quite far enough, failing to engage fully with the indeterminacy and malleability of the very construction of people trafficking itself. IJLC

The assumption, is that as a result state bodies would behave differently. ... Presumably, the People would also have different expectations of government, ... IJLC

On several occasions (author) seems incapable of comprehending how it could be possible to accept that the judiciary look beyond legal ''principles'' in their deliberations. IJLC

This might suggest that (author) sees identity in an atomised sense, but it is clear she does not. IJLC

The impact on rates of donation and the resulting lack of provision for infertile couples is not explored sufficiently. IJLC

The problem with dialogue theories is that neither the courts nor Parliament appear to talk in those terms. CLJ

In particular, the modal verbs, whether or not occurring in paired evaluative acts, were used not only to hedge on the force of the FTA-criticism but also to operate together with other hedges to test reviewers' hypotheses by epistemically acknowledging a variety of plausible judgments in the evaluative discourse. Thus, combining the positively evaluated material with what was still cognitively debatable in the reviewer's assumption and research community had the effect of reducing "the interpersonal damage of critical comments" (Hyland 2004: 55), and maintaining social harmony and solidarity with the author and the reader in face-concerns.

Other attribution

In this strategy, the reviewers in the examples below stood as the immediate readership by commenting on the likely response of any member in the disciplinary community. The mitigating strategy thus allowed them to stand apart from aloof criticism in FTA by seeking some kind of consensus from such readership:

(25) While the analysis is penetrating and thought provoking, readers may get the sense that (author) is attempting to cram everything he has not yet said in this book into this catch-all chapter, as he skirts concepts such as public choice theory, game theory and infinite regress in an often muddled manner. CLJ

Thirdly, and most irritatingly, the table of cases adopts a bizarre dislike of cases in which the first party is named only as A. This means that anyone wishing to see which pages discuss the Belmarsh Detainees case will not find it listed anywhere under "A" and will have to persevere to the "S" section to find it. CLJ

In addition to overt *reader* attribution in Hyland's (2004) analysis of criticism, however, other strategies were identified in the corpus where responsibility for the criticism was attributed to a *specific reader*, *author*, and *future researcher*. In the *specific reader* instances, shifting the agent of the critical comment to some identifiable readers in the research community went some way towards mitigating the effect of the criticism, as in:

(26) Of course, there will be those conservatively minded "purists" to whom this chapter will appear heretical. They will no doubt advert to what was actually decided in relation to intangible property in *OBG* v. *Allen* and (in line with the majority) possibly also argue that *using conversion to protect intangible property is like using chopsticks to eat soup*. They may even say that some ... . CLJ

Here, as yet, not only did the reviewer stand apart from aloof criticism in the discourse, but also attempted to be fair in the criticism by attending to the knowledge-making needs and expectations of the disciplinary readers. Only rarely did reviewers resort to figures of speech, such as in (26) by an explicit simile (*using conversion to protect intangible property is like using chopsticks to eat soup*), used to present detail for comparison, but in any case leaving the audience to determine which features were being expressed as a target of criticism. In other instances, reviewers attributed responsibility of the critical comment to either the author's concerns, reservations or difficulty by reporting the *author's source* (author's responsibility), as in (27), or by deferring open claims and issues in the book to *future* (disciplinary) *researchers*, as in (28):

(27) *As (author) himself points out in Part B*, it is hard to come up with concrete conclusions in this respect (*passim*); however, for the purpose of this review it suffices to say that he concludes that, although both mechanisms appear more or less possible within Article 81 EC, more clarity is needed as to when, where and which of these mechanisms should and can be applied. CLJ

As the author accepts, this is a somewhat elusive concept, especially when issues such as psychological integrity are examined. IJLC

(28) (Author) argues that Viking and Laval (Cases C-438/05 and C-341/05 [2007] ECR I-11767) have shown the economic arguments are still trumping the social welfare ones. It remains to be seen how long this will be the case. CLJ

While in all the examples attributing responsibility to other sources reflected the reviewer's cognitive assessments of materials, the examples (27-28), in particular, show that the reviewers interspersed critical comments between the arguments raised by the authors, while also invoking reader's knowledge about those arguments.

OTHERS

Five other mitigation strategies were detected in the corpus beyond those identified in Hyland's (2004) analysis of criticism in book reviews.

Inclusive *we* v. exclusive *we*

The data in Table 4 show that *I/my* self-mentions, though spreading differently across book reviews, were lower in incidence than first-person plural self-mentions (*we*, *us*, *our*). Considering that the pronoun *we* occurred far more frequently in the corpora in a total of 99 occurrences (CLJ: 5 - IJLC: 94), different semantic references were potentially identified of the pronoun outside its use in quotes.

In a few instances (15 occ.), there were attempts particularly among debating reviewers in IJLC to cast themselves in the role of co-researchers in unambiguously inclusive *we* (Kuo 1999; Tang and John 1999; Hyland 2001a, 2004, 2005a/b; Fortanet 2004; Harwood 2005a/b), which included the author and the reader in a knowledge-sharing perspective. In the following examples, inclusive reviewers assumed that readers knew certain disciplinary issues and carried them along with their evaluations by expressing lack of sufficient knowledge (29), or by contesting the conceptual adequacy of the issue (30), in hedged comments[16]:

[16] In the literature, hedges (or hedging) are most commonly thought to either express a lack of commitment to the truth-value of a proposition (e.g. Lyons 1977; Coates 1987; Markkanen and Schröder 1989; Salager- Meyer 1994; Hyland 1998), or to mitigate the force of the speaker's utterance in order to make it more acceptable to the hearer (e.g. Brown and Levinson 1987; Nikula 1997). The latter function highlights the interpersonal (politeness) aspect of hedging. However, in Hyland's (1998) polypragmatic categories of hedges expressed in everyday speech and scientific writing, 'admitting to lack of knowledge' and 'referring to limitations (of

(29) *We need to know more about* how different African countries are responding to domestic violence. There is only a little on the place of religion and nothing on pagan beliefs which might explain domestic violence. There are many Victoria Climbiés in Africa, and adult ones as well. And what of the role of the media? How prominently does violence against women feature on this in Africa? What views are taken of pornography by African legal systems? We know that violence against women is lowest in cultures which do not link masculinity to actions of dominance, aggression or male honour, and that have flexible gender roles (Levinson, 1989; Sanday, 1981). The Arapesh of New Guinea and the Gusii of the Kenyan highlands have often been compared (discussed briefly by Freeman, 1979, p. 135). The Gusii, according to research conducted fifty years ago (LeVine, 1959), virtually institutionalise rape. Is this still true? IJLC

(30) (Author) emphasises that, if we are to understand the role of conventions in practical reasoning, we need to avoid confusing 'arbitrariness' with 'indifference'. *At this point we may well begin to have doubts about* the soundness of (author)'s proposed extension of the notion of convention. The thought that art is structured by conventions is, of course, a very familiar one. Yet can that thought be fitted without loss to the template proposed by (author)'s analysis? Does the analysis not threaten to have a flattening and impoverishing effect upon our comprehension of art? Christian artists may use blue to represent the Virgin, and we are at first inclined to think of this as a coded way of referring to the Virgin, or identifying a particular figure as the Virgin. IJLC

Following the argument for inclusive *we* "to indicate an intention to reduce personal attributions" (Hyland 2001a: 217), the examples above show that inclusive *we* enabled debating reviewers to lower their personal responsibility for the criticism (i.e. in matters of knowledge lacking and conceptual adequacy) than would otherwise be the case when they projected themselves in the *I* authorial pronoun examined before. Inclusive *we* was also important to mitigate the face-threatening effect of the critical comment made by maintaining interpersonal relationships with other community members in the academic genre. Beyond this pronominal strategy, however, the examples above suggest that inclusive reviewers

---

the model, experimental conditions, or methods)' are part of several other devices classified as hedges (i.e. surface lexical markers and syntactic markers). In my corpus examples, linguistic uncertainty inherent in the hedged comments is associated to two discourse-based hedging strategies in Hyland's (1998) taxonomy: admission to a lack of knowledge in (29) and reference to limitations of the model in (30).

were aware of the disciplinary research spanning international horizons (29), or dancing on the edge of the Religion and Visual Arts branches of the Humanities disciplines (30). In the latter case of the contributing disciplines (noted in Chapter 4), reviewing an essential topic of legal thought realistically was the proper interdiscursive relation between law and other disciplinary forms of thought and expression performed in the discourse of religious and visual arts studies.[17] In this context, therefore, inclusive *we* (in subject position) helped to link the reviewer with the relevant interdisciplinary/interdiscursive issues dealt with in the book by creating new and enlarged knowledge space.

In more instances (82 occ.), however, the pronoun *we* did not seem to lower such responsibility, but defined mainly the reviewer's exclusive voice by informing about the material for the most immediate readership, thus reflecting the informative function identified of book reviews (Gea Valor 2000; Hyland 2004; Salager-Meyer et al. 2005). This can be seen in the set of extracts in (31) below, where exclusive reviewers sought to inform the readers by describing the argument in the book rather than signalling their inclusive presence as co-researchers:

(31) Even given the general fairness and accuracy of the discussion, however, the sheer diversity of the arguments addressed may cause <u>us</u> to wonder, as <u>we</u> read, whether it will be possible for (author) to offer any interestingly unified critique of the neo-liberal position, or whether his counter-arguments will prove to be disconnected and discrete. The answer is revealed by the second half of the book, which aims to develop precisely such a unified critique of neo-liberalism. Here (author) identifies ... .

CLJ

The author acknowledges the problems posed by the idea of 'deep conventions'. For example, <u>we</u> may want to say that Islamic ornamental art and Christian representational art rest on different conventions. But, to apply the concept of 'convention' in this context, <u>we</u> must be able to preserve the thought that the norms are 'arbitrary' (though not, remember, 'indifferent'). To preserve that thought, <u>we</u> must be able to view the

[17] Although apparent from the language use in the sample given (*art, Christian artists, the Virgin*), the phenomenon of interdiscursivity here describes the system by which the conceptual boundary work of interdisciplinary legal research operated in the reviewed book, as noted also about empirical legal research conducted in most research article abstracts (Chapter 4). The reviewer in the sample identified ambiguities or inconsistencies between different lines of thought constructed in other systems of disciplinary discourse, and revealed in the book produced and interpreted by the reviewed author himself.

differing norms as simply diverse ways of achieving basically the same thing. Thus we are told that the notion of convention remains useful in this context: ... . IJLC

This analysis enables us to understand how chess and a host of other activities can be conventionally structured practices without being solutions to pre-existing co-ordination problems. ... But we can say that 'a certain evaluation is constituted by conventions if it is the case that we could not have grasped or come to appreciate the relevant value without understanding the conventions that constitute the relevant practice' (p. 38).
IJLC

Interestingly, however, there were only 2 book reviews (IJLC) where the description of the argument in the book relied on some other background information appearing in the opening lines of the review. This is shown in (32), where the reviewer actually laid the ground to the topic in the book by indicating the most immediate readership the direction towards such topic, and as a consequence *we* potentially functioned as "*I* as guide" category in Tang and John's (1999) taxonomy:

(32) Much of the world that we inhabit relies for its order, stability and familiarity upon rules and understandings that we hold in common but mostly take for granted. We might loosely speak of such things as matters of 'convention'. But the single word 'convention' conceals the diversity and complexity of the phenomena in question. In some contexts the notion of 'convention' is associated with agreement, and 'agreement' is itself ambiguous as between a convergence of opinion (e.g. we agree that the Moon is not made of cheese) and the exchange of promises (we agree to meet next Saturday). Thus we speak of 'conventional beliefs' but also of 'the Hague Convention'. In other contexts 'convention' is not connected with agreement at all, but with shared standards or patterns of conduct that derive a part of their practical force from the very fact that they are shared and regularly complied with. IJLC
[opening lines]

In all these cases, it was clear that reviewers exploited the *inclusive (disciplinary community) 'we' v. exclusive (reviewer) 'we'* ambiguity for their own purposes in the interpersonal dimension of the genre.

Indefinite generic subject *one*

The indefinite generic subject "was an appropriate device for suppressing the identity of the participants in the speech act" (Haverkate 1992: 516) in cases where reviewers projected themselves in the *I* and *we* pronouns. The generalized reference seemed therefore to be "manipulated in order to expand the speaker coordinate of the deictic centre to the extent that its boundaries become indeterminate" (Haverkate 1992: 516-517). In the present corpus, the generic device was defined by its reference to 'any individual (including the reviewer) in the disciplinary community'.

In the examples below (33), where the indefinite device served "to mitigate assertive force" (Haverkate 1992: 516), the device allowed the reviewers to minimize their responsibility for the critical comment and to similarly detach themselves from the face-threatening act, while also securing cooperation from, and stress solidarity with, the readers (Myers 1989):

(33) The book's analyses of the neo-liberal writers are both concise and accurate (this is not to say that one agrees with his interpretations at every point). Given that the author's own political outlook is not friendly towards neo-liberalism, the fairness and lucidity of his discussion is striking. CLJ

There are, in consequence, very few criticisms that one may fairly make of this book without transgressing the fine line between providing an objective review of this book, ... CLJ

One could try to construe the notion of 'co-ordination problem' in an increasingly contrived and abstract way, but this is unlikely to be helpful or enlightening. IJLC

Moreover, the second person reader pronoun *you* was observed in marginal instances (2 occ.) out of a total five, where it occurred within quotes. Although this device seemed to be an alternative for *reader*, it was open to two different potential readings: directly engaging the readership into the evaluative discourse (Hyland 2005a: 151), or referring to the generality of people as *one*:

(34) This brings us to the major worry that permeates every chapter of this book and which undermines the very notion of 'law in context': Which or whose law? Which or whose context? Until you provide answers to these questions, it is very difficult to see how the sociology of law could be any more than a string of simultaneous relativistic accounts, each depending on how the theorists or the theory give meaning to both 'law' and 'law's context', the social environment in which law is seen to operate. IJLC

Questions

The disproportionally higher incidence of questions in IJLC was the result of the wider discursive space of the critical reviews in this journal. Here, the debating reviewers often employed questions as "a key strategy of dialogic involvement" (Hyland 2005a: 153), although viewed as politeness devices, questions also functioned as indirectness strategy (B&L 1987), or as very personal and subjective (Swales and Feak 1994).

Almost all reviewers in the corpus used questions rhetorically to engage and elicit a response from the inquiring, competent reader, who was thus invited to respond to the issue posed by the question in a way that could lead them to the reviewer's viewpoint. Where questions did occur, however, there was often an attempt to create a research niche, make counterclaims and suggest further research within an inclusive evaluation framework, while also sometimes signalling the reviewer's emotional involvement (Heinemann 2006). In example (35) below, showing inclusive *we*, the controversial reviewer used a chain of no-answer questions to alert readers to some other interpretations of the notion of convention treated in the book by creating a research niche:

(35) *At this point* <u>*we*</u> *may well begin to have doubts about the soundness of (author)'s proposed extension of the notion of convention.* The thought that art is structured by conventions is, of course, a very familiar one. <u>Yet can that thought be fitted without loss to the template proposed by (author)'s analysis? Does the analysis not threaten to have a flattening and impoverishing effect upon our comprehension of art?</u> Christian artists may use blue to represent the Virgin, and <u>*we*</u> are at first inclined to think of this as a coded way of referring to the Virgin, or identifying a particular figure as the Virgin. <u>But might another interpretation not offer greater insight? Perhaps the use of that particular colour is intended to alert us to connections with other manifestations of blue, thereby tracing resonances of meaning that exist quite independently of the conventions of art?</u> IJLC

In this and other instances, where hedges also played their own rhetorical role, direct questions allowed the reviewer to go ambiguously off-record with negative comments (FTAs), since they acted as "an "out" by providing himself with a number of defensible interpretations" (Brown and Levinson 1987: 211), and encouraged the reader with an interest in the issue to decide on the reviewer's reservations and interpretations.

On some occasions, however, the debating reviewers provided answers posed either by questions or question-forms that raised an explicit issue through an indirect question. In these cases, the reviewers' exclusive evaluation as Opinion-Holders (Tang and John 1999) limited their answer to a bald-on record FTA in a rather authoritative tone:

(36) *My question is whether* adopting a creationist text would actually make a difference. Would the English or British suspend their habits of mere patriotic acquiescence, suspicion of politics and politicians and concerns about legitimacy just because the text recites that 'We the People' created politics and gave politicians their power? Would politicians behave better because they operate under this written Constitution? *I very much doubt it.* ... *A question then is whether* switching to a written 'We the People' constitution would stop people asking whether the exercise of power is legitimate and cause them to concern themselves only with legality. *My own view is that the British, or at least English, culture runs too deep to be changed merely by a new Constitution.* IJLC

Still, in other few instances where questions were used as lead-in answers, the result was to mitigate the FTA of the comment in inclusive *we* by suggesting a future research in the discipline:

(37) *The question remains:* Could there be uniform codes of marriage in Africa? Would such codes be complied with? Some, Martin Chanock (1991) being one example, advocate this. (Author) responds that 'some cultural practices are immune to top-down legal change' (p. 123). 'Culture' (broadly defined) is to blame. *We need a fuller answer than this.* IJLC

Interestingly, however, there was only one instance (38) where questions departed from the usual practice observed so far:

(38) Their opening claim, that such a book is "long overdue" (p. 1) would scarcely be doubted by academics or practitioners. But can just one book meet the needs of both? After all, most practitioners are likely to want a reliable, comprehensive, expository guide to the law (with occasional critique of controversial or errant judgments) while academics interested in conversion are more likely to be drawn to the fascinating peculiarities of the this tort's evolution, or its strict liability basis and quasi-proprietary nature (which together pose interesting questions for much modern tort theory). *Happily, Green and Randall's splendid book caters splendidly for both (even if a widespread undergraduate readership might be a little too much to hope for given the relative infrequency with which conversion is taught these days).* CLJ

This reviewer set up the reader to expect a negative comment only to be answered positively on an objective feature of the book outside subjective

I/my pronouns seen before, thus wrong-footing the reader in the evaluative rhetorical strategy.

Apology

In the three instances shown in (39), where contrastive relations (*but*) were also used in the overall evaluation, reviewers acknowledged their impossibility or difficulty to cover all issues in the book:

(39) A brief review of this nature could not sufficiently comment on such excellent scholarship. Nonetheless, at the risk of some reductionism, I will focus on three controversial areas. First, (author) explores ... . CLJ

To this reviewer it is rather difficult to cover an issue as wide as the common law. CLJ

This review is too small a space to accurately reflect all of the contributions or everything contained in them *but* some common themes can be drawn out in summary. CLJ

By indirectly admitting their responsibility for such faults in sympathetic sorrow-sounding expressions, these reviewers encoded an apology which implied damage to the reviewer's positive face in context of an offense to the author's face needs (Brown and Levinson 1987: 68-76). Whereas in face-to-face settings an apology has been referred to as a remedy, which is an essential element in a remedial interchange (Goffman 1967: 14)[18], it would appear from the examples that the apology strategy amended the reviewers' preferred images of self, or face, in the interactional conventions of the genre. The reviewer's desire to amend his or her own face and the reviewee's face, as well as the relationship with the reviewee, became therefore the motivating factor to redress the possible debt incurred by the positive/negative face-threatening act. As a result, apology functioned "to restore equilibrium between the apologizer and the offended person" (Holmes 1990: 161).

---

[18] It is worth noting that, in Goffman's (1967) theory, a remedial interchange is treated as a unit which consists of four moves – namely, remedy (i.e. accounts, apologies, or requests), relief, appreciation, and minimization.

Suggestion

Of the total incidence of suggestion in the corpus, nine such instances occurred in the intermediate sections (plus two others in the closings) where suggestions were packed together in 4 BRs, ranging from 1 to 4 such acts, as shown in the set of examples (40) below:

(40) In particular the discussion of least cost avoiders in relation to contractual assumption of risk could have mentioned the reasoning of the House of Lords in *Tsakiroglou* v. *Noblee Thorl GmbH* [1962] A.C. 93 or compensation based on gain after *Attorney General* v. *Blake* [2001] 1 AC 268. It is similarly noteworthy that there is no index of cases. ... While it might have been preferable to divide the chapter on enforcement into civil law and criminal law, the discussion of incentivizing the identification of criminals through the state's payment of informants is an interesting example of the relevance of economic analysis to methods of crime prevention. Perhaps, some commentary on non-market advantages associated with criminal behaviour, such as the recently identified propensity of young men to seek imprisonment as a status symbol, would have enhanced this section as well as provided some scope of originality. CLJ

Exploitation is a difficult and important issue: I would perhaps have welcomed a lengthier and more subtle analysis of it, whether or not couched in the conventional libertarian framework which – contrary to (author)'s assertions – dominates academic discussion as well as public policy in the UK. IJLC

It is rather disappointing that this chapter does little more than set out the case-law in this area. More could have been done to consider the construction of sexual identity revealed in the court judgments. Indeed, a consideration of the treatment of intersex people might have assisted a more radical challenge to the constructions of sexual identity set out in the chapter. ...The discussion in chapter 2 could have been used to consider the extent to which such claims represent genuine desires or are social constructions. ... (Author) provides a fair and thorough explanation of the views of others. There are places where she could have been more explicit in her opinions. IJLC

That sense of frustration was heightened by (author)'s organisational scheme: it would perhaps have been better to have introduced the precise claims of bioequity as a 'new property class for human material' much earlier on than at p. 155 (of 163 pages in the text itself, excluding bibliography and index), and to have avoided what often felt like scattered digressions from the central argument about 'Equity, the common law's virtuous twin' (p. 141). IJLC

In these examples, it is clear that reviewers criticized authors for not attending to some specific aspects of the book, and the modal verbs *might*, *could* and *would* (used with the perfect infinitive structure in personal and impersonal subjects) indicate that reviewers expressed imaginary situations/actions (*would have / I would*) or otherwise speculated about possible actions (*might*, *could*) that did not happen. This way then, reviewers made suggestions for remedy or improvement to the author's book and, whether remedy or improvement derived most possibly from reviewers' experience, it reflected the nature of the book review genre inevitably calling for suggestions as well as criticisms.

Requests, orders, threats, suggestions and advice in the politeness model (B&L) are said to be examples of acts which represent a threat to the author's negative face (i.e. the freedom to act without being impeded by others), since the writer will in some way be imposing on the hearer to do or refrain from doing a specific act, without therefore recognizing that the hearer has a desire to be respected (positive politeness strategy). However, the use of the tentative, epistemic modal verbs coupled with the hedging (epistemic) adverb (*perhaps*) did not seem to pose a threat to the author's (hearer's) negative face of being impeded by others. Thus, suggestions seemed to perform off-record indirect strategies, removing the reviewer from the potential to be imposing in the FTA, and were treated as mitigated (hedged) criticisms. The latter therefore minimized the threat of the judgment, and contributed to the positive social relationship between the author and the reviewer, in regard to remedial action.

Closing sections

Unlike reviewers from almost half (14 BRs) the journals, as noted, reviewers in the other share (12 BRs) of both journals endorsed the objective features of the book in the closing lines, despite mitigating their criticisms in earlier parts of the closings. Although the mitigation strategies were mostly the same as used earlier in the sections, they functioned to redress the various face-threatening acts performed in the intermediate sections in an attempt to maintain social harmony with the author and the reader within a global evaluation framework.

To illustrate this in (41), the reviewer in first person (2 occ. in closings) justified his deliberate choice for not treating all issues in the book, on account of the intricacies involved in the evaluating task. He therefore offered a humble apology (2 occ. in closings) by saving positive face to the author, despite indicating some flaws:

(41) There is much more in this book which *I* will not consider. To cover all the issues across a tapestry of countries with different cultures and economies as well as different religions is no easy task. (Author) must be commended for putting together an excellent survey of ideas and a huge amount of data. Whilst there is little very original in the thesis or the details, this is clearly a book of significance, and certainly one that should command a substantial student market. IJLC

Here, as again, the necessity modals and suasive verbs occurring with intensifiers were the most direct features of persuasion (Biber's Dimension 4, 1988) in the evaluated genre, where the use of the modal *must* seemed to be the reviewer's willingness to declare the author authoritatively as a knowledgeable member in the discipline, as compared to his advisable mode of judgment expressed in the (weaker imperative) *should* modal.

In other cases, such as in (42) below, suppressing the reviewer's co-researcher role in inclusive *we* pronoun in favour of the generalized reference was sufficient for the debating reviewer to syntactically concede disagreement with the author and express suggestion (2 occ. in closings) about possible solutions or actions to some aspects of the book, and thereafter to empathize his concern about further insights into the topic with the author. The reviewer's favourable closing of the material, however, did not save the debating reviewer from raising readers' awareness over a topical question that was not dealt with in the book, and which was possibly deferred to *future researchers*:

(42) Whilst *one* does not necessarily have to agree with all of (author)'s conclusions and his arguments could, at times, be made both clearer and more forcefully, *it is very much hoped that this book is not the end of a much needed discussion.* As (author) observes himself in his overall conclusion, "[t]here is much (difficult) work to do" (p. 319). In the meantime, this book provides a good starting point for the further examination of the important question "Why, how and when might public policy have a part to play in contemporary EC competition analysis?". This is even (and especially) the case at the advent of the Treaty of Lisbon. IJLC

By signalling affective appeals as part of metadiscoursal resources of *pathos* (Hyland 2005a: 81), the reviewer's empathizing pattern above (*it is very much hoped that*) acted as a positive politeness device of evaluation. Affective appeals were not so noticeable in incidence throughout the corpus since they occurred only nine times in the intermediate and closing sections. Where affective appeals did occur, they run along the following lines: *<u>Hopefully</u>, his urgent calls for change will not go unheeded / I hope that / it is hoped that / in the hope that / as one could hope.*

Conclusion

The main findings in this study show that reviewers from both journals were far more positive than fully negative in their evaluations of the books in question, and preferred far easily to mitigate their negative comments. The tendency to heavily avoid bald criticisms (fully negative comments), and to express them only when warranted, led reviewers in each journal to produce two main different evaluation practices: positive and mitigative book reviews. In all cases, the use and function of positive, negative and mitigated evaluations shows that they characterized the various book review sections in regard to the book aspects in focus, even though mitigated evaluations characterized particularly the intermediate sections.

The preference for positive reviews was rather expected on one simple account: the fact that book reviews were solicited implies that they were at least works of merit rather than solely works of personal taste. Regardless of this, the positive preference in CLJ confirms earlier studies of favourable book reviews in the social science and humanities (Green and Spornick 1995; Spink et al. 1998). Indeed, Hyland (2004) notes that reviewers in the "soft" disciplines "were more extensive in their evaluations and generally more critical in their judgments" (2004: 49-50) than reviews in the hard disciplines containing twice as much praise as criticism. Without questioning that the greater use of critical judgments rests with the social sciences and humanities, where inquiry "tends to be treated as a reiterative process" (Hyland 2004: 52), reviewers in my (soft discipline) data revealed that this was perhaps not the case.

Importantly, the findings in this study indicate the reviewers' ability to cognitively read and scrutinize the author's book for its strengths and weaknesses, and the reviewers' interpersonal role in reading and scrutinizing was achieved pragmatically by several types of politeness mitigation strategies. Despite the absence of journal guidelines encouraging reviewers to be bluntly critical of the book for review, the ease in using mitigation strategies enabled the reviewers to shy away from baldly expressed criticisms, and their avoidance was due to the interactional nature of the genre where "criticism becomes a potential source of friction because it can represent a direct challenge to a specific author" (Hyland 2004: 41). Viewed generally, in fact, criticism is a tricky business because very few people are receptive to it or even know how to criticize others outwardly. In the case of the academic book review genre examined, outward criticism could in fact have resulted in harmful effects being caused to both the reviewed author and the academic legal community, in a context where solidarity principles are highly valued in academic communities (Myers 1989; Hyland 2004). Thus, as a result of these social factors implied in baldly criticizing the qualities of the reviewed authors' books, mitigated criticisms proved to be the best rhetorical choice to reduce the stronger reviewer/reviewee's face-threat posed by blunt criticisms.

In addition to the three-dimensional challenge raised with the author, the legal community, and the reviewer, the findings in this study also suggest that writing book reviews represented a challenge to reviewers in their interaction with the media institution which employed them, in a context where business commitment was squarely pursued by such institution. In commending the books for their positive qualities through a variety of expressions, the ostensibly positive reviewers in CLJ were not insensitive to relocating the informative and evaluative genre in the more complex business accounts of disciplinary discourse. Thus, conveying support for the book and the credibility of the author among these reviewers had the effect of implicitly straying the review task towards promotional purposes, by whetting the appetite of the widest readership and encouraging them to buy the published book. This is an indirect consequence of promotional strategies that are part and parcel of the policies pursued by today's media institutions. Here, as a matter of fact, editorial rewards are gained by increasingly looking for people worldwide to read and buy positively appraised books, in a context where value is also clearly put to disciplinary knowledge. Allied with promotional strategies is the content of positively reviewed books in the CLJ, which was delivered via electronic formats as well in print. Consequently, the effects of electronic word-of-mouth advertising became a significant marketing tool for book purchasing decisions, as noted in the literature (Chevalier and Mayzlin 2006, among others). Thus, if we admit that CLJ reviewers in their interaction with the institution also implied a biased positive tendency towards reviewing in addition to objective, clear-sighted scrutiny, then it is fair to say that they allowed the seemingly independent genre to trespass upon, and therefore be *colonized* by, other core promotional genres (Bhatia 2004: 61-67). Obviously, the positive book reviews in the data examined differed from core promotional genres, in terms of the product involved and the use of rhetorical and linguistic resources. Despite this, the positive reviews were still potentially reflected "in the form of a constellation of several closely related genres with an overlapping communicative purpose of promoting a product" (Bhatia 2004: 62).

Quite apart from the attractive/promotional purposes, however, the findings show other important features of the texts produced by CLJ and IJLC reviewers, as suggested by the scope of their criticism based on varying degrees of expertise on the law topic. On the one hand, CLJ reviewers almost lacked self-projection towards some analytical or theoretical issue covered in the book. The reason for this was that they were mainly concerned with an 'outline' of the scope and content of the book under review in ways that the readers could immediately determine the book's interest to them. The end-result was that reviewers opted for 'steering a safe course', as it were, by informing and evaluating along positive descriptions of the books, within the framework of an interactively promotional vision of the legal research product. At the other end of the scale, however, IJLC reviewers went beyond 'outline' descriptions and evaluations, since they often intruded into the author's space by recasting the topic for review and joining the legal debate in the evaluative genre. The end-result here was that the scope of the reviewers' criticisms was widened for debating purposes in order to embrace their own views of some law issues although, admittedly, their criticisms may have also been influenced by some academic school of thought. Therefore, these debating reviewers consciously revealed more intuition and knowledge of some important analytical or theoretical issue in the book than their CLJ counterparts, tending instead to ignore the scope of their criticisms in their 'outline' reviewing formats. By entering into the legal debate to promote new ideas via critique and to create a disciplinary individual argument in "its own persuasive structure" (Becher 1987: 272), IJLC reviewers thus allowed for the discourse in the genre to become a more subjective rhetorical criterion designed to promote new ideas about the status of disciplinary knowledge. As such, the reviewed book strayed towards a short, subjective piece of writing dealing with the law topic speculatively, at least to some degree.

As a result of the different reviewing practices in both journals, the book review genre came to the fore as a variable rhetorical product, suggesting what reviewers themselves thought of their discourse practices and values in the genre. And this, in the politeness framework, shaped a "set of norms or values that crucially influences the volitional and strategic action of individuals" (Bargiela-Chiappini and Harris 2006: 12).

APPENDIXES

APPENDIX 1:
CASE NOTES

[ELJ] – ***Ecclesiastical Law Journal*** **- Cambridge University Press Journals**

Chaplin v Royal Devon and Exeter Hospital NHS Foundation Trust (2011), 13: 242-242

Re St Mary the Virgin, Ashford (2011), 13: 244-244

Re St Mary the Virgin, Monkseaton (2011), 13: 243-243

Re St Barnabus, Erdington (2011), 13: 244-245

Re Holy Trinity, Richmond (2011), 13: 246-247

Re St Michael and All Angels, Isel (2011), 13: 248-248

Re St Mary Magdalene, Reigate (2011), 13: 245-246

Aguilar and others v Secretary of State for the Home Department (2011), 13: 250-250

Bentley v Anglican Synod of the Diocese of New Westminster (2010), 12: 402-403

Re Holy Innocents, Southwater (2010), 12: 121-121

Re St Augustine, Holly Hall, Dudley (2010), 12: 126-126

Re All Saints, Sidmouth (2010), 12: 125-125

Re St Mary, White Waltham (2010), 12: 260-261

Re St Margaret, Halliwell (2010), 12: 256-256

Ladele v Islington Borough Council and Liberty (2010), 12: 261-261

Ladele v London Borough of Islington (2009), 11: 122-123

Johnston v Liverpool Diocesan Board of Finance (2009), 11: 123-124

R (on the application of Baiai) v Secretary of State for the Home Department (2009), 11: 124-125

Gallagher v Church of Jesus Christ of Latter-day Saints (2009), 11: 125-126

Armstrong v Robinson (2009), 11: 127-128

[MLR] – ***The Modern Law Review*** **- Blackwell Wiley**

Complicating Complicity: Aiding and Abetting Causing Death by Dangerous Driving in *R* v *Martin* (2011) 74(5) 767-793

Sienkiewicz v *Greif (UK) Ltd* and *Willmore* v *Knowsley Metropolitan Borough Council*: A Material Contribution to Uncertainty? (2011) 74(5) 767-793

Guiding Principles for Directorial Conflicts of Interest: *Re Allied Business and Financial Consultants Ltd; O'Donnell* v *Shanahan* (2011) 74(4) 596-616

Public or Personal Character in Election Campaigns: A Review of the Implications of the Judgment in *Watkins* v *Woolas* (2011) 74(4) 596-616

Marriage and Divorce in the Supreme Court and the Law Commission: for Love or Money? (2011) 74(3) 430-455

Extending the Confusion About Bayes (2011) 74(3) 430-455

Personal Religious Beliefs in the Workplace: How Not to Define Indirect Discrimination (2011) 74(2) 287-305

Unfair Contract Terms, Unfair Prices and Bank Charges (2011) 74(1) 106-134

Buckland v *Bournemouth University Higher Education Corp*: Statutory Constructive Dismissal and the Implied Term of Mutual Trust and Confidence (2011) 74(1) 106-134

A Negligent Blow to Children at Risk: *MAK and RK* v *United Kingdom* (European Court of Human Rights) (2010) 73(6) 1026-1047

Auctioneers and Misdescription: Between Scylla and Charybdis (2010) 73(6) 1026-1047

European Arrest Warrant Cases and the Principles of Non-discrimination and EU Citizenship (2010) 73(5) 824-857

Special Advocates, Control Orders and the Right to a Fair Trial (2010) 73(5) 824-857

Stone&Rolls Ltd v *Moore Stephens*: An Unnecessary Tangle (2010) 73(3) 487-493

Because You're Worth It: *L'Oréal* and the Prohibition on Free Riding (2010) 73(2) 282-304

Disobedience to Law – Debbie Purdy's Case (2010) 73(2) 282-304

How to Make a Terrorist Out of Nothing (2009) 72(6) 984-1015

Hopes, Expectations and Revocable Promises in Proprietary Estoppel (2009) 72(6) 984-1015

Interpreting the Threshold Criteria under section 31(2) of the Children Act 1989 – the House of Lords decision in *Re B* (2009) 72(3) 463-487

Debating 'Democracy' and the Ban on Political Advertising (2009) 72(3) 463-487

[NILR] - *Netherlands International Law Review* - Cambridge University Press Journals

Dispute regarding Navigational and Related Rights (*Costa Rica* v. *Nicaragua)*, (2009), 55: 287

Arbitration between the Government of Sudan and the Sudan People's Liberation Movement/Army (Abyei Arbitration), (2009), 55: 288

The Prosecutor v. *Krajisnik* (Appeal*)*, (2009), 55: 288-289

The Prosecutor v. *Jokic* (Trial Chamber and Appeal*)*, (2009), 55: 289

Case Concerning Maritime Delimitation in the Black Sea (*Romania* v. *Ukraine*) , (2009), 56: 69

The Prosecutor v. *Haraqija, Morina,* (2009), 56: 69

The Prosecutor v. *Milutinovic, Sainovic, Pavkovic, Lukic, Lazarevic, Ojdanic,* (2009), 56: 70

The Prosecutor v. *Karera* (Appeal)*,* (2009), 56: 70

Case Concerning Pulp Mills on the River Uruguay (*Argentina* v. *Uruguay*), (2010), 57:525-526

Accordance with International Law of the Unilateral Declaration of Independence in Respect of Kosovo (Request for Advisory Opinion) , (2010), 57:526

The Prosecutor v. *Tarculovski and Boskoski* (Appeals Chamber), (2010), 57:526-527

The Prosecutor v. *Seselj* (Appeals Chamber), (2010), 57:527

The Prosecutor v. *Popovic et al.* (Trial Chamber) , (2010), 57:527-528

The Prosecutor v. *Delic* (Appeals Chamber), (2010), 57:528

The Prosecutor v. *Haradinaj, Balaj, Brahimaj* (Appeals Chamber), (2010), 57:528- 529

The Prosecutor v. *Rukundo* (Appeals Chamber), (2010), 57: 529

The Prosecutor v. *Kalimanzira* (Appeals Chamber), (2010), 57: 529-530

Case Concerning Ahmadou Sadio Diallo *(Republic of Guinea* v. *Democratic Republic of the Congo),* (2011), 58: 143

The Prosecutor v. *Šljivančanin* (Appeals Chamber), (2011), 58: 143-144

The Prosecutor v. *Đorđević* (Trial Chamber), (2011), 58: 144

[ECLR] - *European Constitutional Law Review* – Cambridge University Press Journals

Constitutional Ultra Vires Review of European Acts Only Under Exceptional Circumstances; Decision of 6 July 2010, 2 BvR 2661/06, Honeywell (2011), 7: 161–167

Janko Rottman v. Freistaat Bayern, (2011), 7: 138–149

Janko Rottman v. Freistaat Bayern, The Consequences of the Rottmann Judgment on Member State Autonomy – The European Court of Justice's Avant-Gardism in Nationality Matters, (2011), 7: 150–160

The Conseil d'Etat Abandons Its Cohn Bendit Case-Law, (2010), 6: 123–136

Ireland v. Parliament/Council, (2010), 6: 137–157

Judgment in the case of *Sejdić and Finci v. Bosnia and Herzegovina*, (2010), 6: 309–333

Seda Kücükdeveci v. Swedex GmbH & Co. KG, (2010), 6: 293–308

Rhimou Chakroun v. Minister van Buitenlandse Zaken, (2010), 6: 462–480

R v The Governing Body of JFS, 2009 UKSC 15, (2010), 6: 481–502

German Data Retention Provisions Unconstitutional In Their Present Form, (2010), 6: 503–517

APPENDIX 2: LAW RESEARCH ARTICLE ABSTRACTS

[JIEL] -*Journal of International Economic Law* – Oxford University Press Journals

2011, 14(1) pp. 719-892 (Petersmann, Kennedy, Hsieh, Maupin)
2010, 13(4) pp. 969-1147 (Hsieh, Adlung&Morrison, Spears)
2010, 13(3) pp. 525-968 (Lastra& Wood, Gadbaw, Lowenfeld)
2010, 13(2) pp. 287-524 (Flett, Voon)
2010, 13(1) pp. 1-286 (Rolland, Ruse-Khan, Davies)
2009, 12(4) pp. 803-1069(Wolfe, van Aaken & Kurtz, Condon, Reich)
2009, 12(3) pp. 555-802 (Busch&Pelc, Motaal, La Chimia&Arrowsmith, Veel)
2008, 11(4) pp. 705-1034 (Van den Bossche, Petersmann, Biukovic)
2008, 11(3) pp. 507-704 (Diamond, Heymann, Maton & Maton)

[OJLS] - *Oxford Journal of Legal Studies*– Oxford University Press Journals

2011, 31(1) (O'Brian, Ringe & Hellgardt, Tucker, Bosland,Mihai, Kirchengast)
2011, 31(2) (Smith, da Silva, Harding, Johns)
2010, 30(3) (Sherman, Rowan, Gava)
2009, 29(1) (Pattenden,Clarkson, Roberts & Weathered, Mildenberger, Ehrenberg, Chartier)
2008, 28(3) (Beever, Edmond)
2008, 28(4) (Swadling, Eidenmüller et al., Samet)
2007, 27 (1) (Duxbury, Kesby, Himma)
2007, 27(4) (Lamond, Metz)
2007, 27(2) (Kimel)

[BJC] - *British Journal of Criminology*– Oxford University Press Journals

2011, 51(3) (Eisner, Nivette, Johnson)
2011, 51(2) (Bond & Jeffries, Kennelly, Chiu et al., Fleetwood, Besemer et al.)
2011, 51(4) (Lawless, Brooks)

2010, 50(5) (Wing Lo, Miller, Cromby et al.)
2010, 50(4) (Levi, Berko et al., Wilson et al., Weisburd et al.)
2009, 49(2) (Levi, McGloin et al., King, Bennett & Holloway)
2008, 48(4) (Almond, Cammiss, Stride)
2007, 47(1) (McAuley & Macdonald, Moore)
2007, 47(2) (Crewe, Pridemore)
2007, 47(3) (McSweeney et al.)
2007, 47(4) (Dinovitzer & Dawson)

[ILJ] - *Industrial Law Journal* – Oxford University Press Journals
2011, 40(1) (Leighton & Wynn, Boon et al.)
2011, 40(2) (Creighton, Cabrelli, Albin)
2010, 39(4) (O'Sullivan & Macmahon, Rowbottom, Merrett)
2010, 39(3) (Sargeant, Sciarra)
2010, 39(2) (Tucker, le Roux)
2010, 39(1) (Ewing & Hendy, Carr & Lewis)
2009, 38(4) (Manfredi, Vickers, Deakin & Koukiadaki)
2009, 38(3) (Barnard, Davies)
2009, 38(1) (Mccolgan, Sanders)
2008, 37(1) (Fudge)
2008, 37(2) (Davies, Finkin)
2008, 37(4) (Brodie)
2008, 37(3) (Syrpis)
2007, 36(1) (Riley, Barmes, Stone, Davies, Kilpatrick)

[IJTJ] - The *International Journal of Transitional Justice* – Oxford University Press Journals
2011, 5(1) (Thomson, Nagy, Peskin & Boduszyński, Robins, Zunino, Saunders, De Falco)
2010, 4(3) (Dancy, Hamber et al., Backer, Millar)
2010, 4(2) (Aiken, Meertens & Zambrano)
2010, 4(1) (Viaene, Duffy, Nettelfield, Boesten)
2009, 3(2) (Findlay, January)
2009, 3(1) (Bell, Lambourne, Wilcox, Haider, Henry, Horn et al.)
2008, 2(2) (Arriaza & Roht-Arriaza,Zolkos , Klinkner)
2008, 2(1) (Lundy, McGovern, Garcia-Godos, Sivac-Bryant)

APPENDIX 3:
LAW BOOK REVIEWS

[CLJ] – ***The Cambridge Law Journal*** **- Cambridge University Press Journals**

Green, S. / Randall, J. *The Tort of Conversion* (2010), 69: 415-417

Townley, C. *Article 81 EC and Public Policy* (2010), 69: 209-210

Hammond, G. *Judicial Recusal: Principles, Process and Problem* (2010), 69: 205-206

Wiegel, W. *Economics of the Law: A Primer* (2010), 69: 207-209

Plant, R. *The Neo-Liberal State* (2010), 69: 677-678

Dougan, M. / Currie, S. *50 Years of the European Treaties: looking back and thinking forward. Essays in European Law* (2010), 69: 678-680

Mitchell, C. *Constructive and Resulting Trusts* (2010), 69: 680-682

Hickman, T. *Public Law after the Human Rights Act* (2010), 69: 682-684

Goold, I. / Kelly, C. *Lawyers' Medicine: The Legislature, the Courts and Medical Practice 1760–2000* (2010), 69: 685-686

Schneiderman, D. *Constitutionalizing Economic Globalization: Investment Rules and Democracy's Promise* (2009), 68: 231-233

McCahery, J. / Vermeulen, E. *Corporate Governance of Non-Listed Companies* (2009), 68: 233-235

Broude, T. / Shany, Y. *The Shifting Allocation of Authority in International Law: Considering Sovereignty, Supremacy and Subsidiarity, Essays in Honour of Professor Ruth Lapidoth (Studies in International Law)* (2009), 68: 225-226

Beever, A. *Rediscovering the Law of Negligence* (2008), 67: 654-656

Salomon, M. *Global Responsibility for Human Rights: World Poverty and the Development of International Law* (2008), 67: 656 -658

Neff, S. *War and the Law of Nations: A General History* (2007), 66: 461-463

[IJLC] **-** ***The International Journal of Law in Context*** **- Cambridge University Press Journals**

Hoppe, N. *Bioequity – Property and the Human Body* (2010), 6: 397-399

Gordon, R. *Repairing British Politics: A Blueprint for Constitutional Change* (2010), 6: 399-403

Leigh, I / Masterman, R. *Making Human Rights Real: the Human Rights Act in its First Decade* (2010), 6: 403-405

Guchteneire, P. / Pécoud, A. / Cholewinski, R. *Migration and Human Rights – The United Nations Convention on Migrant Workers' Rights* (2010), 6: 405-409

Young, A. *The Scene of Violence: Cinema, Crime, Affect* (2010), 6: 409-411

Marmor, A. *Social Conventions: From Language to Law* (2010), 6: 411-414

Marshall, J. *Personal Freedom through Human Rights Law? Autonomy, Identity and Integrity under the European Convention on Human Rights* (2010), 6: 196-198

Nelken, D. *Beyond Law in Context: Developing a Sociological Understanding of Law* (2010), 6: 198-200

Raffield, P. / Watt, G. *Shakespeare and the Law* (2009), 5: 339-341

Banda, F. *Women, Law and Human Rights: An African Perspective* (2008), 4: 79-83

Askol, H. *Legal Responses to Trafficking in Women for Sexual Exploitation in the European Union* (2008), 4: 285-287

Countouris, N. *The Changing Law of the Employment Relationship: Comparative Analyses in the European Context* (2008), 4: 287-290

Beyleveld, D. / Brownsword, R. *Consent in the law* (2008), 4: 419-422

Fionda, J. *Devils and Angels Youth Policy and Crime* – Waites, M.

The Age of Consent: Young People, Sexuality and Citizenship (2007), 3:77-80

BIBLIOGRAPHY

Ädel, Annelie 2006. *Metadiscourse in L1 and L2 English*. Amsterdam: John Benjamins.

Ädel, Annelie / Mauranen, Anna 2010. Metadiscourse: Diverse and Divided Perspectives. *Nordic Journal of English Studies* 9(2): 1-11.

Anthony, Laurence 2001. Characteristic Features of Research Article Titles in Computer Science. *IEEETransactions on Professional Communication* 44(3): 187-194

Arthurs, Harry W. 1983. *Law and Learning: Report to the Social Sciences and Humanities Research Council of Canada by the Consultative Group on Research and Education in Law*. Information Division, Social Sciences and Humanities Research Council of Canada, Ottawa.

Askehave, Inger / Swales, John M. 2001. Genre Identification and Communicative Purpose: A Problem and Possible Solution. *Applied Linguistics* 22(2):195-212.

Athanasiadou, Angeliki / Dirven, René 1997. Conditionality, Hypotheticality, Counterfactuality. In Athanasiadou, A. / Dirven, R. (eds.), *On Conditionals Again* (pp. 61-96). Amsterdam: Benjamins.

Austin, John L. 1962. *How To Do Things with Words*. Oxford: Oxford University Press.

Ayers, Gael 2008. The Evolutionary Nature of Genre: An Investigation of the Short Texts Accompanying Research Articles in the Scientific Journal Nature. *English for Specific Purposes* 27: 22-41.

Badger, Richard 2003. Legal and General: Towards a Genre Analysis of Newspaper Law Reports. *English for Specific Purposes* 22: 249-263.

Bakhtin, Michail M. 1981. The Dialogic Imagination: Four Essays by M. M. Bakhtin. In M. Holquist (ed.), transl., M. Holquist and C. Emerson. Austin: University of Texas Press.

—. 1986. *Speech Genres and Other Late Essays*. Austin: University of Texas Press.

Bargiela-Chiappini, Francesca / Harris, Sandra 2006. Politeness at Work: Issues and Challenges. *Journal of Politeness Research* 2(1): 7-34.

Barth-Weingarten, Dagmar 2003. *Concession in Spoken English. On the Realization of a Discourse Pragmatic Relation*. Tübingen: Gunter Narr Verlag.

Barton, Ellen 1993. Evidentials, Argumentation, and Epistemological Stance. *College English* 55: 745-769.

Basturkmen, Helen 2009. Commenting on Results in Published Research Articles and Masters Dissertations in Language Teaching. *Journal of English for Academic Purposes* 8: 241-251.

—. 2011. A Genre-based Investigation of Discussion Sections of Research Articles in Dentistry and Disciplinary Variation. *Journal of English for Academic Purposes* 1-11.

Bazerman, Charles. 1985. Physicists Reading Physics: Schema-Laden Purposes and Purpose - Laden Schema. *Written Communication* 2 (1): 3-23.

—. 1988. *Shaping Written Knowledge: The Genre and Activity of the Experimental Article in Science*. Madison, Wisconsin: University of Wisconsin Press.

—. 1994. Systems of Genres and the Enactment of Social Intentions. In Freedman, A. / Medway, P. (1994), *Genre and the New Rhetoric* (pp. 79-101). London: Taylor & Francis.

—. 2000. *Shaping Written Knowledge: The Genre and Activity of the Experimental Article in Science*. WAC Clearinghouse Landmark Publications in Writing Studies. Available at: http://wac.colostate.edu/books/bazerman_shaping/

Bazerman, Charles 2004. Speech Acts, Genres, and Activity Systems: How Texts Organize Activity and People. In Bazerman, C. / Prior, P. (eds.), *What Writing Does and How it Does it: An Introduction to Analyzing Texts and Textual Practices* (pp. 309-339). Mahwah: Lawrence Erlbaum.

Bazerman, Charles / Russell, David (eds.) 2003. *Writing Selves/Writing Societies: Research from Activity Perspectives.* Fort Collins, Colorado: The WAC Clearinghouse and Mind, Culture, and Activity. Available at:http://wac.colostate.edu/books/selves_societies/

Bazerman, Charles / Bonini, Adair / Figueiredo, Débora (eds.) 2009. *Genre in a Changing World. Perspectives on Writing*. Fort Collins, CO, and West Lafayette, In: The WAC Clearinghouse & Parlor Press Available at http://wac.colostate.edu/books/

Beasley, Colin J. 1994. *Picking up the Principles: An Applied Linguistic Analysis of the Legal Problem Genre*. Unpublished MA Paper. Edith Cowan University.

Becher, Tony 1987. Disciplinary Discourse. *Studies in Higher Education* 12 (3): 261-274.

—. 1989. *Academic Tribes and Territories: Intellectual Enquiry and the Culture of Disciplines*. Bury St. Edmunds: Society for Research into Higher Education, Open University Press.

Becher, Tony / Trowler, Paul R. 2001. *Academic Tribes and Territories. Intellectual Enquiry and the Culture of Disciplines* (2nd ed.). Buckingham: The Society for Research into Higher Education and Open University Press.

Bellés-Fortuño, Begoña / Querol-Julían, Mercedes 2010. Evaluation in Research Article Abstracts: A Cross-cultural Study between Spanish and English Medical Discourse. In Lorés-Sanz, R. / Dueñas, P. M. / Lafuente-Millàn, E. (eds.), *Constructing Interpersonality: Multiple Perspectives on Written Academic Genres* (pp. 83-98). New Castle upon Tyne: Cambridge Scholars Publishing.

Belotti, Ulisse 2008. Manifestations of Identity in Economics RA Abstracts. In Di Martino, G. / Polese, V. / Solly, M. (eds.), *Identity and Culture in English Domain-specific Discourse* (pp. 349-366). Napoli: Edizioni Scientifiche Italiane.

—. 2012. Variations of Identity in Single- and Multi-Authored Economics RA Abstracts. In Gotti. M. (ed.), *Academic Identity Traits. A Corpus-based Investigation* (pp. 145-171). Bern: Peter Lang.

Berkenkotter, Carol / Huckin, Thomas 1995. *Genre Knowledge in Disciplinary Communication*. Hillsdale, NJ: Erlbaum.

Bhatia, Vijay K. 1983. An Applied Discourse Analysis of English Legislative Writing. University of Aston in Birmingham, UK: Language Studies Unit.

—. 1993. *Analysing Genre: Language Use in Professional Settings*. London: Longman.

—. 1994. Cognitive Structuring in Legislative Provisions. In Gibbons, J. (ed.), *Language and the Law (*pp.136-155). London: Longman.

—. 1995. Genre-mixing in Professional Communication: The Case of 'private intentions' v. 'socially recognized purposes'. In Bruthiaux, P. / Boswood, T. / Bertha, B. (eds.), *Explorations in English for Professional Communication* (pp. 1-19).Hong Kong: City University of Hong Kong.

—. 1997a. Genre Analysis Today. *Revue Belge de Philologie et l'Histoire* 75 (3): 629-652.

—. 1997b. Introduction: Genre Analysis and World Englishes. *World Englishes* 16(3): 313–319.

—. 2001. Analysing Genre: Some Conceptual Issues. In Hewings, M. (ed.), *Academic Writing in Context: Implications and Applications* (pp. 79-92). Birmingham: The University of Birmingham Press.

—. 2002. Applied Genre Analysis: Analytical Advances and Pedagogical Procedures. In Johns, A. M. (ed.), *Genre in the Classroom: Multiple Perspectives* (pp. 279-284). London: Lawrence Erlbaum Associates.
—. 2004. *Worlds of Written Discourse*. London: Continuum.
—. 2008. Towards Critical Genre Analysis. In: Bhatia, V. K. / Flowerdew, J. / Jones, R. H. (eds.), *Advances in Discourse Studies* (pp. 166-177). London: Routledge.
—. 2010. Interdiscursivity in Professional Communication. *Discourse & Communication* 21(1): 32-50.
—. 2011. Interdiscursive Colonization of Arbitration Practice. *World Englishes* 30 (1): 76-80.
Bhatia, Vijay K. / Gotti, Maurizio (eds.) 2006. *Explorations in Specialized Genres*. Bern: Peter Lang.
Bhatia, Vijay K. / Candlin, Christopher N. / Gotti, Maurizio (eds.) 2003. *Legal Discourse in Multilingual and Multicultural Contexts: Arbitration Texts in Europe.* Bern: Peter Lang.
Bhatia, Vijay K. / Candlin, Christopher N. / Evangelisti Allori, Paola (eds.) 2008. *Language, Culture and the Law. The Formulation of Legal Concepts across Systems and Cultures.* Bern: Peter Lang.
Bhatia, Vijay K. / Candlin, Christopher N. / Gotti, Maurizio (eds.) 2010. *The Discourses of Dispute Resolution*. Bern: Peter Lang.
Bhatia, Vijay K. / Evangelisti Allori, Paola (eds.) 2011. *Discourse and Identity in the Professions. Legal, Corporate and Institutional Citizenship.* Bern: Peter Lang.
Bhatia, Vijay K. / Candlin, Christopher N. / Gotti, Maurizio (eds.) 2012. *Discourse and Practice in International Commercial Arbitration*. Farnham, UK: Ashgate.
Bhatia, Vijay K. / Garzone, Giuliana / Degano, Chiara (eds.) 2012. *Arbitration Awards. Generic Features and Textual Realisations*. New Castle Upon Tyne, UK: Cambridge Scholars Publishing.
Bhatia, Vijay K. / Hafner, Christoph / Miller, Lindsay / Wagner, Anne (eds.) 2012. *Transparency, Power, and Control. Perspectives on Legal Communication*. Surrey: Ashgate.
Biber, Douglas 1988. *Variation across Speech and Writing.* Cambridge: Cambridge University Press.
—. 2006. Stance in Spoken and Written University Registers. *Journal of English for Academic Purposes* 5(2): 97-116.
Biber, Douglas / Finegan, Edward 1989. Styles of Stance in English: Lexical and Grammatical Marking of Evidentiality and Affect. *Text* 9(1): 93-124.

Biber, Douglas / Johansson, Stig / Leech, Geoffrey / Conrad, Susan / Finegan, Edward 1999. *Longman Grammar of Spoken and Written English.* Essex: Pearson Education Limited.

Bloor, Meriel / Bloor, Thomas 1993. How Economists Modify Propositions. In Henderson, W. / Dudley-Evans, T. /Backhouse, R. (eds.), *Economics and Language* (pp. 153-169). Routledge: London/ New York.

Blum-Kulka, Shoshana / House, Juliane / Kasper, Gabriele (eds.) 1989. *Cross-cultural Pragmatics: Requests and Apologies*. Norwood, NJ: Ablex.

Bondi, Marina 2004. The Discourse Function of Contrastive Connectors in Academic Abstracts. In Aijmer, K. / Stenström, A-B (eds), *Discourse Patterns in Spoken and Written Corpora* (pp. 139-156). Amsterdam: Benjamins.

—. 2005. Metadiscursive Practices in Academic Discourse: Variation across Genres and Disciplines. In Bamford, J. / Bondi, M. (eds), *Dialogue within Discourse Communities* (pp. 3-30). Tubingen: Niemeyer.

—. 2006. A Case in Point: Signals of Narrative Development in Business and Economics. In Hyland, K. / Bondi, M. (eds.), *Academic Discourse across Disciplines* (pp. 49-74). Bern: Peter Lang.

—. 2009. Historians at Work: Reporting Frameworks in English and Italian Book Review Articles. In Hyland, K. / Diani, G. (eds.), *Academic Evaluation: Review Genres in University Settings* (pp. 179-196) London: Palgrave-MacMillan.

Bondi, Marina / Silver, Marc 2004. Textual Voices: A Cross Disciplinary Study of Attribution in Academic Discourse. In Anderson, L. / Bamford, J. (eds.), *Evaluation in Oral and Written Discourse* (pp. 117-136). Rome: Officina Edizioni.

Bondi, Marina / Hyland, Ken 2006. Introduction. In Hyland, K. / Bondi,M. (eds.), *Academic Discourse across Disciplines* (pp. 7-17). Bern: Peter Lang.

Bondi, Marina / Cavalieri, Silvia 2012. The Evolution of the Abstract as a Genre: 1988-2008. The Case of Applied Linguistics. In Garzone, G. / Catenaccio, P. / Degano, C. (eds.), *Genre Change in the Contemporary World. Short-term Diachronic Perspectives* (pp. 43-56). Bern: Peter Lang.

Bonn, Vann S. / Swales, John M. 2007. English and French Journal Abstracts in the Language Sciences: Three Exploratory Studies. *English for Specific Purposes* 6: 93-108.

Bowles, Hugo 1995. Why are Newspaper Law Reports So Hard to Understand? *English for Specific Purposes* 14: 201-222.

Breeze, Ruth 2009. Issues of Persuasion in Academic Law Abstracts. *Revista Alicantina de Estudios Ingleses* 22: 11-26.

Brown, Penelope / Levinson, Stephen C. 1987. *Politeness: Some Universals in Language Usage*. Cambridge: Cambridge University Press.

—. 2009. Politeness: Some Universals in Language Usage [Chapter 1, reprint]. In Coupland, N. / Jaworski, A. (eds.), *Sociolinguistics: Critical Concepts* (pp. 311-323) - Volume III: Interactional Sociolinguistics. London: Routledge.

Bruce, Ian 2008. Cognitive Genre Structures in Methods Sections of Research Articles: A Corpus Study. *Journal of English for Academic Purposes* 7(1): 38-54.

—. 2009. Results Sections in Sociology and Organic Chemistry Articles: A Genre Analysis. *English for Specific Purposes* 28(2): 105-124.

Bruce, Nigel 2002. Dovetailing Language and Content: Teaching Balanced Argument in Legal Problem Answer Writing. *English for Specific Purposes* 21(4): 321-345.

Bunton, David 2002. Generic Moves in Ph.D Thesis Introductions. In Flowerdew, J. (ed.), *Academic Discourse*. London: Pearson Education. 57-75

—. 2005. The Structure of PhD Conclusion Chapters. *Journal of English forAcademic Purposes* 4: 207-224.

Burgess, Sally / Martín-Martin, Pedro 2010. Interpersonal Features of Spanish Social Sciences Journal Abstracts: A Diachronic Study. In Lorés-Sanz, R. / Dueñas, P. M. / Lafuente-Millàn, E. (eds.), *Constructing Interpersonality: Multiple Perspectives on Written Academic Genres* (pp. 99-115). New Castle upon Tyne: Cambridge Scholars Publishing.

Bush-Laurer, Ines 2000. Titles in English and German Research Papers in Medicine and Linguistics. In Trosborg, A. (ed.), *Analysing Professional Genres* (pp. 77-94). Amsterdam: John Benjamins.

Buxton, Andrew B. / Meadows, A. Jack 1977. The Variation in the Information Content of Titles of Research Papers with Time and Discipline. *Journal of Documentation* 33 (1): 46–52.

Candlin, Christopher N. / Maley, Yon 1997. Intertextuality and Interdiscursivity in the Discourse of Alternative Dispute Resolution. In Gunnarsson, B-L / Lineel, P. / Nordberg, B. (eds.), *The Construction of Professional Discourse* (pp. 201-222). London: Longman.

Candlin, Christopher N. / Bhatia, Vijay K. / Jensen, Christian H. 2002a. Must the Worlds Collide? Professional and Academic Discourses in the Study and Practice of Law. In Cortese, G. / Riley, P. (eds.), *Domain-specific English: Textual Practices Across Communities and Classrooms* (pp. 101-114). Bern: Peter Lang.

Candlin, Christopher N. / Bhatia, Vijay K. / Jensen, Christian H. 2002b. Developing Legal Writing Materials for English Second Language Learners: Problems and Perspectives. *English for Specific Purposes* 21: 299-320.

Candlin, Christopher N. / Gotti Maurizio (eds.) 2004. *Intercultural Aspects of Specialized Communication*. Bern: Peter Lang.

Cao, Deborah 2007. *Translating Law*. Clevedon: Multilingual Matters.

Card, R. 2002. The Legal Scholar. *The Reporter: Newsletter of the Society of Legal Scholars* 25: 5–12.

Carter-Thomas, Shirley 2007. The 'iffiness' of Medical Research Articles. A Comparison of English *if* and French *si*". In Flottum, K. (ed.), *Language and Discipline Perspectives on Academic Discourse* (pp. 161-188). Newcastle, UK: Cambridge Scholars Press.

Case, Donald O. / Georgeann, M. Higgins 2000. How Can We Investigate Citation Behavior? A Study of Reasons for Citing Literature in Communication. *Journal of the American Society for Information Science* 51: 635-45.

Charnock, Ross 2010. Traces of Orality in Common Law Judgments. In Giannoni, D. S. / Frade, C. (eds.), *Researching Language and the Law* (pp. 113-134). Bern: Peter Lang.

Cherry, Roger D. 1998. Ethos versus Persona: Self-representation in Written Discourse. *Written Communication* 15: 384-410.

Chevalier, Judith A. / Mayzlin, Dina 2006. The Effect of Word of Mouth on Sales: Online Book Reviews. *Journal of Marketing Research* 43(3): 345-354.

Coates, Jennifer 1987. Epistemic Modality and Spoken Discourse. *Transactions of the Philological Society* 85: 100-131.

Coffin, Caroline / Curry, Mary Jane / Goodman, Sharon / Hewings, Ann / Lillis, Theresa / Swann, Joan 2003. *Teaching academic writing: A toolkit for higher education*. London: Routledge.

Cownie, Fiona 2004. *Legal Academics: Culture and Identities*. Oxford and Portland, Oregon: Hart Publishing.

Crevels, Mily 2000. Concessives on Different Semantic Levels: A Typological Perspective. In Couper-Kuhlen, E. / Kortmann, B. (eds.), *Cause, Condition, Concession, Contrast: Cognitive and Discourse Perspectives* (pp. 313-339). Berlin: Mouton de Gruyter.

Crismore, Avon 1989. *Talking with Readers: Metadiscourse as Rhetorical Act*. New York: Peter Lang Publishers.

Crismore, Avon / Markkanen, Rajja / Steffensen, Margaret 1993. Metadiscourse in Persuasive Writing: A Study of Texts Written by American and Finnish University Students. *Written Communication* 10,39-71.

Crompton, Peter 1997. Hedging in Academic Writing. Some Theoretical Aspects. *English for Specific Purposes* 16(4): 271-289.

Crowley, Sharon 1990. *The Methodical Memory: Invention in Current-Traditional Rhetoric.* Carbondale: Southern Illinois UP.

Crystal, David / Davy, Derek 1969. *Investigating English Style.* London: Longman.

Crystal, David 2003. *English as a Global Language* (2nd ed.). Cambridge: Cambridge University Press.

D'Angelo, Larissa 2008. Gender Identity and Authority in Academic Book Reviews : A Metadiscourse Analysis across Disciplines. *Linguistica e Filologia* 27, 205-221.

—. 2010. Exploring Gender Identity in Academic Book Reviews. In Garzone, G. / Archibald, J. (eds.), *Discourse, Identities and Roles in Specialized Communication* (pp. 365-383). Bern, Peter Lang.

Dahl, Trine 2004. Some Characteristics of Argumentative Abstracts. *Akademisk Prosa* 2, 4967. Skrifter fra KIAP, Department of Romance studies, University of Bergen.

Dancygier, Barbara / Sweetser, Eve 1997. *Then* in Conditional Constructions. *Cognitive Linguistics* 2: 109-136.

Dancygier, Barbara 1998. *Conditionals and Prediction.* Cambridge: Cambridge University Press.

Danet, Brenda 1984. Special Issue: Studies of Legal Discourse. *TEXT: An Interdisciplinary Journal for the Study of Discourse.* 4:1/3.

Davenport, Elizabeth / Cronin, Blaise 2000. The Citation Network as a Protoreason for Representing Trust in Virtual Environments. In Cronin, B. / Atkins, H. B. (eds.), *The Web of Knowledge: A Festschrift in Honor of Eugene Garfield* (pp. 517-534). New Jersey: Information Today, Inc.

Devitt, Amy 1991. Intertextuality in Tax Accounting: Generic, Referential, and Functional. In Bazerman, C. / Paradis, J. (eds.), *Textual Dynamics of the Professions: Historical and Contemporary Studies of Writing in Professional Communities* (pp. 336-357). Madison: University of Wisconsin Press.

—. 2004. *Writing genres*. Carbondale: Southern Illinois University Press.

Day, Robert A. 1995. *How to Write and Publish a Scientific paper* (5th ed). Cambridge:Cambridge University Press.

Declerck, Renaat / Reed, Susan 2001. *Conditionals: A Comprehensive Empirical Analysis*. Berlin: Mouton de Gruyter.

Del Lungo Camiciotti, Gabriella / Tognini Bonelli, Elena (eds.) 2004. *Academic Discourse: New Insights into Evaluation*. Frankfurt: Peter Lang.

De Zarobe, Leyre R. / De Zarobe, Yolanda R. (eds.) 2012. *Speech Acts and Politeness across Languages and Cultures*. Bern: Peter Lang.

Dressen-Hammouda, Dacia 2008. From Novice to Disciplinary Expert: Disciplinary Identity and Genre Mastery. *English for Specific Purposes* 27(2): 233-252.

Dubois, Betty L. 1997. *The Biomedical Discussion Section in Context*. Greenwich: Connecticut: Ablex Publishing.

Dunning, Ted 1993. Accurate Method for the Statistics of Surprise and Coincidence. *Computational Linguistics* 19 (1), 61-74.

Duxbury, Neil 2001. *Jurists and Judges. An Essay on Influence*. Oxford: Hart Publishing.

Eemeren, Frans H. van / Grootendorst, Rob 1992. *Argumentation, Communication and Fallacies. A Pragma-dialectical Perspective*. Hillsdale NJ: Erlbaum.

Eggins, Suzanne 1994. *An Introduction to Systemic Functional Linguistics*. London: Pinter.

Facchinetti, Roberta 2001. Conditional Constructions in Modern English Legal Texts. In Gotti, M. / Dossena, M. (eds.), *Modality in Specialized Texts* (pp. 133-150). Bern: Peter Lang.

Fahnestock, Jeanne 2005. Rhetoric of Science: Enriching the Discipline. *Technical Communication Quarterly* 14 (3): 277-286.

Fairclough, Norman 1992. *Discourse and Social Change*. Oxford: Polity Press.

—. 2003. *Analyzing Discourse: Text Analysis for Social Research*. London: Routledge.

—. 2004. *Analyzing Discourse: Textual Analysis for Social Research*. London: Routledge.

Fajans, Elizabeth / Falk, Mary, R. 2011. *Scholarly Writing for Law Students: Seminar Papers, Law Review Notes, and Law Review Competition Papers* (4th ed.). Eagan, MN: West Publishing.

Feak, Christine / Reinhart, Susan, M. / Sinsheimer, Ann 2000. A Preliminary Analysis of Law Review Notes. *English for Specific Purposes* 19: 197-220.

Felstiner, William / Abel, Richard / Sarat, Austin 1980-81. The Emergence and Transformation of Disputes: Naming, Blaiming, Claiming. *Law and Society Review* 15(3-4): 631-654.

Feteris, Eveline T. 1990. Conditions and Rules for Rational Discussion in a Legal Process: A Pragma-Dialectical Perspective. Argumentation and Advocacy. *Journal of the American Forensic Association* 26(3); 108-117.

—. 1993. Rationality in Legal Discussions: A Pragma-Dialectical Perspective. *Informal Logic*, XV (3): 179-188.

Feteris, Eveline T. 2002. A Pragma-Dialectical Approach of the Analysis and Evaluation of Pragmatic Argumentation in a Legal Context, *Argumentation* 16 (3): 349–367.

—. 2005. The Rational Reconstruction of Argumentation Referring to Consequences and Purposes in the Application of Legal Rules: A Pragma-Dialectical Perspective. *Argumentation* 19(4): 459–470.

Flowerdew, John / Gotti, Maurizio (eds.) 2006. *Studies in Specialized Discourse*. Bern: Peter Lang.

Ford, Cecilia E. / Thompson, Sandra A. 1986. Conditionals in Discourse: A Text-based Study from English. In Traugott, E. C. / Meulen, A. / Reilly, J. S. / Ferguson, C. A. (eds.), *On Conditionals* (pp. 353-372). Cambridge: Cambridge University Press.

Fortanet, Inmaculada 2004. The Use of *We* in University Lectures: Reference and Function. *English for Specific Purposes* 23: 45-66.

Freedman, Aviva, and Medway, Peter (eds.) 1994. *Genre and the New Rhetoric*. London: Taylor & Francis.

Garzone, Giuliana 2001. Deontic Modality and Performativity in English Legal Texts. In Gotti, M. / Dossena, M. (eds.), *Modality in Specialized Texts* (pp. 153-173). Bern: Peter Lang.

—. 2002. Tradurre la Convenzione Internazionale: Aspetti Testuali e Pragmatici. In Schena, L. / Snel, T. (eds), *Traduttori e Giuristi a Confronto. Interpretazione Traducente e Comparazione del Discorso Giuridico* (pp. 37-72), Vol. II. Bologna: CLUEB.

—. 2007. Osservazioni sulla Didattica della Traduzione Giuridica. In Mazzotta, P. / Salmon, L. (eds.), *Tradurre le Microlingue Scientifico-Professionali. Riflessioni Teoriche e Proposte Didattiche* (pp. 194-238). Torino: UTET.

Gea-Valor, Maria L. 2000. *A Pragmatic Approach to Politeness and Modality in the Book Review.* València: Universitat de València. SELL Monographs 6.

—. 2010. The Emergence of the Author's Voice in Book Reviewing: A Contrastive Study of Academic vs Non-Academic Discourse. In Lorés-

Sanz, R. / Dueñas, P. M. / Lafuente-Millàn, E. (eds.), *Constructing Interpersonality: Multiple Perspectives on Written Academic Genres* (pp. 117-135). New Castle upon Tyne: Cambridge Scholars Publishing.

Giannoni, Davide S. 2002. Worlds of Gratitude: A Contrastive Study of Acknowledgement Texts in English and Italian Research Articles. *Applied Linguistics* 23(1), 1-31.

—. 2006. Expressing Praise and Criticism in Economic Discourse: A Comparative Analysis of English and Italian Book Reviews. In Del Lungo Camiciotti, G. / Dossena, M. / Crawford Camiciottoli, B. (eds.), *Variation in Business and Economics Discourse. Diachronic and Genre Perspectives* (pp. 126-138). Roma: Officina Edizioni.

Gibbons, John 2003. *Forensic Linguistics. An Introduction to Language in the Justice System*. Oxford: Blackwell.

Gillaerts, Paul / Van de Velde, Freek 2010. Interactional Metadiscourse in Research Article Abstracts. *Journal of English for Academic Purposes* 9: 128-139.

Giltrow, Janet 2005. Modern Conscience: Modalities of Obligation in Research Genres. *Text* 25(2): 171-199.

Goffman, Ewing 1967. *International Ritual: Essays on Face-to-Face Behaviour*. NewYork: Anchor.

Gotti, Maurizio 2001. Semantic and Pragmatic Values of Shall and Will in Early Modern English Statutes. In Gotti, M. / Dossena, M. (eds.), *Modality in Specialized Texts* (pp. 89-111). Bern: Peter Lang.

—. 2003. *Specialized Discourse: Linguistic Features and Changing Conventions*. Bern: Peter Lang.

—. 2005. *Investigating Specialized Discourse*. Bern, Peter Lang.

—. 2008. *Investigating Specialized Discourse* (2nd revised ed.). Bern: Peter Lang.

—. 2011. Identity Traits in Legal Texts. In Baccolini, R. / Chiaro, D. / Rundle, C. / Whitsitt, S. (eds.), *Minding the Gap. Studies in Linguistic and Cultural Exchange for Rosa Maria Bollettieri Bosinelli* (pp. 287-298). Bologna: Bononia University Press.

Gotti, Maurizio / Susan Šarčević (eds.) 2006. *Insights into Specialized Translation*. Bern: Peter Lang.

Gotti, Maurizio / Williams, Christopher J. (eds.) 2010. *Legal Discourse across Languages and Cultures*. Bern: Peter Lang.

Goodrich, Peter 1987. *Legal Discourse: Studies in Linguistics, Rhetoric and Legal Analysis.* London; New York: Macmillan; St. Martin's.

Graetz, Naomi 1985. Teaching EFL Students to Extract Structural Information from Abstracts. In Ulijn, J. / Pugh, A. (eds.), *Reading for*

Professional Purposes: Methods and Materials in Teaching Languages (pp. 123-135). Leuven: Acco.

Greene, Robert J. / Spornick, Charles D. 1995. Favorable and Unfavorable Book Reviews: A Quantitative Study. *Journal of Academic Librarianship* 21, 449-453.

Greenfield, Steve / Osborn, Guy 2006. Law, Legal Education and Popular Culture. In Greenfield, S. / Osborn, G (eds.), *Readings in Law and Popular Culture* (pp. 1-11). London: Routledge.

Grice, H. Paul 1975. Logic and Conversation. In Cole, P. / Morgan, J. (eds.), *Syntax and Semantics* (pp. 41-58), Volume 3. New York: Academic Press.

Gross, Alan G. / Harmon, Joseph E. / Reidy, Michael 2002. *Communicating Science: The Scientific Article from the 17th Century to the Present*. Oxford: Oxford University Press.

Grote, Brigitte / Lenke, Nils / Stede, Manfed 1997. Ma(r)king Concession in English and German. *Discourse Processes* 24: 87-117.

Hafner, Christoph, A. 2008. *Designing, Implementing, and Evaluating an Online Resource for Professional Legal Communication Skills*. Thesis presented for the degree of Doctor of Philosophy in Linguistics, Department of Linguistics, Macquarie University, Sydney.

—. 2010. A Multi-perspective Genre Analysis of the Barrister's Opinion: Writing Context, Generic Structure, and Textualization. *Written Communication* 27(4): 410 -441.

—. 2011. Professional Reasoning, Legal Cultures, and Arbitral Awards. *World Englishes* 30(1): 117-128.

Haggan, Madeline. 2004. Research Paper Titles in Literature, Linguistics and Science: Dimensions of Attraction. *Journal of Pragmatics* 36: 293-317.

Halliday, Michael A. K. / Hasan, Ruqaiya 1976. *Cohesion in English*. London: Longman.

Halliday, Michael A. K. 1994. *An Introduction to Functional Grammar*. London: Edward Arnold.

—. 2004. *An Introduction to Functional Grammar*. London: Arnold.

Hartley, James, 2005. To Attract or to Inform: What are Titles For? *Journal of Technical Writing and Communication* 35(2): 203-213.

—. 2007. Planning that Title: Practices and Preferences for Titles with Colons in Academic Disciplines. *Library and Information Science Research* 29: 553-568.

Harwell, Kevin 2002. Law and Justice. In N. Herron (ed.), *The Social Sciences: A Cross-disciplinary Guide to Selected Sources* (pp. 195-233). Greenwood, CO: Libraries Unlimited.

Harwood, Nigel 2005a. 'Nowhere has anyone attempted … In this article I aim to do just that'. A Corpus-based Study of Self-promotional *I* and *we* in Academic Writing across Four Disciplines. *Journal of Pragmatics* 37: 1207-1231.

—. 2005b. 'We do not seem to have a Theory … The Theory I Present here attempts to fill this gap': Inclusive and Exclusive Pronouns in Academic Writing. *Applied Linguistics* 26(3): 343-375.

Haverkate, Henk 1992. Deictic Categories as Mitigation Devices. *Pragmatics.* 2(4), 505-522.

Heinemann, Trine 2006. Will You or Can't You?: Displaying Entitlement in Interrogative Requests. *Journal of Pragmatics* 38: 1081-1104.

Hemais, Barbara 2001. The Discourse of Research and Practice in Marketing Journals. *English for Specific Purposes* 20(1): 39-59.

Hewings, Martin / Hewings, Ann 2002. "It is interesting to note that …": a comparative study of anticipatory 'it' in student and published writing. *English for Specific Purposes* 21: 367-383.

Hewings, Ann / Lillis, Theresa / Vladimirou, Dimitra 2010. Who's Citing Whose Writings? A Corpus-based Study of Citations as Interpersonal Resource in English-medium National and English-medium International Journals. *Journal of English for Academic Purposes* 9(2): 102-115.

Hinkel, Eli 2001. Giving Examples and Telling Stories in Academic Essays. *Issues in Applied Linguistics* 12: 149-170.

Hoey, Michael 2001. *Textual Interaction: An Introduction to Written Discourse Analysis*. London: Routledge.

Holmes, Janet1988. Paying Compliments: A Sex-Preferential Politeness Strategy. *Journal of Pragmatics* 12: 445-465.

—. 1990. Apologies in New Zealand English. *Language in Society* 19: 155-199.

—. 1995. *Women, Men and Politeness*. London: Longman.

Holmes, Richard 1997. Genre Analysis and Social Sciences: An Investigation of the Structure of Research Article Discussion Sections in Three Disciplines. *English for Specific Purposes* 16(4): 321-337.

Hopkins, Andy / Dudley-Evans, Tony 1988. A Genre-based Investigation of the Discussion Sections in Articles and Dissertations. *English for Specific Purposes* 7: 113-122.

Howarth, David 2004. Is Law a Humanity: (Or Is It More Like Engineering)? *Arts and Humanities in Higher Education* 3(1): 9-28.

Howe, Peter M. 1990.The Problem of the Problem Question in English for Academic Legal Purposes. *English for Specific Purposes, 9*, 215-236.

Huckin, Thomas 2001. Abstracting from Abstracts. In Hewings, M. (ed.), *Academic Writing in Context: Implications and Applications* (pp. 93-103). Birmingham: The University of Birmingham Press.

—. 2006. Abstracting from Abstracts. In Hewings, M. (ed.) *Academic Writing in Context* (pp. 93-103). London: Continuum.

Hultman, Tor G. 2003. *Svenska Akademiens språklära.* Stockholm: Svenska Akademien.

Hunston, Susan 1993. Evaluation and Ideology in Scientific Writing. In Ghadessy, M. (ed.), *Register Analysis: Theory and Practice* (pp. 57-73). London: Pinter Publishers.

—. 1994. Evaluation and Organization in a Sample of Written Academic Discourse. In Coulthard, M. (ed.), *Advances in Written Text Analysis* (pp. 191-218). London: Routledge.

Hyland, Ken 1994. Hedging in Academic Writing and EAP Textbooks. *English for Specific Purposes* 13(3): 239-256.

—. 1996. Writing Without Conviction? Hedging in Science Research Articles. *Applied Linguistics* 17: 433-454.

—. 1998. *Hedging in Scientific Research Articles*. Amsterdam: John Benjamins.

—. 1999a. Academic Attribution: Citation and the Construction of Disciplinary Knowledge. *Applied Linguistics* 20 (3): 341-367.

—. 1999b. Disciplinary Discourses: Writer Stance in Research Articles. In Candlin, C. / Hyland, K. (eds.), *Writing: Texts, Processes and Practices* (pp. 99-121). London: Longman.

—. 2001a. Humble Servants of the Discipline? Self-mention in Research Articles. *English for Specific Purposes* 20: 207-226.

—. 2001b. Bringing in the Reader: Addressee Features in Academic Discourse. *Written Communication* 18(4): 549-574.

—. 2002a. What do they Mean? Questions in Academic Writing. *Text* 22 (4): 529-557.

—. 2002b. Directives: Argument and Engagement in Academic Writing. *Applied Linguistics* 23: 215-239.

—. 2004. *Disciplinary Discourses: Social Interactions in Academic Writing*. The University of Michigan Press, Ann Arbor, MI (first published by Pearson Education Limited, Longman, 2000).

—. 2005a. *Metadiscourse*. London: Continuum.

—. 2005b. Stance and Engagement: A Model of Interaction in Academic Discourse. *Discourse Studies* 7(2): 173-192.

—. 2007. Applying a Gloss: Exemplifying and Reformulating in Academic Discourse. *Applied Linguistics* 28(2), 266-285.

—. 2009. *Academic Discourse*. London: Continuum.

Hyland, Fiona / Hyland, Ken 2001. Sugaring the Pill: Praise and Criticism in Written Feedback. *Journal of Second Language Writing* 10(3): 185-212.

Hyland, Ken / Tse, Polly 2004a. Metadiscourse in Academic Writing: A Reappraisal. *Applied Linguistics* 25 (2): 156-177.

Hyland, Ken / Tse, Polly 2004b. "I would like to thank my supervisor": Acknowledgments in Graduate Dissertations. *International Journal of Applied Linguistics* 14 (2): 259-275.

Hyland, Ken / Tse, Polly 2005. Hooking the Reader: A Corpus Study of Evaluative *that* in Abstracts. *English for Specific Purposes* 24: 123-139.

Hyland, Ken / Bondi, Marina (eds.) 2006. *Academic Discourse across Disciplines*. Bern: Peter Lang.

Hyland, Ken / Diani, Giuliana (eds.) 2009. *Academic Evaluation: Review Genres in University Settings*. Hampshire, England: Palgrave Macmillan.

Iedema, Rick A. 1993. Legal English: Subject Specific Literacy and Genre Theory. *ARAL* 16(2): 86–122.

Iedema, Rick / Rhodes, Carl / Scheeres, Hermine 2006. Surveillance, Resistance, Observance: Exploring the Teleo-affective Volatility of Workplace Interaction. *Organisation Studies* 27(8): 1111-1130.

Ivanič, Roz 1998. *Writing and Identity. The Discoursal Construction of Identity in Academic Writing*. Amsterdam: John Benjamins.

Jackson, Bernard S. 1994. Some Semiotic Features of a Judicial Summing-up in an English Crimimal Trial. *International Journal for the Semiotics of Law*. 7(20): 201-24.

Jenkins, Jennifer 2003. *World Englishes*. London:Routledge.

Jensen, Christian H. 2002. Legal Problem Questions: Analysing Rhetorical Strategies Using 'IRAC. In Candlin, C. N. (ed.), *Research and Practice in Professional Discourse* (pp. 463-498). Hong Kong: City University of Hong Kong Press.

Kanoksilapatham, Budsaba 2005. Rhetorical Structure of Biochemistry RAs. *English for Specific Purposes* 24: 269-292.

Kelsen, Hans 1967. *The Pure Theory of Law*. California: University of California Press, Berkeley (Knight, M. translation).

Kőnig, Ekkehard 1986. Conditionals, Concessive Conditionals and Concessives: Areas of Contrast, Overlap and Neutralization. In Traugott, C. / Meulen, A. ter / Smitzer, R. / Ferguson, Ch. (eds.), *On Conditionals* (pp. 229-246). Cambridge: Cambridge University Press.

—. 1988. Concessive Connectives and Concessive Sentences: Cross-linguistic Regularities and Pragmatic Principles. In Hawkins, J. A.

(ed.), *Explaining Language Universals* (pp. 321-349). Oxford: Blackwell.

Kranich, Svenja 2011. To hedge or not to Hedge: The Use of Epistemic Modal Expressions in Popular Science in English Texts, English–German Translations, and German Original Texts. *TEXT & TALK* 31 (1): 77–99.

Kuo, Chih-Hua 1999. The Use of Personal Pronouns: Role Relationships in Scientific Journal Articles. *English for Specific Purposes* 18(2): 121-138.

Kurzon, Dennis 1985. How Lawyers Tell their Tales: Narrative Aspects of a Lawyer's Brief. *Poetics* 14: 467–481.

Kurzon, Dennis 1994. Linguistics and Legal Discourse: An Introduction. *International Journal for the Semiotics of Law,* 7: 19, 2-10.

Kwan, Becky S. C. 2006. The Schematic Structure of Literature Reviews in Doctoral Theses of Applied Linguistics. *English for Specific Purposes* 25: 30-55.

Labov, William 1997. Some Further Steps in Narrative Analysis. *Journal of Narrative and Life History* 7: 395-415.

Lakoff, George 1987. *Women, Fire and Dangerous Things: What Categories Reveal About the Mind.* Chicago: University of Chicago Press.

Larreya, Paul 2009. Towards a Typology of Modality in Language. In Salkie, R. B. / Johan van der Auwera (eds.), *Modality in English. Theory and Description* (pp. 9–29). Berlin: Mouton de Gruyter.

Lewin, Beverly A. / Fine, Jonathan / Young, Lynne 2001. *Expository Discourse: A Genre-based Approach to Social Science Research Texts.* London: Continuum.

Lim, Jason M. 2010. Commenting on Research Results in Applied Linguistics and Education: A Comparative Genre-based Investigation. *Journal of English for Academic Purposes* 9(4): 280-294.

Lin, Ling / Evans, Stephen 2012. Structural Patterns in Empirical Research Articles. *English for Specific Purposes* 31(3): 150-160.

Lindholm-Romantschuk, Ylva 1998. *Scholarly Book Reviewing in the Social Sciences and Humanities. The Flow of Ideas within and among Disciplines*. Westport, Connecticut: Greenwood.

Lorés, Rosa 2004. On RA Abstracts: From Rhetorical Structure to Thematic Organisation. *English for Specific Purposes* 23: 280-302.

Lyons, John 1977. *Semantics* (Vol. 1-2). Cambridge: Cambridge University Press.

Maley, Yon 1994. The Language of the Law. In Gibbons, J. (ed.), *Language and the Law* (pp. 11-50). London: Longman.

Mann, William C. / Thompson, Sandra, A. 1992. Relational Discourse Structure: A Comparison of Approaches to Structuring Text by 'Contrast'. In Hwang, S. J. / Merrifield, W. R. (eds.), *Language in Context: Essays for Robert E. Longacre* (pp. 19-45). Summer Institute of Linguistics and The University of Texas at Arlington Publications in Linguistics, Publ. 107. Dallas: Summer Institute of Linguistics.

Markkanen, Raija / Schröder, Hartmut 1989. Hedging as a Translation Problem in Scientific Texts. In Laurén, C. / Nordmann, M. (eds.), *Special Language: from Humans Thinking to Thinking Machines* (pp. 171-179). Clevedon: Multilingual Matters.

Markkanen, Raija / Schröder, Hartmut 1992. Hedging and its Linguistic Realizations in German,English and Finnish Philosophical Texts: A Case Study. In Nordman, M. (ed.), *Fachsprachliche Miniaturen. Festschrift für Christer Laurén* (pp. 121-130). Frankfurt am Main et al.: Peter Lang.

Martin, James R. 1984. Genre as Social Action. In *Quarterly Journal of Speech* 7: 151-167.

—. 1992. *English Text: System and Structure*. Philadelphia/Amsterdam: John Benjamins.

—. 1995. Text and Clause: Fractal Resonance. *Text* 15: 5-42.

—. 1998. Linguistics and the Consumer: The Practice of Theory. *Linguistics and Education* 9(4): 411-448.

—. 2000. Beyond Exchange: Appraisal Systems in English. In Hunston, S. / Thompson, G. (eds.), *Evaluation in Text: Authorial Stance and the Construction of Discourse* (pp. 142-175). Oxford, New York: Oxford University Press.

Martin, James R. / Rose, David 2003. *Working with Discourse: Meaning beyond Clause*. London: Continuum.

Martin, James R. / White, Peter R. 2005. *The Language of Evaluation: Appraisal in English*. Basingstoke: Palgrave Macmillan.

Martín-Martín, Pedro 2002. A Genre Analysis of English and Spanish Research Paper Abstracts in Experimental Social Sciences. *English for Specific Purposes* 22(1): 25-43.

Matsuda, Paul K. / Tardy, Christine M. 2008. Continuing the Conversation on Voice in Academic Writing. *English for Specific Purposes* 27(1): 100-105.

Mattila, Heikki E.S. 2006. *Comparative Legal Linguistics*. Surrey: Ashgate.

Mauranen, Anna. 1993. *Cultural Differences in Academic Rhetoric*. Peter Lang: Frankfurt am Main.

McArthur, Tom 1998. *The English Languages*. Cambridge: Cambridge University Press.

McGowan, Jessie / Tugwell, Peter 2005. Informative Titles Described Article Content. *Journal of the Canadian Health Libraries Association* 26: 83-84.

McMenamin, Gerard R. 1993. *Forensic Stylistics*. Amsterdam: Elsevier.

Medway, Peter 2002. Fuzzy Genres and Community Identities: The Case of Architecture Students' Sketchbooks. In Coe, R. / Lingard, L. / Teslenko, T. (eds.), *The Rhetoric and Ideology of Genre*. Cresskill: NJ: Hampton (pp. 123-154). Cresskill, NJ: Hampton Press.

Melander, Björn / Swales, John M. / Fredrickson, Kristin M. 1997. Journal Abstracts from Three Academic Fields in the United States and Sweden: National or Disciplinary Proclivities? In Duszak, A. (ed.), *Intellectual Styles and Cross-Cultural Communication* (pp. 251-272). Berlin: De Gruyter.

Mellinkoff, David 1963. *The Language of the Law*. Boston: Little, Brown & Co.

Miller, Carolyn R. 1984. Genre as Social Action. *Quarterly Journal of Speech* 70: 151-167.

Mills, Sara 2003. *Gender and Politeness*. Cambridge: Cambridge University Press.

Moreno, Ana I. / Suárez, Lorena 2006. The Rhetorical Structure of Academic Journal Book Reviews: A Cross-linguist and Cross-disciplinary Approach. In Pérez-Llantada, C. / Pló, R. / Neumann, C. P. (eds.), *Proceedings of the 5th International AELFE Conference* (pp. 191-196). Zaragoza: Prensas Universitarias.

—. 2009. Academic Book Reviews in English and Spanish: Critical Comments and Rhetorical Structure. In Hyland, K. / Diani, G. (eds.), *Academic Evaluation: Review Genres in University Settings* (pp. 161-178). London: Palgrave-MacMillan.

—. 2010. Academic Book Reviews in English and Spanish: Is "giving reasons for critical comments" a Universal Politeness Strategy? In Lorés-Sanz, R. / Dueñas, P. M. / Lafuente-Millàn, E. (eds.), *Constructing Interpersonality: Multiple Perspectives on Written Academic Genres* (pp. 137-160). New Castle upon Tyne: Cambridge Scholars Publishing.

Motta-Roth, Desirée 1996. Same Genre, Different Discipline: A Genre-based Study of Book Reviews in Academy. The *ESP*, São Paulo 17: 99-131.

—. 1998. Discourse Analysis and Academic Book Reviews: A Study of Text and Disciplinary Cultures. In Coll, J. F. / Fortanet, I. / Palmer, J.

C. / Posteguillo, S. (eds.), *Genre Studies in English for Academic Purposes* (pp. 29-58). Castelló: Universitat Jaume I.

Mur, Pilar 2007. 'I/we focus on...:' A Cross-cultural Analysis of Self-mentions in Business Management Research Articles. *Journal of English for Academic Purposes* 6: 143-162.

Myers, Gregory A. 1989. The Pragmatics of Politeness in Scientific Articles. *Applied Linguistics.* 10, 1-35.

—. 1992a. In this Paper We Report... - Speech Acts and Scientific Facts. *Journal of Pragmatics* 17 (4): 295–313.

—. 1992b. Textbooks and the Sociology of Scientific Knowledge. *English for Specific Purposes* 11 (1): 3-17.

—. 2003. Risk and Face: A Review of the Six Studies. *Health Risk and Society* 5(2): 215-220.

Nicolaisen, Jeppe P. 2002. Structure-based Interpretation of Scholarly Book Reviews. In Emerging Frameworks and Methods - CoLIS 4: *Proceedings of the Fourth International Conference on Conceptions of Library and Information Science* - Seattle, Wa, July 21-25 (pp. 123-135). Greenwood Village, Colo: Libraries Unlimited Incorporated.

Nikula, Tarja 1997. Interlanguage View on Hedging. In Markkanen, R. / Schröder, H. (eds.), *Hedging and Discourse: Approaches to the Analysis of a Pragmatic Phenomenon in Academic Texts* (pp. 188-207). Berlin: Walter de Gruyter.

Nwogu; K. Ngozi 1990. *Discourse Variation in Medical Texts: Schema, Theme and Cohesion on Professional and Journalistic Accounts.* Nottingham: Department of English Studies, University of Nottingham.

Nwogu, K. Ngozi 1997. The Medical Research Paper: Structure and Function. *English for Specific Purposes* 16(2):119-138.

Osborn, Guy 2001. Borders and Boundaries: Locating the Law in Film. *Journal of Law and Society* 28 (1): 164-176.

Orlikowski, Wanda J. / Yates, JoAnne 1994. Genre Repertoire: The Structuring of Communicative Practices in Organizations. *Administrative Science Quarterly* 39: 541-574.

Ozturk, Ismet 2007. The Textual Organization of Research Article Introductions in Applied Linguistics: Variability within a Single Discipline. *English for Specific Purposes* 26(1): 25-38.

Palmer, Frank 2001. *Mood and Modality.* Cambridge: Cambridge University Press.

Palmer, Jerry / Pearce, Frank 1983. Legal Discourse and State Power. *International Journal of the Sociology of Law* 11: 361.

Paltridge, Brian 2001. *Genre and the Language Learning Classroom.* Ann Arbor, MI: The University of Michigan Press.

—. 2002. Thesis and Dissertation Writing: An Examination of Published Advice and Actual Practice. *English for Specific Purposes* 21: 125-143.

Peacock, Matthew 2002. Communicative Moves in the Discussion Section of Research Articles. *System* 30 (4): 479-497.

Pickard, Valerie 1995. Citing Previous Writers: What Can We Say Instead of "say"? *Hong Kong Papers in Linguistics and Language Teaching* 18: 89-102.

Posteguillo, Santiago 1999. The Schematic Structure of Computer Science Research Articles. *English for Specific Purposes* 18 (2): 139-60.

Quirk, Randolph / Greenbaum, Sidney 1973. *A University Grammar of English*. London: Longman.

Quirk, Randolph / Sidney, Greenbaum / Geoffrey, Leech / Jan, Svartvik 1972. *A Grammar of Contemporary English*. Harlow, UK: Longman.

Quirk, Randolph / Greenbaum, Sidney / Leech, Geoffrey / Svartvik, Jan 1985. *A Comprehensive Grammar of the English Language*. London: Longman.

Rudolph, Elisabeth 1996. *Contrast: Adversative and Concessive Relations and their Expressions in English, German, Spanish and Portuguese on Sentence Level and Text Level*. Berlin/New York: Mouton de Gruyter.

Sala, Michele 2010. Interrogative Forms as Professional Identity Markers in Legal Research Articles. In Garzone, G. / Archibald, J. (eds.), *Discourse, Identities and Roles in Specialized Communication* (pp. 301-320). Bern: Peter Lang.

Salager-Meyer, Françoise 1990. Discoursal Flaws in Medical English Abstracts: A Genre Analysis Per Research-and Text Type. *Text* 10(4): 365-384.

—. 1992. A Text-type and Move Analysis Study of Verb Tense and Modality Distribution in Medical English Abstracts. *English for Specific Purposes* 11(2): 93-113.

—. 1994. Hedges and Textual Communicative Function in Medical English Written Discourse. *English for Specific Purposes* 13(2): 149-171.

—. 1997. 'I think that perhaps you should': A Study of Hedges in Written Scientific Discourse. In Miller, T. (ed.), *Functional Approaches to Written Text: Classroom Applications* (pp. 127-143). Washington: United States Information Agency.

Salager-Meyer, Françoise / Zambrano, Nahirana 2001. The Bittersweet Rhetoric of Controversiality in 19th- and 20th- Century French and English Medical Literature. *Journal of Historical Pragmatics* 2(1): 141-173.

Salager-Meyer, Françoise / Alcaraz Ariza, María Ángeles / Zambrano, Nahirana 2003. The Scimitar, the Dagger and the Glove: Intercultural Differences in the Rhetoric of Criticism in Spanish, French and English Medical Discourse (1930-1999). *English for Specific Purposes* 22 (3): 223-247.

Salager-Meyer, Françoise / Alcaraz Ariza, María Ángeles 2004. Negative Appraisals in Academic Book Reviews: A Cross Linguistic Approach. In Candlin, C. N. / Gotti, G. (eds.), *Intercultural Aspects of Specialized Communication* (pp. 149-172). Peter Lang: Bern.

Salager-Meyer, Françoise / Alcaraz Ariza, María Ángeles / Berbesí Pabón, Maryelis 2005. The Prosecutor and the Defendant: Contrasting Critical Voices in French- and English-written Academic Book Reviews. In Flottum, K. (ed.), *Language and Discipline Perspectives on Academic Discourse* (pp. 109-127). Newcastle: Cambridge Scholars Publishing.

Salager-Meyer, Françoise / Alcaraz Ariza, María Ángeles / Berbesí Pabón, Maryelis 2007. Collegiality, Critique and the Construction of Scientific Argumentation in Medical Book Reviews: A Diachronic Approach. *Journal of Pragmatics* 39: 1758-1774.

Salmi-Tolonen, Tarja 2008. *Language and the Functions of Law: A Legal Linguistic Study*. Rovaniemi: Painosalama Turku.

Salvi, Rita 2002. The Intertextual Dimension in the Teaching of Legal English. In Schena, L. / Snel Trampus, R. (eds.), *Traduttori e Giuristi a Confronto* (pp. 73-95), Vol. 2. Bologna: CLUEB.

Samraj, Betty 2002a. Disciplinary Variation in Abstracts: The Case of Wildlife Behaviour and Conservation Biology. In Flowerdew, J. (ed.), *Academic Discourse* (pp. 40-56). London: Pearson.

—. 2002b. Introductions in Research Articles: Variations across Disciplines. *English for Specific Purposes* 21(1): 1-17.

—. 2005. An Exploration of a Genre Set: Research Article Abstracts and Introductions in two Disciplines. *English for Specific Purposes* 24: 141-156.

Santos, Mauro B. 1996. The Textual Organization of Research Paper Abstracts in Applied Linguistics. *Text* 16(4): 481-499.

Sarangi, Srikant 2006. The Conditions and Consequences of Professional Discourse Studies. In Kiely, R. / Rea-Dickens, P. / Woodfield, H. / Clibbon, G. (eds.), *Language, Culture and Identity in Applied Linguistics* (pp. 199-220), British Studies in Applied Linguistics 21. London: Equinox.

Sarangi, Srikant / Brookes-Howell, Lucy 2006. Recontextualising the Familial Lifeworld in Genetic Counselling Case Notes. In Gotti, M. /

Salager-Meyer, F. (eds.), *Advances in Medical Discourse Analysis: Oral and Written Contexts* (pp. 197-225). Bern: Peter Lang.

Šarčević, Susan (ed.) 2009. *Legal Language in Action: Translation, Terminology, Drafting and Procedural Issues*. Zagreb: Globus.

Searle, John 1975. *Indirect Speech Acts*. In Cole, P. / Morgan, J. (eds.), *Syntax and Semantics III. Speech Acts* (pp. 59-82). New York: Academic Press.

Smith, Richard 2000. Informative Titles in the BMJ. *British Medical Journal* 320 (7239): 915.

Soler, Viviana. 2007. Writing Titles in Science: An Exploratory Study. *English for Specific Purposes* 26: 90-102.

Spink, Amanda / Robins, David / Schamber, Linda 1998. Use of Scholarly Book Reviews: Implications for Electronic Publishing and Scholarly Communication. *Journal of the American Society for Information Science* 49: 364-374.

Spinuzzi, Clay 2004. Four Ways to Investigate Assemblages of Texts: Genre Sets, Systems, Repertoires, and Ecologies. *SIGDOC '04: Proceedings of the 22nd Annual International Conference on Design of Communication* (pp. 110-116). New York: ACM Press.

Stotesbury, Hilkka 2003. Evaluation in Research Article Abstracts in the Narrative and Hard Sciences. *Journal of English for Academic Purposes* 2: 327-341.

—. 2005. Focus on Business Abstracts: Considerations of Rhetorical, Lexico-Grammatical and Interpersonal Perspectives. In Kuure, Leena / Saarenkangas, Maarit (eds.), *Kieli Ja Sosiaalinen Toiminta – Language and Social Action* (pp. 321-334). AfinLA Yearbook. Publications de L'association Finlandaise de Linguistique Appliquée 63.

—. 2006a. Gaps and False Conclusions: Criticism in Research Article Abstracts across the Disciplines. In Hyland, K. / Bondi, M. (eds.), *Academic Discourse across Disciplines* (pp. 123-148). Bern: Peter Lang.

—. 2006b. From Interdisciplinary to Intradisciplinary and Beyond: Subfield-specific Differences within Research Article Abstracts in Economic Sciences. In Bhatia, V. K. / Gotti, M. (eds.), *Explorations in Specialized Genres* (pp. 79-97). Bern: Peter Lang.

Svartvik, Jan / Olof, Sager 1996. *Engelsk Universitetsgrammatik.* Stockholm: Liber AB.

Swales, John M. 1981. *Aspects of Article Introductions.* Birmingham, UK: The University of Aston, Language Studies Unit.

Swales, John M. / Najar, Hazem 1987. The Writing of Research Article Introductions. *Written Communication* 4: 175-192.

Swales, John M. 1990. *Genre Analysis: English in Academic and Research Settings*. Cambridge: Cambridge University Press.

—. 2004. *Research Genres: Explorations and Applications*. Cambridge: Cambridge University Press.

Swales, John M. / Feak, Christine B. 1994. *Academic Writing for Graduate Students*. Ann Arbor: The University of Michigan Press.

Swales, John M. / Burke, Amy 2003. It's Really Fascinating Work: Differences in Evaluative Adjectives across Academic Registers. In Leistyna, P. / Meyer, C. F. (eds.), *Corpus Analysis, Language Structure and Language Use* (pp. 1-18). Amsterdam, New York: John Benjamins.

Swales, John M. / Feak, Christine B. 2003. *English in Today's Research World. A Writing Guide*. Ann Arbor: University of Michigan.

Swales, John M. / Feak, Christine B. 2004. *Academic Writing for Graduate Students: Essential Tasks and Skills* (2nd ed.). Ann Arbor, MI: University of Michigan Press.

Swales, John M. / Feak, Christine B. 2009. *Academic Writing for Graduate Students*. Ann Arbor: University of Michigan Press.

Sweetser, Eve 1990. *From Etymology to Pragmatics: Metaphorical and Cultural Aspects of Semantic Structure*. Cambridge: Cambridge University Press.

Szczyrbak, Magdalena 2009. Genre-based Analysis of the Realisation of Concession in Judicial Discourse. *Studia Linguistica, Universitatis Iagellonicae Cracoviensis* 126(1): 127-148.

Tang, Ramona / John, Suganthi 1999. The 'I' Identity: Exploring Writer Identity in Student Academic Writing through the First Person Pronoun. *English for Specific Purposes* 18: 23-39.

Tardy, Christine M. / Swales, John M. 2008. Form, Text Organisation, Genre, Coherence, and Cohesion. In Bazerman, C. (eds.), *Handbook of Research on Writing* (pp. 565–582). New York: Lawrence Erlbaum Associates.

Tessuto, Girolamo 2006. Opinions of Counsel: An Exploratory Survey of Generic Features. In Bhatia, V. K. / Gotti, M. (eds.), *Explorations in Specialized Genres* (pp. 291-309). Bern: Peter Lang.

—. 2008a. Discourse Systems in English Arbitration Awards. In Bhatia, V. K. / Candlin, C. N. / Engberg, J. (eds.), *Legal Discourse across Cultures and Systems* (pp. 181-197). Hong Kong: Hong Kong University Press.

—. 2008b. Writer Identity in the Introduction Section of Academic Law Research Articles. *Linguistica e Filologia* 27: 39-58.

—. 2011a. Legal Problem Question Answer Genre across Jurisdictions and Cultures. *English for Specific Purposes* 30(4): 298-309.

—. 2011b. Developing Genre-based English Legal Writing Literacy in Italian Law Faculty Contexts: *Law Essays*. Research Principles and Pedagogic Applications. In Desideri, P. / Tessuto, G. (eds.), *Il Discorso Accademico. Lingue e Pratiche Disciplinari* (pp. 253-297). Urbino: Edizioni QuattroVenti.

—. 2012. Arbitration Awards: A Genre-oriented Linguistic Description of Professional Discursive Practices. In Bhatia, V. K. / Garzone, G. / Degano, C. (eds.), *Arbitration Awards. Generic Features and Textual Realisations* (pp. 109-136). New Castle Upon Tyne: Cambridge Scholars Publishing.

Thompson, Dorothea K. 1993. Arguing for Experimental "facts" in Science. *Written Communication* 10: 106-128.

Thompson, Geoffrey / Hunston, Susan 2000. Evaluation: An Introduction. In Hunston, S. / Thompson, G. (eds.), *Evaluation in Text: Authorial Stance and the Construction of Discourse* (pp. 1-27). Oxford: Oxford University Press.

Thompson, Geoffrey 2001. Interaction in Academic Writing: Learning to Argue with the Reader. *Applied Linguistics* 22(1): 58-78.

Thompson, Paul 1999. Exploring the Contexts of Writing: Interviews with PhD Supervisors. In Thompson, P. (ed.), *Issues in EAP Writing Research and Instruction* (pp. 37-54). Reading: University of Reading.

—. 2000. Citation Practice in PhD Theses. In Burnard, L. / McEnery, T. (eds.), *Rethinking Language Pedagogy from a Corpus Perspective* (91-101). Frankfurt: Peter Lang.

Thompson, Paul / Tribble, Chris 2001. Looking at Citations: Using Corpora in English for Academic Purposes. *Language, Learning and Technology* 5(3): 91-105.

Thompson, Paul 2005. Points of Focus and Position: Intertextual Reference in PhD Theses. *Journal of English for Academic Purposes* 4: 307-323.

Tibbo, Helen R. 1992. Abstracting Across the Disciplines: A Content Analysis of Abstracts from the Natural Sciences, the Social Sciences, and the Humanities with Implications for Abstracting Standards and Online Information Retrieval. *Library and Information Science Research* 14(1): 31-56.

Tiersma, Peter M. 1986. The Language of Offer and Acceptance: Speech Acts and the Question of Intent. *California Law Review* 74(1): 189–232.

—. 1999. *Legal Language*. Chicago: University of Chicago Press.

Tiersma, Peter 2010. *Parchment, Paper, Pixels: Law and the Technologies of Communication*. Chicago: The University of Chicago Press.

Tiersma, Peter / Solan, Lawrence, M. (eds.) 2012. *The Oxford Handbook of Language and Law*. Oxford: Oxford University Press.

Tognini Bonelli, Elena / Del Lungo Camiciotti, Gabriella (eds.) 2005. *Strategies in Academic Discourse*. Amsterdam: John Benjamins.

Toolan, Michael J. 2009. *Narrative Progression in the Short Story: A Corpus Stylistic Approach.* Amsterdam/Philadelphia: Benjamins.

Trosborg, Anna 1995. Statutes and Contracts: An Analysis of Legal Speech Acts in the English Language of the Law. *Journal of Pragmatics* 23: 31–53.

—. 1997. *Rhetorical Strategies in Legal Language: Discourse Analysis of Statutes and Contracts*. Tübingen: Gunter Narr Verlag.

Tse, Polly / Hyland, Ken 2008. 'Robot Kung Fu': Gender and Professional Identity in Biology and Philosophy Reviews. *Journal of Pragmatics* 40: 1232-1248.

Van Schooten, Hanneke 1999. Instrumental Legislation and Communication Theories. In Van Schooten, H. (ed.), *Semiotics and Legislation: Jurisprudential, Institutional and Sociological Perspectives* (pp. 185-211). Liverpool: Deborah Charles.

Vande Kopple, William J. 1985. Some Exploratory Discourse on Metadiscourse. *College Composition and Communication* 36, 82-93.

Vassileva, Irena 1998. Who Am I/Who Are We in Academic Writing? *International Journal of Applied Linguistics* 8(2): 163-190.

Ventola, Eija 1994. Abstracts as an Object of Linguistic Study. In Cmejrkova, S. / Danes, F. / Havlova, E. (eds.), *Writing vs Speaking: Language, Text, Discorse, Communication* (pp. 333-352). Conference Proceedings, Czech Language Institute of the Academy of Sciences of the Czech Republic (Prague, 14-16 October 1992). Tübingen: Gunter Narr Verlag.

Volokh, Eugene 2010. *Academic Legal Writing: Law Review Articles, Students Notes, Seminar Papers and Getting on Law Review* (4th ed.). New York: Foundation Press.

Wagner, Anne / Werner, Wouter / Cao, Deborah (eds.) 2007. *Interpretation, Law and the Construction of Meaning. Collected Papers on Legal Interpretation in Theory, Adjudication and Political Practice*. New York: Springer-Verlag.

Wagner, Anne / Broekman, Jan M. (eds.) 2011. *Prospects of Legal Semiotics*. New York: Springer-Verlag.

Wagner, Anne / Cheng, Le (eds.) 2011. *Exploring Courtroom Discourse. The Language of Power and Control*. Surrey: Ashgate.

Wang, Yan / Bai, Yongquan 2007. A Corpus-based Syntactic Study of Medical Research Article Titles. *System* 35: 388-399.

Watson, Roger 2010. Editorial: What's in a Title? *Journal of Clinical Nursing* 19: 2-3.

Webber, Pauline 1994. The Function of Questions in Different Medical English Genres. *English for Specific Purposes* 13: 257-268.

Williams, Christopher J. 2005. *Tradition and Change in Legal English: Verbal Constructions in Prescriptive Texts*. Bern: Peter Lang.

—. 2006. Fuzziness in Legal English: What Shall We Do With *Shall?* In Wagner, A. / Cacciaguidi-Fahy, S. (eds.), *Legal Language and the Search for Clarity* (pp. 237-263). Bern: Peter Lang.

—. 2009. Scottish Parliament and Plain Language Legal Drafting. In Šarčević, S. (ed.), *Legal Language in Action: Translation, Terminology, Drafting and Procedural Issues* (pp. 301-312). Zagabria: Globus Publishers.

Wong, Song Mei L. 1994. Imperatives in Requests: Direct or Impolite-observations from Chinese. *Pragmatics* 4: 491–515.

Wood, Alistair 2001. International Scientific English: The Language of Research Scientists around the World. In Flowerdew, J. / Peacock, M. (eds.), *Research Perspectives on English for Academic Purposes* (pp. 71-83). Cambridge: Cambridge University Press.

Yang, Ruiying / Allison, Desmond 2003. Research Articles in Applied Linguistics: Moving from Results to Conclusions. *English for Specific Purposes* 22: 365-385.

Yitzhaki, Moshe 1997. Variation in Informativity of Titles of Research Papers in Selected Humanities Journals: A Comparative Study. *Scientometrics* 38 (2): 219-229.